ANDHRA PRADESH

Glimpses of Library Movement and Public Library Development in Andhra Pradesh

Glimpses of Library Movement and Public Library Development in Andhra Pradesh

Prof. A.A.N. Raju
Formerly Head, Dept. of Library & Information Science
Osmania University, Hyderabad - 500 007

Ess Ess Publications
New Delhi

Glimpses of Library Movement & Public Library Development in Andhra Pradesh

ISBN: 978-81-7000-615-2

Rs.1200/-

First Published 2010

Published by:
Ess Ess Publications
4837/24, Ansari Road,
Darya Ganj,
New Delhi-110 002.
INDIA
Phones: 23260807, 41563444
Fax: 41563334
E-mail: info@essessreference.com
www.essessreference.com

Cover Design by *Patch Creative Unit*

Printed and bound in India at Salasar Imaging Systems.

Dedicated to the sacred memory of the

PIONEERS OF LIBRARY MOVEMENT IN ANDHRA PRADESH

SRI IYYANKI VENKATA RAMANAYYA
(1890-1979)

SRI GADICHARLA HARISARVOTHAMA RAO
(1883-1960)

SRI PATURI NAGABHUSHANAM
(1907-1987)

SRI VAVILALA GOPALA KRISHNAYYA
(1906-2003)

SRI KODATI NARAYANA RAO
(1914-2002)

Contents

FOREWORD

Public libraries have significant roles to play in the socio-economic, cultural and spiritual development of all communities in all parts of the world, more so in the developing countries. In national democratic governance, equity and justice call for facilitation of the participation of all persons of all communities (directly and/or through their elected representatives) in the governing process and enjoyment of the benefits of socio-economic development. International organizations, such as, the United Nations Educational, Scientific, Cultural Organization (UNESCO) and the International Federation of Library Associations and Institutions (IFLA) have reiterated and emphasized these matters in their manifestos and other documents on public policy and public library development.

In India, as in many other countries, the roots of the 'public library' can be traced back decades if not centuries before a 'public library movement' was initiated and became visible as a service institution to the people at large. In India on a national level and at the level of constituent States the late Dr. S.R.Ranganathan had made yeomen contributions for the cause of public libraries - through his writings, establishing model public library services, public library legislation (preparing memoranda, bills, acts, etc) and assisting in the enactment of the bills through the respective legislatures. Even before this, in some States, such as, the Andhra Pradesh there have been social development-oriented stalwarts who initiated and supported library service to the public at large.

Prof. A.A.N Raju in his book Glimpses of *Library Movement and Public Library Development in Andhra Pradesh* describes and documents in some detail the library movement, more particularly the public library movement in Andhra Pradesh, one of the progressive constituent States of India The structure of the public library system under the related legislation - from the State Central Library, through the Regional Libraries, down to the Zilla Gramdhalaya Samsthas - is explained. The functions and role of the associated Library Committees - the Review Committee for public libraries (the Ekbote Committee) and the Vavillala Committee for private libraries - are described. There is a useful set of supplementary details about the contributions of (1) professionals associations and organizations, (2) education and training of library and information professionals in Andhra Pradesh, and (3) the Raja Rammohun Roy Library Foundation, Kolkata, that has supported and immensely contributed to library development programmes in India.

I am sure Professor Raju's work will be appreciated and well used by students and teachers of library and information science and also by practising public library professionals. Public policy makers and legislators will also find valuable information in the book.

Bangalore **A. Neelameghan**

PREFACE

Library movement is one of the most important social movements witnessed in our Country in general and Andhra Desa in particular since the beginning of the twentieth century. The movement which originated and developed in the three regions i.e. Coastal Andhra, Rayalaseema and Telangana of the present Andhra Pradesh carved out for itself a most significant and prominent place in the annals of library movement of the whole Country.

In the present work *"Glimpses of Library Movement and Public Library Development in Andhra Pradesh"* an attempt has been to study in the origins, aims and objectives of library movement and development and spread of the movement in the three regions of the State. The study has taken into account the impact of library movement on social, political and cultural developments in the three regions and paving the way for emergence of enlarged State of Andhra Pradesh.

After independence the then Madras Presidency took initiative for bringing out for the first time for the entire Country library legislation in 1948 which paved the way for orderly development of public libraries in the State of which Andhra Pradesh was part of it. The then Hyderabad State followed suit and brought out Hyderabad Public Libraries Act in 1955. After the formation of enlarged State of Andhra Pradesh in 1956, an integrated library act, the Andhra Pradesh Public Libraries Act, 1960 came into being which resulted in orderly development of public libraries in the State.

As a result of A. P. Public Libraries Act, 19660 a network of public libraries have been functioning in the State. The Public Library system consists of the State Central Library (SCL) at the top followed by the Regional Libraries (RLs) and at the district level, the District Central Libraries (DCL) and further down the system the Branch Libraries (BLs), Village Libraries (VLs), Book Deposite Centres (BDCs) and Mobile Libraries (MLs). In the present work an attempt has been made to provide glimpses of the activities of those various types of libraries and at the district level the District Central Libraries (DCLs) under the authority of Zilla Grandhalaya Samsthas (ZGSs).

In order to assess the working of A. P. Public Libraries Act, 1960 a review Committee was appointed in 1976 under the Chairmanship of Justice Gopal Rao Ekbote and a second Committee was appointed in 1978 under the Chairmanship of Sri Vavila Gopala Krishnayya to look into the state of affairs of private libraries in the State. These two Committees submitted their reports with far reaching recommendations for the development of public library system in the State and rejuvenation of private libraries. The present work briefly deals with these two reports.

Professional associations and organizations played a prominent role in the genesis and sustenance of the library movement and public library development in the State. The Andhra Pradesh Library Association (APLA) played a prominent role in the origin and spread of library movement during the beginning of the twentieth century and later after independence, the enactment of library legislation and public library development in the State. There are other professional associations which have contributed in no small measure for the growth and development of public libraries and emergence of library profession in the State. The contributions of these associations have been briefly presented in the present volume.

Lastly the present volume deals with LIS education in

the State and the Institutions which have been concerned with LIS education at different levels and courses offered by them to turnout the required trained manpower to manage the public library system in the State. The present work concludes with a brief note on Raja Rammohun Roy Library Foundation (RRRLF) which was established by the Government of India during 1972 to promote public library movement and development in the Country by extending necessary financial support.

For the first time an attempt has been made to present the glimpses of library movement and public library movement in the State of Andhra Pradesh covering various facets with facts and figures. It is hoped that the present publication will serve as one of the basic and important sources of information on the subject and go a long way in meeting the information requirements of those interested in library movement and public library movement in Andhra Pradesh.

Hyderabad — **Prof. A. A. N. Raju**

ACKNOWLEDGEMENTS

At the outset I would like to thank very sincerely Prof. A. Neelameghan, well known Library and Information Scientist and currently Member Secretary, Sarada Ranganathan Endowment for Library Science, Bangalore, who readily acceded to my request and wrote a foreword for this book.

I would be failing in my duty if I do not thank Smt. S. Venkamma, Director, Dept. of Public Libraries, Government of Andhra Pradesh for permitting me to peruse the annual reports of Zilla Grandhalaya Samsthas and Regional Libraries in the State for collecting required information. In this regard Sri Bugga Reddy, the concerned Officer in the Department of Public Libraries painstakingly provided the required annual reports. I am thankful to him. Sri. Y. Narasimha Rao, retired Superintendent, West Godavari Zilla Grandhalaya Samstha, Eluru, who with great effort provided information on norms for Branch Libraries and I am grateful to him.

Special thanks are due to Dr.(Smt) R. Sarada, Hon. General Secretary, Andhra Pradesh Library Association and R.V.S. Siva Rama Krishna, Lecturer, Paturi Nagabhushanam School of Library Science, Vijayawada for providing the required photographs of SCL and of Zilla Grandhalaya Samasthas. Thanks are also due to Sri P. V. Malleshwar, Joint Secretary, A. P. Library Association for providing photograph of State Regional Library, Guntur. I would also thank Sri T. V. Prafullachandra, who is a source of strength to me in my research and publication endeavors and who prepared the relevant maps. I acknowledge and record my sincere appreciation of the support and assistance rendered by Sri M. Madhusudan, who typed the preliminary pages and index of this publication.

Lastly but not the least I whole heartedly thank Sri Sumit Sethi, the young and dynamic Chief Executive, M/s Ess Ess Publications, New Delhi, who came forward to publish this work.

— Prof. A. A. N. Raju

A
Library Movement in Andhra Pradesh

A.1. Introduction

The genesis and development of library movement and public library development in Andhra (including Rayalaseema) and Telangana regions of Andhra Pradesh is the main focus of this books. Social developments combined with the political struggle for freedom lead certain special characteristics to the period and the Library movement has been studied against this background. The seeds for the spread of Library movement were sown as early as in 1886 with the establishment of Saraswathi Grandhalayam at Visakhapatnam. From that time, a few libraries sprang up until the beginning of the 20 century. The establishment of Sri Krishna Devaraya Andhra Bhasha Nilayam, in 1901, at Hyderabad had great significance and impact, later on the spread of library movement in Telangana and Andhra Desa. The renaissance movement in Telangana region sprouted after the establishment of this premier institution. Gradually, the movement in the two regions gained momentum along with the freedom struggle. After Independence, the former Nizam's State was integrated with the Indian Union after Police Action in 1948. A separate Andhra State was formed in 1953. Later, the Andhra and Telangana regions were integrated to form the enlarged state of Andhra Pradesh in 1956. Thus, the library movements in the two regions were merged and transformed into an integrated library movement.Before the movement took the shape of a larger mass movement after the formation of Andhra Desa Grandhalaya Sangham in 1914, many libraries had been established by individuals or groups of enthusiasts for the spread of knowledge among the people through the medium of libraries. It has been estimated that as many as 163 libraries were established before 1914 in Andhra Desa.[1] After the formation of Andhra Desa Library Association in 1914, the movement spread vigorously to the rural areas in Andhra Desa, thanks to the pioneering work done by the leaders of the movement.

In Telangana also, the movement started with the establishment of Sri Krishna Devaraya Andhra Bhasa Nilayam in 1901. The movement quickly spread as a part of the freedom movement against the Nizam's autocratic rule. The movement received an institutional support with the formation of Andhra Jana Sangham in 1921.

Definition of the Library

While all the modern concepts of a library cannot be found in the same form and extent in the past, the essentials of a Library in thought and action could be seen from the earliest date in this study. A mere assembly or collection of books is not a library, nor is a library alone a place where books are kept. A library in its true sense is an organisation, a system designed to preserve and facilitate the use of graphic records. It is a social instrument created to form a link in the net-work of communication system essential to the healthy growth of any society or culture. As an institution, the library has, from time to time, assumed certain marginal functions, but its basic function remains unaltered as a link in the chain of synchronic and diachronic communication, and it is the custody of recorded knowledge embodied in diverse graphic materials. The fundamental concern of the library is "communication of knowledge, ideas, thought, but those intangibles are embodied in physical objects, i.e., books and other graphic records."[2] Therefore, collection, preservation and dissemination of knowledge embodied in documents becomes the primary function of the library.

Several definitions of the library emphasise the utilitarian aspect of the library. Thus *Encyclopedia Britannica*,[3] defines it as "a collection of written, printed or other graphic material (including films, slides, phonograph records and tapes) organised for use." *The Librarian's Glossary*[4] defines library as a "(I) collection of books and other literary material kept for reading, study and consultation; (2) a place, building, room or rooms set apart for the keeping and use of a collection of books etc."

The library was a product of civilization. It emerged when people had reached a point where they had writing materials, a written language and records to preserve human thought. "It progressed in size, complexity and elaborateness as civilization itself advanced."[5] Next to schooling or formal education, the library assumed a very important role in the dissemination of knowledge. The accumulated knowledge of a society or generation is far greater than the content of the curriculum in formal education either in school, college or in university. Therefore, any member of the society has the opportunity and access to the whole gamut of accumulated knowledge in the library and can choose any subject or get any type of information for study and learn matters that are not included in any scholastic curriculum.[6] In the course of its development through centuries,the library has become the chief instrument, so far, perfected for accumulation and dissemination of knowledge for the benefit of society. The library enabled man to depend on letters instead of live memory and spoken word alone.[7] Man has vastly increased his capacity for communication with written documents largely because of the library.[8] Thus, the institution of library has become a perfect and principal vehicle in the process of communication by carrying forward and making available the intellectual resources (i.e., documents) which it accumulates for use for the present and future generations.

Public Library : Definition, Objectives and Functions

It is necessary to explain the word Library and in what connotation it has been used in this study. The word "Library" does not cover merely public libraries but all types of libraries such as national, academic (school, college and university), special, industrial and technical libraries, which have emerged for the last two hundred years. But the present study is confined to the library movement which means the public library movement. Therefore, as a preliminary step, the definition, objectives and activities of a public library are briefly discussed in the following sections.

Definition

The public library as we understand it today is an Anglo-Saxon idea. It developed in England and America at about the same time and was original in both the countries.[9] It is a Western idea based on the progress of society under Western democracy. The modern public library "with all the paraphernalia that the term carries with it is not a very familiar picture to us and is never indigenous to us."[10] Let us examine its meaning in some detail.

The word "public" has been used with various shades of meaning. For example, "a public school in the U.S. is a free school, supported by the public. In England it is a school in which tuition is charged but which is open to all on the same conditions. But the librarians have universally tended to restrict the term Public Library to those which are provided through the rates or other forms of taxation."[11] The public library inthe United States is "either owned or controlled by the public or freely accessible to the public or it has two of these features or all three of them."[12]

Jast defines the public library as a "public institution supported by taxation, one that opens its collection, facilities and services without distinction to all citizens."[13] More than a century ago Poole, the librarian of Chicago Public Library, wrote :

> the public library is established by state laws, is supported by local taxation and voluntary gifts, is managed by public trust, and every citizen of the city and town which maintains it has an equal share of its privileges of reference and circulation.[14]

The concept of the public library is something new in India. Though libraries have been in existence from time immemorial, the idea of the public library as a social institution took firm roots only after the advent of the British in India. The Advisory Committee for Libraries states that

> the British came to dominate India, but they brought with them an ideology and literature embodying ideals of the common man with which the whole of Europe was imbued at the time. They could not rid themselves in India of ideas in which they were brought up in England. Inevitably they inspired though they may not have actively encouraged the setting up of public libraries in the country.[15]

The Ekbote Committee[16] appointed by the Government of Andhra Pradesh in 1976 to review the working of A.P. Public Librarians Act, 1960, supports this view by stating that

> although there was the tradition of learning in India and there were a few notable libraries, the concept of public libraries was brought to India from England. Britishers came to India with an ideology and literature embodying of the common man with

which the whole of Europe was imbued at that time.[17]

Public libraries in the UK, the USA' and the Scandinavian countries have been established by state laws and supported by local taxation and voluntary gifts. But the situation is different in India. Under the British rule, that is, until 1947, the library movement did not get any State support and had to depend merely upon initiave, imagination, planning and enthusiasm of individuals or groups in different parts of the country. This was more so in the case of the library movement in Andhra Desa and the Telangana region of the former Nizam's state. It was essentially a people's movement. The public library in this context may be defined as "the library open to the public, run by representatives of the public, who had their hand on the pulse of the people's urges and aspirations with the fullest public support."[18]

Objectives

Public libraries have established themselves as an indispensable element in the life of the community. They provide information which is essential for the progress of the community and provide relaxation and refreshment for every class of the population. The great French writer Andre Maurois,[19] emphasised the need for the public library service to every individual in the community so as to transform him as a valuable member of the society. The UNESCO Public Library Manifesto[20] first issued in 1949 and revised in 1972, proclaims its belief in the Public Library as a living force for education, culture and information and as an essential agent for fostering of peace and understanding between people and between nations. It also sets out the basic services which the public libraries should provide, how they should be provided, administered and financed.

Leigh[21] stated the objectives of the Public Library as follows:

(i) to assemble, preserve and administer books and related educational materials in organised collections, in order to promote, through guidance and stimulation and enlightened citizenship and enhance personal lives ;

(ii) to serve the community as a general centre of reliable information ;

(iii) to provide opportunity and encouragement for children young people, men and women to educate themselves largely.

In 1971, the Library Association (UK) set out the following objectives for Public Library Services :

(a)*Ed ucation* : to foster and provide means for self development of the individual group at whatever age of education, closing the gap between the individual and recorded knowledge ;

(b) *Information* : to bring to the individual group accurate information quickly in depth particularly on topics of current concern ;

(c) *Culture* : to be one of principal centres of cultural life and promote a keener participation, enjoyment and appreciation of all arts ; and

(d) *Leisure* : to play a part in encouraging the positive use of leisure and providing material for change and relaxation.[22]

Functions

The UNESCO Manifesto[23] describes the public library as a "democratic agency for education, a vital community force, and the people's University." The Manifesto enjoins that the public library should provide :

(i) Books, Pamphlets, Magazines, Newspapers, Maps, Pictures, Films, Music scores and recordings and give guidance to their use ;

(ii) the Public Library should offer children, young people men and women opportunity and encouragement;

(iii) to educate themselves continuously ;

(iv) to keep abreast of progress in all fields of knowledge;

(v) to maintain freedom of expression and constructively critical attitude towards all public issues ;

(vi) to be better social and political citizens of their country and of the world;

(vii) to be more efficient in their day-to-day activities;

(viii) to develop their creative capacities and powers of appreciation in arts and letters ;

(ix) to aid generally in the advancement of knowledge ;

(x) to use their leisure time to promote personal happiness and social well being.

The Roberts Committee Report[24] states the essential functions of the Public library as follows :

(i) to supply any reader or group of readers, the books and relative material for which they may ask ;

(ii) to satisfy, and to promote the desire for books ;

(iii) the public library is an obviously suitable centre for exhibitions, lectures, adult education classes and discussions groups.

The Ekbote Committee[26] summarised the functions of the public library as collection, organisation, distribution, interpretation and guidance of documents.

To realize its aims and to perform effectively the functions stated above the public library evolved different departments within its fold. The best known and the most important of these are reference and information work, home reading service for children and young people, periodicals, bibliographical services, and such specialist departments as audio-visual work, and archives and local history studies. Other areas which help in the growth of the public libraries and in the extension of their activities are : branch and mobile libraries, lectures, exhibitions and other extension work services to special classes of users such as hospital patients, the blind, seamen and prisoners.

Library Movement

The word "movement" has been defined by the Oxford English Dictionary as "a series of organised activities working towards an objective."[26] The word "movement" has been used to indicate a variety of social movements such as workers, religious, literary, linguistic, sectarian, caste, peasant, tribal, ethnic, feministic and student movements, which the world has witnessed since the beginning of the nineteenth century. The term "social movement" or its equivalent in the Western language is being used to denote "a wide variety of collective attempts to bring about a change in certain social institutions or to create an entirely new order."[27] The term "social movement" has been used in the present study in a wider connotation to include any movement which tries to bring about a change in the society.

Features

The basic feature of a social movement is collective action as distinct from individual action. When the collective action is somewhat sustained as distinct from a sporadic occurrence, it takes the form of a movement. The collective action should be able to create an interest and awakening in a fairly large number of people. Hence "a social movement essentially involves sustained collective mobilization through either informal or formal organisation."[28] The second important feature is that a social movement is generally oriented towards bringing about change either partial or total in existing system of relationships, values or norms. The third important feature of a social movement, according to Rao,[29] is ideology which forms an important component of a social movement. In terms of these three features, a social movement has been defined as "an organised attempt on the part of a section of a society to bring about either partial or total change in society through collective mobilization based on an ideology."[30] There have been several attempts to classify social movements using one characteristic or the other.[31] Depending on their purpose movements may be described as oriented either towards bringing about a reform in some area of life or towards bringing about revolutionary changes in all spheres of life and in all basic values.[32] Thus, on the basis of "mission" and characteristics, movements have been classified as linguistic, literary, religious, sectarian, peasant, feministic and student movements.[33] Social movements have also been classified on the basis of the geographical area under purview. While some may be international, others may be national, regional or local.[34]

The Library movement in general, either in the USA, UK or in India have the basic features of a movement, viz., collective mobilization, change orientation, presence of ideology and organisation. The movement in these countries had been launched and propagated by enthusiastic workers and took the shape of a popular movement. It was directed to achieve change in the existing condition of the society with respect to the level of education and dissemination of information. The ideology[35] or the aim of the movement was to spread knowledge among the people through the establishment of the social institution, namely the library. To spread the ideology or to achieve the objective, and for the sustenance of the movement, an institutional arrangement was sought and the result was the establishment of library associations.

In the USA, the library movement was spearheaded by stalwarts like C.J. Jewatt, Melvil Dewey, W.F. Pool, CA. Cutter and scores of others, during the second half of the nineteenth century. The main object of the movement was "conservation and organisation of world's resources of recorded thought and fact so as to make them available for the present and future uses."[36] For sustaining the movement, the stalwarts visualized an institutional support and established the American Library Association (ALA) in 1876, the first professional library association in the world. It was formed for the purpose of promoting the library movement in the country by exchanging views, reaching conclusions and inducing cooperation in all departments of bibliotechnical science and economy.[37] The founding of the ALA had great impact on similar movements in other parts of the world. The establishment of the ALA attracted attention of Great Britain and the result was an International Library Conference in London held in 1877 and the consequent founding of the Library Association of the United Kingdom.[38]

In the United Kingdom, the library movement was launched by the pioneers like Thomas Carlyle, who helped in the establishing the London Library in 1841, Edward Edwards, William Ewart and J.D. Brown to mention a few during the second half of the nineteenth century.[39] The library movement by these pioneers, which attained the character of a popular movement, resulted in the passing of first British Public Libraries Act in 1850.[40] The basic objective of the movement was intellectual advancement of the population through the establishment of public libraries in the country.[41] To sustain this movement, the Library Association (UK) was founded, in 1877, with the following objectives: a) to unite all persons engaged or interested in library work by holding conferences and meetings; (b) to promote the adoption of public libraries acts in any city, borough or district within the United Kingdom; (c) to promote the establishment of reference and lending libraries for use by the public.[42]

In India the library movement was the product of general national awakening and particularly of the Swadeshi movement. The Swadeshi movement led by Bipincbandra Pal and Lala Lajpat Rai helped the library movement to spread.[43] The free public library movement started by Maharaja Sayaji Rao Gaekwad of Baroda in 1910, confined to this princely state only.[44] It was not a mass movement but purely an official effort and received support from its enlightened ruler. This did not spread to other states in India. But the leaders of the library movement in other parts of the country, specially from Andhra Desa and Telangana appreciated the efforts made in Baroda State.

The seeds for the popular Library Movement were first sown in Andhra Desa. The establishment of "Saraswati Grandhalayam" in the year 1886 at Visakhapatnam marks the genesis of the concept of Public Library. Since then numerous public libraries sprang up with individual or group effort throughout the length and breadth of Andhra Desa. It was estimated that as many as 163 libraries sprang up before the first library Conference.[45] When the number of these libraries multiplied and the field of their activities widened, it became necessary to bring together the men responsible for their organisation so as to work together for collective benefit and advancement. As a result of this move, the first Conference of representatives of libraries of Andhra Desa was held on 10th April 1914, under the auspices of Ram Mohan Library, Bezawada.[46] The prime organisers of the Conference were Ayyanki Venkata Ramanayya, Suri Venkat Narasimha Sastri, Nalam Krishna Rao and Mocharla Ramachandra Rao. Nearly 200 delegates from Andhra Desa and Telugu speaking districts of the Nizam's state attended the Conference. The Conference decided to form Andhra Desa Library Association (ADLA) with the main object of spreading the public library movement in Andhra Desa and organising it on sound lines. The movement was the product of the efforts of ordinary men, intellectuals, students and peasants in the villages."[47] Chilakmarthi Lakshmi Narasimham,[48] an illustrious Telugu scholar and writer who presided over the first Conference of representatives of libraries of Andhra Desa put forth a miniature manifesto (Grandhalaya Vedam) of the library movement.[49]

The Andhra Desa Library Association which was leading

the library movement in Andhra Desa took steps for the spread of the movement in other parts of the country. The first All India Public Library Conference was convened along with the sixth session of the Provincial Andhra Desa Public Library Conference in November 1919 at Madras.[50]

Thus, we find that the library movement either in Andhra Desa or in other parts of British India had the characteristics of a social movement viz. sustained collective action for bringing about change, an organisation and a manifesto. The movement took strong roots during the national awakening and helped to establish numerous libraries in Andhra Desa and other parts of the country.

Background of the Library Movement in Andhra and Telangana Regions

Before tracing the genesis and development of library movement in the Andhra and Telangana regions during the beginning of the twentieth century it is useful to have a glimpse, as a background of the general conditions that obtained in the two regions.

Andhra Region

The advent of British rule in India heralded a new epoch not only in the history of India but in that of the Andhra region also. The internal squabbles among the Indian rulers and their short-sighted and selfish policies facilitated the establishment and consolidation of British Power in India.[51] The English East India Company, in order to achieve the expansion of their political suzerainty, wiped out the French rule from Andhra by defeating the French in the battle at Chandurti near Rajahmundry, in 1758,[52] and one year later, by the seizure of the Fort of Masulipatnam, one of the strong holds of the French in Andhra, in 1759.[53]

As a result of the defeat of the French, the East India Company acquired Northern Circars of Eluru, Mustafa Nagar,

Rajahmundry and Srikakulam in 1776 and Guntur in 1788 from the Nizam of Hyderabad in return for which they promised to help the Nizam against his enemies.[54] In the year 1800, the Nizam also through Subsidiary Alliance, ceded the districts of Cuddapah, Kurnool, Anantapur and Bellary to East India Company.[55] Thus, at the beginning of the nineteenth century, the whole Andhra Desa decisively came under the Company's rule.

However, the local rulers i.e., the Rajahs, Zamindars and Poligars who had their own military forces, had set up opposition and did not accept the Company's supremacy.[56] It took some years for the Company to put down these local revolts and establish its authority. By 1840 Andhra Desa became practically free from local rebellions. The great uprising in North India in 1857 and its ruthless supression had little effect in Andhra. A few disturbances in the agency area[57] and intermittent raids organised by Rohillas and Arabs from the Nizam's territory were promptly put down.[58] The suppression of the 1857 rebellion and assumption of power by Queen Victoria from East India Company resulted in passing of the Andhra region under the direct rule of the British crown in 1858. This assumption of power directly by the crown brought about vital changes in the economic, social and administrative set-up of the country.[59]

Administration

One of the important changes initiated was the introduction of a uniform system of administration. Its distinguishing feature was an enlightened bureaucracy, strictly secular in character and highly centralized.[60] For administrative convenience, the Presidency was divided into districts, talukas and villages with a hierarchy of trained officials to carry on the administration. The district administration was headed by a collector, usually a European, who was also entrusted with judicial and police powers. Administration at the taluka level was, however, in the hands of Tahsildars who were invariably Indians[61] Administration of justice was an important aspect of the British rule. They were responsible for undertaking rule of law which gradually eliminated nepotism, casteism and communalism in the dispensation of justice and established a good measure of equality among the people in the eyes of law.

Economic Situation

One of the chief features of the economic policy introduced by the British administration was the collection of land revenue. They introduced the system of permanent settlement, the underlying principle being ensuring a fixed sum to be paid into the state exchequer. With this end in view, the Zamindari and Ryotwari systems of tenure were introduced. But, the system, with many loop holes, brought untold suffering to the peasantry.[62]

The commercial interests of the British stood paramount in shaping the economy of the country. It was formulated and geared primarily to the growth of industries in England by exporting raw materials from India and importing finished goods from England. For the success of their policy, the British felt the need for better transport and communication facilities. Therefore, laying of new roads and railway lines were undertaken and important places were connected. But communication facilities in rural areas remained in a bad shape.[63]

The dumping of machine-made goods from England into the local markets in India had a disastrous effect on the indigenous industries which could not withstand the competition of foreign machine-made goods. While some industries succumbed to their onslaught, others slowly disintegrated.[64] A large number of artisans and skilled workers were thrown out of employment. No industries were established to absorb them. Many artisans and skilled workers left the country in search of livelihood for South-East Asian countries.[65]

Many unemployed workers, particularly from artisan classes, took to agriculture.[66]

The Indian economy was very much dependent on agriculture. But the irrigation facilities in the country were far from satisfactory. The construction of anicuts across the rivers Godavari (1847), Krishna (1853) and Pennar (1806) and the digging of the Kurnool-Cuddapah Canal and a few other minor irrigation facilities brought large tracts of land under irrigation but had no significant impact on the lives of agriculturists as a greater part of the country depended on rainfall alone and irrigation works were not in a good shape.[67] The taxes imposed by the Government added to the misery of the people. For example, the Salt Tax of Rs. 2-8-0 per maund severely affected the middle and lower income groups. The other taxes such as Income Tax and Profession Tax, brought greater hardship to artisan and non-agriculturist classes.

The policies pursued and administrative measures initiated in land revenue, commerce, irrigation and taxation ruined the people. The frequent famines also proved fatal. The Famine of 1802 hit the Northern Circars, while the one which broke out in 1804 in the Ceded Districts caused untold suffering. The Guntur Famine of 1833 was disastrous.[68] Famines occurred in 1854 and 1865 also. Another devastating famine which broke out in 1867 gravely shook the people in the Circars and Ceded Districts. A prolonged Famine occurred in Andhra from 1900 to 1903. The economic policies pursued by the British administration made the people unhappy and by the end of the nineteenth century, they started agitations against land revenue collections, famine and taxation policies.[69]

Education

From the second half of the nineteenth century, western education slowly spread to the Andhra districts owing to the efforts of the Government, Christian missionaries and philanthropic Zamindar.[70] With the establishment of University of Madias in 1857 higher education began to gain ground in Andhra. The Government of Madras established colleges at Rajahmundry (1873), Nellore (1877), Vizianagaram (1877), Visakhapatnam (1878), Berhampur (1879) and Pithapuram (1892). The educational policy of the Government was so designed as to diffuse western thought, philosophy and literature.

The Christian missionaries undertook, as part of their evangelical work to start institutions for imparting western education and the Zamindars did so as a mark of their philanthrophy. In 1843, the Church Missionary Society[71] under the leadership of Rev. Noble started a school at Machilipatnarn for imparting western education. In 1864, it was upgraded into a college. The Society also started two more high schools, one at Eluru and another at Vijayawada.

The spread of western education in Andhra created a new class of elite imbued with liberalism of the west. It helped intellectual generation. It had also helped the educated to give up their attitude of uncritical deference to authority, tradition and custom. The impact of western thought and spread of western culture was two-fold. Firstly, some among the educated opted to work in social reconstruction and religious reforms of the Hindu society and became pioneers in these spheres. Secondly, it sowed the seeds of nationalism which in the twentieth century grew into a full-fledged freedom movement.[72]

Reform Movement

The reform work in the Hindu society started with the starting of Brahmo Samaj movement in Bengal by Raja Ram Mohan Roy (1744-1833). The movement popularised theistic worship and its theism was a synthesis of the essential truths and basic ideals of the great religions not only of India but also of the whole world.[73] It preached against caste system, evils of drinking, concubinage and supported widow re-marriages and encouraged women education. The movement soon spread to other parts of India including Andhra too. Brahmo Samaj units were established in Rajahmundry (1878), Masulipatnam (1882), Kakinada (1883), Vijayawada (1888) and Guntur (1898). The Brahmo Samaj movement greatly influenced the thoughts and aspirations of young men all over Andhra. In fact, most social reformers from Andhra, in the nineteenth century, were staunch followers of Brahmo Samaj.[74]

In the field of social reform in Andhra, Kandukuri Veeresalingam Pantulu (1848-1919) stands foremost. He was greatly influenced by the writings of Raja Ram Mohan Roy. He dedicated himself to the upliftment of society. In the words of V.R. Narla.

> he shook them out of their medieval stupor, he whipped them out of their ignorance, he purged them of many of their superstitions and he gave an altogether modern progressive and humanistic turn to their life and thought,[75]

He excelled in the Telugu literary field in several spheres. He was the first author to write in Telugu a novel, a drama, and on natural science and history and prose for women. Through his special activities like education of women, widow remarriages, and through his contributions for the growth of Telugu journalism, he heralded the "renaissance movement" in Andhra. He laid the foundations for the renaissance by his multifarious activities and writings which prepared the minds of the people for achieving social reforms and political advancement in the twentieth century.[76]

Journalistic activity

The second half of the nineteenth century witnessed the rise and growth of Telugu journalism. A number of vernacular newspapers steadily increased after the great rebellion of 1857 and gradually took a militant tone. The first Telugu journal *Satyadoota* was published by a Christian Association of Bellary for the propagation of Christianity. To counter this missionary propaganda, a few Telugu news papers were started, the most prominent among them being the *Tatva Bodhini* started by the Vedasamaj of Madras in 1864." In 1874 Veeresalingam started a weekly called *Vivekavardhani* from Rajahmundry for propagating his ideas and reforms in social and literary fields. He also started a separate journal for women called the *Sahiti Bodhini*, *Hasya Vardhini* and *SatyaSoma Vardhini* for the propagation of his reform movement.[78] The first Telugu political news weekly *Andhra Prakasika* was started, in 1885, with Parthasarathy Naidu of Madras as editor. By 1905, as many as 20 journals were published in Telugu.[79] The most popular among them were *Andhra Prakasika*, *Sasilekha*, *Krishna Patrika*, *Vivekavardhani*, *Deshabhimani*, *Rasikollasini*, *Lokaranjani* and *Purushardha Pradayani*. These papers boldly criticised the Government for its failure in administration.[80] They also highlighted the economic distress of the people resulting from inequitous taxation, imperialistic wars financed by the Indian tax payer, racial discrimination, rising prices, heavy land revenue and a host of other grievances.[81]

The spread of education and the growth of Telugu journallism contributed to the growth of a new awareness among the people. Many associations were founded for political and other purposes. The Madras Mahajana Sabha was founded, on 16th May 1884, by Rangayya Naidu and Anandacharyulu who were its President and Secretary respectively. The Sabha was the first attempt by the English educated Indians to get together for an exchange of ideas on questions of vital interest and for a joint action. Many delegates from the Telugu districts attended the first conference of the Sabha.[82] Among the literary associations, the Cocanada Literary Association was prominent. This association also took an active interest in public affairs.

Indian National Congress

The formation of Indian National Congress in the year

1885 was another land-mark and gave great impetus to the political awakening in Andhra. Andhras evinced great interest in the Congress. The first session which was held at Bombay was attended by Rangayya Naidu and Anandacharyulu.[83] The Indian National Congress movement gave great impetus for the establishment of various district associations. In 1892, the Krishna District Association was formed and it was the first of its kind not only in Madras Presidency but also probably in the whole of India.[84]

The British rule in India and the changes that had been effected in administration, judiciary, education, social and economic conditions, and intellectual life of the country in the nineteenth century prepared the ground for public awareness and brought consciousness for the assertion of self respect and individual rights among the people and led to the emergence of a new class of intelligentsia. The material conditions created by the British Government also contributed for the awakening of the Andhra intelligentsia.[86] Thus, by the turn of the century, the stage was set for a relentless struggle for freedom and social regeneration of the people through several movements like upliftment of women, Harijan upliftment, Temperance work, Swadeshi movement and last but not least the Library and adult education movement. The Library movement spread with the establishment of libraries throughout Andhra Desa for the spread of knowledge among the people.

Telangana Region

The Hyderabad State was established in 1724 by Nizam-ul-Mulk Asafjah. It comprised the present State of Andbra Pradesh and portions of Tamil Nadu, Orissa, Maharashtra and Karnataka. The French General, Bussy, acquired the Northern Circars from the Nizam, in 1753, for the maintenance of French troops in the Deccan.[86] When the French were defeated by the English, the East India Company acquired Northern Circars of Eluru, Mustafanagar, Rajahmundry and Srikakulam in 1776 and Guntur in 1788, from the Nizam in return for the help they promised him against his enemies. The Nizam also ceded to the English East India Company, the districts of Cuddapah, Kurnool, Anantapur and Bellary, in the year 1800, when he entered into the Subsidiary Alliance with them for protecting him against internal and external dangers.[87]

By the end of the eighteenth century, Andhra Desa was broken and the Northern Circars and Ceded Districts became part of Madras Presidency under the British rule while the rest of the Telugu districts remained under the control of the Nizam under the name of Telangana.[88] As a consequence of this historical separation, the two regions came under two different and distrinct political systems. Therefore, from the beginning of the nineteenth century and onwards, political, social and cultural developments in the two regions took two distinct paths.[89]

The total area of Hyderabad State comprised 87, 700 sq. miles. The State was divided into 16 districts for administrative convenience and its total population was approximately 181/2 million[8"] of which Telugu speaking people were about 10 million. Marathi and Kannada speaking people were 4 million and 2 million respectively. The remaining two and half million comprised the Hindustani and Urdu speaking people. The population of the State was overwhelmingly rural in character. Of the total population, less than 6 per cent lived in towns. The bulk of the population had agriculture for occupation. The total percentage of Hindus in the State was 85 per cent while that of the Muslims was 10.5 per cent.[91]

Several factors such as political changes, social and religious movements, growth of education, economic changes and journalistic activities contributed for the slow beginning of the public awakening in the Hyderabad State. As the State was being ruled by an autocratic ruler with few avenues for social, educational and economic development, the seeds of public awakening germinated very slowly. In contrast, in British India it was quick and fast as a result of direct impact of western ideas and institutions. This was evident from the fact that public awareness regarding political, economic, educational, social and religious reforms was only in the formative stages by the end of the nineteenth century in the Nizam's State while such reforms were already under way in the British India.[92]

Political Conditions

The great rebellion of 1857 in North India had its impact on the people of Hyderabad State. Nizam's aloofness and apathy to the revolt caused public resentment against his regime. The cessation of Berar, Osmanabad and Raichur Districts in 1853, to the British for stationing of British troops in Nizam State provoked resentment against the British. The events of 1857 further aggravated the resentment against the British.[93] The reverberation of 1857 revolt, British machinations, Nizam's indifference to people's reactions, his bad policies—all contributed for the spread of anti-British and anti-Nizam movements and for the growth of political awakening among the public during the later part of the nineteenth century.[94]

Economic Conditions

The feudal system was the basis for the Nizam's State. In the Telangana region, big chunks of land was owned by big landlords and the majority of poor farmers owned small land holdings. The characteristics of this situation was exploitation and ill treatment of small farmers, Vettichakiri and dominance by the Zamindars. The frequent occurrance of famines, squeezing of money by the Arabs, Rohillas and Marwadi merchants affected the economy of the State adversely and caused great hardship to the people. The State borrowed money from the Hindu and Muslim aristocracy as well as from the Arab and Marwadi merchants. The indebtedness of the Government increased and the economic condition was far from satisfactory.[95] As regards communications in the State, the

Hyderabad-Sholapur road was completed in 1860. The Bombay-Madras line touching the parts of the State like Gulbarga and Wadi was laid in 1868. By 1878, Hyderabad city was connected by broadgage line running from Hyderabad to Wadi with the Bombay-Madras Railway.[96] The Chanda Railway scheme which went against the interest of the State was completed in 1886, and sparked a public agitation in 1883. The educated class of Hyderabad had set up a committee known as "The Committee to consider the Chanda Railway scheme"under the leadership of Aghornath Chattopadhyaya and Mulla Abdul Qayum.[97] With this agitation, the growth of public opinion in the state could be said to have started in 1883.[98]

Language and Education

Language and education are two vital necessities of the people on which their social and cultural progress depends much. They also help the educated to communicate their ideas. Telugu was spoken by 10 million people out of a total population of 181/2 million. The Government's policy of making Urdu as the medium of instruction in the middle schools and high schools was greatly responsible for the stunted growth of the Telugu language and as also for the educational backwardness of the Telugu speaking people.[99] As Ramanuja Rao states :

> as a result of 250 years rule of Asafzahis, Andhras became nonentity. They had to be initiated to education with Persian. Urdu became the official language. From elementary school level to university level the medium of instruction being Urdu, Telugu language, for decades had to go into exile.[100]

Urdu was introduced as the language of the courts in 1884, and later extended to all branches of administration, in 1886.[101] This dealt a severe blow to the development of the

Telugu language and the representation of Telugu people in the stateadministration had been severely curtailed.[102] The Government, did not encourage the establishment of private educational institutions To curb the private initiative, the Government had imposed severe restrictions. The deterrent rules and regulations dampened the enthusiasm of individuals and private bodies interested in the establishment of educational institutions of their own.[103] The policies of the government not only came in the way of development of education but also in the physical development of the people as it imposed severe restrictions on the establishment of private gymnasiams or Akhadas.[104]

In spite of these restrictions, a number of educational institutions were established in twin cities of Hyderabad and Secunderabad, by 1885. Apart from the government schools, Christian missionaries and private organisations had also started establishing educational institutions. The growth of educational institutions attracted a number of educated persons to Hyderabad from other parts of the country. Eminent persons, like Aghornath Chattopadhyaya, played a significant part in the intellectual and social growth of Hyderabad.[105]

According to the Administration Report of the Nizam's State[106] for the years 1894-1898, there was one first grade college with 66 students, one second grade college with 4 students. There was one Oriental college with 83 students and there were 13 high schools and 49 middle schools with 3,425 and 8,635 pupils respectively. There were 708 primary schools for boys and 67 schools for girls with 46,581 and 3,812 students respectively.

Social and Religious Conditions

The majority of the population of the state were Hindus. But the state was a Muslim state. The society in general was plagued by several social evils such as superstitions, child marriages, casteism, prevention of widow marriages, purdah system, practice of Sati, and exploitation of the poor by Zamindars.[107]

A number of enlightened individuals took initiative and established a number of organisations to eradicate the social evils. The social policy of the British India had its impact on the Nizam's state. Consequently, the practice of Sati was banned in 1848. Selling of children was legally prohibited in 1856.[108] In the domain of Hindu religious reforms, Arya Samaj which was established in Hyderabad in 1892, played a significant role. Through its multifarious activities, it countered certain orthodox Hindu religious practices. It organised Ganesh Utsavs, Bhajans, gymanisiums and arranged lectures which promoted social awakening.[109] The Theosophical Society was established in 1892 by Ramaswamy Iyengar, at Chanderghat. The Society, as a centre of discussion on religious and cultural matters, attracted the elite of the city.[110] The Young Men's Improvement Society (YMIS, 1879), the Albert Reading Room, Secunderabad, the Malawala Maha Sabha, the Hindu Social Club also took active interest in the social development of the people."[111] In the field of social and political awakening of the State, Aghornath Chattopadhyaya's contribution was singular. Ever since he came to Hyderabad in 1878 he bad been connected with all intellectual, social and political activities of the State. He encouraged inter-caste and widow marriages, worked for the abolition of child marriages, encouraged education of depressed classes and emancipation of women.[112] Another notable figure in the social and political awakening in Hyderabad during the last two decades of the nineteenth century was Mulla Abdul Qayum. He, along with Aghornath Chattopad hyaya, played a significant role in the social and political affairs of the state. He pleaded for Hindu-Muslim unity and took a keen interest in Ganesh Utsav celebrations. In the words of Sarojini Naidu, "he was not only the messenger but the living message of Hindu-Muslim unity."[113] Thus, by the end of the nineteenth century the social and religious awakening of the people was in formative stages when compared with its counterpart in British India.[114]

Journalistic Activity

Journalistic activity in the second half of the nineteenth century also contributed for the social and political awakening in the state. A number of newspapers in Urdu, Persian, Telugu, Marathi and English were started during the period. These newspapers boldly commented against the administration and faced many difficulties from the state authority.[115] Mention may be made of *Gulbarga Samachar, Bhageshya Nagar, Champavati* (Marathi), *Hyderabad Telegraph, The Deccan Standard, The Hyderabad Record, The Deccan Times, The Deccan Punch* (English) and *Dina Vartamani* (Telugu). By the end of the nineteenth century, there were only 22 papers in the State, whereas in Madras Presidency there were 161 papers in the corresponding period. In the Nizam's state, the journalistic activity was very slow when compared with various presidencies in the rest of India.[116] *The Hyderabad Record* championed the cause of the National movement and the uderdog.[117]

Establishment of Indian National Congress

The establishment of the Indian National Congress in 1885, had a profound effect on the enlightened and educated classes of Hyderabad. Intellectuals like Aghornath Chattopadhyaya, Mulla Abdul Qayum, Ramachandra Pilley, Muthyala Ramanna and others welcomed the formation of the Congress. Public opinion was sympathetic to this new political awakening. But the Government adopted critical attitude against this new development.[118] Among the Muslims, Mulla Abdul Qayum was the first to join the Indian National Congress. He also pleaded that all Muslims should join the Indian National Congress.[119] The press, in general, notably *The Hyderabad Record* championed the cause of building public opinion in favour of National movement in India.

During the nineteenth century in general, and from the second half of the century in particular, State of Hyderabad witnessed the rise of an educated middle class, development of communications, growth of the press, spread of educational institutions, and social and religious reformist movements which greatly contributed for the public awakening in the state. However, it should be pointed out that the public awakening in the Nizam's state was in formative stages when compared with that in British India. The supressive policies by the Nizam government and the educational, social and economic backwardness of the people were responsible for this sorry state of affairs.[120]

By the end of the nineteenth century, the political and social movements in British India in particular, and the activities of national leaders, in general, had greater impact on the thinking of the people of Hyderabad.[121] The developments in British Andhra also had their impact on the developments in Hyderabad during the beginning of the twentieth century. To spread knowledge among the people, to restore the lost prestige of the Telugu language, literature and culture, and to establish cultural links between the Telangana and Andhra regions, the Library movement was started in the beginning of the twentieth century.[122]

References

1. Suri Venkata Narasimha Sastri in his Presidential address to the 6th Andhra Desa Library Conference held at Madras on 19th November 1916 quotes this figure. See *Grandhalaya Pragati*, Part 1 (Vijayawada : Andhra Pradesh Library Association, 1962), p. 83.
2. *ALA Encyclopedia of Library and Information Science* (Chicago ' ALA, 1980), p. 315.
3. *Encyclopedia Britannica* (Chicago : Britannica, Inc., 1973), v. 13, p. 1031.
4. L.M. Harrod, ed., *The Librarian's Glossary*. 4th ed. (London : Andre Deutsch, 1977), p. 673.
5. E.D. Johnson, *Communication* (New York : The Scarecrow Press, 1955), p. 15.

6. S.K. Mookerjee and B. Sengupta, *Library Organisation and Library Administration*, 2nd ed. (Calcutta : The World Press, 1977), p. 4.

7. CM. White, "The Intertwined destiny of literate society and librarianship," in *Bases of Modern Librarianship* (Oxford : Pergamon Press, 1961), vol. 1, pp. 1-12.

8. The word "document" has been defined as a "record of work on paper or other material fit for physical handling, transport across space and preservation through time. See *Glossary of classification Terms* (New Delhi : ISI, 1964), p. 24.Introduction 29

9. L.S. Jast, Libraries and Living : *Essays and Addresses of Public Librarians* (New York : Book for Libraries Press, 1969), p. 45.

10. S.K. Mookerjee, *Development of Libraries and Library Science in India* (Calcutta : The World Press, 1969), p. I,

11. K.C. Harrison, *The Library and the Community*, 3rd rev. ed. (London : Andre Deutsch, 1977), p. 11.

12. A.E. Bostwick, *The American Public Library*, 3rd rev. ed. (New York : D. Appleton & Co., 1923), p. 20.

13. L.S. Jast, *Libraries and Living*, p. 15.

14. W.F. Poole, "The Origin and Management of Public Libraries" in *Public Libraries in the USA, their histosy, consolidation and management* (Washington : Government Printing Office, 1876), p. 477.

15. *Report of the Advisory Committee for Libraries* (New Delhi : Ministry of Education, Govt. of India, 1961), p. 1.

16. The Government of Andhra Pradesh in 1976 appointed the A.P. Public Libraries Act Review Committee under the Chairmanship of Justice Gopal Rao Ekbote.

17. *Report of A.P. Public Libraries Act Review Committee* (Hyderabad : Department of Public Libraries, Government of A.P., 1978), p. 1.

18. *Report of the Committee on Private Libraries* (Hyderabad : Department of Public Libraries, Govt. of A.P., 1978), p. 9.

19. Andre Maurois, *Public Libraries and their mission* (Paris : UNESCO, 1969).

20. "Public Library Manifesto," *UNESCO Bulletin for Libraries*, May-June 1972.

21. R.D, Leigh, *The Public Library in the United States*, (New York : Columbia University Press, 1950), p. 12.

22. *A.L.A. Encyclopedia of Library & Information Science* (Chicago ; ALA, 1980), p. 315.

23. "Public Library Manifesto," *UNESCO Bulletin for Libraries*, May-June 1972.
24. The Government of United Kingdom set up a Committee under the Chairmanship of Sir Sydney Roberts to study the structure of Public Library Service in England and Wales. The Report is popularly known as Roberts Report.
25. *Report cfA.P. Public Libraries Act Review Committee*, p. 8.
26. *Oxford English Dictionary*, (London : Oxford University Press, 1961), p. 728.
27. *International Encyclopedia of Social Sciences* (New York: The Macmillan & Co., 1968), 14, p. 438.
28. M.S.A. Rao, "Conceptual Problems in the Study of Social Movements" in *Social Movements in India*, ed. M.S.A, Rao (New Delhi : Manohar Publications, 1978), 1, p. 2,
29. Ibid., p. 2.
30. Ibia., p. 2.
31. H. Blumer, "Social Movements" in *An Outline of the Principles of Sociology*, ed. Robert E. Park (New York : Barnes & Noble, 1939).
32. T.H. Green, *Contemporary Revolutionary Movements* (Englewood Cliffs, N.J. : Prentice-Hall, 1974).
33. R.R. Evans, ed., *Social Movement* (Chicago ; Rand McNally, 1973).
34. J.R. Gusfield, "The Study of Social Movements," in *International Encyclopedia of Social Sciences*, ed., David Sills (New York : Macmillan, 1968), pp. 445-450.
35. The term "Ideology" means integrated assertions, theories and aims that constitute socio-political programme. In the context of library movement it may refer to aims and objectives of the movement.
36. R.D. Leigh, *The Public Library in the United States*, p. 12.
37. Allen Kent and Harold Lancour, eds., *Encyclopedia of Library and Information Science* (New York; Marcel Dekker, 1968), 1, p. 267.
38. A.E. Bostwick, *The American Public Library*, 3rd rev. ed., p. 356.
39. K.C. Harrison, *Public Library Today* (London : Crosby Lockwood, 1963), p. 1.
40. Ibid., p. I.
41. W.J. Murison, *The public library ; its origin, purpose and significance as a social institution* (London : George G. Harrop, 1955).
42. *Royal Charter of Library Association* (London : The Library Association, 1895).

43. K. Narayana Rao and J J. Ramachandra Rao, *Rise and Growth of Public Library Movement in India* (Eluru : Ayyanki Library Awards Committee, 1981), p. 4.
44. Newton Mohan Dutt, *Baroda and its libraries* (Baroda : Central Library, 1928).
45. *Sarvajanika Puithakalayamulu mariyu Andhra Desa Grandha Bhandagara Prathinidhula Maha Sabha* (Bezawada : Andhra Desa Library Association, 1914).
46. Ibid.
47. V. Gopala Krishnayya, *Library Movement in Andhra Pradesh* (Hyderabad : Director of Information and Public Relations, Government of A.P., 1974), p. 3.
48. Ch. Lakshmi Narasimhatn, "Presidential Address," in *Grandhalaya Pragati*, ed. P. Naga Bhusanam (Vijayawada ; A.P. Library Association, 1962), 1, p. 17.
49. The "manifesto" states that "knowledge should be available to all as universally as air we breath, the water that quenches thirst and the sun's energy that sustains the cycle of life."
50. *Grandhalaya Sarvaswamu*, v. 4, 1919.
51. M. Venkatarangaiya, ed., *The Freedom Struggle in Andhra Pradesh (Andhra) (1800-1905 AD)* (Hyderabad: A.P. State Committee appointed for the compilation of history of freedom struggle in A.P. (Andhra 1965), 1, p. 12.
52. Ibid., p. 16.
53. Ibid., p. 17.
54. Ibid., p. 18.
55. Sarojini Regani, *Highlights of Freedom Movement in Andhra Pradesh* (Hyderabad : Ministry of Cultural Affairs, Govt. of A.P., 1972), p. 41.
56. M. Venkatarangaiya, ed., *The Freedom Struggle in Andhra Pradesh*, p. 44.
57. Ibid. p. 60
58. Sarojini Regani, *Highlights of freedom movement in Andhra Pradesh*, p. 6.
59. Ibid., p. 12.
60. B. Kesavanarayana, *Social and Political Factors in Andhra* (Thesis), p. 3.
61. H.H. Dodwall, *The Cambridge History of India* (New Delhi : S. Chand, 1969).

62. A.V. Rama Rao, *Economic Development of Andhra Pradesh* (1766-1957) (Bombay : Popular Book Depot, 1958).

63. Ibid., p. 249.

64. Ibid., p. 184.

65. P.R. Rao, *History of Modern Andhra*, 2nd rev. ed. (New Delhi : Sterling Publishers, 1983), p. 61.

66. M. Venkatarangaiya, "British Government" in *Andhra vigjnana Sarvaswamu* (Hyderabad : Telugu Bhasasamithi, 1959), 3, p. 456.

67. A.V. Rama Rao, *Economic Development of Andhra Pradesh*, p. 237.

68. B. Kesavanarayana, *Social and Political Factors in Andhra* (Thesis), p. 9.

69. Ibid., p. 10.

70. K.V. Narayana Rao, *The Emergence of Andhra Pradesh* (Bombay : Popular Prakashan, 1973), p. 8,

71. G. Hibbert-Ware, *Christian Missions in the Telugu Country* (Madras Christian Literature Society, 1970).

72. B. Kesavanarayana, *Social and Political Factors in Andhra* (Thesis), p. 13.

73. B.B. Rakshit, Brahmoism and universal worship, in *Diamond Jubilee Report of Kakinada Brahmosamaj*, 1949), p. 204.

74. B. Kesavanarayana, *Social and Political Factors in Andhra* (Thesis), p. 15.

75. Narla Venkateswara Rao, *Veeresalingam* (New Delhi : National Book Trust, 1963), p. 10.

76. B. Kesavanarayana, *Social and Political Factors in Andhra* (Thesis), p. 20,

77. Sarojini Regani, *Highlights of Freedom Movement in Andhra Pradesh*, p. 18.78. Ibid., p. 18.

79. P. Raghunadha Rao, *History of Modern Andhra*, 2nd rev. ed. (New Delhi : Sterling Publishers, 1983), p. 73.

80. M. Venkatarangaiya, ed., *The Freedom Struggle in Andhra Pradesh*, (Andhra) (1800-1905), p. 80.

81. M. Pattabhi Rama Reddy, "Aspects of Awakening in 19th century Andhra", *Itihas*, 4 (January-June 1976), 165.

82. Ibid., pp. 212-13.

83. M. Venkatarangaiya, ed., *The freedom struggle in Andhra Pradesh*, p. 239.

84. M. Bapineedu, *Andhra Sarwaswamu* (Rajahmundry, 1961), p. 459.

85. M. Pattabi Rama Reddy, "Aspects of Awakening in 19th century Andhra," p. 165.
86. Sarojini Regani, *Highlights of freedom movement in Andhra Pradesh*, p. 4.
87. M. Venkatarangaiya, ed., *The Freedom Struggle in Andhra Pradesh*, pp. 18-20.
88. Sarojini Regani, *Highlights of freedom movement in Andhra Pradesh*, p. 5.
89. Ibid.
90. *Census of India, 1941*, v. 21, H.E.H. The Nizam Dominians (Hyderabad State), pp. 237-241.
91. Ibid.
92. Y. Vaikuntam, "Public Awakening in the Nizams Dominions in the Second Half of the 19th Century," *Itihas*, 6 (July-December 1978), 19.
93. D. Ramanuja Rao, *Telugu Secmalo Jaatiyodhyamalu* (Hyderabad : The Author, 1967), p. 19.
94. Y. Vaikuntam, "Public Awakening in the Nizam's Dominions in the second half of the 19th Century," p. 97.
95. S. Pratapa Reddy, *Andhrula Sanghika Charitra* (Hyderabad: Andhra Saraswati Parishad, 1950), pp. 440-443.
96. *The Freedom Struggle in Hyderabad (1857-1885)* (Hyderabad : Hyderabad State Committee appointed for the compilation of a history of the Freedom Movement in Hyderabad, 1956), 2, p. 285.
97. Ibid., p. 285.
98. Sarojini Regani, *Highlights of the Freedom Movement in A.P.*, p. 168.
99. Sarojini Regani. "The Social background for the rise of Andhra Mahasabha movement," p. 182.
100. D. Ramanuja Rao, *Telugu Seemalo Jaatiyodhyamalu*, p. 44.
101. *The Freedom Struggle in Hyderabad*, p. 323.
102. D. Ramanuja Rao, *Telugu Seemalo Jaatiyodhyamalu*, p. 44.
103. Sarojini Regani, "The social background," p. 182.
104. Ibid.
105. *The Freedom Struggle in Hyderabad*, p. 311.
106. *Report of the Administration of H.H. The Nizam's Dominions for four years from 8-10-1894 to 7-10-1898*, v. I, pp. 222-242.
107. Y. Vaikuntam, "Public Awakening in the Nizam's Dominions in the Second Half of the 19th century," p. 100.

108. S. Pratapa Reddy, *Andhrula Sanghika Charitra*, p. 433.
109. *Freedom Struggle in Hyderabad* (1885-1920) v 3 1957 p 54
110. Ibid., p. 17.
112. Ibid., pp. 229-230.
113. Sarojini Naidu, "A tribute to the memory of Abdul Qayum" in *The Freedom Struggle in Hyderabad* (1885-1920), v. 3, 1957, pp. 72-73.
114. Y. Vaikuntam, "Public Awakening in the Nizam's Dominions in the Second half of the 19th Century, p. 98.
115. *The Freedom Struggle in Hyderabad*, 3, 1957, p. 27.
116. Y. Vaikuntam, "Public Awakening in the Nizam's Dominions in the Second half of the 19th century," p, 98.
117. *The Freedom Struggle in Hyderabad*, v. 3, 1957, p. 30
118. Ibid., p. 1.
119. Sarojini Regani, *Highlights of the Freedom Movement in AP* p. 169.
120. Y. Vaikuntam, "Public Awakening in the Nizam's Dominions in the Second Half of the 19th Century, p, 110
121. Ibid., p. 110.
122. D. Ramanuja Rao, *Telugu Seemalo Samskritika Punarujjivanam*, 5th edn. (Hyderabad : The Author, 1972), pp. 86-89.

A.2. Origins, Aims and Objectives of Library Movement

Factors Contributed to the Origin and Spread of Library Movement

Libraries have been established in Andhra Desa as a part of people's movement, while in the other parts of the country they were established with the active support and initiative of Europeans. Libraries in Andhra Desa have been established owing to the initiation, enthusiasm and drive of selfless individuals and groups of dedicated workers willing to work at the grassroot level for the spread of the movement.[1] The democratic character of the movement was proclaimed in Grandhalaya Vedam (Library Manifesto) by the noted scholar and writer Chilakamarthi Lakshmi Narasimham, when he said that "knowledge should be available to all as universally as the air we breathe, the water that quenches our thirst and the Sun's energy that sustains our cycle of life."[2] The urge to educate themselves and spread knowledge among the people through library service appeared during the last quarter of the nineteenth century and steadily rose like a groundswell which none could prevent or stop.[3] Several factors contributed to the origin and spread of the Library Movement by the people.

1. The introduction of printing in Telugu in 1806 gave impetus for the spread of publication activity. The first Telugu book was printed in 1834. Gradually new printed books started appearing in Telugu. As the number of printed books increased, the establishment of public libraries, reading clubs, school and college libraries and even personal libraries also steadily increased.
2. The spread of English education through primary and secondary schools contributed for the growth of literacy among the population. In the industrial units and government offices the number of educated employees grew steadily. The need for reading rooms and libraries

was felt strongly in view of the reading requirements of these educated employees and other classes in the population in their leisure time, and also those of the Europeans.

3. The partition of Bengal in 1905, and the political awakening in the country had its own impact on Andhra Desa. Stalwarts like Lala Lajpat Rai and Bipin Chandra Pal entered freedom movement and toured the whole country including Andhra Desa and awakened and inspired the people to dedicate themselves to the cause of freedom. The Vandemataram movement had great impact on the social and political movements in Andhra Desa. Inspired by these political stirrings, the youth felt the need for a "temple" where they could decide their future programmes. People in general felt the need for more libraries and centres of information in different places in the state.[6]

4. The Andhra Movement which had begun in 1913 led to great awakening throughout Andhra Desa. The movement manifested itself in several forms and contributed for the genesis of several other sister movements. Preparations for the Native Conference (Deshiya Maha Sabha) at Visakhapatnam, establishment of a Sanskrit school at Kovvur, the first Andhra Desa Library Representatives Conference at Bezawada, publication series such as "Vijnana Chandrika Grandha Mandali", "Andhra Bhashabhivardhini", "Andhra Pracharini", "Veguchukka", establishment of national education institutions at Rajahmundry and Masulipatnam, and conducting Social Reform Conferences annually in the Ceded districts—are all the manifestations of Andhra Movement. Naturally, the Andhra Movement which was all-pervasive also contributed for the origin and spread of library movement in Andhra Desa.[8]

The goal of this new awakening was to liberate and enlighten the individual. Its influence cannot be described in a few words. Its effects were far reaching. It also manifested itself in the movement for a separate Andhra State, a new society for Social Reformers, books to language reformers and knowledge to intellectuals. Library workers felt that by opening more libraries they would be able to serve the Goddess of learning with purity of heart.[7]

This new awakening helped in infusing new energy and enthusiasm into the people of Andhra Desa. The stalwarts of the movement wanted to channelise this new energy for the progress and welfare of the people of the country. To achieve this progress, they felt there Were only two methods. One was to depend upon the Government and the other was to rely on self help. As K. Nageswara Rao stated the Library movement was the best example which entirely depended upon self-help and was able to do yeomen service for the benefit of the people. However, he pointed out that the political and social conferences of the day ended up with high sounding resolutions and with out any follow up action. But Library Conferences start with a programmes of action and become stepping stones for achieving desired results. The delegates to the Library Conferences are library workers and organisers. They are action-oriented but not speech oriented. They believe in rendering service to others. They are young and dynamic. They love their mother tongue. The youth should serve their mother land and the mother tongue through library movement.[8]

5. The origin and spread of library movement in the West had its general impact on the library workers of Andhra Desa. Chilakamarthi Lakshmi Narasimham, in his presidential address to the delegates of the first Andhra

Desa Library Representatives Conference held at Bezawada in 1914, referred to the spread of library movement in the West, particularly in Europe and America. The example set up by the metropolitan libraries of Paris, London, New York and Washington each with its rich collections of books and other reading materials and the services it rendered to all types of readers had greatly inspired people to strive for the spread of education and growth of literacy. Further, in these countries, they established technical libraries to meet the requirements of skilled and semi-skilled workers and artisans, libraries for the blind, libraries for prisoners and these achievements did also contribute indirectly to the spread of library movement. Also, to meet the requirements of people in the rural areas, mobile libraries were introduced. Not only governments, but also philanthropists had come forward with munificient donations for the establishment of libraries. This public library movement in the West had its impact on the educated youth who felt the urgent need for the establishment libraries in Andhra Desa.[9] K, Nageswara Rao, too, in his presidential address at the third Andhra Desa Libraries Representatives Conference held at Nellore from May 12-13, 1916, referred to the enormous book collections possessed by the libraries in the West and appealed to the delegates to strive hard for the development of libraries.[10]

6. During this period in the princely state of Baroda under its enlightened ruler Sayaji Rao Gaekwad, supported the establishment of public library system in his state with the expertise of William Borden, an American. The library development in Baroda state, immediately attracted the attention of the social workers and intellectuals of the rest of India.[11] The library workers in Andhra Desa was no exception to this influence.

7. The Renaissance movement started by Kandukuri Veeresa Lingam through his numerous publications, lectures and propagation of social reforms had already shown its impact on the minds of the people throughout Andhra Desa. Educated youth attracted by the activities of Veeresa Lingam, came forward to work for the eradication of social evils. The social movement ushered in a new awakening and thinking in the society.

8. Further, the language movement launched by Gidugu Rama Murthy Pantulu had also contributed for the spread of the library movement. This language movement, popularly known as "Vyavaharik Bhashodyamam" (Movement for the use of Colloquial Telugu), propagated the spread of the colloquial Telugu language by waging a war against the conservative and orthodox champions of the Classical Telugu which was known as "Grandhika Bhasha." Consequently, many publications were brought out in the colloquial language and this contributed for the growth of reading habits among the common people.[12]

9. Besides, the spread of a communication network by road, by rail and by post resulted in an increase of agricultural production by making necessary information accessible to the villagers and, in this respect, the libraries played a vital role and created a new awareness among the rural population.[18]

   For the genesis and growth of any movement in any country the support of the youth is essential. The youth of Andhra Desa, in order to strengthen their constructive activities and improve their knowledge felt the need for libraries and extended their unstinted support to the Library Movement.[14]

10. The Library workers also felt the need for the propagation of Telugu which was the only way to spread knowledge among the people a majority of whom did not know any

other language than Telugu. The educationists and the patriots of the country also emphasised this point. K. Nageswara Rao, for instance, stressed the need for the development of Telugu and stated that it should be introduced in schools and colleges as medium of instruction. Untill then, he said, it was not possible to spread knowledge among the people. He pointed out that propagation of mother tongue and creation of love and effection for it among the people had to be done by libraries in the region. He further, observed that the youth came forward with confidence, self-help, sacrifice, motto of service, love for mother tongue, spreading libraries and their consolidation, the libraries in Andhra Desa would become centres of learning and instrumental for the growth of the language and spread of knowledge among the people.[15] Thus, as the love for the mother tougue and need for its development increased among the people, the establishment of new libraries also steadily increased. V. Ramadasu Pantulu referred to the growth of the libraries and stated that

> Many free libraries, Telugu libraries, Telugu newspapers, Telugu library Associations, had been established and conferences organised in the state. From 1914 onwards, the library movement steadily spread in the entire state so that by 1920, there were as many as 600 libraries in Andhra Desa and all of them were affiliated to Andhra Desa Library Association.[18]

Origins of Library Movement

The success of public library movement in Andhra Desa can be traced to the beginning of the 19th century. It grew steadily in the subsequent decades. In the year 1800, a private library belonging to Paravasthu family was declared open for the public. It was subsequently developed as Arsha

Grandhalaya. In 1820, the Saraswati Mahal Library was established at Thanjavur by Raja Sarfoji, Raja Rameshwar Rayalu's (1821-1865) library was also opened to the public at Wanaparthy.

In Rajahmundry a public library was opened by Justice James Thomas, in 1839. The Theosophical Society opened a library at Guntur in 1850. Mudigonda Sankaradhya promoted the Sankaranda Library in Secunderabad in 1872. In 1886, Saraswati Nilayam was started by Manthane Adinarayana Murthy, a school teacher. Historically this library was the first public library ever conceived and started by a single individual in Andhra Desa.[17]

In the Telangana region of the former Hyderabad State, a Library was established by Mulla Abdul Qayum, a nationalist and a patriot and Moulvi Syed Hussain Bilgarmi (Nawab Emadul Mulla), in the year 1886. This was later acquired by the Nizam's Government and declared open to the public. This was named "Asafia Library" and converted into State Central Library, in 1892.[18] Slowly and steadily, libraries and reading clubs sprang up in several parts of Andhra Desa. The following can be mentioned as examples: the Saraswathi Vilasamu, Pulivendula, Cuddapah district (1892) ; C.V.N. Library, Ongole (1890); the Simhachalapathi Rao Library, Vijayanagaram (1894); the Naoroji Club, Undi(1895); Veeresalinga Kavi Samajam, Kumudavalli (now in West Godavari district) (1897); Gautami Grandhalayam, Rajahmundry (1898); Vardhamana Samajam, Nellore (1906); the Reading Club, Kolluru (in Guntur district) (1899); the Youngmen's Literary Association, Guntur (1900).

The partition of Bengal in 1905 and the political awakening which developed in the wake of this partition during 1907-1908, led to a growing demand from the people for more libraries and centres of information in different parts of the state.[19] Thus, Ram Mohan Library was established at Vijayawada by Ayyanki Venkata Ramaniah in 1911, the

Andhra Grandhalayam by M. Ramachandra Rao at Kurnool in 1920 and Saraswata Niketanam by V.V. Shreshti at Vetapalem, in 1911.

Thus, by 1914, there were nearly 163 libraries scattered all over Andhra Desa without any central authority or organisation to coordinate their activities or foster their growth. Nor was there any attempt made to establish cooperation amongst them with a view to serving the needs of the people more efficiently. Many libraries were in a highly disorganised condition. Therefore, there was an urgent need for the preservation of the existing libraries and the revival of those which were falling into disuse due mainly to lack of financial support.[20] Due to the foresight of Ayyanki Venkata Ramaniah and Suri Venkata Narasimha Sastri the first Andhra Desa Librarians representatives conference was convened on 10 April 1914 under the auspices of Ram Mohan Library, Vijayawada.[21] About 200 delegates representing various libraries in Andhra as well as in Telangana attended the first conference. Chilakamarthi Lakshmi Narasimham in his presidential address made a fervent appeal for the spread of knowledge throughout the length and breadth of the land.[22] The Conference passed several resolutions concerning the spread of library movement and establishment of a standing committee under the name of "Andhra Desa Grandhalaya Sangham."[23] The Association formulated the following aims and objectives in a Conference held in July 1918 : (1) to establish a central library at Vijayawada ; (2) to work for the spread of education ; (3) to organise lectures and audiovisual programmes like film shows, and magic lantern shows ; (4) to organise touring libraries, etc.[24] Form 1914, holding of annual conferences at different places in Andhra Desa for popularisation of library movement, became a regular feature of the Association.[26] Furthermore the Association acted as standing committee and tried to follow-up the resolutions adopted at the annual conferences, from time to time. These conferences also provided an opportunity for the library workers to meet at different places to discuss problems of mutual interest and spread the message for the establishment of new libraries, Educationists; social workers, poets and officials were invited to preside over the annual conferences.[26] After the establishment of the Association, the library movement gained momentum in Andhra Desa.

In the former state of Hyderabad of which Telangana formed a part, as in the then British India, library movement paved the way for and gave strength to political, social and cultural renaissance of the people.[27] Against the peculiar conditions obtaining under the Nizam's autocratic rule in Hyderabad state, the library movement helped in forging an awareness and unity among the Telugu people to fight the oppression by feudal forces. The rulers wanted to suppress the library movement by issuing the notorious Circular (No. 53) which banned establishment of a library, school or Vyayamashala without Government's prior permission. In practice, obtaining such permission became a very difficult task.[28]

The origins of public library movement in Telangana can be traced to the beginning of 20th century. Private libraries belonging to rich individuals became a common feature of Hyderabad state, during the nineteenth centutry. During this period, a few libraries which may be called public libraries were established. In the year, 1872 Sankarananda Library was established by Sri Mudigonda Sankararadhya in Secunderabad. The year 1886 witnessed the origin of the present State Central Library with the efforts of Mulla Abdul Quayyum a nationalist and a patriot, and Moulvi Syed Hussain Bilgrmi. This was later taken over by the Nizam's Government and declared open to the public. The Bharat Guna Vardhak Samstha was established in 1895. At the beginning of the twentieth century (i.e., 1901) Sri Krishna Devaraya Andhra Bhasha Nilayam was established as a result of the devotion and dynamism of Ravichettu Ranga Rao, Kommaraju Laxman Rao and Raja Nayani Venkata

Ranga Rao, the Raja of Munagala. From 1901 onwards, the library movement in the Hyderabad state became a popular movement. It derived its motivation, strength and direction from the people themselves.[29]

With the establishment of Sri Krishna Devaraya Andhra Bhasha Nilayam, the library movement gained momentum and libraries were established at several other places in Telangana. Mention may be made of Sri Raja Raja Narendra Andhra Bhasha Nilayam (1904) established in Hanumkonda by the efforts of Madapati Hanumantha Rao, the Andhra Samvardhani (1905) at Secunderabad, Andhra Vijnana Prakashini Grandha Nilayam (1917) at Suryapet, Sri Vemana Andhra Bhasha Nilayam (1923) at Siddiambar Bazar, Hyderabad, Balasaraswati Andhra Bhasha Nilayam at Afzal Ganj, Hyderabad; Prataparudra Andhra Bhasha Nilayam (1924) at Manikonda ; Desodharaka Andhra Bhasha Nilayam (1925) at Kukkunuru and Vijnana Niketanam, (1936) at Khammam. By the year 1925, under the dynamic leadership of Madapati Hanumantha Rao, nearly 100 libraries were established throughout Telangana.[30] Suravaram Pratapa Reddy, another notable personality, through his journalistic activity rendered valuable services for the spread of library movement in the Telangana region. The notorious circular Gashti Nishan 53 which was promulgated in 1929 came in the way of people's enthusiasm for the establishment of libraries and the spread of library movement.[31] In spite of these hurdles and restrictions on the movement by the Nizam's government, the library movement did spread throughout the Telangana region.

Aims and Objectives

The aim of the library movement is to disseminate knowledge among the people and ameliorate their pathetic condition for better living. The old idea that a public library is a mere storehouse of books and the librarian is its custodian only became outdated. The library movement conceived that a public library is a "People's university." In the words of S.V. Narasimha Sastri, "its aim is to unfold the varied faculties of every individual comprised in the body politic, man or woman, child or adult, rich or poor, literate or illiterate by adopting appropriate means and methods in each case in accordance with the idio-syncracies, tastes, environment, intellectual equipment and the like."[32] He also stated that libraries were established to create political and social awakening in the country. The libraries established during the first stage of the spread of the movement, were those like Sri Veeresalinga Kavi Samajam established at Kumudavali, Bhimavaram Taluk then in Krishna District, with a hospital, cooperative Society, prayer hall as its adjuncts. During the second stage of development of the movement, libraries such as Sri Gautami Library, Rajahmundry, and Sri Krishna Devaraya Andhra Bhasha Nilayam, Hyderabad, were established. These libraries introduced and propagated lending books to houses for ladies free of cost, conducted competitions for the development of reading habits among women, and brought out pamphlets beneficial to the common man. These library services were open not only to those who visit the libraries but also to others and thereby helped in the spread of knowledge among all sections of people. During the third stage of development, the libraries which were established were conceived not merely as store houses of knowledge but also as institutions where several programmes cultural and welfare were undertaken. These libraries expanded their service activities by establishing night schools, recitation of holy scriptures during the evening hours, staging dramas, conducting puppet shows, organising service guilds, holding competitive examinations and sports events for which prizes were awarded, arranging lectures and magic lantern shows, and celebrating national festivals and death anniversaries of eminent Indians.[33] The movement was neither a sporadic attempts for the spread of knowledge among people nor was it spearheaded by the leaders immersed in politics.

Libraries were not started on an adhoc basis to achieve temporary results. They were to carry out their activities throughout the year without any break or hindrance. Inspired by the national movement and ready to serve the nation, the youth became the backbone of the library movement.[34]

The aim of the library movement elsewhere was mainly to undertake activities for the intellectual development of the people. But the library movement in Andhra Desa including Telangana aimed at achieving an overall development of human personality and to realize the objective that the library was used as an effective means.[35] The movement wished to spread knowledge among the people and thereby awaken the "atma" of the individual steeped in ignorance and inertia and help him in leading a truthful and purposeful life in society.[88] This objective was kept as paramount in the spread of library movement in Andhra Desa.[37]

The leaders of the Library Movement felt that the country cannot progress with a few individuals acquiring knowledge. Efforts were to be made to provide knowledge to the general public. This could only be possible through the establishment of an adequate number of libraries and reading rooms. The enormous potential of libraries for the spread of knowledge and for enlightenment was recognised by the leaders of the movement. They visualised that "Association with books indirectly leads to association with authors. This association brings immense benefit to the readers. It also encourages non-readers to read books. If a few readers assemble in a library, they start discussing books, those who listen to them will also be attracted to read books, themselves, and benefit greatly by acquiring knowledge. Therefore, the sooner the establishment of libraries the better for the country. Vigorous efforts have been made in the Western countries for the establishment of more libraries and these libraries have been rendering good service to the people."[38]

One of the important objectives of the library movement

was to develop literature which promotes enlightenment and social improvement of the people. This fact was emphasised by B. Venkatapati Raju in his presidential address at the Fourth Andhra Desa Library Representatives Conference held at Baruva, in 1917.[39] He stated that already Bengalis and Maharashtrians took the lead in the development of their literatures and benefited very much. We also started publishing daily newspapers, weeklies, monthlies, book series and established educational institutions. Unless Telugu language and literature develops, it would be futile to think that the libraries would develop. To reach new heights through libraries, we need a good number of books. They should be written in an easy and attractive style covering several disciplines. Then alone literature develops. It is the duty of all lovers of the Telugu language to see that good books are published and sold quickly. Unless this is done new authors and publishers will not come forward. There is no end for writing good books because there are a number of areas to be covered. As the readership increases the publication of books also increases simultaneously. If there are good books in libraries, readership will increase. Therefore readers and authors should serve the cause of literature.

The stalwarts of the movement recognised the role of libraries as centres of social and cultural activities of society and emphasised the fact that the success of the social movements very much depended upon the importance given to libraries in the national reconstruction. K. Nageshwara Rao emphasised this fact and stated :

> Unless due importance is given to libraries in the activities of national reconstruction, they cannot become useful for the country, language and the people. Libraries should become the means to organise several social movements which help develop the individual. Reading of books and periodicals is one of the advantages of libraries.

> Libraries and reading rooms should become centres for physical culture, social services, education, arts, recreation and culture. Then only they can become excellent means of national reconstruction. Libraries should strive hard for the enlightenment of social life of the people.[40]

By establishing libraries throughout the Andhra Desa, the leaders of the movement wanted to achieve two important aims of the movement. The first aim was to render free library service to all classes of people in the society. To achieve this, libraries had to meet the reading requirements of all classes of people, all types of professions and all men and women according to their requirements by providing various types of suitable reading material.

The second aim was to undertake library publicity very vigorously. Through library publicity, uses and advantages of the libraries had to be made known to the people. Even people residing in remote villages should be benefited by the library movement. To achieve these two important aims of the movement, V. Ramadasu Pantulu suggested : "we must establish a central library with its branches in important cities and towns including libraries in the villages,'[41]

Through the various functions of the libraries, the organisers wanted to expand the scope of the movement. The movement stressed and propagated that libraries should not confine their activity to merely acquiring books and making them available to the public. The scope of their activities should be expanded so as to cover the social and literary life of the people. Through libraries, the movement aimed at preserving and protecting the sources of ancient culture and civilization by acquiring rare and unpublished manuscripts and other documentary sources. In the course of his Presidential Address to the Fifth Andhra Desa Library Representatives Conference held at Visakhapatnam, in 1918, V. Ramadasu Pantulu stated in clear terms :

> In Andhra Desa, in every region we find invaluable and unpublished manuscripts. Old palm leaf manuscripts and rare old publications must be acquired. The purchase of old and valuable manuscripts by the foreigners and carrying these materials with them, must be prohibited. Our libraries should come forward to acquire them. Old coins, old and broken sculptures and other antiques should be acquired by libraries. Sources dealing with local histories, stories narrated by villagers, folk songs, wise sayings and proverbs, should see that lending of books to men and women is carried on systematically. Good writers should be encouraged by libraries by way of giving them some help. Libraries should open schools for the spread of education.[42]

The movement also aimed at achieving the upliftment of the population by establishing libraries in the rural areas. Through their activities, the movement wanted to meet the varied requirements of the rural population, so as to bring a change and progress in their lives. This fact was emphasised during the fourth annual conference of Andhra Desa Library Association held at Barua from May 6-7, 1912. B. Venkatapati Raju stated that

> India lives in her villages. Agriculture is the main occupation in the villages. Libraries in the rural areas must acquire more books on agriculture and impart new methods and techniques to agriculturists for improvement. Likewise, libraries should make efforts to acquire books on weaving, carpentry, smithy, basket-making, business, medicine and other village industries and trades and make them used by the village artisans and craftsmen and women so that they can lead a happy life. This should be the prime aim of libraries

and to achieve this, the library workers should work hard.[43]

The libraries which have been established as a result of the movement acted as centres to disseminate information relating to contemporary, political, social and scientific activities. Promotion of Swadeshi goods and Khadi, encouragement for writing dramas, patronising music and other fine arts, establishment of national printing houses, training voluntary service workers like scouts and guides, revival of national physical culture, celebration of national festivals and all other activities became auxiliaries to library movement.[44]

The organisers of the movement felt that if the movement had to be consolidated and continued on sound lines, the libraries in Andhra Desa should cooperate with each other in acquisition, lending, collection, development and sharing of resources. Emphasising this fact, S.V. Narasimha Sastri pointed out that "No Library is self-sufficient, therefore, each library in the region should specialize in a particular subject area and try to acquire all types of books and other reading materials in that subject. This will enable them to conserve their meagre financial resources and render immense service. Libraries could cooperate with each other for lending of books and sharing resources. To strengthen the movement it was necessary to establish a Central Library and District and Taluk Libraries. At the Conference held at Visakhapatnam it was resolved to upgrade the Ram Mohan Library at Bezawada and designate it as Central Library. There was also a need for establishing District Library Associations in each district and the District Central Libraries should function under the District Library Association concerned.[45]

The library movement either in Andhra Desa or in Telangana region was not a weak and isolated movement, but a spontaneous, strong and all-embracing socio-linguistic and political movement which tried to provide free and universal library service to all people.[46] The universal nature of this service was very succinctly but categorically put forth in the library manifesto of the library movement by Chilakainarthi, the illustrious Telugu scholar and writer, who presided over the first Andhra Desa Grandhalaya Mahasabha at Vijayawada held in 1914.[47] He laid emphasis that the formal agencies of education, i.e., schools will not ameliorate the degradation of intellectual or otherwise of the people. He visualized a network of fullfledged libraries that could help people to rise from the soggy morass of illiteracy.[48]

The movement was launched by ordinary Telugu youth who did not have any English education and contact with the British intelligentsia. In Andhra Desa the movement had its genesis and growth on its own with the support of enthusiastic youth and spread throughout the Andhra and Telangana regions. Therefore the movement in Andhra Desa was termed as "Swayambhuvu", which means the movement originated on its own without the support of others,[49] a term generally used referring to temples or icons indicating that they were not established by humans.

The youth who spearheaded the movement belonged to the rural areas and they were inspired by the social and political movements of the times. Therefore the library movement, from the beginning, dedicated itself for the spread of rural library service. The leaders of the movement realized the need and importance of the spread of knowledge and thereby educating rural population, which would contribute ultimately to the development of the country. Therefore streneous efforts were made for the spread of library movement in the rural areas. Hundreds of libraries were established in the rural areas and support and cooperation was extended for their efficient functioning. Thus, the library movement aimed at removing illiteracy, superstition, social evils, backwardness and stagnation prevalent in the rural areas and providing the rural people with a better life.[50]

The objectives of the library movement were very clearly

put forth by S.V. Narasimha Sastri in his presidential address at the Sixth Annual Conference of "Andhra Desa Grandhalaya Sangham" held at Madras on 16 November 1919. He stated that: (1) A library is no longer a place where books are merely stocked and made available to visitors nor a librarian, a custodian. It is a centre where the tastes and initiations of each individual are noticed and every individual reader is served according to (a) his aptitude, (b) the stage of his intellectual development and (c) social purpose he attempts to serve; (2) Books should be taken to the needy without waiting for them to call at the library ; (3) Library service should help in the full development of the individual's personality ; (4) A movement fulfils its mission only when it has the innate capacity to anticipate new forces that surface from time to time and to channelise them in the right direction. (5) A library should arrange for every reader a book of his taste and a suitable reader for every book in the stocks.[61] (6) To cover the entire Andhra Desa one Association at State level would be inadequate. Every District should have a district association.[52,53]

In the Telangana region the library movement gained momentum with the establishment of Sri Krishna Devaraya Andhra Bhasha Nilayam in the year 1901. Gradually, several libraries were established in several parts of Telangana and these libraries, through their activities, helped the cause of the Telugu language. The library movement paved the way for the beginning of Andhra Movement with the establishment of Andhra Jana Sangham[64] at Hyderabad in 1921. Slowly, several Andhra Sanghas were established in other parts of Telangana. To coordinate and regulate the activities of these local Sanghas and spread the movement vigorously a cultural body known as "Andhra Jana Kendra Sangham" was established in 1923.[ss] The first conference of the Kendra Sangham was held at Hyderabad on 27 July 1923. This conference listed the following activities to be undertaken by the Andhra Jana Sanghas;"

(i) to establish libraries, reading rooms and schools;

(ii) to honour scholars and poets;

(iii) to support and encourage students;

(iv) to acquire palmleaf manuscripts, inscriptions and rare documents and to encourage research ;

(v) to publish pamphlets, booklets and lectures to spread knowledge; and

(vi) to make all efforts for the spread and propagation of the Telugu language.

The libraries which had been established throughout Telangana before and after the formation of Andhra Jana Kendra Sangham broadly formulated their aims and objectives in such a way as to undertake the above mentioned activities suggested by the Kendra Sangham. The first library Conference which was held on 22nd February 1925 at Madhira reiterated these activities to and gave a call for spreading library movement more vigorously. The Conference appointed a sub-committee to suggest a policy and programme for spreading the movement in a broad-based manner.[57] The second library conference which was held at Suryapeta from 30th June to 1st July 1929, also reiterated the above activities to be performed by the libraries and passed 15 resolutions for the spread of library movement in the Telangana region. The Conference through its resolution No. 11, emphasised the role of Andhra Jana Kendra Sangbam for the spread of library movement in Telangana and appealed to the public to come forward to establish more libraries.[58]

References

1. C. Gopinatha Rao, *Library Movement in Andhra Pradesh* (Hyderabad : Department of Public Libraries, Govt., of A.P., 1981), p. 1.

2. C.H. Lakshmi Narasimham, "Presidential Address to First Andhra Desa Library Representatives Conference," held at Bezawada on 10 April 1914. *See Grandhalaya Pragati*, Part 2 (Vijayawada : A.P. Library Association, 1962). p. 17.

3. V. Gopalakrishnayya, *Library Movement in Andhra Pradesh* (Hyderabad, Dept. of Information and Public Relations, Govt. of A.P., 1977), p. 1.
4. B. Venkatapati Raju, "Presidential Address to Fourth Andhra Desa Library Representatives Conference" held at Baruva on 6-7 May 1917. In *Grandhalaya Pragati*, Part I (Vijayawada : A.P. Library Association, 1962), p. 46.
5. V. Venkatappaiah, *Andhra-Telangana Grandhalaya Pragati* (Eluru : Sanchelana Sahiti, 1973), pp, 10-12.
6. C.H. Lakshminarasimham "Presidential Address to First Andhra Desa Library Representatives Conference" held at Bezawada on 10 April 1914. *See Grahdhalaya Pragati*, Part I (Vijayawada : A.P. Library Association, 1952), p. 2.
7. K. Nageswara Rao, "Presidential Address to Third Andhra Desa Library Representatives Conference" held at Nellore on 12-13 Hay 1916. *See Grandhalaya Pragati* Part I (Vijayawada : A.P. Library Association, 1962), p. 44.
8. Ibid., pp. 42-43.
9. Chilakamarthy, Ibid., pp. 6-7.
10. K. Nageswara Rao, "Presidential Address to the Third Andhra Desa Library Representatives Conference" held at Nellore on 12-13 May, 1916. *See Grandhalaya Pragati*, Part I (Vijayawada : A.P. Library Association, 1962), p. 37.
11. Newton Mohan Dutt, *Baroda and Its Libraries* (Baroda : Central Library, 1928).
12. V. Venkatappaiah, *Mana Grandhlaya Udyamamu*, 1900-1950 (Manuscript, 1984), p. 56,
13. Ibid.
14. Ibid.
15. K. Nageswara Rao, "Presidential Address to the Third Andhra Desa Library Representatives Conference" held at Nellore on 12-13 May 1916. *See Grandhataya Pragati*, Part I (Vijayawada : A.P. Library Association, 1962), p. 43.
16. V. Ramadasu Pantulu "Presidential Address to the Tenth Andhra Desa Library Conference" held at Peda Cherukuru on 28 June 1928. Ibid., pp. 137-138.
17. I. Venkata Ramanayya, *Grandhalaya Jyoti*, (Vijayawada Saraswati Samrajya Prachurana Trust, 1967), p. 61.
18. *The Freedom Struggle in Hyderabad*, Vol. 3 (Hyderabad : Hyderabad State Committee for the Compilation of a History of the Freedom Movement in Hyderabad, 1957), p. 67.

19. V. Gopalakrishnayya, *Library Movement in Andhra Pradesh*, p. 2.
20. *Grandhalaya Saravaswamu*, Nos. 3 & 4, 1918, p. 184.
21. *Grandhalaya Pragati*. Part I (Vijayawada : A.P. Library Association, 1962), p. 3.
22. P. Naga Bhusanam, *Andhra Pradesh Grandhalayodhyamamu* (Vijayawada : A.P. Library Association, 1957), p. 3.
23. *The Hindu*, 21 April 1914.
24. *Grandhalaya Saravaswamu*, 3 (1918), 118.
25. The Presidential address of the Annual state level as well as District and Taluka level Conferences and other details have been published. These sources throw light on the efforts made by the Association for the spread of the library movement. See *Grandhalaya Pragati*, 3 parts (Vijayawada : A.P. Library Association, 1962, 1969 and 1964).
26. B. Kesavanarayana, "*Social and Political factors in Andhra, 1900-1956*" (Thesis). 1966, pp. 218-19.
27. V. Gopalakrishnayya, *Library Movement in Andhra Pradesh*, p. 9.
28. *Report of the Committee on Working of A.P. Public Libraries Act 1960* (Hyderabad : Dept. of Public Libraries, Govt. of A.P- 1978), p. 6,
29. Ibid.
30. V. Gopalakrishnayya, *Library Movement in Andhra Pradesh*, p. 10.
31. M. Hanumantha Rao, *Telangana Andhrodhyamcmu*, Vol. 1 (Hyderabad : Andhra Chandrika Grandha Mandali 1949), p. 49.
32. S.V. Narasimha Sastri, "Public Library Movement in India" in *The Library Movement: A Collection of Essays* (Madras : Madras Library Association, 1929), p. 31.
33. S.V. Narasimha Sastri, "Presidential Address to the Sixth Andhra Desa LibraryJConference" held at Madras on 16 November 1919, in *Grandhalaya Pragati*, Part I (Vijayawada : A.P. Library Association, 1962), pp. 81-82.
34. I. Venkata Ramanayya, *Grandhalaya Jyoti*, p. 53.
35. Ibid., p, 54.
36. Ibid.
37. Ibid.
38. P. Ramarayanim, "Presidential Address to Second Andhra Desha Representative Conference" held at Raja 1915, in *Grandhalaya Pragati*, Part I (Vijayawada : A.P. Library Association, 1962), p. 21.
39. B. Venkatapati Raju, "Presidential Address Desa Library Representatives Conference'' held at Rajamundry on 9-10 May 1915, in *Grandhalaya Pragati*, Part I (Vijayawada : A.P. Library Association, 1962), p. 21.

40. K. Nageswara Rao, "Presidential Address to third Andhra Desa Library Representatives Conference" held at Nellore on 12-13 May 1916. Ibid., p. 43.
41. V. Ramadasu Pantulu "Presidential Address Desa Library Conference" held at Peda Cherukuru to the fifth Andhra 1928. Ibid., pp. 135.
42. Vikrama Deva Varma, "Presidential Address to fifth Andhra Desa Library Conference" held at Visakhapatnam in 1918 Ibid., pp. 56–57.
43. B. Venkatapati Raju, "Presidential Address to the fourth Andhra Desa Library Conference" held at Barua from 6–7 May 1917. Ibid., pp.56–57 to the sixth Andhra.
44. Ibid.
45. S.V. Narasimha Sastri, "Presidential Address to the sixth Andhra Desa Library Conference" held at Madras on 16th November 1919. Ibid., pp.93.
46. V. Gopalakrishnayya, *Library Movement in Andhra Pradesh* p. 3.
47. *Grandhalaya Pragati*, Part I (Vijayawada : tion, 1962), p. 17.
48. V. Gopalakrishnayya, *Library Movement in Andhra Pradesh*, p. 3.
49. I. Venkata Ramanayya, *Grandhalaya Jyoti*, p.52.
50. K. Sarada, "Andhra Grandhalayamamu : Vartamana Parisilana," *Grandhalaya Sarvaswamu*, December 1975, p. 9.
51. It is interesting to note that this statement made as far back as in 1919 gave rise later to S.R. Ranganathan'second and third laws of library science. See S.R. Ranganathan, Five laws of the library Science, 2nd ed. (Bombay : Asia Publishing House, 1931)
52. S.V. Narasimha Sastri, "Presidential Address to Grandhalaya Maha Sabha" held at Madra4 See *Grandhalaya Pragati*, Part I (Vijayawada : A.P. Library Association, 1962), pp. 78-97.
53. V. Gopalakrishnayya translated these objectives in to English and Presented in his booklet entitled Library Movement in Andhra Pradesh (Hyderabad : Dept. of Information and Public Relations, Govt. of A.P., 1977), pp. 5-6.
54. M. Hanumantha Rao, *Telangana Andhrodhyamamu*, p. 19.
55. Ibid., p. 30.
56. Ibid., pp. 31-32.
57. D. Ramanuja Rao, *Teluguseemalo Samskritika Punarujjivanam* (Hyderabad, The Author, 1983), p. 63.
58. *Golakanda Patrika*, 9 June 1929, p. 5.

B

Development of Library Movement

B.1 Coastal Andhra

As stated in the previous chapter, library movement gained momentum only after the establishment of Andhra Desa Library Association in 1914. It was estimated that by the end of 1913, there were nearly 163 libraries functioning in' different parts of Andhra Desa.[1] These libraries were completely isolated and disorganised with no central authority to guide, coordinate and organise their activities and help their growth. No attempts were made earlier to establish cooperation among them so that the needs of the people could be fulfilled more effectively and efficiently.[2] The need to improve the conditions of these libraries and to call for a conference of library workers for discussion of the situation was first identified by Ayyanki Venkata Ramanayya. So, along with S. Narasimha Sastri, he issued an appeal which states interalia : (a) to discuss common problems faced by library workers ; (b) to find out ways and means for sustaining the libraries which had been already established ; (c) to establish new libraries ; (d) to foster brotherhood among the library workers ; (e) to develop cooperation and coordination among fellow libraries; and (f) to spread the message of library movement vigorously throughout Andhra Desa.[3]

In response to this appeal, about 200 delegates representing different libraries in Andhra as well as Telangana attended the first Andhra Desa Library Workers Conference held on 10 April 1914 under the auspices of Ram Mohan Library at Bezawada. At the outset, Vemuri Sri Rama Sastri, Satavadhani performed invocation. S. Venkata Narasimha Sastri, Chairman Reception Committee, welcomed the gathering. Chilakamarthi Lakshmi Narasimham in his Presidential address made a fervent appeal for the spread of knowledge throughout the length and breadth of the land. While concluding his address, he proclaimed that "knowledge should be available to all as universally and as freely as the air we breathe, the water that quenches thirst and the sun's energy that sustains the cycle of life."[4] Ayyanki Venkata Ramanayya described these words as "Grandhalaya Vedam'' (a miniature manifesto) which ever since has inspired and guided the library workers for the spread of library movement in Andhra Desa.[5]

The conference passed several resolutions concerning the spread of library movement, government's responsibility, financial assistance for opening and maintenance of libraries, establishment of standing committee under the name of'Andhra Desa Grandhalaya Sangham' appointment of paid Secretary and starting of a periodical as an official organ for the spread of library movement.[6] The conference elected Mocherla Ramachandra Rao as President, Chilakamarthi Lakshmi Narasimham and Suri Venkata Narasimha Sastri as Vice-Presidents, and Nalam Krishna Rao and Ayyanki Venkata Ramanayya as General Secretaries of the Association.[7] As a result of the Fourth resolution Andhra Desa Grandhalaya Sangham was founded on April 10, 1914 and it was the first library Association of its kind for the whole country.[8]

After the formation of the Library Association, Ayyanki Venkata Ramanayya and S.V. Narasimha Sastri took effective steps for the spread of library movement. The Association initiated action for the establishment of libraries in several parts of Andhra Desa. As a result of their efforts, the number of libraries increased from 163 in 1913 to 212 in 1915 and to 474 in 1918, to 586 in 1919 and to 600 in 1934.[9] The years that followed 1942, witnessed a steady increase in the number of libraries owing to the greater attention paid by the library workers besides the governmental aid and the contributions made by the public.[10] The district-wise figures in 1953 were : West Godavari (110), Visakhapatnam (53), Krishna (80), Kurnool (52), Anantapur (132), Nellore (104), Srikakulam (28), East Godavari (124), Guntur (118), Bellary (97), Cuddapah (42) and Chittoor(139).[11]

Role of Andhra Desa Library Association for the Spread of Library Movement

The Association through its publicity programmes such as meetings, conferences, library pilgrimages, Vasanthothsavas (garden dinners), propagated the significance of the role of libraries in social and economic development. It cultivated and spread the notion that library is a centre of knowledge and information and therefore, of great public concern and interest. It emphasised the democratic and public character of libraries in that they shall be accessible to all readers.[12] The Association encouraged the establishment of special sections for children and women in libraries and five special libraries for women were established in 1915.[13] Ayyanki Venkata Ramanayya who studied the Baroda Library Movement of 1917, introduced special divisions for women and children in the libraries and devised a scheme for classifying the Telugu books on the basis of the Baroda scheme.[14]

Decline of the Movement

The various activities of Andhra Desa Library Association referred to in the preceeding sections had greatly contributed for the spread of the movement in Andhra Desa. But the movement had its ups and downs through its chequered history. Political conditions obtaining in the country also had their impact on the people of Andhra Desa. Many stalwarts of the movement joined the freedom struggle and this hampered the onward march of library movement. The situation was voiced by Nalam Krishna Rao in his presidential address to the delegates of 11th Andhra Desa Library Conference held at Eluru in 1926. He stated that "after 1926, there appears to be a decline in the spread of Library Movement. One of the main reasons for this decline being the political situation in the country and everybody turned his attention to politics rather than library movement.[15]

The organisation of library conferences alongwith political conferences had a negative effect on the spread of library movement. The library conferences lost their individuality and could not project properly the image of the movement. This fact was brought by N. Krishna Rao to the notice of the delegates of the eleventh Andhra Desa Library Association LibraryConference held at Eluru, in 1926. He stated that "in the beginning, for some years, library conferences were held independently. Later on these conferences were conducted along with Andhra Sabha, Mandala Sabhas or State Conferences. Due to this situation, library conferences lost their individuality. If we want to make library conferences independent and respected by all types of people we should not hold our conferences with political conferences. We should take steps to conduct our conferences independent of political conferences. [16] To salvage the library movement from its decline N. Krishna Rao suggested that "the movement should be organised by the government, the public or by both. The third method was the most important. But due to the foreign rule it will not be possible in our country. There is a wide gap between the government and the people. Unless we achieve complete freedom the gap between the government and the people cannot be filled."[17]

Concern was also expressed over the decline of the

movement in other annual conferences of Andhra Desa Library Association. B. Seshagiri Rao referred to this aspect in his presidential address at 14th ADLA Conference held at Guntur, in 1931. He stated that

> there is no doubt that some sort of slowness crept not only into our library movement but also into other movements. Spread of education has also slowed down. In the last 10 years, due to the vigorous political activity, stalwarts and other workers who actively helped the spread of the movement got tired and diverted their attention to something else.[18]

Besides the political conditions, and the non-participation of library workers, there were some other reasons for the decline of the movement. During the early days of the movement, libraries bad been established at various places by mutual emulation. Just like sports associations, recreation clubs, youth associations, dramatic associations, libraries had also been established by uneducated rich people as one of the recreational institutions. But these libraries declined soon for want of knowledgeable persons to manage them. Consequently, the support from the uneducated rich was also not forthcoming. The libraries established as auxiliaries to recreation clubs became centres of pleasure and recreation of the youth and these libraries, in certain cases, led to controversies in the villages.[19] Stressing the need to revive the libraries which declined and to give a fillip to the library movement. B. Seshagiri Rao pointed out that "a lot of enthusiasm is shown for lecturing on the methods of organising library associations, methods of book acquisition, preparation of book lists, arrangements for organizing annual conferences. If at least 10 per cent of that enthusiasm had been shown by our leaders of the library movement on teaching how to read a particular book to get the maximum benefit, how to find information in a particular part, what the classics are to be read to know different aspects of knowledge, the library movement would not have reached the present state of decline."[20]

The decline and revival of the movement due to political movements was also referred to by S. Ramaswamy Chowdhary in his presidential address at 20th ADLA Conference, held in 1935. He stated that "due to political movements, library movement of late has slackened. But now the movement is being revived with vigour and enthusiasm. District and taluk Conferences are being organised. Educationists and patriots should come forward to support the library movement and thereby help spread knowledge among the people. Even though there is no government support, the movement has been launched by the people and spread with their unstinted support. Our movement set an example for the rest of British India. The movement has yet to cover several thousands of villages. We have to revive those libraries which are in a bad shape.'[21]

Revival and Spread of the Movement

The stalwarts of the movement felt the need for revival and spread of the movement. Their first task was to see that the existing libraries functioned properly. The second task was to find out the reasons for closure or inefficient functioning of certain existing libraries and help in reviving them to work efficiently. Opening of new libraries was the third task. Consolidation and improvement of existing library services and making efforts to increase readership was the fourth task. M. Ramachandra Sastri suggested the following steps for the spread and consolidation of library movement and for an effective functioning of libraries.[22]

1. For the last several years in the annual conferences numerous resolutions have been adopted to prepare lists of books available in big and small libraries. So far this work has been done. On the basis of experience and with the help of *Andhra Vagmaya Suchi* (Andhra

Bibliography) small bibliographies consisting of titles between 100 and 800 should be prepared. These bibliographies should include, biographies of eminent people, natural sciences, different professions, historical novels, select poetry and dramas.

2. Useless books and periodicals and undesirable collections should be eliminated from the libraries.
3. Efforts should be made to get books written in Telugu on agriculture, weaving, planet earth, water, electricity, personal and social ethics. These books should be supplied to the libraries at a cheaper prices.
4. Copper inscriptions, old coins, pieces of sculpture manuscripts, antique implements, and other curious objects should be collected and preserved in libraries.
5. Efforts should be made to educate readers on good habits, manners and behaviour.
6. While staging puppet shows or street dramas, the organizers must ensure that there is no place for vulgar and raw satire and harsh language. Likewise in respect of Harikathas, recitation of puranas, lectures, it should be ensured that there is no place for hecklings and undesirable and unwarranted criticism.
7. Efforts should be made to get donations to libraries from the village common fund, temples, cooperative societies, and also from philanthropists, local bodies and the government.
8. Village libraries should cooperate and compete with one another for rendering good and effective service to the society.
9. Libraries should possess instruments for the measurement of day temperature, rainfall, wind directions, gramophones, magic lanterns. First Aid kits and medicines should be collected and kept in libraries. If possible, a radio should also be made available.

10. Night schools and summer schools should be organised for educating adults. This will prevent the partly literate youth to relapse into illiteracy.
11. Children should be taught new things by showing them picture books, telling stories, conversing with them, and making them play different games. Suitable reading material should be provided for this purpose.
12. Separate collections should be developed for ladies. These books should be lent freely to them for home reading. Special lectures should be arranged for their enlightenment. This will enable them to take care of the education of their children.
13. Health is wealth. This should be improved among villagers through sports. Those who take part in sports and develop physical culture protect not only their health but also that of the whole village.
14. Lectures by eminent scholars on religious tolerance, morality and ethics should be arranged for the benefit of the people. Telugu should be taught. Bhajans also should be arranged.
15. Undesirable elements should not be allowed to enter the library.
16. Library workers should strive hard to eliminate rivalries and enemity in the villages. They should be neutral and should not take sides. They should try to realize Village Swaraj which has been forgotten.
17. In villages where there are no libraries, they should be opened in the schools run by District Boards. These libraries should be made really useful.
18. In villages where there are no schools, the District Board authorities should run mobile libraries.
19. Good books and periodicals should be selected and acquired. Libraries should also subscribe to *Indian*

Library Journal, Andhra Grandhalayam and *Divyajnana Dipika.*

20. Library workers should be trained to manage the libraries as in the West.

The above mentioned activities and in addition other things which are in confirmity with our culture and tradition should be undertaken by ADLA, All India Library Association, district library associations, taluka library associations, village libraries, town libraries, District Boards, Municipalities, Panchayat Boards, religious endowment associations, Education Department of the Government, Congress and Justice Parties, religious heads, educational institutions and patriots. Even if others keep quite, libraries and library associations should come forward to work for the spread of the movement. For this, Andhra Desa Library Association should show the way to other library associations.

S. Pratapa Reddy also suggested certain measures for the revival of the movement. He found that the efforts that were being made in Coastal Andhra, Rayalaseema and Telangana were not adequate. For the spread of the movement the following suggestions were putforth by him in his Presidential address at 23rd ADLA Conference held at Pedapalem, in 1942.[23]

Collection of Folksongs and Tales

For each and every country folksongs and folk tales are very important. Hindusthanies, Bengalis, Maharashtrians and Kannadigas have done significant work by collecting folk songs and printing them. In our region we find a good number of folk songs, ballads, folktales, Kaifeeyats, etc. We must make concerted efforts to collect this folk literature and to publish it.

Scientific Attitude

We have not yet developed the scientific attitude. Our approach should change. Through English, we can know about the literature of any language in the world, information about all nationalities, on any aspect. Books on scientific knowledge, geography, history, are being published in large numbers. Are there such publications in our language ? We do not have even a complete encyclopedia. The Telugu Encyclopedia launchedby K.V. Lakshman Rao remains incomplete. Philanthropists should come forward to give monetary support for the completion of this encyclopedia.

Encouragement for the Publication of Good Books

We find that so many sub-standard books are being written by many people. Strangely enough many donors are coming forward to assist the printing such sub-standard books. Our Zamindars, Rajas, Maharajas and rich people should come forward to give Rs. 500 as prize money annually for the publication of good books. For giving such prizes an endowment should be created.

Support for Journalistic Activity

The journalistic activity in Telugu is far from satisfactory. It is not on sound lines. Telugu periodicals should improve themselves in content and quality like English periodicals. Then alone will people start reading Telugu periodicals. Certain weeklies and monthlies in Telugu are not up to the mark and they are useless. The irony is that some of our eminent journalists are working as editors for prominent English newspapers in India. It is regrettable that we do not have a single english newspaper in Andhra Desa.

Learning other Sister Languages

Those who wish to render service to the Telugu language must learn such sister languages as Tamil and Kannada. Ignoring the sister languages not only shows our narrow mindedness but also makes us unable to render any service to our own language.

Publication of Book Selection Lists

Libraries should not be contented by merely acquiring books. Those who manage rural libraries do not know which books are good to be ordered for the library. Therefore we must publish a booklet containing an annotated list of good books with which will serve as a tool for book selection.

Libraries and Village Upliftment

In the rural areas, libraries should serve as centres of village activity. Those who are willing to come forward to propagate adult education freely for some years should act as heads of libraries. Along with adult education, health and sanitation, cooperation, village panchayat affairs should be propagated among the villagers. Through newspapers and reading of books, geography, history, lives of great men, sciences etc., should be taught to the villagers. In some libraries indoor games are being organised. Along with indoor games, gymnasium should be organised as an auxiliary to the library. If we proceed in this manner, we can reshape our villages on the desired lines within a short span of time.

Other Facets of the Movement

Library movement in Andhra Desa not solely confined to the establishment of libraries and rendering library service to the people. The leaders of the movement realised that the success of the movement very much depended upon the spread of literacy, the telugu language and literature, publication of good books in telugu, encouragement to telugu authors, establishment of higher educational and research institutions, journalistic activity and the amelioration of social and economic conditions of the people. These aspects were given due importance in the policies and programmes of ADLA and were discussed in several conferences and necessary action was initiated. Thus, library movement in Andhra Desa was not confined only to the establishment of libraries and many other related aspects were taken into its fold and transformed it into an entirely popular movement.

The organisers of the movement wished to work closely with other educational, social and cultural institutions and organisations so that the movement could be consolidated and spread vigorously for the benefit of the people. The manuscript library established by Andhra Sahitya Parishad at Kakinada, was functioning aloof without any cooperation or coordination with the library movement. To bring it into the main stream of the library movement, Nalam Krishna Rao suggested :

> It would be more appropriate if the Parishad publishes rare manuscripts possessed by it for the benefit of the educated people of Andhra Desa. The headquarters of the Parishad should be shifted from Kakinada toRajahmundry and this will be more convenient to use its collection.[24]

He also stated that :

> there are some important libraries with rich collection of telugu manuscripts and old printed books, which are not easily accessible to Andhras. For example, the Madras Oriental Manuscript Library, Connemara Library and Madras University Library, are all located in the city of Madras. These are not within the reach of the Andhras. Therefore important sections of book collections concerning the telugu language, culture, literature and history should be transferred to the Andhra University Library[25]

He further suggested that

> Andhra University must make concerted efforts to develop its own library. For, a good library is more important than the buildings, galleries, professors and even the vice-chancellor.[26]

Andhra University was established when the Colloquial

language movement was at its peak in Andhra Desa. One of the important aims of the University is "to promote the development of Telugu, Kanarese, Urdu and Oriya and their use as media of instruction and examination.[27]. In this context, Nalam Krishna Rao observed :

> it would be a happy thing if Andhra University strives to develop and propagate the Telugu language. In this respect libraries should not forget their responsibility and strive vigorously for the development of Telugu. If Andhra University does not encourage Telugu it will merely stand as an institution for swallowing people's money. It will also, like Madras University become useless to the people's needs and turns out, like a machine, merely graduates to meet the requirements of foreign rulers. With that type of machine we do not have any truck.[28]

Telugu Libraries and Telugu Language

Establishment and improvement of Telugu libraries was one of the important objectives of Andhra Library movement. This fact was emphasised in the annual conferences of ADLA. Nalam Krishna Rao stressed that

> Libraries in Andhra Desa should take necessary steps for acquiring all the books published in Telugu. If the libraries have sufficient resources they should encourage and support eminent authors to write books and publish them. In addition, distinguished scholars may be invited to deliver lectures in Telugu on Telugu literature, history and science. All the avenues and opportunities must be explored for the development of Telugu.[29]

He also stated that

> the development of the Telugu language is, to a large extent, depends upon the development of

> other languages. Equal importance should be given for the development of the Sanskrit language. Therefore, Telugu libraries should acquire Sanskrit works so as to spread knowledge in Telugu.[30]

Library Movement and Educational Policy

The movement recognised the value of educating the masses so that knowledge could be spread through libraries effectively to rural masses. As such, the organisers wanted to bring the library movement closer to the activities of educational institutions. B. Seshagiri Rao in his Presidential address at the 14th ADLA Conference held in 1931, stated :

> There are two methods by which library movement can be brought closer to the activities of other educational institutions. (1) to link libraries someway or the other with Andhra University. When the headquarters of the University were located at Vijayawada, K. Ramalinga Reddy, the then Vice-Chancellor prepared a plan to bring libraries closer to University extension policy. But the government rejected this plan on the ground that extension policy does not fall under the purview of the university education. (2) to associate libraries with the activities of autonomous and independent educational institutions functioning in Andhra Desa. The courses offered by these institutions can be formulated in such a way that the libraries have a definite role to play in the formulation of the syllabi, teaching and conduct of examinations.[31]

The movement stressed the need for educating the villagers through effective library service. This was to be realized through acquisition of books dealing with histories of villages and their administration, by arranging lectures on these topics and also acquisition of ancient family histories of the villages and by bringing to their notice, the gifts made by ancestors to the villagers. To be successful in this endeavour, B. Seshagiri Rao suggested that

> efforts should be made to acquire books which deal with special programmes for the development of villages. Whenever occasion arises lectures should be arranged on these programmes. During the leisure time of the villagers, libraries should arrange recitation of ancient scriptures, lectures on world history and contemporary developments and they should acquire books on these topics. Libraries also should train the villagers in acquiring knowledge in different arts and crafts. If libraries take steps to show the path of knowledge to villagers they will win the love and affection of the villagers. The villagers also will have the benefit of their association with the libraries which will ultimately help them to lead their life in a fruitful manner.[32]

School Library Movement

The movement not only concentrated on the establishment of free libraries in urban and rural areas of Andhra Desa but strove hard for the opening of more libraries in the primary schools all over Andhra Desa. ADLA tried for the establishment of libraries in 10,000 schools functioning in 12 districts ofAndhra Desa.[33] D. Trivikrama Rao in his Presidential address at 19th ADLA Conference held in 1934 emphasised the need for opening more school libraries so as to accelerate the spread of library movement. For an effective management of these school libraries he suggested that

> the teachers should be trained properly for the organisation of these libraries. The administration of these libraries should be left to the District

> Boards. The primary school should be used as a centre for the spread of the movement systematically and gradually. For mobilization of resources required for social movements we should not depend upon individuals. The government which collects taxes from the public should come forward to assist schools and libraries. It is the duty of the Education Department to help the children and adults for acquiring knowledge. But the present government is not coming forward to help spread library movement. Therefore, stalwarts of the movement, legislators, social reformers should bring pressure on the government for patronizing the libraries as per the requirements of Andhra Desa.[34]

P. Appalaswamy in the course of his welcome address at the, 14th Kalinga Grandhalaya Maha Sabha held in 1933, suggsted that the library movement should be linked with school libraries so as to accelerate the movement. He stated that

> in big villages we find school libraries. These libraries should be brought into the fold of our library movement. In this way we can get help from Taluka Boards. They must be requested to support the movement and to help financially for its progress.[35]

Libraries and Publication of Good Books

One of the important objectives of the library movement was to develop publication activity in Telugu so as to bring out good Telugu books covering different disciplines. This will in turn, enhance the value of the collections in the libraries. But the situation that obtained during the second phase of themovement was not encouraging. Due to lack of good writers, highly educated people, support from the publishers and the government, good books were not forth coming in Telugu. To remedy the situation, N. Krishna Rao suggested that

> a committee consisting of 5 members should be constituted by ADLA. These members should be elected in the Annual Conferences of the Association. The author should send 3 copies each of their publications with a registration fee of Re. 1 per book. The sub-committee should go through these new publications and select standard works. The list of selected works should be published every month in *Grandhalaya Sarvaswamu and Dharma Grandhalaya Patrika*. The list of selected books with evaluation reports should be sent to all the libraries affiliated the ADLA. These libraries should purchase those books selected by the sub-committee. Out of the three copies received from the author, one copy should be retained in Andhra Central Library and the remaining two copies must be sent to the two libraries selected by the Association for this purpose. This method will ensure the sale of at least 500 copies of a new publication brought out by the authors. This method also will enable to develop at least three good libraries in Andhra Desa.[36]

Urban Library Movement

The workers of the library movement strove hard for the spread of the movement not only in the rural areas but also in the urban areas, for they felt the spread of knowledge in urban areas was equally important because there are also several uneducated people. Even for the educated, library services were very essential to sustain their literacy. For the success of these efforts to spread knowledge, support and co-operation from the Municipalities and other government agencies was very essential. B. Sitarama Raju, in his presidential address at the 15th ADLA Conference held in 1933, suggested that

> Urban associations which are acting as cultural points for rural service should undertake activities which will be useful to urban and rural areas. For doing this, the urban centres should be in a position to have sufficient resources. The associations should be in a position to acquire the required number of good books, appoint properly trained library personnel for efficient management of libraries and patronize enthusiastic library workers for the spread of library movement. It is very essential that those who are educated and well acquainted with library problems should be appointed as library employees. In order to coordinate various efforts that are being made at rural and urban areas in a systematic way and bring in cooperation and mutual dependence between urban and rural libraries, the state and national library associations should watch the situation carefully and work closely for the success of the movement. These associations should, on behalf of the people know what is presently being done and think what should be done in the future and find out the means for the success of the programme. It is very essential that all the associations should organise conferences for the formulation of policies which will make the movement the successful.[37]

Libraries and other Publicity Organisations

The movement tried to establish close cooperation and rapport between the libraries and other publicity organisations. It was visualized that a library should function as a fountain head of the associations and institutions concerned with the knowledge. For the purpose, Ch. Bhanu Murthy in his presidential address at Guntur 13th ADLA Conference held at in 1928 suggested that

> a library should act as a main organ of the body and all other associations/institutions should act as sub-organs. Therefore institutions such as schools, village associations, and other media institutions

such as book series, newspapers should closely work with libraries as the aims and objectives of these institutions are common. For public awakening and consciousness,publicity organisations are very important. Through publicity in the villages by posters, pictures, magic lanterns, and other equipment, new developments in agriculture, chemistry, naturopathy can be communicated to the villagers. Therefore, it is very essential to establish many publicity organisations to assist the library in realising this objective. In this respect, the library should function as head of all such associations and institutions.[38]

Libraries and Spiritual, Moral Development

The movement not only strove hard to spread knowledge among the common people for the eradication of illiteracy and improvement of physical conditions of the people but also tried for their spiritual and moral development, by building up appropriate collections of books in libraries by and various extension activities. The movement also emphasised the fact that a time had come for India to shed lethargy and inaction and work for the spiritual and moral reformation of its people and provide leadership to the world for the attainment of self-enlightenment and establishment of a welfare society. These aims can be achieved through libraries. S.R. Ranganathan suggested the following two ways for achieving this objective.

(1) Libraries should help to make available our classics in philosophy and religion which have been bequeathed to us and rest of the world by our ancestors.

(2) In order to increase philosophical and spiritual knowledge among the readers we have to introduce new methods in our library organisation. The library profession in our country should follow the path shown by our ancient sages and help spreading our spiritual and philosophical

knowledge to the rest of the world. This way, India can do service for the development of library movement in the rest of the world.[39]

Peoples Movement

The library movement in Andhra Desa was primarily a people's movement. The characteristics of the movement were very succinctly put forth by Ranganathan when he stated that

> Library movement in Andhra Desa was not a government affair. It was not organised under the supervision of a University for there was no University in Andhra Desa at the beginning of the movement. The Library Movement has originated entirely due to people's enthusiasm and initiative. It strengthened due to people's effort. The thirst for knowledge among the common people in Andhra Desa promoted the genesis and spread of the library movement.[40]

During the initial stages of its development, the government did not bother to take congnisance of the movement. Later the government suspected the libraries as centres of political activity bringing political and social awareness among the people. The government rejected the applications submitted by individual libraries for grants. The first Andhra Desa Library Association Conference held in 1914 appealed to the government to permit District and Taluk Boards and Municipalities to give grants to libraries and reading rooms.[41] Due to the efforts of Andhra Desa Library Association few local bodies in Andhra Desa supported the libraries with annual grants. The municipalities of Bezawada, Guntur and the Taluka Board of Tadepalligudem established their own libraries. The District Boards of Krishna and Godavari sanctioned grants for the construction of library buildings.

Inspired by the message of library movement, individuals started establishing libraries in their own humble way in the villages. Mention may be made of efforts of Vavilala Gopala-krishnayya and his friends for the establishment of Sarada Library at Sattenapalli, on 11th December 1924. Likewise, many enthusiastic youth started establishing libraries in the villages without the support or financial assistance from the government.[42] The libraries so established by the youth in the villages used to face now and then financial problems. To overcome the financial difficulties, there was no other way than appealing for governments grants. The government grant in-aid rules, stipulate that the library which applied for grant should have been registered according to the Registration ofSocieties Act. The fee fixed by the government for registration was Rs. 50. Many libraries were not in a position to play this amount of Rs. 50 towards registration as they had no funds whatsoever.[43] Therefore, the Andhra Desa Library Association appealed to the government through several of its resolutions to reduce the registration fee. At last, as a result of these appeals the government finally reduced the fees to Rs.5.[44] In 1920, Konda Venkatappayya, Member of the Madras Legislative Council, moved a resolution in the Council seeking government's helping hand and support for the growth of libraries.[45]

By the time the country achieved independence in 1947, the library movement in Andhra Desa was at its zenith. Many libraries had been established in different parts of Andhra Desa. Local bodies like Municipalities, Panchayats, Cooperative Societies, Voluntary organisations and many other institutions established libraries. Further, under the Firka Development plan of the then government of Madras, some more libraries were established.

No statistics are available with regard to the library development in Andhra Desa. Stray statistics available from a few sources indicate that on the eve of the formation of Andhra state in 1953, there were 976 "aided" libraries[46] in Andhra

Desa. This figure rose to 1127 on the eve of the formation of Andhra Pradesh in 1956.[47]

References

1. *Grandhalaya Pragati*, Part 1 (Vijayawada : A.P. Library Association 1962), p. 83.
2. *Grandhalaya Sarvaswamu*, Nos. 3 & 4, 1918, p. 184.
3. *Andhra Desa Grandhalaya Charitra 1914, Vrittantamu* (Bezawada : Andhra Desa Grandhalaya Sangham, 1915).
4. *Grandhalaya Pragati*, Part 1, p. 17.
5. *Andhra Desa Grandhalaya Charitra 1914 Vrittantamu* (Bezawada : ADGS, 1915).
6. A. Venkata Ramanayya, *Grandhalaya Jyoti* (Vijayawada : Saraswati Samrajyamu, 1977), p. 273.
7. *Andhra Desa Grandhalaya Charitra 1914 Vrittantamu.*
8. Ibid.
9. *Grandhalaya Sarvaswamu*, January 1934.
10. *Grandhalaya Sarvaswamu*, August-November 1953.
11. Ibid.
12. K. Sarada, *A.P. Library Association*, (Waltair : Andhra University Press, 1978), p. 66.
13. S.V. Narasimha Sastri, "Andhra Grandhalayodhyamamu," *Grandhalaya Sarvaswamu*' VI, p. 2.
14. A. Venkata Ramanayya, *Grandhalaya Jyoti*, pp. 215-233 and 332-334.
15. Nalam Krishna Rao, "Presidential Address to Eleventh Andhra Desa Library Conference" held at Eluru on November 30 1926 In *Grandhalaya Pragati*, Part 2 (Vijayawada, A.P. Library Association, 1969), p. 8.
16. Nalam Krishna Rao, "Presidential Address, p. 11.
17. ibid., pp. 11-12.
18. B.Seshagiri Rao, "Presidential Address to 14th ADLA Library Conference held on 30 June, 1931 at Guntur. In *Grandhalaya Pragati*, part 2, (Vijayawada, ADLA, 1969), p. 143.
19. B. Seshagiri Rao, "Presidential Address to 14th ADLA Conf., p. 147.
20. Ibid., p. 148.
21. S. Ramaswamy Choudhary, "Presidential Address to 20th ADLA Conference held on 25th Nov. 1935 at Vishakapatnam. Ibid.

22. M.Ramachandra Sastri, "Presidential Address to 22nd ADLA Conference" held from 14-16 January, 1941 at Rajahmundry, See *Grandhalaya Pragati*, part 2, pp. 101-106.
23. S. Pratapa Reddy, "Presidential Address to 23rd ADLA Conference held from 27-28 May, 1942 at Pedapalam. In *Grandhalaya Pragat*, part 2 (Vijayawada, ADLA, 1969), pp, 126-131.
24. Nalam Krishna Rao, "Presidential Address to the 11th ADLA Conference, 1926, p.10.
25. Nalam Krishna Rao, "Presidential Address, p. 11.
26. Ibid., pp. 11-12.
27. Quoted by Nalam Krishna Rao in his Presidential address to 11th ADLA Conference held on 30th November 1926 at Eluru. In *Grandhalaya Pragati*, Part 2. p. 18.
28. Nalam Krishna Rao, Presidential Address, pp. 18-19.
29. Ibid, p. 17.
30. Ibid, pp. 17-18.
31. B. Seshagiri Reo, "Presidential Address to 14th ADLA Conference held on 30th June 1931 at Guntur. In *Grandhalaya Pragati* Part-I (Vijayawada, APLA, 1969), pp. 159-160.
32. B. Seshagiri Rao, pp. 153-54.
33. *Grandhalaya Pragati*, Part-2, Vijayawada, APLA, 1969, p. 63.
34. D. Trivikrama Rao, "Presidential Address to 19th ADLA Conference held from 24-25 December 1924 at Madras. See *Grandhalaya Pragati*, Part-2, p. 63.
35. P. Appala Swamy, "Welcome Address to 14th Kalinga Desa Grandhalaya Maha Sabha, held at Visakhapatnam on 6 May 1933. See *Grandhalaya Pragati*, Part-3, p. 126.
36. N. Krishna Rao, "Presidential Address", pp. 16-17.
37. B. Sitarama Raju "Presidential address to 15th ADLA Conference.. In *Grandhalaya Pragati* part 2. pp. 40-41.
38. C.H. Bhanumurthy, "Presidential Address to 13th ADLA Conference held at Guntur on 28th July 1938. *Grandhalaya Pragati*, Part 2, pp. 30-31.
39. S.R. Ranganathaa,"Presidential Address to 24th ADLA Conference, held at Hindupur in 1942. In *Grandhalaya Pragati*, Part 2, pp. 139-40.
40. Ibid., p. 133,
41. *Grandhalaya Pragati*, Part 1 (Vijayawada : A.P. Library Association, 1962), pp. 146-147.

42. A Venkata Ramanayya, *Grandhalaya Jyotl*, p. 66.
43. V. Venkatappaya, *Mana Grandhalaya Udyamamu*,. p. 79.
44. K. Sarada, *A.P. Library Association*, p. 79.
45. V. Gopalakrishnayya, *Library Movement in Andhra Pradesh*, p. 7.
46. Libraries established out of initiative drive, imagination, planning and enthusiasm of individuals and groups dedicated to library Movement were erroneously termed as "private" or "aided" ibraries with the advent of Madras Public Libraries Act in 1948. See *Report of the Committee on Private Libraries* Hyderabad. Dept. ofPublic Libraries, Govt. of A.P., 1978), p. 97.
47. *Teluguseemalo Grandhalaya Pragati* (Chittoor : K.B. Reddy, 1983), pp. 80-81.

Appendix

List of some of the prominent libraries in Coastal Andhra region in 1930's.

Visakhapatnam District

1. Sri Mahatma Grandhalayam (1929), Bobbili
2. Sri Mahadeva Grandhalayam (1927), Ponduru

Anakapalli (Tq)

3. Sri Sarada Grandhalayam, Anakapalli

Vizianagaram (Tq)

4. Adidamu Surakavi Andhra Grandha Niketanam (1938), Pusupatirega

Visakhapatnam (Tq)

5. Andhra Grandhamandali (1925), Visakhapatnam
6. Godenarayana Gajapati Hindu Reading Room, (1925), Visakhapatnam

Salur (Tq)

7. SriRama Grandhalayam (1921), Sivaramapuram

Sompeta (Tq)

8. Vivekapradhayini Sancharaka Grandhalayam & Pathana Mandiramu (1936), Sompeta

Sringavarapukota (Tq)

9. Sri Venkateshwara Vilasa Pustakabhandagarmu (1920), Upamaka Agraharam, Nakkapalli (P.O.)
10. Sri Sarma Pustakabhandagaramu (1912) Yelamanchili.

East Godavari District

11. SriVenugapala Pustakabhandagaramu (1927), Vulapalli, Dwarapudi (P.O)
12. Sri Jatiyochitapathana mandiramu (1930), Artamuru, Mandapeta (P.O)

Amalapuram (Tq)

13. Andhraratna Gopalakrishna Bhandagaramu (1926), Buchammapeta Agraharam, Amalapuram
14. Sri Sarada Pustaka Bhandagaramu (1929) Jagannadha Puram Agraharamu

Kakinada (Tq)

15. Sri EshwaraPustaka Bhandagaramu (1916), Ramaraopata, Kakinada
16. Sri Rama VilasaGrandhalayamu, Samarlakota

Pitahapuram (Tq)

17. Srichelikani Achutaraya Pustaka Bhandagaramu (1928), Chitrada
18. Sri Suryaraya Vidyananda Grandhalayamu (1935), Pitahpuram

Peddapuram (Tq)

19. SriSivaji Grandhamandali (1927), Peddapuram
20. Sri Mahatma Gandhi Pustaka Bhandagaramu, Somavaramu

Bhadrachalam (Tq)

21. Sri Sabarigautamisangamananda Grandhalayamu (1938), Kunavaramu

22. Sri Kalpavalli Grandhalayamu, Bhadrachalamu Raja mahendravaramu (Tq)
23. Sri Satyanarayana Pustaka Bhandagaramu (1917), Dhavaleshwaramu
24. Sri Gautami Grandhalayamu (1898), Rajamahendravaramu
25. Sri Veeresalinga Grandhalayamu, Town Hall, Rajamahendravaramu
26. Hindusamaja Grandhalaymu, Innispeta, Rajamahendravarama

Rajolu (Tq)

27. Sri Ramachandra Pustaka Bhandagaramu (1920), Palagummi, Amabajipeta (P.O.)
28. SriVeeresalinga PustakaBhandagaramu (1919), Mori.
29. Vishwasahiti Nilayamu (1935), Munganda Agraharam, Ambajipeta (P.O)

RamachandraPuram (Tq)

30. Saraswati Samajamu (1910), Alamuru
31. Sri Saraswati Vilasa Grandhalayamu (1910), Narisipudi, Alamuru (P.O)

West Godavari District

Elumu (Tq)

33. Sri Ramakrishna Paramahansa Grandhalayamu, (1930), Vatluru
34. Sri Balabharati Grandhalayamu (1920), Punugollu, Pedapadu (P.O)
35. Sri Vanipustaka Bhandagaramu (1928), Satyavolu

Korvuru (Tq)

36. Sarvaraya Pustaka Bhandaguramu (1928), Annadevarpeta.
37. Sri Gandhiji Grandhalayamu (1938), Tyajampudi,

Potavaram (P.O)

38. Jawahar Grandhalayamu (1936), Singavaramu, Nidadavolu (P.O)

Tanuku (Tq)

39. Sri Vemanapustaka Bhandagaramu (1937), Aravalli, via, Attili

40. Sri Gopala Krishna Grandhalayamu (1938), Surampudi, Velpuru (P.O)

Tadepalligudem (Tq)

41. Sriveeresalinga Grandhalayamu (1939), Umamaheswarapuram

42. SriNageshwara Grandhalayamu (1928), Ganapavaramu

43. Sri Chittaranjana Grandhalayamu (1935), Badampudi

Bhimavaram (Tq)

44. Sri Veeresalinga Kavisamaja Grandhalayamu (1897), Kumudavalli, Palakoderu (PO)

45. Sri Motilal Pustaka Bhandagaramu (1931) Konitiwada.

46. Sri Krishna Devaraya Pustakalayamu (1916), Cherukumilli

47. Sri Peddanamatya Grandhalayamu (1932), Jakkramu

Narasapuram (Tq)

48. Sri Ramachandra Grandhalayamu (1914), Poduru, Palakollu (P.O)

49. Sri Pardhasaradhi Pustaka Bhandagaramu (1914) Ballipadu

Krishna District

Gannavaram (Tq)

50. Sri Jitendradasu Grandhalayamu (1930), Kaluvapamula Indupalli (P.O)

51. SriVemana Grandhalayamu (1933), Telaprolu,

Gudivada (Tq)

52. Yuvajana Bharati Grandhalayamu (1934), Kanumuru
53. Sri RamaMohanGrandhalayamu (1936), Chinaparupudi, Vuyyur (P.O)
54. Sri Dayananda Grandhalayamu (1933), Yalamarru

Tiruvuru (Tq)

55. Sri Vivekananda Grandhalayamu (1935), Daliparru, Gantasala (P.O)
56. Sri Kamala Nehru Pathanamandiramu (1937), Chinamuktevi

Nandigama (Tq)

57. Sri Krishna Devaraya Grandhalayamu, Chintalapadu
58. Sri Tirupatamma Grandhalayamu, Penuganchibrolu

Nuzvidu (Tq)

59. Sri Sobhanachala Pathana Mandiramu, Agirapalli
60. Sri Balasaraswati Grandhalayamu, Ramanakkapeta

Bandaru (Tq)

61. Sri Venugopala Grandhalayamu (1923) Kankata, Gudur (P.O)
62. Sri Umamaheswara Grandhalayamu (1929), Patapeta, Pedana.

Bezawada (Tq)

63. Sri Rammohan Dharma Pustaka Bhandagaramu (1911), Bezawada.
64. Sri Velidandla Hanumantharaya Grandhalayamu (1934), Bezawada.
65. Sri Mahatma Gandhi Grandhanilayamu (1937), Mylavaramu

Guntur (Dt)

Ongole (Tq)

66. Andhra Bhasha Nilayamu (1930), Koniki

67. Sri Chittaranjandas Grandhalayamu (1926), Kottapattanamu
68. Sri Saraswati Grandhalayamu (1918) Ongole

Guntur (Tq)

69. Sri Tikkana Grandhalayamu, Pata Guntur, Guntur
70. Sri Maheswara Grandhalayamu (1930), Tulluru
71. Sri BalaBharati Dharma Patanamandiramu (1931), Mangalagiri

Tenali (Tq)

72. Sri Radhakrishna Grandhalayamu (1937), Evuru, Kolluru (P.O)
73. Sri Tilakjatiya Grandhalayamu (1933), Chinapalemu, Perakalapudi (P.O)
74. Srikrishnamohana Grandhalayamu (1928), Nazarupeta, Tenali
75. Andhrabala Bharati Grandhalayamu, (1932), Vetapalem

Narasaraopeta (Tq)

76. Sri Gandhi Saraswatanilayamu (1937), Kanuparru, Satuluru (P.O)
77. Andhra BhashaPustaka Bhandagaramu (1938), Gannavaramu, Jagarlamudi (P.O)

Palnadu (Tq)

78. Andhra Grandhalayamu (1914), Rentachintala
79. Sri Lakshmichennakesavavilasa Grandhalayamu, (1916), Karempudi

Bapatla (Tq)

80. Andhraratna DharmaPathanalayamu (1937), Chirala
81. Saraswata Niketanamu (1918), Vetapalemu

Repalle (Tq)

82. Sri Vaanivijnana Nilayamu (1933), Dhulipudi, (via) Repalle

83. Andhra Ratna Gopala krishna Grandhalayamu (1938), Peteru, (via) Repalle

Sattenapalli (Tq)

84. Sri SaradaNilayamu (1925), Sattenapalli

85. Sri Desodharaka Grandhalayamu (1936), Medikonduru

Source : P. Nagabhushanam, *Comp.* AndhraDesa Grandhalayamula Pattika (Bezawada, AndhraDesa Grandhalaya Sangham, 1939)

B.2. Talangana

The establishment of Sri Krishna Devaraya Andbra Bhasha Nilayam in 1901, at Hyderabad is a landmark in the history of library movement in the Telangana Region. This paved the way for the revival of Telugu and the genesis and development library movement which was truly the first Andhra movement in the region.[1] Gradually, the movement spread to other areas of Telangana and many libraries were established. By the year 1927, when the Bhasha Nilayam entered its Silver Jubilee year, it has been estimated that 7 libraries in Hyderabad, 4 in Secunderabad 2 in Attrapubalda, 15 in Warangal, 9 in Karimnagar, 13 in Nalgonda, 5 in Mahboob Nagar districts, 1 each in Adilabad and Raichur districts,—a total of 63 libraries - hadbeen established in the Telangana region.[2] These libraries through lectures, meetings, conferences, poets gatherings, annual celebrations, and numerous other activities awakened the people of Telangana who were in a deep slumber and instilled in them the thirst for acquiring knowledge and information for the betterment of their lives.[3] In spite of the Nizam's government's policy against the library movement, and the impediments put forth in the growth of library movement, these libraries strove hard for the spread of library movement. These libraries helped create nationalistic ideas and moulded the people as patriotic citizens and prepared them for the struggle against Nizam's autocratic and oppressive rule. These libraries spread not only knowledge among the people but also sowed the seeds of revolution for the struggle against the Nizam's autocratic rule[4].

Andhra Jana Sangham

While in Andhra Desa (i.e., the Andhra region) where the activities of individual libraries were channelized, coordinated and guided by the establishment of Andhra Desa Library Association in 1914, the activities of individual libraries in the Telangana region were coordinated, channelised and guided during the early stages by Andhra Jana Kendra Sangham and later by Andhra Maha Sabha.

The Andhra Jana Sangham was formed on 12th November 1921 with only eleven members. Prominent among them were Madapati Hanumantha Rao, B. Ramakrishna Rao, M. Narasinga Rao, T. Ranga Rao and A. Veerabhadra Rao. Very soon, the membership of the Sangham rose to a hundred and its first General Body meeting was held on 14th February 1922 at Reddy Vidyalaya under the Chairmanship of K.V. Ranga Reddy.[5] Later, two General Body meetings of the Sangham were held on 17th March and 4th April 1922 under the chairmanship of K.V. Ranga Reddy and in these meetings aims, objectives and rules of the Sangham were finally approved and the executive formed.[6] The formation of Andhra Jana Sangham was the beginning of Andhra movement in Hyderabad state. The Sangham stood for social and cultural upliftment of the people of Telangana and brought about general enlightenment among them by establishing associations and institutions, by helping the existing institutions and societies, by arranging lectures, and by conducting meetings and conferences.[7] The Sangham had worked right earnestly since its inception for the spread of Andhra movement. It arranged lectures and meetings in several parts of Hyderabad city. Soon several Andhra Sanghas sprouted at several places in the Telangana region. In order to broad base the movement and coordinate the activities of these Sanghams, there was a need for a Kendra Sangham (central association). A meeting of the representatives of the Sanghams was convened on 1st April 1923 at Hanamkonda to prepare a constitution for the Kendra Sangham and the meeting was presided over by Rao Bahadur Samala Venkata Reddy. The meeting approved the constitution of the Kendra Sangham.[8]

After the approval of the constitution the first conference of the Kendra Sangham was held at Hyderabad on 27th July 1923, nearly four months after the Hanumkonda meeting.

Seven out of 13 representatives from the districts and invitees from the districts and Hyderabad City attended the first conference. In this first conference the bye-laws for the Kendra Sangham were approved. These bye-laws include the following.[9]

(i) to establish libraries, reading rooms and schools,

(ii) to collect palm-leaf manuscripts, inscriptions and to conduct research,

(iii) to spread knowledge through pamphlets, booklets and lectures;

(iv) to honour eminent poets and scholars;

(v) to initiate necessary steps for the propagation of the Telugu language.

(vi) to support and encourage students.

The second conference of the Kendra Sangham was held at Nalgonda on 21st March 1924, and it was presided over by its President Rao Bahadur Venkata Reddy. Seven representatives from the districts along with fifty other invitees attended the conference. The important decisions taken in this conference were: (1) to create a fund named "Nizam Rashtra Andhra Nidhi" for the spread of the movement; (2). to appoint a paid 'pracharka' (a person who propagates); (3) to transfer management of Parisodhaka Sangham (research wing) of Hyderabad Andhra Sangham to Kendra Sangham, (4) to honour the candidates who passed B.A. Examination in the First division with Telugu as a subject, by awarding Gold and Silver Medals, and (5) to conduct examinations for the propagation of the Telugu language and literature.[10]

The third conference of the Kendra Sangham was held at Madhira on 21st February 1925 under the chairmanship of Rao Bahadur Venkata Reddy. Nineteen Andhra Jana Sangha representatives, twenty library representatives and 100 invitees attended the conference. The important decisions taken in this conference were (1) to elect executive for the Andhra Research

Association; (2) to award Gold Medals to Telugu students who pass Medical and Engineering examinations in distinction; (3) to award a prize of Rs. 25 for the writer of the best essay on "Nizam Rashtrandhrula Abhivridhi Margamulu" ("the Developmental Activities of the Andhras of the Nizam State") and to publish it for distribution.[11]

The fourth conference of the Kendra Sangham was held on 30th May 1928 at Suryapeta under the chairmanship of K.V. Ranga Reddy. Important decisions taken in this conference were : (1) to award gold medals to the top rank Telugu studenis in B.A. and Intermediate examinations of Osmania University; (2) to take steps to get admissions to the Telugu students of Osmania University in the colleges affiliated to Andhra University. During this conference several lectures were arranged for the cause of Andhra movement.[12]

Afterwards 5th, 6th, 7th and 8th conferences of the Kendra Sangham were held at Jogipeta, Devarakonda, Khammam and Sirisilla respectively. These conferences endorsed the resolutions adopted in the Andhra Maha Sabha conferences and tried to impliment them. Therefore, after the fourth annual conference, pratically no conferences of the Andhra Jana Kendra Sangham were held. After the adoption, of constitution and bye-laws for Andhra Maha Sabha at Sirisilla the Kendra Sangham receded in to the background.[13]

The Andhra Jana Kendra Sangham, through its activities helped to establish schools for the cause of Telugu language in the rural areas.[14] In order to spread the movement, the Kendra Jana Sangham accomplished the following four activities : (1) it published pamphlets and booklets; (2) it appointed paid "pracharakas" for propagation of the movement and to develop rapport with the public; (3) it arranged public meetings and lectures; and (4) it circulated newspapers.

In order to spread knowledge among the people, the following books were published by the Kendra Sangham, during the first eight years which constitute the first phase (1923-1930) of the Andhra movement.[15]

1. *Nizamrashtra Andhrulu*
2. *Nizamrashtra Abhuridhi Margamulu* by Vadlakonda Narasimha Rao
3. *Vartaka Swatantriyam* by M. Ramachandra Rao
4. *Mohatarpha—Maggamupannu* by Mateti Papayya
5. *Nizamrashtra Jana Pariganam.*

During the second phase of the movement, 19 books were published between 1930 and 1935 and of these four publications constitute the reports of the conferences of Andhra Maha Sabha held at Jogipeta, Devarakonda, Khammam and Sirisilla. Of the remaining 15 publications, information about the following 9 publications is available.[16]

1. *Vyavasayakulilu Konni Suchanalu* by Sarvothama Rao.
2. *Nyayasthanamulu—Desha Bhashalu* by M. Narayana Rao.
3. *Madhya Panamu.*
4. *Grandhalayamulu* by Suravaramu Pratapa Reddy.
5. *Mana Vakswatantryamu.*
6. *Gastinishan 53 yokka vivaranamu*
7. *Raitula Runabadhavivaranam*
8. *Mana Vidyasamasyalu* by K. Subba Rao.
9. *Nizam Rashtrapu Jana Pariganamu*

Publicity is a very important factor for the success of any movement. The leaders of the Andhra movement recognised this fact and took steps for effective publicity of the aims and objectives of the movement, especially in rural areas. The Andhra Jana Kendra Sangham appointed Unnava Venkata Ramayya (1921-1928) the only paid "pracharaka" for popularising the movement. But the credit of spreading the message of the movement rightly goes to honorary "pracharakas". Mention may be made of Puwada Venkatatappayya (Suryapeta),T.K. Bappayya (Nizamabad), Chatrati Lakshmi Narasamma (Khammam) and Gangula Sai Reddi who carried on tremendous publicity work and brought laurels to the Andhra movement.[17] Puwada Venkatappayya vigorously spread the message of Andhra movement in the areas of Suryapeta, Devarakonda, Nallagonda, Bhuvanagiri and Karimnagar. The people of these areas were greatly enlightened by the publicity campaign launched by Seshagiri Rao and this contributed very much for the spread of Andhra movement.[18]

Spreading knowledge through lectures and conferences was one of the important methods adopted for the spread of the Andhra movement. But it encountered several impediments from the Nizam's autocratic rulers. The government promulgated several orders which prevented free arrangement of lectures and meetings. Mention may be made of the notorious Gastinishan 53 promulgated in 1929, which prohibited holding of meetings and conferences without Nizam's prior permission.[19] Golakonda Patrika in its editorials dated 18-2-1933 strongly pleaded for the repeal of this draconian order.[20]

Newspapers played a prominent role in spreading the cause of Andhra movement during the first phase. Mention may be made of the role of *Nilagiri Patrika* (24-8-1922), *Telugu Patrika* (27-8-1922), and *Golakonda Patrika* (10-5-1926). These newspapers, notwithstanding of several odds, gave prominence in their columns, to Andhra movement and library movement and published information emanating from different parts of the Telangana region.[21]

Library Conferences

After Andhra movement began, several libraries were established in different parts of the Telangana region. With the objective of bringing library workers together at one place for exchange of ideas and to create fellowship among them and also to give further push to library movement, the first Andhra Libraries conference was convened at Madhira on 22 February 1925 along with Andhra Jana Kendra Sangham's 3rd annual conference.[22] The first conference was presided over by Pingili Venkata Rama Reddy. Library representatives from all parts of Telangana right from the capital to the villages attended the first conference. In his presidential address Venkata Rama Reddy cautioned the library workers not to dissipate their energies for the cause of other movements and thereby weaken the library movement. He advised the Kendra Sangham to make three special efforts through its library section : to coordinate the activities of libraries, and to spread library movement, and while doing so, not to harm the autonomy of the individual libraries.[23] The conference appointed a sub-committee for broadening the phase of library movement.

The Second Libraries Conference held from 30th May to 1st June 1929 along with the fourth conference of Andhra Jana Kendra Sangham at Suryapeta, was presided over by Deshabhakta Vaman Naik. Representatives from 29 libraries attended the second conference. Vaman Naik in his Presidential address identified three activities for the spread of education, viz. (1) opening of schools ; (2) arranging lectures and meetings and (3) establishment of libraries. He appealed to the library workers to establish hundreds of libraries in the state for the cause of education and spread of knowledge. He also wished that there should be one Central Library.[24] The conference adopted fifteen resolutions for the spread of library movement. Mention may be made of some of the important resolutions which state : (1) as in the Baroda State, a separate department for libraries should be created for the development of libraries in the state (Resolution No. 3), (2) allocation of at least 12 per cent from the local fund revenue for assisting library movement (Resolution No. 5) ; (3) for the spread of knowledge among the people, the government should supply, free of cost, annual reports and other publications brought out by various departments of the government, to all libraries in the state (Resolution No. 8), (4) the conference would support and encourage the managements of libraries which celebrated anniversaries, published annual reports, arranged lectures and meetings, contributed for the growth of reading of books and periodicals by the villagers and helped the development of library movement in the region (Resolution No. 13); (5) the conference appealed to the government to remove hurdles being created by the local police and other government officials to the meetings and conferences conducted by the libraries (Resolution No. 14).[25]

After this conference, no separate libraries conference was held. However, the cause of library movement was taken up by Andhra Maha Sabha. Its first conference was held from 3-5 March 1930, at Jogipeta. From 1930 to 1946, thirteen conferences of Andhra Maha Sabha were held at different places in Telangana. These conferences helped create a new and great awareness among the people of Telangana. But most of the resolutions adopted in these conferences deal with political, educational and social aspects.[26] However, in some of the conferences, the need for spread of library movement was discussed and a few resolutions were adopted. They were as follows.

The first Andhra Maha Sabha conference held at Jogipeta from 3rd-5th March 1930 resolved to appeal to the government firstly, for the withdrawal of Gastinishan 53 promulgated in 1929 which prohibited holding of public meetings and conferences, (Resolution 2). Secondly, the library movement in the Telangana region was essentially a people's effort which contributed for the growth of education. Therefore it appealed to government to support the movement for further growth as was done in Baroda state. Thirdly it resolved to open separate sections for Telugu, Marathi and Kannada in the state central library.[27] (Resolution 5).

The second Andhra Maha Sabha conference held at Devarakonda, from 3rd to 5th March 1931, resolved to appeal to the government to extend financial support to the libraries managed by the public and take steps to establish more public libraries for the spread of library movement as was done in the Baroda State.[28] (Resolution 10).

The third Andhra Maha Sabha conference held at Khammam, in 1934, resolved to reiterate its appeal to the government to establish a public library system in the state on the lines of that in Baroda State and to give grants from the state exchequer, local fund and municipal finances to the public libraries presently working in the state.[29] (Resolution 2). The fourth conference was held at Sirisilla from 30th December 1935 to 1st January 1936. Nandagiri Venkata Rao, suggested a plan for the consideration of the 4th Conference which aimed for the revival of defunct libraries and spread of education in rural areas. The plan suggested the following structure for the development of public libraries and library movement in the state.

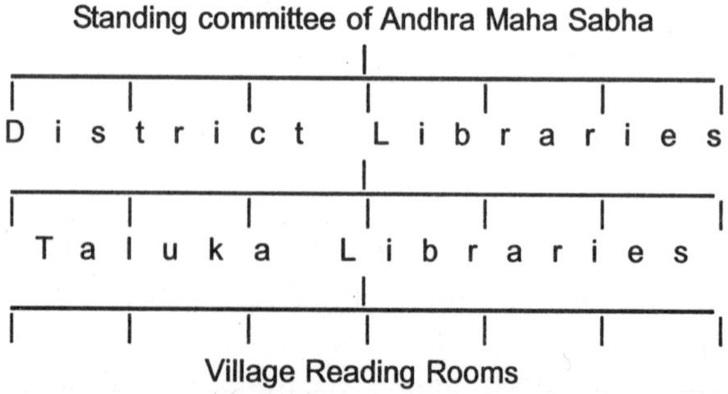

He further suggested that until the revival of Nizam State Library Conference, the Standing Committee of Andhra Maba Sabha could appoint a sub-committee which would act as a „ centre and take care of the library movement in the state.[30] Another delegate, suggested to this conference the need for appointment of special propagandists for the development of libraries and spread of library movement in the state. He also suggested the need for holding regularly library conferences along with Andhra Maha Sabha Conferences. [31]The fourth conference resolved to recognise the existing public welfare institutions and libraries as "Andhra Jana Sanghas" and, through them, to implement the aims and objectives Andhra Jana Sangha, to appoint a special propagandist for a period of one year, for at least in one Taluka in each district under the control of the district Association, to undertake the activities of spread of library movement, literacy, improvement of health and sanitation in the villages.[32] (Resolution 3). The 5th conference of the Andhra Maha Sabha held from 15th to 17th December 1936, at Shadnagar resolved to appoint a subcommittee to look into the state of affairs of libraries and reading rooms, revival of those which were in badshape and develop mutual help and cooperation among them126 (Resolution 6). The 6th conference held at Nizamabad, from 6th to 8th December 1937, resolved to request the government to withdraw immediately "Gastinishafl 53" which was coming in the way of spreading knowledge among the people.[33] (Resolution 3).

After the Nizamabad conference, seven more conferences ofAndhra Maha Sabha were held between 1940 and 1946 at different places in Telangana. It appears that political, educa-cational, social and economic aspects dominated' these conferences and library movement receded to the background.

The Andhra movement which started initially as a linguistic, literary and scientific movement gradually transformed into a political movement aiming at the achievement of responsible government.[34] After the Kandi conference (1946), the Andhra Maha Sabha merged with Hyderabad State Congress in 1946, to fight against the Nizam's government and to bring about the merger of Hyderabad State with the Indian Union.[35]

Thus, the efforts of Andhra Jana Kendra Sangham and Andhra Maha Sabha for the spread of library movement in the

Telangana region was significant. During the first phase of Andhra movement (1923-1930) as well as in the second phase i.e., from the first Andhra Maha Sabha Conference held at Sirisilla in 1930, to the 9th conference held at Nizamabad, in 1937 library movement received active support and cooperation from the library workers and leaders alike. It was at the Nizamabad conference held in 1937 that K. Lakshmiranjanam, I. Sita Rama Rao and others started Nizam State Library Association. But the activities of this Associaation were shortlived and it did not make any significant impact on the library movement.[36]

Library Legislation

After Police Action in 1948, Hyderabad State was merged into the Indian Union. In 1951, Hyderabad Library Association was formed. Through the efforts of Hyderabad Library Association, the state Assembly adopted Hyderabad Public Libraries Act in 1955 and became the second Library Act in India. The provisions of the Act remained in force in the 9 districts of the Telangana region.[37] The year 1956 saw the reorganisation of states on linguistic basis and the formation of Andhra Pradesh. For four years thereafter, the two Acts viz. Madras Public Libraries Act 1948 was in force in the 11 districts of the Andbra region and Hyderabad Libraries Act 1955 in the 9 districts of the Telangana region of the enlarged state of Andhra Pradesh presenting peculiar difficulties in their implementation and this compelled the government to think of an unified comprehensive legislation. It was against this background that the Andhra Pradesh Public Libraries Act 1960 emerged on the scene replacing the two predecessor Acts in force till then in the state.[38]

Merger of two streams of Library Movement of Telangana and Andhra Regions

Cooperation between the library workers of Andhra and

Telangana regions existed right from the formation of Andhra Desa Library Association in 1914. Representatives from the Telangana region, M. Ramakoteswara Rao (Warangal); A. Gururaja Rao (Hanamkonda) and B.V. Subrahmanyam (Secunderabad) attended the first Andhra Desa Library workers conference.[39] Afterwards, such stalwarts in the library movement as Madapati Hanumantha Rao, Suravarm Pratapa Reddy, Burgula Rama Krishna Rao, Vaman Naik, K.V. Ranga Reddy, Kodati Narayana Rao, Kaloji Narayana Rao, and V. Alwarswamy and many others actively participated in the activities of Andhra Desa Library Association. Likewise, from the Andhra region, Gandhicherla Harisarvothama Rao, Ayyanki Venkata Ramanayya, Paturi Nagathusanam, Vavilala Gopal-krishnayya and scores of others established close contacts and actively associated themselves with the library movement in the Telangana region.[40]

Participation in Library Conferences

Suravarm Pratapa Reddy presided over the 23rd Andhra Desa Library Association conference held at Pedapalem from 27-28th May 1942. In his presidential address Pratapa Reddy emphasised the need for collection and preservation of folk songs, inculcation of scientific knowledge among the readers by providing new books on science and technology, and guiding the rural libraries in acquiring suitable books for the villages, and preparation of library catalogues.[41]

G. Harisarvothama Rao, P. Nagabhusanam, Ch. Narasimham and others participated in the annual celebrations of Vijnana Niketanam, Khammam held in 1944, and inspired the library workers in the region. The 25th Andhra Desa Library Association conference was held at Singareni colleries in 1944, and it was presided over by B. Ramakrishna Rao. Such stalwarts as Ayyanki Venkata Ramanayya, G. Harisarvothama Rao, Ch. Narasimham and Paturi Naga Bhusanam participated in this conference. V. Gopalakrishnayya observed that

> This conference stands as a great landmark in the history of library movement in the area. It was at Singareni that the two streams, one from British India and the other from Hyderabad state merged to become a bigger stream.[42]

The objective of this conference was to strengthen the library movement in the Andhra and Telangana regions and establish closer contacts between the library workers of the two regions. Accordingly, Andhra Desa Library Association established its branch office at Khammam on 18th April 1945. G. Harisarvothama Rao, President of Andhra Desa Library Association while opening the branch stated that

> though Andhras were separated and living in different regions, they have common links of language and culture. Eventhough there is no possibility of establishing political links, there is every possibility for establishing literary, cultural and scientific links between the two regions.[43]

On the whole, the 25 and 26 conferences laid strong foundation for the realization of 'Visalandhra' (Greater Andhra). Many scholars and poets from Rayala Seema also attended the conference. This enabled to arrange for gatherings of poets and scholars during the conference.[44]

The twentysixth conference of Andhra Desa Library Association was held at Kyaturu (near Alampur) in 1946, and it was presided over by P. Venkata Rama Reddy. The 27th Conference of Andhra Desa Library Association was held at Suryapeta from 7th to 9th April 1950 and it was presided over by P. Rama Murthy. Commenting on this conference, *Golakonda Patrika*[45] in its editorial dated 3-4-1950 stated that these conferences enabled library workers from the Andhra region to visit Telangana and instilled new enthusiasm among the library workers for the spread of library movement. This conference strove hard to remove regionalism and propogated the idea of Visalandhra. The 29th Conference of Andhra Desa

Library Association[46] was held at Janagama from 18th to 20th September 1953, and it was presided over by S. Bhagavantam, Vice-Chancellor of Osmania University. Nearly two thousand people attended the first day conference. The government of Madras, for the first time, in the history of library movement, issued orders to enable the local bodies and local library authorities to send the delegates to this conference. M. Chenna Reddy in his inaugural address paid glowing tributes to the efforts made by the stalwarts like Ayyanki and Gadhicherla for the spread of library movement in the Andhra region. He appealed to the library workers for opening more libraries in the rural areas for the spread of literacy. S. Bhagavantam in his presidential address stated that as the country attained independence, there was a greater need for giving more importance to the development of Science and Technology. To achieve this libraries had to play a greater role.[47] Commenting up on the conference *Golakonda Patrika* in its Editorial dated 22-9-1953 reminded the need for dedicated workers for sustaining the library movement which was at present in its lowest ebb. Activities such as literary and adult education programmes had to be undertaken so as to create interest among the public and see that library became an important factor in the daily life of the individual. To achieve this is required well trained and action-oriented library workers and librarians.[48]

The conference adopted resolutions which concerning: (a) modification of grant-in-aid rules for libraries formulated by government of Hyderabad, (b) starting of a diploma course in library science at Osmania University ; (c) free supply of government publications, periodicals and annual reports to all libraries in the state, and (d) conducting examinations in oriental languages by Andhra and Osmania Universities.[49]

The impact of these conferences resulted in a greater recognition of library movement in Telangana. The four state level conferences and other conferences held at the district level revived the library movement and generated great enthusiasm among the people. Though library movement quite often faced the wrath of Nizam's government, it was able to retain its distinct individuality and continued to serve the spread of knowledge among the people. It strove hard and fought the autocratic rule of the Nizam and indirectly supported the political movement in the state culminating in the merger of the Hyderabad state in the Indian union after Police Action, in 1948. It is necessary to take note that many of the libraries which had been established during the movement suffered from lack of proper buildings and the required number of books. They were not able to get proper support from the government. Many of them were struggling hard to stand on their own legs. There was an urgent need for library legislation to improve the state of affairs of libraries. The Hyderabad Library Association established in 1951, took initiative in this regard.[50]

References

1. B. Ramakrishna Rao, "Presidential Address to Golden Jubilee Celebrations of Sri Krishna Devaraya Andhra Bbasba Nilayam, 1 Sept. 1952. In *Suvarnothsava Sartchika* (Hyderabad : SKDAD Niiayam, 1955), p. 24.
2. Sri Krishna Devaraya Andhra Bhasha Nilayam, Hyderabad, *Rajathothsava Satichika*, 1927, pp. 96-101. .
3. B. Ramakrishna Rao, Presidential Address, p. 24.
4. Gayitri, "Telanganalo Grandhalayodhyamamu, Sadhinchina apoorva Pragati." *Andhra Jyoti*, 8 December 1968, p. 11.
5. M. Hanumantha Rao, *Telangana Andhrodhyamamu*, Part 1, (Hyderabad : Andhra Chaodrika Grandhamala, 1949), pp. 19-20.
6. Ibid., p. 20.
7. Ibid., p. 21.
8. Ibid., pp. lii-19. .
9. Ibid., pp. 31-32. .
10. Ibid., pp. 33-34. .
11. Ibid., pp. 37-38. .
12. Ibid., pp. 41-43. .

13. Ibid., pp. 43-44.
14. Ibid., pp. 83-86..
15. Ibid., pp. 87-90.
16. Ibid., pp. 91-92.
17. Ibid,, pp. 93-98.
18. *Golakonda Patrika*, 24 June 1927, p. 6. .
19. M. Hanumantha Rao, *Telangana Andhrodhyamamu*, Part 1, pp.99-128.
20. *Golakonda Patrika*, 18 February 1933, p. 6. .
21. "Nizamrashtramuloni Andhra Patrikalu," *Golakonda Patrika*, 7 May 1927, p. 2.
22. M. Hanumantha Rao, *Telangana Andhrodhyamamu*, Part 1, pp. 62-63.
23. *Grandhalaya Pragati*, Part 3, p. 8.
24. *Golakonda Patrika*, 4 July 1929, p. 9. ,
25. *Golakonda Patrika*, 9 June 1929, p. 5.
26. D. Ramanuja Rao, *Telanganaloo Jatiyodhyamalu* (Hyderabad : The Author, 1967), pp. 51-52.
27. M. Hanumantha Rao, *Telangana Andhrodhyamamu*, Part 2 (Hyderabad : Andhra Chandrika Grandhamala, 1950), pp, 234-235.
28. Ibid., p. 249.
29. Ibid., p. 259.
30. Nandagiri Venkata Rao, "Andhra Grandbalayalu—Andhra Maba Sabha", *Golakonda Patrika*, 30 December 1935, pp. 4 and 18.
31. *Golakonda Patrika*, 19 December 1935, p. 3.
32. M. Hanutnantha Rao, *Telangana Andhrodhyamamu*, Part 2, p. 269.
33. Ibid., p. 285.
34. D. Ramanuja Rao, *Telanganaloo Jatiyodhyamalu*, p. 57.
35. Sarojini Regani, *Highlights of Freedom Movement in Andhra Pra-desh* (Hyderabad : Ministry of Cultural Affairs, Govt. of A.P., 1972)., p. 182.
36. A.A.N. Raju, "Telangana Grandhalayodhyamamu" in *Vajrothsava Sanchika* (Hyderabad : Vemana Andhra Bhasha Nilayam, 1983).
37. R.S. Sastry and N.B. Inamdar, "Library Legislation in India : Andhra Pradesh Experiment," in Supplement to 27th All India Library Conference Papers (Delhi : Indian Library Association, 1981), p. 3.
38. C. Gopinatha Rao, *Library Movement in Andhra Pradesh* (Hyderabad: Dept. of Public Libraries. Govt. of A.P., 1981), pp. 4-5.
39. *Pradhama Andhradesa Grandha Bhandagara Pratinidhula Maha-sabha*

Vrittantamu (Bezawada : Andhra Desa Library Association, 1915).

40. K. Narayana Rao, "Telanganalo Grandhalayodhyamamu" in *Andhra Pradesh Avtaranadinothsava Sanchika*, 1956.
41. *Grandhalaya Pragati*, Part 2 (Vijayawada : A.P. Library Association, 1969), pp. 129-131.
42. V. Gopalakrishnayya, *Library Movement in Andhra Pradesh*, 1977, p. 11.
43. *Golakonda Patrika*,26 April 1945, p. 2.
44. K. Narayana Rao, "*Telanganalo Grandhalayodhyamamu*", p. 72.
45. *Golakonda Patrika*, 3 April 1950, p. 2.
46. P. Nagabhusanam, *Andhra Pradesh Grandhalayodhyamamu*, p. 48.
47. *Golakonda Patrika*, 20 September 1953, pp. 2 and 4.
48. Ibid., 22 September 1953, p. 2.
49. Ibid., 29 September 1953, p. 2.
50. D. Ramanuja Rao, "Grandhalaya Udyamamu—Yuvajanula—kartavyamu". *Teluguvani*, November 1982;

Appendix

List of some prominant libraries in Telangana region of former Hyderabad state in 1930's

Khammammet District

1. Sri Vijnana Niketanamu, *Khammammet*
2. Sri Vishnu Vardhana Andhra Bhasha Nilayamu *Burgumpadu* (via) Dornakal
3. Sri Venkataramraya AndhraBhasha Nilayamu *Mandavalli*, Palvancha P.O
4. Sri Sitaramanjaneya Hinduvarthaka Grandhalayamu (1930), Singareni Collaries.

Atrapubalda District

5. Sri Hanumodandhra Grandhalayamu, (1924) Arutla
6. Sri Balabharati Nilayamu (1917) Shamashabad

Karimnagar District

7. Osmania Andhra Grandhalayamu (1928), Karimnagar
8. Sri jagdishwara Grandhalayamu (1923), Jagtyala
9. Osmania Grandhalayamu (1923), Manthena
10. Sri Narayanandhra Bhasanilayamu (1925) Sirisilla
11. Sri Balasaraswatti Nilayamu (1928), Manthena
12. Sri Vishweshwar Andhra Bhasha Nilayamu (1922) Huzurabad.

Nallangonda District

13. Andhra Saraswati Nilayamu (1918), Nallagonda
14. Bharatiyandhra Grandhalayamu (1921), Nallagonda
15. Andhravijnana Prakashini Grandhalayamu (1917), Suryapata.

Nizamabad District

16. AndhraBhasha Nilayamu (1927), Nizambad

Mahabubad District

17. SriKrishna Grandhalayamu, Mahabubad

Mabboobnagar District

18. Andhrabhasha Nilayamu (1930), Vindavelli, Alampur (Tq)
19. Andhrabhasha Nilayamu, Jadhcherla
20. Sri Anjanay Andhrabhasha Nilayamu, Badepalli station, Jadcherla

Medak District

21. Sri Ramachandra Sanskrit Andhra Grandhalayamu, Jogipeta
22. Sri Joginatha Andhragrandhalayamu (1924), Jogipeta
23. Sri Sachidananda Andhragrandhalayamu, Dakuru
24. Andhrabhashasnajivani Grandhalayamu (1928) Medak
25. Sri Rangeswar Andhrabhasha Nilayamu (1938), Ranagampeta.
26. Umamaheswar Andhra Grandhalayamu (1922), Siddipeta

Warangal District

27. Sri SaivaPracharini Grandhalayamu (1924) Aijan
28. Mahabubia Grandhalayamu, (1911) Yerrupalem
29. Sri Sabhdanusasana Grandhalayamu, (1918) Warangul
30. Sri Desodharaka Andhrabhasha Nilayamu (1925) Kukkunuru, Kunavaram (P.O) via Bhadrachalam
31. Sri Viratraya Andhrabhasha Nilayamu (1912) Nelakondapalli, Khammam (Tq)

32. Sri Prataprudra Andhra Grandhalayamu (1924), Madikonda
33. Osmania Grnahdalayamu (1923), Madhira
34. Sri Saraswati Library, Madhira
35. Sri Hanumadrama Grandhalayamu, Mahadevapuram, Madhira
36. Sri Sidhamalleswara Grandhalayamu (1913) Remdicharla
37. Sri Venugopalapustakabhandagaramu, (1935) Venrusuru (via) Madhira
38. Sri Rajaraja Narendra Andhrabhasu Nilayamu (1904), Hanumakonda

Secundrabad District

39. Andhrasmavardhani Grandhalayamu (1905), Imambaveedhi, Secundrabad
40. Sri Krishna Grandhalayamu (1929), Nalabazaru, Secundrabad
41. Deccan Vysyasanghanilayamu (1926), station road, Secundrabad
42. Madduri Raghavalu Bhasha Kalpavalli Grandhalayamu, (1920) Shubrakveedhi, Secundrabad
43. Sri Saivabharati bhavanamu (1927), 4268, Sajanlal street, Secundrabad
44. Sanskruta kalavardhani Grandhalayamu (1913), Aipan, Secunderabad
45. Sanskrit Andhra Grandhalayamu (1872) (Sri Panditaradhyaswamy Mattam), Secundrabad

Hyderabad District

46. Sri Balasaraswati Nilayamu, Gowaliguda, Hyderabad
47. Sri Gaurisankara Andhra Grandhalaymu (1938), Musherabad, Hyderabad

48. Reddy Grandhalayamu, Hyderabad
49. Sri Vermana Andhrabhasha Nilayamu (1923), Nampally, Hyderabad
50. Sri Balasaraswati Grandhalayamu (1922), Afzalganj, Hyderabad
51. Sri Krishna Devaraya Andhrabhasa Nilayamu, (1901), Sultan Bazar, Hyderabad

Source : P. Nagabhusanam, *comp. Andhradesa Grandhalayamula Pattika* (Bezawada, AndhraGrandhalaya Sangham, 1939) pp. 124 – 132.

B.3. Rayalaseema

Historical Background

Hyderabad State was established in 1724 in the Deccan by Nizam-ul-Mulk Asafjah. The Northern circars and the districts of Cuddapah, Kurnool, Anantapur and Bellary came under the control of Nizam of Hyderabad. The Nizam gave these districts to the French General Bussy for the maintenance French troops in Deccan in the year, 1753. The French was defeated by the English and the East India company acquired Northern circars in 1776 from the Nizam in return for which the British promished military support. The Nizam also ceded to the English East India Company on 20th October 1800 the districts of Cuddapah, Kurnool Anantpur and Ballary when he entered into subsidiary alliance with the East India company for protecting his dominion against external and internal dangers[1]. Since then these districts were known as ceded districts.

Since the year 1800 and onwards the Northern Circars and ceded districts of Andhra Desa became part of Madras presidency while the remaining Telugu speaking areas known as Telangana region remained under control of Nizams.

The Andhra state was fromed in 1953 comprising the Telugu speaking areas of Madras Presidency. Later the enlaged State of Andhra Pradesh was formed on Ist November 1956 by merging the Telangana Districts with the Andhra region. The present Andhra Pradesh state constitutes three district regions viz., Coastal Andhra Rayalaseema and Telangana. Rayalaseema region in Andhra Pradesh consist's of four districts viz : Kadapa, Kurnool, Anantpur and Chittoor. The following paragraphs briefly lead with the library movement in Rayalaseema.

Like, other two regions of Andhra pradesh ie., Coastal Andhra and Telanagana, the library movement in Rayalaseema was closely associated with the freedom movement and other social and adult literacy movements of the region. Shri

Gadicherla Hari Sarvottam Rao the first political prisioner from Andhra was in the forefront of library movement. He devoted his early part of his life for freedom and home rule movement and later attracted to adult education and library movement[2]. He along with band of enthusiastic collegues propagated the idea of establishing libraries and reading rooms in the Rayalaseema districts and also in the other regions of the state. The library workers especially from Coastal Andhra and also from Telangana region had closer contacts with library movement leaders of Rayalseema region.

Estabilishment of Libraries : 19th Century

The earliest, reading club – 'Book club of European Gentlemen' was established at Kurnool in the year 1864. This was supposed to be the first reading room not only for Rayalaseema but also the entire Andhradesa. Later, American Mission Freeding Room was established at Madanapalle, Chittoor District in the year 1870. Another reading room American Mission Free reading room was established in chittoor in the year 1880. Slowly the movement spread to the other districts of the region. In the year 1881 Reddijana Grandhalayam was established at Jammalamadugu, Cuddupah, District. Anantpur district followed suit. In the year 1883 a reading was established in Anantpur and another was estblished in the same year at Nandyala, Kurnool district. A Public Library was established at Proddatur in 1884 followed by Saraswati Vilasa Mandiram Library at Pulivendula in the year 1889. The American Mission at Chittoor estblished a reading room in the year 1890. In 1884 News paper clubs ware started at Penukond and Kambadur. In 1893 the Edward Coronation Reading Room was established at Dharmavaram. These have been rendering useful library services eventoday to the public at large. The Edward Coronation Reading Room had celebrated contenary of service in the year 1992[3].

SriVenkatakrishna Nilayam Reading Room was

established at Markapur, Kurnool District in the year 1899. Between the years 1883 and 1900 library reading rooms were established in saveral places in Kurnool district such as : Alur, Adoni, Nandyala, Pyapili, Yemmiganur and Kosigi.

20th Century

The begining of the 20 century witnessed the establishment Sujanananda Library at Rajampeta in Cudapa district. This library was followed by the establishment of Ramakrishna Paramhansa Memorial Reading Room at Cuddapah in 1910. From 1912, local bodies such Panchayat Boards and Municipalities came foward to establish libraries and reading rooms in the Anantpur district. The earliest among them was the one started at Veldurthi in 1912 and 1913 at Lepakshi, in 1915 at Enumoladoddi, in 1916 at Cholasarmudram and in 1919 at Hindupur. Later the District Board started a library at Anantpur in 1928. From 1929 onwards the Muncipalities in the district came forward to establish and maintain libraries and reading rooms. Mention may be made of Hindupur Muncipality which took over the management of existing public library in 1929-1930 and in 1938 Tadipatri Muncipality established a Free Reading Room and Public Library. Later during the year 1947-1948 Anantpur Muncipality established few Reading Rooms cum Libraries[4].

In the year 1917 Free Library and Reading Room was established at Cuddapah followed by Arya Vysya Pathalayam and Libraryal, Proddatur in 1919.

In the year 1923 Polepalli Venganna Shreshty established "Sri Sita Ramchandra Grandha Bahandagarmu" at Vallur near Cuddapah. The library established itself well among the public by rendering valuable library services. This library was merged with the C.P. Brown Memorial Library at Cuddapah in the year 1991.

It was established to Perpetuate the memory of C.P. Brown, the famous laxicographer who revived and enriched

Telugu language and literature with his legendary works and who worked as an Assistant to the collector of Cuddapah in 1820. Under the inspiring lead ershings and guidence of Dr. J. Hanumath Sastri a new library building was constructed in place where Brown lived 175 years ago and the library in the new building started functioning from 1992 and onwards, but officially inaugrated on 25th November, 1995[5].

The District Board, Cuddapah, established a district library at Cuddapah during 1930-31 and between the years 1939 and 1947 some major Panchayats in the district viz; Nandyala, Jammalmadugu, Pulivendula and Rajampeta established libraries for the Public. Mention could be made of the Hanuman Library Association established in 1917 at Narayanawanam and the Theosophical library at chittoor.

Other Notable Libraries

The other notable libraries established in Anantpur district were Aravinda Library and Arya Vysya Library at Tadipatri, Sarada Mitramandali Grandhalayam at Bethapalli in Gooty taluk. Thimmapuram Sevamandir Grandhalayam at Beluguppa, Rayalaseema Sahakara Sikshanalaya Grandhalayam at Anantpur town and Sri Krishna Devaraya Grandhalayam at Hindpur. It has been established that a total of one hundred and thirty libraries were functioning in Ananatpur District[6].

In the year 1915 it was estimated that the number of libraries in Kadapa district were (4), Kurnool (2) Bellary (2) Anantapur (5) and chitoor (2). These figures were compiled by Andhra Desa Library Association[7].

Kurnool district was not lagging behind in the matter of library movement. In addition to voluntary effort by the stalwarts of the library movement Panchayats, Municpalities Cooperative institutions, voluntary organisations have established more than sixty libraries during the first four decades of the 20th century. The doyen of library movement in Andhra desa and president of Andhra Desa Grandhalaya Sangham Gadicherla Harisarvotama Rao who was native of Kurnool district toured the district from 1936 and onwards and inspired library workers to establish libraries and propogate adult education in the urban and rural areas of the district. As a result of his sojurn in the villages such as Patakota, Nandavaram 'Balabharti Libraries' were established. The voluntary organisations have also established libraries in places like : Brahmankotkuru, Velugodu, Velpanuru, Parumanchala, Komidela, Murvakonda, Vadlarama Puram, Dhone, Pyapal Rangapuram, Devana konda, Karumanchi, Tuggali, Pattikonda, Koyilakuntal, Avuku, Mukkamala, Alakonda, Dornipadu, Nandyala, Santajuturu, Allagadda, Jambuladinne Narsapuram Giddaluru Racharla, Mundlapadu, Kamabam, Dupadu, Badinehali, Adoni, Emmigarunu, Mahadeva Puram, Karivena, Peddadevala puram, Betamcherla, Errakota, and Kurnool town. In Peravali, Cooperative Society established a library[8].

In addtion to above mentioned libraries the following libraries were listed in the book titled *Andhradesa Grandhalya Charitra* district wise. In Anantapur district Vidyabhivardhini Sangham (1912), Indravathi, Uravakonda (PO); JnanabhivardhaniSangham (1916), Chinnamusturu, Uravakonda (PO). Dharmagrandha Bhandagarmu (1913) Hindupur, Srikriya shakti wodayaru Grandha Niketa, (1915) Dharmavaramu, Srikrishnadewarya pustaka Bhandguramu (1914) Penugonda, have been established Incuddapah district the following libraries were established.

Andhrabhasabhi Vardhani Samajamu (1912) Proddatur, Srivagwadhunilaya Grandha Bhandagarmu (1915) Nermalladinne. Under Kurnool district the following libraries were listed. Andhrapustaka Bhandgaramu (1914), Panneru, Sri Krishnapustakabhandagaramu, Ouku, Kovelakuntla (T.q.) In Chittoor district the following libraries were established : Sri Ram Chandrapustaka Bhandagarmu (1915) Chittoor, Sri Lakshmi Venkateshwara Dinanandana Samaja Andhra Pustaka

Bhandagaramu (1914), Tirupati. In Bellary District which was part of the Madras presidency and contigious district of Rayalaseema the following libraries were established. Mitramandali (1905) Bellary, Vivekavardhani Pustaka Bhandagaramu (1915) Anegondi Samsthanam. In the said document the following libraries were also listed whose history was not known. These were Sadhusamajamu Varadayapalli, Anantpur(Dt), Andhrasarada nilayam, Nandyala, Kurnool (Dt) Gokhale Dharma pustaka Bhandagaramu, Sodam, Chittor(Dt). Maruti Vilasatmaka pustak bhandagaramu, Kudutu, Bellary(Dt)[9].

Yathagiri Lakshmi Vanketa Ramana in his book litled "Grandhalayodhya mamu" (Library movement) published in 1923 has listed 13 libraries in Cuddapah district. These were : Vagwadunilaya Grandhalayam, Jammalamadugu, Sri Ramakrishnasamajam, Cuddapah, Praja Grandhalayam, Pulivendula, Veena Pustaka Grandhayalam, Maidukuru, Andhra Bhashabhi Vardhani samajam, Proddaturu, Veenbraham Samajapustakabhandagaram, Kandi-mallayapuram, Ramchandrasamajam, Maidukuru, Sujnana Vardhanisamajam, Verrakutnla and, Kalyana sundarishwari grandhalayam, Proddulturu[10].

No. of Libraries in 1930's

The establishment of public libraries slowly gained momentum in the four districts of Rayalaseema in the 1930's. The booklet entitled *Andhradesa Grandhalayamula Pattica* (List of libraries in Andhra Desa) lists out libraries functioning in the districts of Ralayaseema. The district wise breakup was as follows : Anantpur 27, Kadapa 11, Kurnool 29 and Chittoor 9. The names these libraries is given in the Appendex.

As per the appendix a total member of 76 libraries were established by managements of government local bodies such Panchayats District Boards, Muncipalities, Cooperative societies, and Peoples Committees, and were functioning the districts of Rayalaseema in 1930's of the four districts, and Kurnool district ranks first with (29) libraries followed by Anantpur (27), Kadapa (11) and chittoor (9).

References

1. Sarojini Ragani. *Highlights of Freedom Movement in Andhrapradesh* (Hyderabad, Ministry of culture, Govt. of Andhra pradesh, 1972).
2. J. Hanumath Sastri 'Library movement in Rayalaseema' In *National Conference on Re-orientation of Library Services in India*, 18-20, August, 2007. Vijayawada Souvenir, Ed.by C. Raghava chari, etal (Vijaywada, A.P., Library Association, 2007) P. 47.
3. P. Kamaiah and G.Sarojini Paul. 'Library movement in Rayalaseema in Andhrapradesh : A new look. In *Library movement and library management in India*. 39th All India Library conference Bangalore, Jan 7-10,1994. Seminar Papers (New Delhi, ILA, 1994) Pp. 32-42.
4. P.Kamaiah and G. Sarojini Paul, Ibid, P. 33.
5. J.Hanumath Sastri 'Ugadipachadi'. In *Mondigodalanundi Mahasaudham daaka*.(C.P. Brown Grandhalayam. Ed by B. Nagesh Babu (Kadapa, C.P. Brown Memorial Trust, 2005) P. XIV.
6. V.Ramachandriah."*An Analytical Bibliography of the holdings of the Edward Coronation Reading Room and Saraswati Nilayam* (Estd. 1910), Dharamvaram, Anantpur, A.P, M.phill Thesis. Submitted to DLIS, S.K. University, Anantpur, 1977.
7. *Andhradesa Grandhalayacharitra*. (Bezawada, Andhradesa Grandha Bhandagara Sangham, 1916). Table before page 1.
8. A Lalita. Andhra Pradesh lo Grandhalaya Samasthalu : Kurnool Zilla. *Grandhalayam Survaswamu*, V63, N8, November 2002, p. 3.
9. *Andhradesa Grandhalayam Charitra*, op.cit, pp. 105-117.
10. Yathagiri VenutalakshmiRamana. *Grandhalayodhyamamu* (Bezawada, Andhradesa Grandhalya Sangham, 1923).
11. P. Nagabhusamam, Comp. *Andhradesa Grandhalayamula Pattika* (Bezawada, Andhra desa Grandhalaya Sangham, 1939), 136p.

Appendix

List of some prominent libraries in the four districts of Rayalaseema in 1930's.

Anantapur District

1. Sri Janardhana Grandhalayamu, Timmanacherla. (Via) Anantapur.
2. Friends Union uchitapathana Mandiramu (1929) Tadipatri.
3. Sri Bharati Grandhayalamu. Tadipatri.
4. Madakasiraa union Dharma Gandhayalamu (1922) Madakasiraa.

Kadiri (Tq)

5. Sri Vasantamma Grandhalayamu, Kadiri.
6. Sri VaniGrandhalayam (1929) Kokkanti.
7. Srikodanda RamaGrandhalayamu, Tanakallu.
8. SriSarada Pustaka Bhandagaramu (1903), Nagireddi-Palley.
9. Sri Vemanayogi Pustaka Bhandagaramu (1926), Reddipalle.
10. Sri Saraswati Pustaka Bhandagaramu (1929), Seshayyagari palley.

Kalyandurgam (Tq)

11. Kalyanduraga Reading Room, Kalyanduragamu (Tq).

Gutti (Tq)

12. SrividyabhiVardhani Dharma Grandhalayamu (1912) Indravati, Urvakonda (PO).
13. Sri Bala Vidyavardhini Grandhalayamu (1934), Uravakonda.

14. Sri Bharati Grandhalayam (1936), Guntakallu.
15. Sri Jnanabhivardhani Sangham, Chinamusturu, Uravakonda (PO).
16. Sri RamakrishnaGrandhalayamu,Sarimollu, Uravakonda (PO).

Dharmavaram (Tq)

17. Srikriyasaktivodayar Grandhalayamu (1915). Dharmavaram.
18. Sri Saraswati Nilayamu (1921), Dharmavaram.
19. Sri Siriyala Bhashabhivardhani Sangham, Naga Sammudramu.

Penugonda (Tq)

20. Srikrishna Devaraya Grandhayalamu, Penugonda.

Hindupuram (Tq)

21. Andhra Jaatiya Grandhalayamu, Kalluru.
22. Kalluru Gramapanchayati Grandhalayamu (1931), Kalluru.
23. Sri Maruti Grandhalyamu (1927), Manepalli, Tebidanuru (PO).
24. Sadvidya mandiramu, Lepakshi, Hindpuram (PO).
25. Gramapanchyati Pustaka Bhandagaramu, (1929), Somaghattu, Bagepalli (PO).
26. Purapalakasangha Sarvajana Grandhalayamu and pathana mandiramu (1919), Hindupuramu.
27. Sri Sarada Uchita Grandha pathanaalayamu (1927), Hindupuramu.

Kadapa (Dt)

28. Zillaboard Grandhalayam, Kadapa.
29. Sripadmanabhaswamy Pathana Mandiramu, Patakadapa, Kadapa (PO).

30. Sri Ramakrishna Samajamu, Kadapa.
31. Sri Veena Pustaka Bhandagaaramu, Maidukuru.
32. Sri Sitaramachandra Pustaka Bhandagaramu, Velluru.

Jammalamadugu (Tq)

33. Sri Bhagannilaya Samajamu, Nemaladinne, Jammala madugu (PO).
34. Sri Saraswati Vilaya Mandiramu, Pulivendala.

Prodduturu (Tq)

35. Andhra Bhasabhivardhani Sangamu, Prodduturu.
36. Aryavysya sabha, (1919), Prodduturu.
37. Sri Veerabrahma Samaja Pustaka Bhandagaarumu, Kandimallayapuram.
38. Reading room, Badwelu.

Kurnool (Dt)

39. Sri RamaMohana Grandhalayamu (1910) Uravakonda.
40. Sri Surabhi Venkata Lakshmanaraya Grandhalayamu, (1921) Kolhapuramu, Jataprolusamstanamu, Uravakonda (PO).
41. Sri Sachidananda Grandhalayamu (1928), Gajjalakonda.

Kambham (Tq)

42. Reading Room & Library, Gilddaluru.
43. Sri Varadarajamma Grandhalayamu, (1928) Bestavarapeta.
44. Sri Veeranjaneya Grandhalayamu, Yekunampeta.

Kurnool (Tq)

45. Andhra Grandhalayamu (1923) Kottapeta, Kurnool.
46. Town Hall & Public Library, Kurnool.
47. Purapalaka Sangha Grandhalayamu, Kurnool.

48. Bharata Yuvajana Sangham (YMIA), Kurnool.

Dronachalam (Tq)

49. Reading Room & Library, Dronachalamu.
50. Reading Room & Library, Pattikonda.

Koyilakuntla (Tq)

51. Reading Room & Library, Koyilakuntla.
52. SriSitanath Grandhalayamu (1935), Timmanayanipeta.
53. Andhra Vijanana Grandha Nilayamu (1935), Nosamu.
54. Sri Sarada Grandhalayamu (1935), Perusomula.

Nandikotkur (Tq)

55. Reading Room & Library, Nandikotkuru.
56. Sri Balabharati Grandhalaymmu (1928), Pratakota.

Nandyala (Tq)

57. Sri Bharati Grandhalayamu, Kaanala.
58. Edward Coronation Library, Nandyala.
59. Guruvidyakalasala Pustaka Ghandayalamu, Hindu Ashramamu, Nandyala.
60. Sri Bala Bharti Pustaka Bhandagarmu (1925), 5th street, Nandayala.
61. Sri Victoria Reading Room & Library, Nandayala.
62. Sri Vasavi Grandhalayamu, Nandyala.

Markapuram (Tq)

63. Sri Vivekananda Grandhalayamu, Markapuram.
64. Reading Room & Library, Markapuram.
65. Srikanayaka Pustaka Bhandagaramu (1928), Mittapalemu, Yerragondu Palem (PO).

Sirivella (Tq)

66. Sri Balabharti Grandhalaymu, Chagalamarri.
67. Sri Saraswati Pustaka Bhandagaramu, Rudravaramu.

Chittoor (Dt)

68. PurapalakasanghaPathanamandiram & Grandhalayamu, Chittoor.
69. Purapalaka Sangoa Dharma Pathnamandiramu & Grandhalayamu, Chittoor.
70. Uchitapattana mandiramu, Narayana Vanamu.
71. Sri Hanumad grandhalayamu, Narayana Vanamu.
72. Sri Goshan Pustakabhandagaramu, Punganuru.
73. Yuvajana Sangahama Pathana mandiramu, Punganuru.
74. Aryavysyabhivrudhi Samajamu, Madanapalley.
75. Pattanasahakara Parapattisangham Grandhalayamu, Madanapalley.
76. Union Panchyati Board Grandhalayamu, Madanapalley.

Source : P. Nagabhusanam, *Comp. Andhradesha Grandhalayamula Pattika* (Bezawarda, Andhradesa Grandhalaya Sanghamu,1939) Pp.2-16, 70.

C

Public Library Development in Andhra Pradesh

After independence, the Central and State governments iniated action for the orderly development of public libraries in the country. The UNESCO Public Library manifesto and its revised Versions of 1949, 1972 and 1994, the IFLAS[2] memorandum on Development of Public Library Services prepared in1955 and the Regional Seminar or Library Development in South Asia, 1960[3] all unanimously emphasised the need for library legislation for orderly development of public libraries and fulfil the objective of providing free and equal services to all the members of the communities regard less of race, religion, colour, nationality, age, sex, language, status or educational attainment.

Library legistation or library law is essential tool to laydown the structure, ensure its development on an approved pattern and prevents haphazard growth. It enables to set up the required infrastructure for proper management of public library system and provides for an authority responsible for its implementation. It also provides for financial support on stable footing and progressive basis. The structure, managment and finances are essential ingrediants for public library service. The need for public library legislation has been recognised by all the progressive countries of the world[4].

Sinha Committee appointed by govt. of India in 1959 to look into the state of affairs of libraries (public libraries) in the country in its report opined that library law should provide the following :

(a) "Free public library service with the following objectives :

1. To house materials giving reliable information and wholesome recreation
2. To organize them so as to promote their use,
3. To stimulate non-readers to be readers and readers to be purposive students.

(b) A library rate of six naye paise [now paise] in a rupee of property fax to be levied by local bodies and panchayats.

(c) The State Government will aid the local bodies by a matching formula. The law may be bought into operation gradually within a period of twenty years,

(d) There will be Block Library Funds and Municipal Library Funds, but the district would be regarded as a unit of library service.

(e) The various units of library service will have their own library committees...

(f) The state governments will organise a Department of Libraries. The functions of the Department will be generally on the lines indicated in the Report.

(g) The state governments will recognise library associations and provide adequate a assistance to them.

(h) Books will form the bulk of library stocks, which must also include newer media of mass communication, like audiovisual materials, etc[5]".

C.1. Library Legislation in Andhra Pradesh

The orgigins of library legislation in Andhra pradesh can be traced to 1930's. During 1934-1936, the Madras Library

Association (MALA) adopted a model bill prepared and presented by Dr. SR. Ranaganathan in 1930 at the Asian Educational conference held at Banaras. Vavilada Gopala Krishanayya published a draft bill in 1938 which attempted to provide among other things for :) a separate registration for all the libraries for getting a grant as in the case of cooperative societies free of cost, 2) establishment of regional libraries for each linguistic region of the then composite Madras state, 3. Constitution of separate fund for giving aid to libraries and 4) building up of a copyright collection in the regional libraries[6].

After independence the opportunities for library legislation were brightened up. The iniative and advice of Dr. S.R. Ranaganathan, the enthusiasm of Avinashalingam Chettiar, the then Education Minister of Madras state, helped in putting the first ever Act on the statute book in Madras in 1948. The Act came into force in April 1950 in the entire state of Madras. The provisions of the Act were in force till 1960 in the 11 districts of Andhra.

The advent of Madras Public Libraries Act, 1948 had its impact on other states of India. Library enthusiasts of Hyderabad State established Hyderabad Library Association in 1951. Under the dynamic leadership of K.M. Ujlambkar, Gen Secretary of the Library Association and with the active support of Gopal Rao Ekbote, Education Minister, the draft bill was published on August, 1954 in Govt. of Hyderabad Gazette Extraordinary for eliciting public opinion. Gopal Rao Ekbote introduced the bill in State Assembly in 1955 and was approved by the Assembly. The provisions of this Act remained in force in the 9 districts of Telanagana region untill the enactment of A.P. Public Libraries act 1960.

The year 1956 saw the states reorganisation on linguistic basis and the formation of enlarged state of Andhra pradesh in 1956. For four years there after two acts continued to be in force in the enlarged state posing peculiar difficulties in the implementation. The government iniated action for an integrated and comprehensive library legislation. The Andhra Pradesh Public Libraries Act, 1960 emerged on the scene. N B. Inamdar and R.S. Sastri opined that "the community owes it to the unremiting hardwork put in by the groups of wokers in Andhra Pradesh lead by Sri Vavilala Gopala krishanayaya and supported by Sri. S.B. Pattabhi RamaRao, the then Education Minister in Andhra Pradesh[7].

Important Provisions of Andhra Pradesh Public Libraries Act, 1960

The Andhra Pradesh Public Libraries Act, 1960 (Andhra Pradesh Act, No. VIII of 1960) received the assent of the Governor on the 18th February, 1960 and first published in A.P. Gazette dated 25th February, 1960. The Preamble of the act states "An act to consolidate and amend laws relating to establishment and maintenance of Public Libraries in the state of Andhra Pradesh and matters connected there with."

Chapter I : Preliminary : deals with definition of words such as 'aided libraries', committee, director, district, public library, state central library, state regional library and soon.

Chapter II : The state Library committee. This was replaced by the Andhra Pradesh Grandhalalya with Parishad with an amendment brought out in the year 1989 and the amendments were published in A.P. Grazette, Part IV - 3 Extraordinary dated April 20, 1989. This amended chapter deads with the establishment and composition of Andhra Pradesh Grandhalaya Parishad, powers and functions, funds for the parishad.

Chapter III deals with Department of Public Libraries and its constitution.

Chapter IV deals with constitution of Local Library Authorities (LLAS), its composition, terms of office of members of LLA and so on. The LLAS were replaced by Zilla Grandhalaya Samasthas (ZGSS) for the district and City

Grandhalaya Samastha for Hyderabad city (HCGS) by an amendment in 1969.

Chapter V deals with Finance and Accounts which includes library cess, library fund.

Chapter VI deals with reports, returns and inspection.

Chapter VII deals miscellaneous aspects such as :

Power to make rules, power to remove difficulties and amendments to the Press and Registration of Books Act, 1867, in its application to the state of Andhra Pradesh.

Specialities of the new Act

The new act came into force on Ist April 1960 through out Andhra Pradesh. The Act contain certain specialities than the former two Acts ie Madras and Hyderabad Public Libraries Acts. These are :

1. A separate Department of Public Libraries was created for expansion and management of public library system in the state.
2. The Librarian of District Central library (DCL) will also function as Secretary to Zilla Grandhalaya Samastha (ZGS),
3. The term of office of members of ZGS has been extended from 3 to 5 years;
4. Library cess was enhanced from 3 paise to 4 paise per rupee and with the permission of the state government it can be from 4 paise to 8 paise,
5. A separate Director for the department of public libraries.

Important amendments

The Act was inforce for the past five decades. During the course of its operation certain difficulties were noticed in the working of the Act. In order to remove these difficulties certain amendments were brought into the Act. Some of the most important amendments, which had far reaching consequences on the working of the act and development of public library system is briefly presented in the following paras.

1. The first amendment was carried out in 1964 to Section (13) sub section, which deals with powers and functions of Zilla Grandhalaya Samastha. A clause was inserted at subsection as "Nothing in subsection (1) shall apply to a library maintained by the Government." Another important a mendment was carried out in 1969.
2. The expression of 'Local Library Authority and 'Local Library Authorities' in the entire Act were substituted by 'Zilla Grandhalaya Samastha' and 'Zilla Grandhalaya Samasthas' by Section of the A.P. Public Libraries (Announcement) Act of 1969. In addition to responsibility of book selection hither to vested with ZGSS was taken over the government itself.
3. The 1960 Act provides for certain percentage of elected members to the ZGSS. This provision was there in the earlier Acts Madras (1948), and Hyderabad (1955). This provision was aimed at strengthening at democratic norms. But the government through an amendment in February 1987 (Act No. 13 of 1987) abolished the then existing bodies and resorted to plant nominated bodies. Event the chairmen of ZGSS were nominented by the government.
4. The most important amendment brought out by the Government in 1989 was constitution of 'Andhra Pradesh Grandhalaya Parishad' in Chapter II of the Act. (Act No. 11 of 1989). The Parishad will be the principal policy making body in respect of public libraries in the state. The objectives of Parishad include : promotion of library services in the state with short and long term development plans. As the principal policy formulating apex body of the public library system the Parishad will have powers to determine quality and standards of

library services and to implement the developmental programmes in accordance with the guidelines issued by the government.

5. Another amendement brought out in 1990 was another example of Policitisation of the working of the public library system in the state. (Act No. 16 of 1990). This amendement removes the specified three year term of the chairmen of ZGSS and have to continue in office as long as they enjoy the sweet will and pleasure of the government.

There were other amendments brought into the Act by the Government to meet the requirements of changing environment of the public library system in the State in the course of last fifty years.

References

1. *IFLA UNESCO Public Library Manifesto.* (Paris, UNESCO, 1994)
2. *Development of Public Library Services*, IFLA, 1956.
3. Regional Seminar of Library Development in South Asia. *Proceedings* (Pairs, UNESCO, 1960).
4. N.B. Inamdar, 'The Andhra Pradesh Public Libraries Act, 1960 : An Evaluation, '*Librarys Librarian* V1, N2, Dec. 1977, Pp. 18-24.
5. *Reports Advisory Committee For Libraries.* (Sinha committee Report), (New Delhi, Ministry of Education, govt. of India, 1961), Pp. 118-119.
6. V.Venkatappayya *Andhra Pradesh Grandhalaya Chattam.* (Vijayawada, Navaratna Book Centre, 1985) P.9.
7. R.S. Sastry and N.B. Inamdar. "Library Legislation in India; Andhra pradesh Experiment." *ILA Bulletin* V17, N1, Jan-March 1981. Supplement P.3.
8. A.A.N. Raju, 'A look into the problems of public library services in Andhra pradesh'. *In Librarianship in Deve lofing Countries*, ed by N.Guru Swamy Naidu.(New Delhi, Ess Ess Publications, 1992) Pp. 165-173.

C.2. Structure of Public Library System

The Public Library structure of the state is implied in chapters II to IV of the Act, which include Grandhalaya Parishad, Department of Public Libraries and Zilla Grandhalaya Samastha (ZGSS). At the top of the structure is the State Central Library (SCL), the apex library in the system whose existence is only obliquely referred to in section 2(11) of the Act and followed by six regional libraries referred to in section 2(12) of the Act established and functioning at Visakhapatnam, Guntur, Warangal, Nizamabad, Tirupati and Rajahmundry. Lower down the structure are District Central libraries (DCLS) and Branch Libraries (BLS). Further Below BLS are village libraries (VLS), Book Deposit Centres (BDCS) and Mobile Libraries (MLS). The inter relationship of all these to one another has not been spelled out in the act. The functions, role and responsibilities of State Central Library (SCL) and its relationship with Regional Libraries (DLS) and Districts Central Libraries (DCLS) has not been clearly specified in the Act. The place of Regional Libraries in the system has not been clearly stated in the Act. Their organic relationships with the SCL at the top and DCLS below has not been spelled out in the Act. They function as individual lending libraries duplicating the functions of DCLS in the region. It was only at the district level and lower down some element of structure interms of management by single line of control, supervision and direction are in evidence. The DCL supervises and controls the functions of BLS, RLS, BDCs and MLS in the district public library system.

The gaps in the public library structure according to R.S. Sastri and N.B. Inamdar resulted in (a) duplicating of functions; (b) absence of coordination of working of several units; (c) wastage of scarce resources; (d) non-availability of adequate resources at points when they are most needed; (e) lack of an overall sense of direction and (f) absence of a planned integrated approach for future development. The organisational structure of Public Library System (PLS) as presently obtained in the state is as follows.

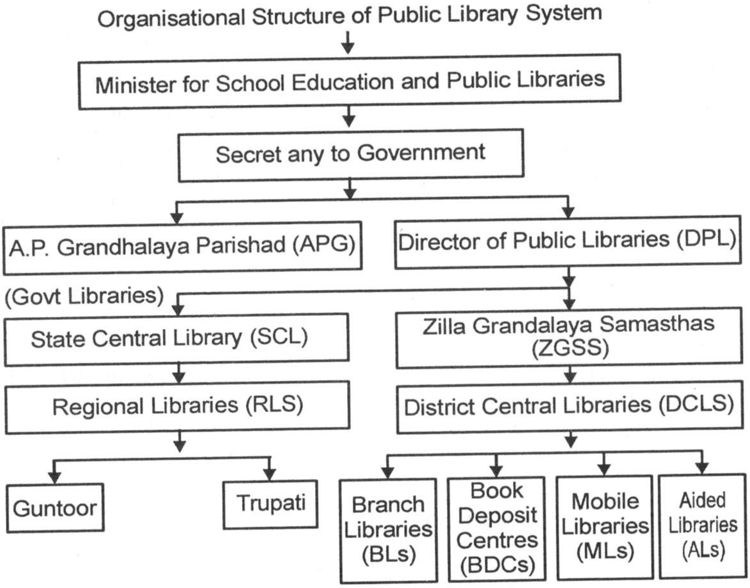

No. of Libraries

The number of libraries functioning in the state during the year 2005-06 was as follows.

S.No.	*Types of Libraries*	*No. of Libraries*
1.	State Central Library (SCL)	1
2.	Govt. Regional Libraries (RLS)	6
3.	City/District Central Libraries (DCLS)	23
4.	Branch Libraries (BLS)	1449
5.	Village Libraries (VLS)	357
6.	Mobile Libraries (MLS)	99
7.	Book Depport Centres (BDCS) (Santioned BDCS 1401; still 390 to be opened)	1011
8.	Aided Libraries (ALS)	1955
	Total	4901

Source : Govt of A.P. Dept of Public Libraries. State Administration Report for the year 2005-06.

Branch Libraries (BLS) : Norms

Branch libraries (BLS) are important links in the chain of public library system in the state and play vital role in the dissemination of information in semi urban and rural areas in the state. There are three types of libraries viz; Grade I, Grade II and Grade III functioning in the state. The following norms were formulated for the establishment of BLS under ZGSS in the state. These were formulated at a work shop of Secretaries of Zilla Grandahalaya Samasthas (ZGSS) held from 8 th to 10th May, 1978 at the State Central Library (SCL) Hyderabad[2]. The recommendations of the said workshop were forwarded to the government for approval. No decision was taken by the Government on these norms since then.

	Population	*Book Stock*	*Borrowers*	*Visitors*
Grade I	20,000	6,000	400	250 persons.
Grade II	10,000	4,000	200	150 persons.
Grade III	upto 10,000	1,500	75	100 persons.

Staff norms

The staff norms for DCL, BLS (Grade I, II and III) are as follows.

District Central Library

1.	Dist. Central Librarian	1
2.	Grade I Librarians	2
3.	Grade II - do-	2
4.	Typist	1
5.	Card writers	2
6.	Attenders	2
7.	Binders	2
8.	Record Assitants	4
9.	Operator	1
10.	Gardener	1
11.	Helper to the Binder	1

Grade I Library

1.	Grade I Librarian	1
2.	Grade III Librarian	1
3.	Record Assistant	1
4.	Attender	1
5.	Watchman	1

Grade II Library

1.	Grade II Librarian	1
2.	Record Assistants	2
3.	Attender	1
4.	Watchman	1

Grade III Library

1.	Grade III Librarian	1
2.	Record Assistant	1
3.	Attender	1
4.	Watchman	1

Office of the ZGS

1.	Superintendent	1
2.	UD clerks	2
3.	L.D. clerks	2
4.	Typist	1
5.	Record Assistants	3
6.	Attenders	3

One more L.D.C. clerk has to be provided for every 30 additional Branch Libraries (BLS).

A. P. Public Libraries Rules, 1961

The Government of Andhra Pradesh had formulated A.P. Public Libraries Rules, 1961 for the administration of public library system in the state. As per section 16(4) of the rules one District central library (DCL) ie the main library of the district headquarters town in all the districts except Hyderabad, where the DCLs shall be located at Vikarabad. The DCLS are the nucleus of all the library activities in the Districts. Their functions includes acquisition, processing and supply of books to BLS and VLS.

As per section 16(4) (b) one Branch Library (BL) for each panchayat with a population of 5000 and above and in exceptional cases, with the permission of the Government, a Branch Library may be provided for a panchayat with a population of less than 5000. As per section 16(4) (c) of AP Public Libraries Rules 1961, the ZGSS shall open one Delivery Station. [Now called Book Deport Centre] for each village or group of villages with population between 1000 to 5000 and if possible one Delivery Station for each village with less than 1000 populataion[3].

References

1. R.S.Sastry and NB.Inamdar. Library Legislation in India. Andhrapradesh Experiment. *ILA Bulletin* V 17, NI, Jan-March 1981. Supplement. P.5.
2. *Report of the Workshop of Secrateries, Zilla Grandhalaya Samasthas* held from 8th to 10th to May, 1978. Pp. 29-30. (Mimeo graphed)
3. PAV Narasimham and M.A. Majeed Khan. *Andhra Pradesh Public Libraries Act, 1960*; with latest amendments commentaries. (Hyderabad. A.P. Public Library Association, 1980). P.46.

C.3. Present Scenario

As on 31.03.2006, The type and number of Libraries working under the Department of Public libraries, Govt. of Andhra Pradesh is as follows :

Type of Libraries	*No. of Libraries*
1. State Central Library (SCL)	1
2. Regional Libraries (RLS)	6
3. City/District Central Libraries (DCLS)	23
4. Branch Libraries (BLS)	1449
5. Mobile Libraries (MLS)	99
6. Village Libraries (VLS)	357
7. Book Deposit Centres (BDCS)	1011
8. Aided Libraries (ALS)	1955

The State Central Library is the apex library of the Public Library system obtaining in the state. As on 31.03.2005 the total stock consists 4, 5.2, 740 books of which English 1.45 lakhs, Telugu 1.44 lakhs, Hindi 0.44 lakhs, Urdu, Arabic and Persian, 0.82 lakhs and other langnages 0.37 volumes. It is subscribing to 108 periodicals and 186 periodicals are received as gratis. It has a total membership 23,411 as on 31.03.06. A total of 2,68,547 readers attended the library during the year 2005-06.

Besides SCL, there are six Regional Libraries (RLS) managed by government and functioning as reference and lending libraries and supposed to act as linkages between the SCL and District Centre Libraries (DCLS).

The performance indicators of the six regional libraries for the 2005-06 is as follows :

Indicator	*Year 2005-06 (in lakhs)*
Membership	9.26
Readership	938.43
Book stock	201.49

Books issued	48.52
Books Consulted	87.56

A total number of 136.08 lakhs books were used by the readers in Government libraries and ZGSS libraries during the year 2005-06.

Book stock

The total book stock obtainable as on 31.03.2006 six Regional Libraries and the SCL is shown in the following table:

Languages	*SCL*	*SRL Guntur*	*SGRL Rajah mundry*	*RL Nizamabad*	*RL Trupati*	*RL Vizag*	*RL Warangal*
Telugu	1,44,156	39,545	60,497	25,982	31,806	20,394	22,483
English	1,45,095	67,076	13,718	24,4993	20,458	23,069	
Hindi	44,121	8,122	2,039	5,983	5,167	4,946	7,588
Urdu	82,297	1330	359	1760	159	418	5190
Other languages	37,071	2,917	654	67	1597	230	-
Total	4,52740	11,8990	77,267	55,163	63,722	46,446	58,338

During the year 2005-06 a total 136.11 lakhs books were consulted in the library premises of above Government libraries.

District Central Libraries (DCLs)

All the 23 revenue districts in the state have District Central Libraries (DCLS) including City Central Library at Hyderabad which were set up in Andhra region under the provisions of Madras Public Libraries Act 1948 and in the Telangana region in 1958 under the provisions of Hyderabad Public Libraries Act, 1955. The DCLS located at the district head quarters towns are the nerve centres of all library activities in the districts. Besides rendering reference service and lending of reading materials to the reading public in the district through BLS, VLS, BDCS and MLS, the DCLS have other functions to perform such as acquisition and the distribution of book to the BLS, VLS, BDCS and MLS and supervision and inspection of the public libraries in the district and organising cultural, social and educational programmes and activities, seminars and conferences to enlighten the reading public and also to attract more readers for the services offered by the district library system.

As on 31.03.2006 the 23 ZGSS and seven government libraries have a total of 9.56 lakhs registered borrowers. A total of 438.43 lakh readers attended 23 DCLS and serven government libraries. A total of 87.58 lakhs books were consulted and 48.53 lakhs books were issued for home reading.

Branch Libraries (BLS)

Branch Libraries (BLS) act as an important links in the public library system. These have been functioning since 1952-53 in the state and rendering library services to various towns and villages. As on 31.03.2005 there were 1449 BLS functioning and covering mostly Mandal headquarters. These function as independent administrative units under the direct supervision and control of the City/District Central Librarian concerned. The Branch Librarian supervise the work of VLS, BDCS and MLS such as mobile vans, rickshaw/cycle libraries. The inspection of aided libraries which apply for grant in-aid is also entrusted to the Branch Librarian. Some BLS have children, text book and reference sections. For example Tagore Reference and Research Centre (aBL), Vijayawada is fully equipped with reference material and AV aids for research scholars and student community.

Village Libraries (VLS)

These have been functioning since 1974-75 on an adhoc basis to provide library services to rural areas. As on 31.03.2006 there were 357 VLS functioning in the state. The VLS work for about four hours a day under the charge of part time worker who is paid a monthly remuneration Rs 1250/-

There are 357 VLS functioning in the state as on 31.03.2006.

Book Deposit Centres (BDCS)

The Book Deposit Centres (BDCS) or delivery stations as they are called were opened in villages with the population between 1000 and 5000. These are located in school premises or Panchayat buildings which are on rent free basis. There are 1011BDCS functioning in the state as on 31.03.2006.

Mobile libraries (MLS)

The Hyderabad City Grandhalaya Samastha (HCGS), has been maintaining three Mobile Libraries (MLS) known as 'Sanchara Bharti' to provide library services to reading public in various localities in the twin cities of Hyderabad and Secandrabad, where BLS were not opened. The first mobile van was introduced in 1973-74. These vehicles ply 12 hours a day covering 60 to 70 points every week.

A few DCLS and BLS in the state were rendering library services to women, senior citizens and disabled persons in rural areas by means of van/rickshaw/bicycle mobile libraries. For example in Guntur city 23 localities were covered by a mobile library van (station wagon). There are about 48 rickshaw and 54 bicycle mobile libraries which supply books to readers at their door steps.

Aided Libraries (ALS)

These are also knowns privately managed libraries established by voluntary organizations. Andhra Pradesh is a land of privately managed libraries. Some of them have been established during the 19th century. The ZGSS support some of these recognised private libraries with grant in aid. There are 1955 recognised aided libraries functioning in the State during the year 2005-06.

Status of Library Buildings

The libraries are housed in their own buildings or rented or rent free buildings. The following table provides the status of accomodations as obtained during the year 2005-06.

Types of Library	*No. of Libraries*	*Libraries functioning in*		
		Own Building	*Rent free Building*	*Rented Building*
1. Govt. Libraries	07	05	0	02
2. DCLS	23	23	0	0
3. BLS	1449	633	588	228
4. VLS	363	59	298	0
Total	1842	720	892	230
%		39.09	48.10	12.81

During the year 2005-06, fifty four (54) library buildings were under constrution at the cost of Rs. 2.16 crores. To have own buildings mostly for BLS, 138 sites were acquired for construction of library buildings.

Staff Strength

The sanctioned strength of posts for the ZGSS during the year 2005-06 stood at 3852 which includes Technical 1303, Ministerial 82 and others 2467.

Of the total strength, 1425 posts were vacant which includes librarians 394, ministerial 28, village librarians 195 and other posts 808. As regards government libraries the sanctioned strength of posts stood at 259 which includes Gazatted 17, Librarians 73 and other posts 91. Of the total strength, 259 posts were vacant which includes Gazetted 05, Librarians 30, Ministerial 20 and others 24.

Filling up of the existing vacancies is a major issue as well a problem faced by both zilla grandhalaya samasthas and government run libraries. The government is not comming forward to lift the ban on filling up of existing vacancies. Many of BLS are being managed by Parttimers and in some cases by Attenders.

Library Cess Dues

Collection of library cess due from the local bodies is an another major problems faced by the ZGSS. An amount of Rs 35.02 crores was due from the local bodies upto 31.03.2004. Of the total amount, an amount of Rs 1221.10 lakhs was due from Municipal corporations, Rs 1125.55 lakhs from Municipalities and Rs 1155.17 lakhs due from GramPanchayats.

Non remittance of library cess due to the ZGSS by the local bodies in the state is another major problem faced by the ZGSS. They were not able to take up more developmental activities such as opening of new BLS, strengthening existing DCLS and BLS with new books, required trained staff, infrastructure facilities, computerization of at least DCLS, constructing own library buildings and offering effective library services by offering text book and competitive exams book sections in BLS also.

Many of the ZGSS were not able to pay salaries to their staff on time and there were instances where some of the ZGSS paid salaries once in three months. The same situation obtains in payment of pensions and post retirement benefits to the retired employees.

The genesis and development, book collections, staff strength, library buildings, readership, books consulted, books lent for home reading, library services, extension activities, development indicators and future plans of SCL, RLS, DCLS of Zilla Granhalaya Samasthas has been briefly presented in the suceeding sections D to F.

Source : Department of Public Libraries, Govt. of Andhra Pradesh, *State Administration Report 2005-06*. (Mimeographed)

D

State Central Library (SCL), Hyderabad

STATE CENTRAL LIBRARY (SCL) AND
REGIONAL LIBRARIES (RLs)

Genesis and Development

The State Central Library (SCL), the apex library in the public library system of Andhra Pradesh had its genesis in the year 1885. It was formally known as 'Asafia Library' and founded jointly by Moulvi Syed Hussain Bilagrami (Nawab Imad-ul-muk) and Mulla Abdul Qayyam. The library was later taken over by the Nizam's government and declared open to public in 1891[1]. Since it inception, many private libraries belonging to certain distinguished persons of Hyderabad was merged with the collections of this library either by donation or by purchase. The libraries of Nawab Imadul Mulk and Nawab Azamyar Jung were donated by their generous owners and the libraries Hakeem Syed Mohib Hussain and Hakeem Syed Quasim Bijapuri were purchased[2].

The library was located in the office of the Directorate of Public Instruction at Malguzari Road. Lateron it was shifted to a rented building and then to a government building at Abids, Hyderabad. During the reign of Nizam VII MirOsman Alikhan, a new building was constructed exclusively for housing the library at a cost of Rs 2.5 lakhs and additional amount of

Rs 37000/-was spent for acquisition of furniture, fittings and fix wires etc. In the year 1936 the library was shifted to the new building located at Afzulganj on the bank of river Musi. The total area of the building and open space is 16, 046 sq. yards[3].

After 1940, several changes were introduced in the administration of the library. The Nizam's government started showing interest in the development of library collections such as books and journals concerning Telugu, Marathi, Kannada and Hindi, to cater to the needs of dominant linguistic groups in the state, were acquired and added to the library collections. Common man was allowed to use the library. Holidays were reduced and working hours were increased. Rules and regulations were modified to make it only a public library[4].

Then Nizam's government recognised the library as Hyderabad Government Central Library. In the year 1941 it celebrated it Golden Jubilee on a grand scale under the chairmenship of Nawab Hafiz Sir Ahmed Sayyad Khan Bahadur, the chairman of the Executive Council[5]. After the enactment of Hyderabad Public Libraries Act, 1955, the library has been redesignated as State Central Library, Hyderabad State. After the formation of Andhra Pradesh in 1956 and as consequent to the enacting integrated A.P. Public Libraries Act, 1960, the library has been redesignated as 'State Centre Library' of Andhra Pradesh. An annex to the existing very imposing library building was constructed at a cost of Rs 9 lakhs and was declared open by Damodaram Sanjivayya, the than chief Minister of Andhra Pradesh on July 9, 1961. The Office of the Director of Public Libraries is also located in the first floor of the annex[6].

Objectives and Functions

During the initial decades of its establishment, the main objectives was to provide facilities to general scholars and supply rare and useful material to the research scholars. With this objective inview rare and valuable MSS in classical and modern languages were acquired through donations and puchase and thereby putting an end to the out flow of the literary treasures of the state to the outside world. The second objective was publication of rare and valuable MSS on Islamic and Hindu civilization and culture. This was to prevent the sale of valuable MSS and printed books their owners for trifling sums of money[8].

The A.P. Public Libraries Act, 1960 has not stated the role and functions of the SCL and vis-a-vis its relationships with other libraries in the system especially the regional libraries. Section2 (11) of the Act merely states that "State Central Library means a library establishment by the Government as the State Central Library." The Advisory committee for Libraries (Sinha committee) recommended that "Every state should have a State Library consisting of the wings the state central library and the state lending library. The important functions of the SCL should among others, be as follows :

(a) build upon exhaustive collection of all publications, official and non-official in the state;

(b) undertake bibliographical work, including special bibliographies for the use of scholars and research workers;

(c) maintain a union catalogue of the important libraries is the state.

(d) maintain a strong reference collection and service;

(e) act as clearing house of information on the Five Year Plans of the country etc;

(f) organise book exhibitions and professional conferences;

(g) be the centre of inter-library loan within and without the state;

(h) promote library works with children."[9]

Justice Gopal Rao Ekbote Committee which was

appointed by the Government of Andhra Pradesh in 1976 to review the working of A.P. Public Libraries Act, 1960 has observed that the State Central. Library which is an apex library should provide leadership in all metters of library activities to all libraries in the state, some times acting as the central organ of a state library service. It is an institution in its own right, performing functions from its special position and character[10]. The committee has identified a number of functions to be performed by the SCL. Some of the important functions are as follows [11]:

1. To collect all literary, scientific, technological and other material concerned and produced in the state both current and historical. It would include the copyright collections of books published in the state.
2. To be conservatory of materials concerned with the Andhra and Indian composite culture.
3. To be the main source in the state of reference materials for scholars and research workers.
4. To act as an authority for the compilation of State bibliography of all the books, periodicals, newspapers and other reading materials in Telugu and other lanaguages spoken in the state.
5. To serve the focal point and organising agency for inter-regional, inter-state loans of books and other library materials. It should be the centre of inter-library cooperation.
6. To be the agency for compiling and maintaining the state union catalogue.
7. To maintain a strong reference collection and service it should contain all standard works of national and international reference as well as all the publications of the state and central government.
8. To organise book exhibitions and professional and library conferences.

9. To centralise at the state level cataloguing and classification of publications and ensure distribution of catalouge cards or catalogues published by libraries.
10. To make provision for in-service training of librarians.
11. To select books and other library materials for all the libraries in the state.
12. To mainitain and service the books recieved under the Press and Ragistration of Books Act, 1867.
13. To main sections for children and blind.

The review committee further observed that "the position today is that State Central Library is not performing these functions to a satisfactory level. It does not provide any leadership to any other library and not even to Regional Libraries functioning in the state."

In the light of preceding observation the committed has recommeded inter alia the following :

1. "The State Central Library should be developed only as a reference and research library;
2. It should stock books, periodicals and other non-book materials for reference and research
3. It should develop reprographic section by acquiring the most modern equipment
4. The bibliographical work, the union catalogue work and bibliography of childrens literature and for the blind should be carried out by the State Central Library in coordination with Regional Libraries. The Government should give special grant for this important and urgent work.
5. The classification and cataloguing should be centrally organised by the State Central Library in coordination with the Regional Libraries and District Central Librarians.
6. The book selection work, the selection of periodicals and

news papers should be entrusted to the State Central Library which would constitute a book selection committee and do the work in consultution with the District Central Libraries and Regional Libraries.

7. It should organise a survey and research unit and continuously carry on survey and research on different aspects of the library work.
8. The State Central Library ought to provide documentation and information services to all and in particular to the Legistlative House and other Departments of State Government.
9. The State Centre Library should be responsible for production of literature for neo-literates and children of different age groups and blind people and supervise the work of book production council.
10. There should be State Central Library Authority for the State Central Library and the Regional Libraries. Its composition should be on the lines suggested by us...[12]

Computerisation of library operations were an important aspect in the present day library management. The review committee has not given thought to this important aspect. Perhaps in 1970s when the Review committee submitted report this aspect was not gained momentum as it was as decade ago. Even now to computerisation of library operations were not given due importance.

Collection Development

The library since its inception started collection of rare and valuable MSS in classical and modern languages through donations and purchases. From time to time many private collections belonging to Nawabs of Hyderabad were acquired either by dontation or by purchase. MSS were also acquired from countries like Egypt, Syria and the Middle East. Special provisions were also made for the library in the budget of Public Instruction from year 1891. A Royal Firman was issued by

Nawab MirMahboo Ali khan in this regard. The firman was published in the StateGazette dated 13th April 1891[13]. According to H.N. Venkata Swamy formerly Sub-librarian of the SCL, the collection of the library in 1930 stood at 15,373 printed books in Arabic Persian and Urdu and manuscripts. The English Section including French and German consisted 6,800 volumes. The MSS which are special features of this library include many rare ones; of the tow MSS of a rare Arabic work existing in the world and was available in this library[14].

The Oriental Section of the library consisted books and MSS in Arabic, Persian, Urdu and Sanskrit. Subsequently, Occidental section was opened with the additional books on English and other European languages. In the year 1940 a new section for regional languages was opened. This Section comprises books on Telugu, Marathi, Kannada and Hindi.

Until 1967, the library was holding 17, 060 MSS which included five palm leaf (Hindu Telugu, Tamil) of rare and immense value. A few of them were unique and date back to 11th and 12th centuries A.D. Among the rare and valuable of MSS the library possessed were: Masnavi Gavasi, Diwan-E Hussain, Guldasta, Masnavi Behramuo- Gul Andam, Arrar E-Ishq, Keerajnama and Qasasul-Ambai[15]. The entire MSS collections have been transferred to Oriental MSS Library and Research Institute established by the Govt. of Andhra Pradesh in 1967.

As on 1999, the library possessed 4,10,005 printed books in all languages and subscribed to 176 journals and 30 newspapers. The break up of printed books language wise in the year 1987 was English 93,812 Telugu 83,484, Urdu 75,037, Hindi 30,762, Marathi 16,124, Kannada 14,144 Sanskrit 2,689 and Tamil 10,44. The back volumes of periodicals and news papers are preserved in a separate back volumes section. News papers are like the Hindu and Times of India are available from 1944 and onwards. But this section unfortunately is maintained badly where in most of back volumes are dumped with out systematic arrangement.

By the end of the year 2005-06, the total book collection in the library stood at 4,59,280 and language wise breakup is as follows :

English	1,46,856
Telugu	1,46,597
Hindi	46,174
Urdu	69,619
Marathi	17,419
Kannada	15,073
Sanskrit	3,368
Tamil	1,223
Arabic	6,459
Persian	6,492
Total	4,59,280

During the same year the library subscribed to 104 periodicals and the languagewise break up is as follows :

Telugu	26
English	59
Hindi	7
Urdu	8
Marathi	2
Kannada	2
Total	104

The library during the year 2005-06 subscribed 30 daily news papers and languagewise break up is as follows :

English	14
Telugu	6
Urdu	3
Hindi	3
Kannada	1
Marathi	3
Total	30

During the year 2006-07 a total of 21,001 books were added to the existing collection and the collection by the end of 31-03-07 stood at 4,80,281. During the year 2007-08 a total of 4960 books were added and the total collection stood at 4,85,241.

Membership

The membership of the library increased impressively and by the end of 2005-06 stood at 23,577. During the year 2006-07, 6354 new members were enrolled and during year 2007-2008, 1092 were added. Thus by the end of 31.03.08 the total membership stood at 31,023.

Readership

The total readership during the year 2004-05 was 2,68,547 and it decreased in the year 2005-06 to 253,778. During the year 2006-07 the total readership stood at 3,74,460 and during the year 2007-2008 it stood at 4,25,235.

Books Consulted

The total number of books consulted within the library during the year 2004-05 stood at 158033 and slumped to 137955 during the year 2005-06. During the year 2006-07 it stood at 2,23,460 and during the year 2007-08 it stood at 2,15,935.

Book Lending

Being the State Central Library located in the west of the city it attracted more members who be come registered borrowers and borrowed books for home reading. In the year 2004-05, 10,231 books were lent and for the year 2005-06 the figure stood at 8156, a decrease of 2075 books. In the year 2006-07 a total of 4976 books were lent and in the 2007-08 a total of 5122 books were lent for home reading.

Book Recieved Under RRRLF Scheme

During the year 2005-06 the library recieved 656 books in Telugu, English, Urdu, Hindi, Sanskrit, Kannada and Marathi from the Director of Public Libraries, Govt. of AP under RRRLF scheme. Likewise the library recieved a total of 2032 books in Telugu, English, Urdu, Hindi and Tamil during the year 2005-06 from the Director RRRLF, Kolkata.

Source : State Central Library, Hyderabad, Annual Report for the Year 2005-06.

Printed Catalogues

The library had in the past broughtout printed catalogue of books available in oriental section in 4 volumes between 1914 and 1936. A descriptive catalogue of titles "Fihriht-E-Mashrooh" of rare and valuable MSS was published in two volumes in 1938. A catalogue of English books were published in 1927 with a supplement in 1941. This was republished in 2 volumes as classified catalogue with author and title indexes[16].

Functions

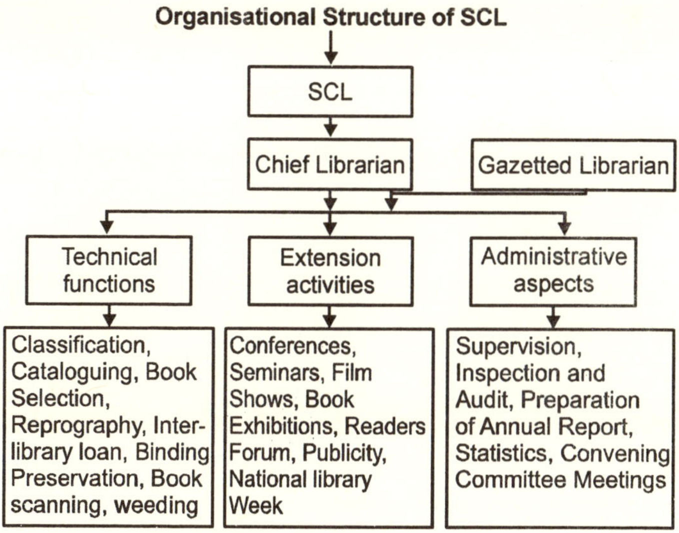

Source : Annual Report of SCL, 2005-06.

The library carries its functions under fourteen sections viz., 1. Acquisition, 2. Accounts, 3. Establishment, 4.Miscellaneous, 5. Reference, 6. Circulation, 7. Periodical, 8. Text books, 9. Children, 10. Braille, 11.Social Education, 12. Binding, 13. Reprography and 14. Stacks (for different languages). It offeres reference and reprographic services to user community. Through the extension works and public relations it has been organizing very regularly 'National Library Week' from 14-20 November every year by arranging lecturers, book exhibitions, book talks, film shows, seminars, symposia, numerous cultural programmes, essay writing and debating competition for students to publicise its services and attract more readers.

It has brought out a quarterly journal entitled *Library Herald* to provide information about services. working hours, sections of the library, lending rules, activities, arrangement of books on the shelves, new additions to the library and other relevant information. It ceased publication in 1986. It was expected to bring out 'State Bibliography' ie list of Telugu books recieved at the Central Reference Library, Kolkata. It has brought out the language bibliography for the 1960-61 and 1973-74[17].

Staff Strength

The SCL is functioning and offering varried library services to the reading public with a staff strength of 133 posts comprising Grade I, II and III Librarians, intermediary staff and class IV employees. In addition to 3 types of librarians, the staff consist of Classifiers, Senior Assistants, Jr. Assistants, Book keepers, Card writers, Supervisers, Book Binders, Book clearnes, Attenders, Gate keepers, Sweepers, Chowkidars and Kamatans. Of the total 133 sanctioned posts of various categories 49 post were vacant by the end of 31.03.2006.

Universal Digital Library Project (UDL)

The purpose of Universal Digital Library (UDL) Project is to digitize books of common interest to the societies and make them available in a location, languages and time independent way. The Carnegie Mellon university, USA under the leadership of Prof. Raj Reddy has launched two projects in India. Under the overall supervision of Director of Public Libraries, Govt of Andhra Pradesh the Project was launched at the State Central Library, Hyderabad in the year 2002. The following table provides figures for books scanned at State Central Library (SCL) form 01.12.2002 to 30.03.2007.

Language	*Scanned*		*Cropped*		*OCR*	
	Books	*Pages*	*Books*	*Pages*	*Books*	*Pages*
English	9165	3552144	8728	3442907	8718	3442907
Persian	4225	1137482	4233	1132396	0	0
Urdu	5185	1322878	5173	1314087	0	0
Arabic	6774	2162788	6661	2160275	0	0
Telugu	459	74028	271	46711	0	0
Hindi	48	10756	44	10284	0	0
Sanskrit	0	0	0	0	0	0
Total	25886	8260076	25110	8106660	8718	3442907

Computerisation of SCL

The RRRLF, Kolkata during the year 2003-04 has sanctioned a sum of Rs 10.00 lakhs towards Purchase of computers. With this grant the SCL has purchased 2 servers, and 9 computers and the work of computerisation of inhouse operations has just started.

An Estimation of Library

The State Central Library which is supposed to be an apex library of the public library system in Andhra Pradesh has to play a leadership role for other types of public libraries in the state. But in reality it has no administrative control or other wise over the libraries in the system viz. Regional Libraries, District Central Libraries and Brand Libraries. There are no linkages with the Regional Libraries in the state. It has been functioning in isolation with out showing any leadership and direction to other libraries in the system. It is still following outdated manual operations to offer effective information services to the user community.

The recommendations of the Ekbote Committee needs to be implemented at the earliest so as to create a new image of State Central Library. L.S. Ramaih while critically analysing the collections and services of SCL offered the following suggestions for its revitalisation.

1. The government should provide proper place for SCL in the Public Library system of A.P.,
2. SCL should be completely reorganised;
3. To work the public library system and the SCL effectively proprofessionally qualified person with vast experience should be appointed at the helm of affairs,
4. SCL should be developed with necessary infrastructure so as to serve the scientists and scholarly communities,
5. To have bibliographical control of publications emanating from the state, the SCL should bring out state bibliographies,
6. There is need for developing book and periodical collections of the library. The present collection needs proper preservation and conservation. The periodical collections piled up for the last four decades needs to properly bounded and made available to the researchers,
7. The present annual budget of rupees six lakhs needs to be enhanced to rupees one crore and all the divisions of the library should be computerised and proper place should be given in vision 2020[18].

The transfer of valuable MSS collections to Govt. Oriental MSS Library and Research Institution in 1967 is a big blow to the value, importance and rarity of collections it possessed. The library should stop lending its valuable collections. It should be converted as reference library at the state level as recommended by Ekbote Committee. The valuable back volumes of periodicals and newspapers should be retrieved and properly maintainted for the benefit of research and scholarly community. Lastly but not the least, the amendments suggested by the Ekbote committed to A.P.Public Librarians Act, 1960 be affected so as to make the State Central Library truly an apex library in the state public library system[19].

References

1. *Freedom struggle in Hyderabad Vol.* 3(1885-1920). (Hyderabad, the Hyderabad state committee appointed for the complilation of history of freedom movement in Hyderabad, 1957) P. 67.
2. Mirkaremat Ali 'A short note on Arabic, Persian and urdu of MSS of our library. *VijnanSaraswati* VI, NI, 1984, p. 75.
3. Mohd Burahanuddin. State central library, Andhra Pradesh. A study. M.Lib.Sc dissertation, 1987 (Mimeographed) p. 7. Submitted to DLIS, Osmania Univ. Hyderabad.
4. V.Venkatappayya. *Managrandhalayu* (Our Libraries) (Nellore, Sairam Publications, 1987) p.97.
5. Ibid., p.97.
6. Mohd, Burhanuddin. opcit. p. 75.
7. Mirkaramat Ali. opcit. p.75.
8. Mohd Burhamuddin. opcit. p. 7.
9. *Report of Advisory Committee for Libraries.* (New Delhi, Ministry of Education, govt. of India, 1961) pp. 53-54.
10. '*Report of the Committee appointed by the govt. of Andhra Pradesh in Feb. 1976 to Review the working of A.P. Public Libraries Act, 1960* and to suggest amendments to the Act'. (Hyderabad, Dept of Public Libraries, 1978) pp. 28-29.
11. Ibid., p. 29.
12. Ibid., pp. 31-32.
13. Mohd. Burhanuddin, opcit., p. 7.
14. M.N. Venkata swami *One hundred one essays on social and literary subjects* (Madras, The Golden & Co, 1932), pp. 120-122.
15. S.A. Usmani and Z.R. Khan. 'Oriental Libraries in India'. In *Perspective of Library and Information Science.* VI. Ed by S.N. Agarwal etal. (Lucknow, Print House, 1982) p. 139.
16. Mohd. Burahanuddin. opcit. pp. 9-10.
17. A.A.NRaju, *Documentary Heritage of Indian Libraries.* (New Delhi, Ess Ess Publications, 2003) p. 28.
18. L.S. Ramiah. 'Rasthra Kendra Grandhalayam.' *Grandhalaya Sarvaswamu* V60, N10, Octo. 1999 p. 11.
19. A.A.N Raju *Documentary Heritage of Indian Libraries.* Opcit. p.29.

E

REGIONAL LIBRARIES

E.1. Regional Library Concept

The concept of 'Regional Library, (RL) is not of recent' origin in our country. Before the states reorganisation in 1956, the need for establishing regional libraries to serve the needs of linguistic groups in multilingual states was felt by the then state governments. Even before independence the government of Bombay appointed Library Development Committed in December 1939 headed by A.A.A Fyzee, Principal, Government Law College, Bombay for the purpose of establishing a Central Provincial library in the city of Bombay and three Regional Libraries for each linguistic centres viz., Poona, Ahmedabad and Dharwar obviously for the three regions of the state for the spread of library service in the Bombay presidency. The committed submitted its report in 1940 and recommended that "no separate Government Regional Libraries be opened, but that at Ahmedabad, the Municipal Library, at Poona, the City Central Library and at Dharwar, the Karnataka Vidya Vardhak Sangh should be entrusted with the functions of the regional libraries and should receive the copyright books of the particular language represented in the region, that is, Gujarati, Marathi and Kanarese respectively."[1] The committee further recommended that "the functions of the Regional Library also will be approximately the same, with it is difference that its sphere of action will be limited its Region, it will be under the general guidence of the central library and it will necessarity have to develop the Library movement in the districts."[2]

The Advisory Committee for Libraries appointed by Government of India in 1958 stated that "in bilingual states, Regional Libraries will fulfil all the functions of the state library, and the Regional Librarians will take place of State Librarian, except that the Library Department will laydown that the technical processes in the public libraries shall be uniform throughout state."[3]

Genesis of Regional Libraries

The Andhra state was formed in 1953 by carving out Telugu speaking districts from the composit Madras State and left with out a state central library and therefore the State Central Library (SCL) was established at Visakkapatnam in 1954. Andhra Pradesh was formed in 1956 by merging 9 Telugu speaking districts of former Hyderabad state with the Andhra area. As per the provisions of Hyderabad Public Libraries Act, 1955, then Asafia Library was declared as State Central Library. When the two regions came together they had each a State Central Library. Therefore the state central library at Hyderabad was declared as the state library of enlarged state of Andhra Pradesh. The State Central Library at Visakkapatnam was shifted to Guntur in 1954 prior to the decalaration of Hyderabad State Central Library as SCL of Andhra Pradesh. After the formation of Andhra Pradesh, the State Central Library of Guntur was convented as State Regional library in 1958. This was the first Regional Library in the state. Till the end of 1963 this was only the Regional Library in the state catering to the information needs of coastal districts. But the two other regions of the state viz., Rayalaseema and Telanaga were without a State Regional Library. In order to provided efficient library services for the two regions and also to northern coastal districts of the state four more regional libraries were established at the educational centres such as Tirupati,

Warangal, Visakkhapatnam and Nizamabad. The Gautami Library at Rajahmundry was taken over by the government in the year 1979 and converted as Gautami Regional Library. Thus currently the state has six regional libraries. The table below shows the dates of establishment and the districts to be covered with effective library services.

S. No.	Place	Date of Establishment	Districts to be covered
1.	Guntur	01-10-1954*	(Originally State Central Library Andhra state, Visakkapatnam) Guntur, Prakasam and Nellone.
2.	Warangal	04--2-1964	Warangal, Nalgonda, Khammam and Mahbooknagar.
3.	Tirupati	09-10-1964	Chittoor, Anantpur, Kaddapah and Kurnool.
4.	Visakapattnam	06-9-1965	Vishakkapatnam, Srikakulam and Viziangananam.
5.	Nizamabad	04-08-1966	Nizamabad, Adilabad, Medak, Karim Nagar, RangaReddy and Hyderabad.
6.	Rajahmundry	19-02-1979	Krishna, East and West Godavari Districts.

* After the formation of Andhra Pradesh in 1956, the State Central Library, Hyderabad state, was declared as State Central Library. Andhra Pradesh hence the State Central Library of former Andhra state located at Visakhapatnam was shifted to Guntur in May-June 1958 and declared as State Regional Library Guntur.

Aims and Objectives

The facilities to be provided in modern servicing public library have been enormously increased in various directions. It was felt that the ZGSS cannot satisfactorily cater to the needs of user community, not only because of their meagre book resources and finance but also for want of required trained manpower. It was therefore contemplated that the Regional Libraries established in various parts of the state as shown in the Table be entrusted with the following aims and objectives :

1. Collection and preservation of MSS of importance, rarity and volume in their respective regions.
2. Provision of research facilities to the scholars and learned people by strengthening library resources.
3. Implementation of inter library loan and regional library cooperation.
4. Setting high standards of library and information services and to act as model for District Central Libraries (DCLS) and other Branch Libraries (BLS) in the region., and
5. Functioning as a leader and provide leadership and guidence to other libraries in the region[4].

B.V. SubbaRao identified the following objectives for Regional libraries.

"1. For collection and Preservation of reading materials (including manuscripts) on various subjects and provide facilities to the research scholars and other reading public in their respective regions.

2. To promote inter library loan between the Regional Libraries and the State Central Library at Hyderabad on the one hand and between the Regional Libraries and District Central Libraries on the other.

3. To set standards and guidence to the District Central Libraries and their branches in technical matters."[5]

Functions of Regional Library

The A.P. Public Library Act, 1960 at section 2(12) merely defines what State Regional Library means. It states that 'State Regional Library' means a library established by the Government as a State Regional Library. It neither specified the functions nor the relationship with other libraries in the system ie state central library and district central libraries. The note circulated to the second Andhra Pradesh Public Libraries Conference held at Hyderabad from 12th to 13th August 1972 enumerated the following services to be rendered by the

Regional Libraries.

1. To have good collection of text books and reference whcih cannot usually be purchased by the Regional Libraries within their area;
2. To prepare bibliographies in coordination with State Central Library (SCL);
3. To lend books to the libraries situated in the area of their jurisdiction for which purpose a few districts may be alloted for the Regional Library;
4. To supervise the technical work of the District Central Libraries (DCLS), their branches and other libraries.
5. To work as Regional offices for the Department[6].

The Review committee appointed by the Govt of Andhra pradesh in 1976 identified the following functions to be performed by a Regional Library;

"1. Collection and preservation of MSS available in the region and rare and valuable books which ZGSS may not be able to purchase. All reference books must be stocked,
2. Provide facilities for research,
3. Organise Inter-Library Cooperation including inter-library loan,
4. Set standards for the Zilla Grandhalaya Samasthas and their branches, book deposit centres and mobile library services,
5. Compilation of bibliography for the region as well as the preparation of union catalogue for the region,
6. Inspection and supervision of ZGSS in the region and to provide them technical advice and assistance,
7. Serve as an essential link between the SCL on the one hand and ZGSS in their region on the other,
8. Plan the development of library service in the region and

implement the same in a phased manner,

9. Prepare and submit annual reports on the working of the libraries in the region"[7].

Present Position

The Regional libraries in Andhra Pradesh have been functioning for the past five and half decades starting with State Regional Library, Guntur. The aims and objectives for which these libraries have been established in the state were not fulfilled so far. It is generally felted by the professional experts that these libraries were not actually functioning as per the expectation of the authorities. They become just mere appendages to the Director of Public Libraries. It was well known that the position and status of these libraries were not properly defined in the Act. There is no clear mention in the Act about the establishment and management of these libraries. The Act simply states that the Director of Public Libraries shall "supervise the State Central Library and branches of such library". It is not clear whether the Regional Libraries are deemed as 'branches' to the State Central Library or they have different status altogether. The position of these libraries in the Act is not clear on this point. These libraries were established by executive orders and are not controlled by the Librarian of the SCL but the Directory Public Libraries. These were not able to realise the aims, objectives and perform the functions identified by the experts and as suggested by Review Committee. The reasons for this state of affairs are : 1. the staff in these libraries is inadequates, 2. the status of Regional Librarians is low, 3. the accomodation is insufficient and 4. the bookstock is poor and insufficient[8].

After going into the working of these libraries, their position and status the Review Committee made the following recommendations :

"1. There should be only three Regional Libraries : one at Guntur, the other at Tirupatti and the third at Warangal.

They shall as at present be wholly financed by the state government.

2. Reference books and other library material of that nature existing in the Visakkhapatnam and Nizamabad Regional Libraries be transferred to Guntur and Warangal. [note : when the report was submitted in 1978, Sri Gautami Library at Rajahamudry was not taken over by government].
3. The status of Regional Librarians should be that of Assistant Director.
4. The Regional Libraries at Visakhapatnam and Nizamabad be developed as Branch Libraries of the concerned District Central Library :
5. The Regional Libraries should be reference libraries and should not be lending libraries except to the extent permitted for the reference section and that too to an institution recognised for the purpose.
6. The functions of the Regional Libraries will be as mentioned above. The powers and duties will be as stated earlier.
7. The growth of all the three Regional Libraries suggested by us should be ensured on equal basis and discrimination of every kind should be avoided, so that the people of the three regions will have equal access to reference and research material."[9]

What lies ahead

The position of Regional Libraries in the so called 'Pyramidical structure' of public library system in the state is not clearly and properly visualized and pronounced. So far the recommendations made by the Review Committee were not implemented. These libraries have failed miserally in fulfilment of their aims and objectives for which they have been established. They have more or less become 'sick' and struggling hard to survive. The Second Andhra Pradesh Public Libraries conference held in 1972 at Hyderabad resolved that "the Regional Libraries should be integrated with the state library system and should function as effective link between the state central library and district central libraries in the region. The Regional Libraries should also share the functions of the State Central Library such as supervision, technical work in the District Central Libraries in the region and their branches."[10]

P. V. Malleshwar who surveyed the working of Regional Libraries in Coastal Andhra Pradesh has concluded that "the Regional Libraries have to work as model libraries for District Central Libraries in the State and in reality it was not so. The reason for this was that DCLS have more financial resources than RLS. Therefore RLS were not able to develop vis - a - vis DCL's. The revenue receipts for DCLs was more than RLS. The DCLs were in a comfortable position with respect to infrastructure, staff and facilities than RLS. Therefore RLS cannot be model libraries and a lead the DCLS. The DCLS were far ahead of RLS. For lack of sufficient staff, infrastructure and finances the services of RLS were shrinking year after year. The RLS were not able acquire regionally available valuable MSS and save our documenting heritage. These were not able to meet information requirements of historians"[11].

There is a need to integrate these libraries into the public library system and necessary steps have to be iniated by the Government for the implementation of recommendations made especially by the Review committee. The following sections briefly deal with the six individual Regional Libraries functioning in the state.

References

1. *Report of the Library Development Committee, Bombay, 1939-1940* (Bombay, the Government Central Press, 1941) p. 58.
2. Ibid, p. 21.
3. *Report of Advisory Committee For Libraries* (New Delhi, Ministry of

Education, Govt of India, 1961) p. 43.

4. A.A.N Raju Regional Libraries in Andhra Pradesh. *ILA Bulletin* V9, N1, Jan-March 1973, p. 9.

5. B.V. SubbaRao. 'Regional Libraries in Andhra Pradesh' In *Hyderabad City Grandhalaya Samastha Silver jubilee (1961-1986). Souvenir.* (Hyderabad, City Grandhalaya Samastha, 1986).

6. Department of Public Libraries, Govt of Andhra Pradesh. *Agenda Papers* (Presented to the Second A.P. Public Libraries Conference, Hyderabad, 12th and 13th August 1972) (Mimeographed).

7. *Report of Committee appointed by the Government of Andhra Pradesh* in February, 1976 to review working of the Andhra Pradesh Public Libraries Act, 1960 and to suggest amendments to the Act. (Hyderabad, Director of Printing, Govt of Andhra Pradesh, 1978) p. 37.

8. A.A.N. Raju Regional Libraries in Andhra Pradesh. Opcit. p. 10.

9. *Report of the Committee appointed by the Government of Andhra Pradesh* in February 1976 ... opcit. p. 101.

10. Department of Public Libraries, Govt of Andhra Pradesh. *Agenda Papers*. opcit. p. 77.

11. P.V. Mallashawar. 'Samachara Samajam lo, Prantiya Grandhalaya Patra. Andhra Pradesh ... *Grandhalaya Sarvasvamu*, V60, N7, Octo. 1999, pp.13-14.

E.2. State Regional Library, Guntur

Genenis and Development

Andhra state was formed in 1953, and Kurnool as its capital, by carving out eleven telugu speaking districts from composite Madras State. The Madras Public Libraries Act, 1948 was inforce in the eleven telugu speaking districts of newly formed Andhra state. Since the state Central Library for composite Madras State was located at Madras, the Andhra State had to establish a state centre library as per the provisions of Madras Public Libraries Act, 1948 and therefore established state central library at Visakkhapatnam on Ist September 1954. The enlarged state of Andhra Pradesh was formed on Ist November 1956 by merging the telugu speakings areas of former Hyderabad State with Andhra State. The former Hyderabad State had enacted Hyderabad Public Libraries Act, 1955 and as per the provisions of the Act Asafia Library located at Hyderabad was declared as State Central Library of Hyderabad State. When Andhra Pradesh was formed there were two state central libraries at two regions of the state in Andhra and Telangana regions. The State Central Library, at

Hyderabad was declared as State Central Library of Andhra Pradesh and the State Central Library at Visakkhapatnam was shifted to Guntur in May-June 1958 redesignated as State Regional Library Guntur. Since then it has been functioning as State Regional Library, Guntur[1].

Book Collections

When the library was shifted from Visakkhapatnam to Guntur in May-June 1958 it had initial collection of 15, 217 books and 9 staff members. By the time the library completed its silver jublee (1958-1982) in the year 1982, the collection has grown impressively touching already 90,000 books. The following table shows the growth of the library between the years 1960-61 and 1980-81.

S.No	*Indicators*	*1960-61*	*1980-81*
1.	Book Stock	25,768	87,487
2.	Periodical Subscription145		225
3.	Staff	11	38
4.	No. of visitors per day	250	1,200
5.	No. books consulted per year	48,500	2,91,715
6.	No. of books issued for home reading	8,700	4,56,022
7.	No. of actual registered borrowers	342	4,258
8.	Total budget	100,000/-	4,20,000

Source : Silver Jublee Souvenir, 1982. p. 2.

Sections of the library

In order to meet the growing information needs of user community the library has been functioning under the following sections and these have been briefly presented below :

Lending Section

The total collection of nearly 87,000 books cover various branches of knowledge including 4000 books donated by American Culture Centre in 1968, which was closed in that year. From this section book are lent for home reading for members who pay Rs 30/ and of Rs 50/ for foreign publications. Books costing of 150/ and above are not issued for home reading.

Text Book Section

This section was opened in the year 1978-79 for the benefit of student community. The collection is exhaustive and meets the requirements of students. This section works from 8.00 AM to 12.00 midnight. More than 15,000 reference books area made available in the section.

Union Catalogue Section

The library has taken up preparation of Union catalogue of books available in 21 district central libraries in Andhra Pradesh in 1960. The work has progressed to certain extent and not completed. It has brought out Telugu section of Indian National Bibliography for two years 1958 and 1959. It has also broughtout descriptive catalogue of children's literature under the title "Balasahitimala" and published in 1963 which was a commedable effort on the part of the library.

Periodical Section

The library subscribes to 225 periodicals and magazines including 15 daily newspapers in different languages. Some of the daily papers and magazines like *Hindu*, *Andhrapatrika*, '*Bharati*' (which now ceased publication) are bound and the volumes are preserved for posterity[2]. The library also possers maps of survey of India which are kept under restricted use.

Social Educationwing

This section was opened in 1966. Cultural activities for the benefit of society is being carried out by this section. The section has cinemetography projector and arranges film shows every wednesday and sunday. The library over the years arranged numerous cultural programmes, public meetings to celebrate the birth and death of anniversaries of national and internation personalities, debating, essay writting contests for students of schools and colleges, exhibition of paintings, photographs dolls and chess and other tournaments. Lectures and discussions are held on topics of current interest. Every year the library celebrated National Library Weeks during 14th 20th November.

Book Selection Committee

In order to select relevant, useful and quality books for the library, Government has constituted two committees for selection of English and Telugu books consisting scholars, academicians and men of letters from different fields of human endeavour. The English book selection committee consisting 10 members and Telugu book selection committee consisting 9 members with the State Regional Librarian as Member/ Secretary.

Library Advisory Committee

The Government has also constituted an Advisory Committee for the library with the Joint collector as its chairman and State Regional Librarian as its Member/Secretary. The committee consists of eminent people drawn from higher education, public life, journalism, library and information science. The Advisory committee had the honour of having Sri Vavilala Gajala Krishanayya as its member for several years.

Library Building

In the year 1967 the Town Hall building was acquired by the government to house the library. The collections of the library and sections have been increased bringing pressure on the available space in the building and effecting the services. In the year 1975-76 the government has sanctioned a sum of Rs 33,000/ for providing additional accommodation in the library. With the sanctioned amount a hall was constructed on the northern side of the main building. With a grant of Rs

200,000/ from Coastal Andhra Development and Planning Committee a new block on the Southern side of the main building was constructed in 1981.

Library Staff

At the time of Silver Jublee Celebrations in the year 1982 the staff position of the library was as follows :

S.No	Type of Post	Nos
1.	Gazetted Librarian	1
2.	Asst. Librarians Gr-I	2
3.	Asst. Librarians Gr-II	9
4.	Book Keepers	... 3
5.	Film Operator	... 1
6.	Binder	... 1
7.	Headclerks	... 1
8.	Jr. Assistants	... 2
9.	Typists	... 2
10.	Record Assts	... 2
11.	Attenders	... 11
12.	Contigent Staff	... 3

Progress of the Library

The State Regional Library has made impressive progress since its inception in 1958. The following table provides decade wise figures for the years 1961-62 to 1980-81 with respect to 'visitors, books consulted, bookslent home and registered borrowers[3].

Year	No. of Visitors	No. of Books consulted	No. of Books lent for home reading	No. of registered borrowers
1961-62	139400	49,500	9700	551
1970-71	149643	231784	48861	1428
1980-81	20,4487	291715	25602	3897

Book Collections

As on 31.03.2003, the total book collections of the library stood at 1,17,305. The break up of the collections is shown in the following table :

Language	*Total Book Collection*
Telugu	39,777
English	65,822
Hindi	7,583
Urdu	1,262
Other languages	2,861
Total	1,17,305

Periodicals Subscribed

During the year 2002-03, the library subscribed to a total of 102 Periodicals of various frequencies. The following table provides languagewise and frequency wise breakup of periodicals.

Mode of Acquisition	*Telugu*			*English*					*Total*
	D	*W*	*M*	*D*	*W*	*H*	*Q*		
By Subscription	6	6	18	5	8	3	0	4	77
By Donation by public			11				8		19
Gratis			3				3		6
Total	6	6	32	5	8	4	1	4	102

Membership

As on 31.03.2003, the total membership of the library stood at 10,183 and there has been an increase of 28% in the membership than the year 2001-02.

Readership

As on 31.03.2003, the total readership of the library stood at 1,91,806 and there has been an increase of 17.5% in the readership than the previous year 2001-2002.

Books Consulted

During the year 2002-03, a total of 3,22,240 books were consulted by the readers. The books include : reference books, books on competitive examinations, astrology, medicine, biochemistry, physiotherphy, food technology, hotel management, electronics and computer sciences.

Books Lent for Home Reading

During the year 2002-03, a total of 8107 books were lent for home reading, and there has been an increase of 12.89% of readership than the previous year 2001-02.

Books Acquired

During the year 2002-03, the library acquired books by purchase, and received from DPL/RRLF scheme, Director, RRRLF and as gratis from the public. The following table. provides figures for books from these sources.

Sources of acquisition	*Total books received*
By Purchase	327
From DPL/RRRLF	694
From Director, RRRLF	142
By Gratis	736
Total	1899

Extension activities

During the year 2002-03, the library has arranged 25 extension activities which included celebration of national events, birth anniversaries of eminent Indians, national library week celebrations, essay and debating completitions, general quiz programmes and yoga classes.

Conclusion

The Regional Library, Guntur is the second larger public library established by the Government of Andhra Pradesh in

1958 and rendering library services to the region covering the districts of Guntur, Prakasam and Nellore. It caters to the needs of school and college going students and others who prepare for competitive examinators, besides serving other sections of the society. One of two important functions of this library is the preservation of old news papers, gazettes and some important periodicals. Its extension activities are note worthy and striving hard to inculcate reading habits and competitive spirit among its reading community. It has also actively participated in the government programmes such as : Janma bhoomi, Neeru Meeru and digging of watershade's, with the cooperation of staff members.

References

1. S.S. Deshmukh, 'Silver Jubilee Report of State Regional Library, Guntur.' *Silver Jubilee Sonvenir*, 1982. (Guntur, State Regional Library, 1982). p. 1.
2. V. V. Vekatappayya. *Mana Grandhalayalu : Parisodhana Kendralu*. (Nellore, Sairam Publications, 1987) p. 678.
3. V.Gopalkrishnayya, 'Our Regional Library' In *Silver Jubilee Sonvenir*, 1982. (Guntur, State Regional Library, 1982), p. 15.

Additional Source : Regional Library, Guntur : *Annual Report* 2002-2003 (Mimeographed).

E.3. Regional Library, Warangal

Genesis

The Regional Library, Warangal was established in the year 1964 at Warangal to meet the information needs of the user community residing in the districts of Warangal, Khammam, Kareemnagar and Adilabad districts Warangal is one of the reputed educational centres in Telangana region nent only to Hyderabad city.

Library Building

The library is honored in its own building. The total area consists of 2,268 sq. yards of which the constructed area comprises 752 sq.yds and with an open area of 1, 516.28 sq. yds. The accommodation consists of reading room, stake room, administration wing, social education wing, reference section, children's section, Periodical section and Internet facility room.

Library Staff

By the end of 31.03.08 the total staff of the library consists of 8 people which include Gazetted Librarian (Temporary), Asst. Librarian, Grade I, Asst. Librarian, Grade II, Card writer P, Book keeper Record Asst, Watchman and Sweeper.

Book Collections

The total book collections by the end of 31.03.08 stood at 64,014. The break-up of this collection is as follows :

Children's books	6,208
Reference books	10,913
Text books	17,035
Fiction books	11,428
Non fiction books	18,430

The library had also received total of 25,486 books RRRLF. Kolkata from 1972 to 31.03.08. The language wise of break-up of the collection is as follows :

Telugu	24,603
English	25,237
Hindi	8,981
Urdu	5,193

During the year 2007-08 the library has subscribed to 65 periodicals and received 6 periodicals as gratis. The break-up was 14 dailies and 57 non dailies.

Registered Borrowers

By the end of 31.03.08 the registered borrowers of the library stood at 4,285. The break-up is : Men 3,620 and women 665. The registered borrowers consist of professionals (276), Farmers (135), Business men (232), House wives (152), Employees (372) and unemployed (491).

Readership

A total of 68,773 readers visited the library during the year 2007-08 with an average of 241 readers per day of the total figure 56,888 readers used the Periodical section and 11,885 readers used Reference Section.

Books Consulted

A total of 11,885 books were consulted within the library during the year 2007-08, with an average of 42 books per day. The type of books consulted by the readers in as follows : Text books 1,575; Reference books 9,976 and other non fiction books 334.

Books Lent

A total of 1,296 books were lent for home reading during the year 2007-08 at an average of 5 books per day. The type of books text were lent for home reading consist of non-fiction books (1,194) and fiction books (102).

Extension Activities

During the year 2007-08 the library has organised two book exhibitions, arranged 22 T.V. and filmshows, 3 lecture programmes and 7 other extension activities.

Source : 2007-2008 State Administrative Report. Govt. Regional Library, Warangal.

E.4. Regional Library, Tirupati

Genesis

The Regional Library, Tirupati was established in the year 1964 to serve the information needs of people of Rayalaseema region covering the districts of Kurnool, Kadapa, Anantapur and Chittoor districts.

Objectives

The main objectives of the library are as follows :

1. To meet the information requirements of students children and general public of Rayalaseema region.
2. To collect, maintain and preserve the rare books and manuscripts available in the region.
3. To provide facilities for research scholars and perform administrative functions such as inspection and supervision of libraries in the region.
4. To serve as a link between the State Central Library at the top and all types of libraries, especially the public libraries in the region.
5. To develop book collections and other reading materials relating to the region.

Library Building

The Library is functioning in a rented building. A site belonging to Sri Buggmutt was purchased in the year 1981 with a plinth area of nearly 237 anknams. A plan for the library building was prepared with a cost about Rs 46.5 lakhs.

Library Staff

The total staff strength the library was eight on 31.03.06 of which three posts were lying vacant. The following table provides information about no of posts sanctioned and number of vacancies as on 31.03.06.

Category of Post	*Sanctioned Posts*	*Posts Vacant*
Gazetted Librarian	01	–
Asst. Librarian Grade I	01	–
Asst Librarian Grade II	01	01
Record Asst	01	–
Card Writer	01	–
Book bearer	01	–
Watchman	01	–
Sweeper	01	01

Book Collection

The total book collection of the library stood at 65,557 as on 01.04.2006. The break-up language wise is ; Telugu 32,626, English 25,665, Hindi 5507, Urdu 172 and other languages 1597. The total number of periodicals subscribed as on 31.04.07 was 72 of which 38 Telugu, 29 English and 01 Hindi. The language wise, frequency wise break-up is shown in the following table.

	Telugu D W F N M	*English* D W F N M	*Other Languages* D W F N M	*Total*
Purchased	0706 0 3 2	1 4 0 5 0	1 1 9 0 2	02

Membership and Readership

The total membership at the end of the year 2005-06 stood at 4059 and readership stood at 62,678.

Books Consulted, Lent for Home Reading

During the year 2005-06 a total of 2,02,026 books were consulted within the library and a total of 4739 books were lent for home reading.

Books Purchased for the Library

In addition to purchase of books from its own budget, the library received books from the DPL under RRRLF scheme, the Director, RRRLF Kolkata and from public as gratis.

The following table provides figures for books received from these sources during the year 2005-06.

Sources	*No. of Titles*	*No. of Books.*
By Purchase	128	128
DPL under RRRLF	576	576
Director RRRLF	620	620
Gratis from the Public	511	511

Extension Activities

Every year the library has been celebrating National Library Week during the month of November. During the year 2005-06 also the library celebrated National Library Week from 14th to 20th November. In addition, it has also celebrated Dr. S.R. Ranganathan and Pandit Jawaharlal Nehru birthday.

Source : *Administrative Report of Government Regional Library*, Tirupati 2005-06.

E.5. Regional Library, Visakhapatnam

Genesis

The Government Regional Library, Visakhapatnam came into being in the year 1965 to meet the information needs of Northern Coastal Andhra districts of Srikakulam, Vizianagaram and Visakhapatnam of Andhra Pradesh. It is supposed to act as a link between the District Central Libraries (DCLs) of the region and the State Library, the apex library at Hyderabad. It is housed in a rented building of Muncipal Corporation situated at Nehru Bazar, upstairs of Muncipal Elementary School, Dwarakanagar.

Objectives

The objectives of the library are as follows :

1. To cater to the information and educational needs of the user community in general and research scholars in particular.
2. To provide reference and reprographic services to the readers.
3. To provide opportunities of self education to all types of readers.
4. To build up library collections through purchase and gratis.

Library Building

The library is honoured in a rented building of Municipal Corporation of Visakapatnam.

Library Staff

The sanctioned posts by the end of the year 2004-05 were 10 of which two posts were vaccant. The following table provides various categories of posts sactioned and posts vaccant.

Category of Post	*No. of Ports sanctioned*	*No. of Ports Vacant*
Gazetted Librarian	1	0
Asst. Librarian Gr I	1	0
Asst. Librarian Gr II	1	1
Card Writer	1	1
Typist	1	0
Record Asst.	1	0
Attender	1	0
Day Watchman	1	0
Night Watchman	1	0
Part time Sweeper	1	0

Book Collection

The total book stocks in the library by the end of 31.03.2005 was 46,446 and the languagewise break-up is as follows : Telugu 20,394, English 20,458, Hindi 4946, Urdu 418 and other languages 230. The library was also subscribing to 104 periodicals during the year 2004-05. The language and periodicity wise break-up is shown in the following table.

Telugu				*English*				*Total*
D	*W*	*FN*	*M*	*D*	*W*	*FN*	*M*	
8	6	3	25	5	9	6	41	104

Membership and Readership

The total membership and the readership of the library by the end of 31.03.2005 stood at 3780 and 65057 respectively. There was 70% increase in the membership and just 08% increase in the readership.

Book consulted and lent

The number of books consulted during the year 2004-05 stood at 37413 with 3.75% increase. Likewise the number of books lent for home reading stood at 31894 with 4% decrease when compared with year 2003-04.

Books added during the year

In addition to purchase books from its own budget the library has been receiving books from the DPL under RRRLF scheme and directly from the Director, RRRLF, Kolkata and also gratis from the public. The following table provides figures for books received from these sources during the year 2004-05.

Sources	*No. of Titles*	*No. of Books*
By Purchase	1910	1910
DPL/RRRLF	1159	1159
Director/RRRLF	145	145
By gratis	160	160

Extension activities

The library actively participated in the extension activities such as participation in total literacy campaign, Janambhoomi and clean and green programmes and also celebrate only National Library week during the month of November and celebration of Dr. S.R. Ranaganathan birthday. In addition to these programmes conducted during the year 2004-05, it has also organised discussions, child and woman programmes and conducted competition programmes for students.

Source : *Annual Report of Govt. Regional Library, Visakhapatnam for the year 2004-05.*

E.6. Regional Library, Nizamabad

Genesis

The Regional Library, Nizamabad was established in the year 1966 to render library services in the region covering Nizamabad, Adilabad, KarimNagar and Medak districts. Presently the library is functioning at chandrasekhar nagar colony of Kamateshwar residential area and in its own building.

Objectives

The main objectives of the library is as follows :

1. To meet the information needs of user clientele particularly students, research scholars and general public.
2. To provide effective reference services to the user community.
3. To provide in addition to books, newspapers and magazines.
4. To increase membership and readership.

Management

The library is headed by Gazetted Librarian and supported by technical and ministerial staff such as Asst. Librarian Grade I, Card writer and Attender. The library has office wing, Technical wing and sections such as Periodical, Text book, Reference and Issue and Membership.

Library Building

The library is housed in its own building with an area of 1404 sqmeters. The Library building consists of one reading room, two big stack rooms. One small room for C.E.R.U. section, small varandha for paper reading and one room for Computer/Librarian.

Staff

The number of sanctioned posts as on 31.03.05 was six of which two ports are vacant. The following table provides category of ports, number of posts sanctioned and vacant.

Category of Post	*Sanctioned Posts*	*Posts Vacant*
Gazetted Librarian	1	1
Asst. Librarian Grade I	1	0
Card Writer	1	0
Attender	1	1
Night Watch man	1	0
Sweeper	1	0
Total	6	2

Book Collection

By the end of 2004-05 the total collection in the library was 55163. The languagewise break-up is; English 21,371, Telugu 25,982, Hindi 5983, Urdu 1760 and Sanskrit 67. It was subscribing to 35 Telugu periodicals and 14 English totaling 49 periodicals and magazines. Of the total 49 peroidicals, 30 periodicals are Telugu and the break-up is 05 daily, 10 weekly, 05 fotnightly, 10 monthly and the remaining 17 are in English and break-up is : 04 daily, 09 weekly and monthly.

Membership

By the end of the year 2004-05, the total membership of the library stood at 1858.

Readership

The total readership by the end of the year 2004-05 stood at 70166 an increase of 4.22%, when compared with the year 2003-04. A total of 4762 readers used the periodical section and 22540 visited the book section. A total of 37596 readers consulted books during the year 2004-05. A total of

4772 books were lent for home reading during the year 2004-05.

Books Purchased for the library

In addition to purchase of books from its own budget, the library received books from the DPL under RRRLF scheme, the Director of RRRLF, Kolkata and also from the public as gratis. The following table provides figures of books received from these sources during the 2004-05.

Sources	*No. of Titles*	*No. of Books*
By Purchase	–	2499
DPL under RRRLF	1133	1133
Director, RRRLF	205	205
Gratis from the Public	417	417

Extension Activities

The library actively participated in the National Library week celebrations held from 14th to 20th November 2004. During the year 2004-05, the library organised 14 conferences/seminars and children programmes, organised two book exhibitions and conducted five literacy activities.

E.7. Sri Gowtami Regional Library, Rajahmundry

Genesis and Development

The present Gowtami Regional Library had its origins in the Gowtami Library which in turn had its origins in 1898, and acquired the name in 1920 by merger of three libraries, namely, Veeresalinga Grandhalayam, Vasuraya Pustaka Bhandagaramu and Ratnakavi Grandha Nilayam.[1] It was registered as No.2 in 1920 under the Act 21 of 1860. The new library, due to the efforts of the management and contributions made by philanthropists, acquired its own premises in the heart of Rajahmundry town and shifted to its new premises in 1923.[2] In this spacious building, the library started growing in its collection and expanded its services. K. Ramachandra Rao, a philanthropist, constructed Babayamma Memorial Hall named after his daughter for organising women welfare activities in the library premises. The total area of the library premises is 3,100 sq. yards or 2,790 sq. meters. The structures on the premises were as follows: 1. The Main Library Building which was

Sri Gowtami Regional Library, Rajahmundry

residential building of a British officer before the library acquired it with a tiled roof and in a dilapidated condition. It was almost a century old. 2. The Babayamma Memorial Hall. 3. An AC sheet shed. 4. A two-room structure. This is an RCC construction. Two tiled verandhas adjacent to Babayamma Memorial Hall. The tiled roof old building was vacated after Government of Andhra Pradesh took over the management of the library on 9th February 1979 and renamed it as Sri Gowtami Regional Library. The Babayamma Memorial Hall is double storied building with a tiled roof. The ground floor is being used for reading and lending sections of the library. The AC sheet shed is used for children's section. The two room RCC structure is used for library office room and stack room for keeping books and other reading materials. The front verandha adjacent to Babayamma Memorial Hall is used for newspaper reading room and the back verandha for dumping broken furniture and other property of the library. Recently out of the funds received from constituency development fund of the local MP from Rajahmundry, a ground floor was constructed in front of Babayamma Memorial Hall. The office of the library and the reference collection is shifted to this new structure.

Aims and Objectives

The following are the aims and objectives of the library:[3]

1. To secure all books in Telugu language and as far as possible books in Sanskrit, English, Hindi and other languages;
2. To secure old manuscripts written on palmyra leaves and print such of those as are important and have not yet been printed;
3. To get newspapers and magazines in Telugu, Hindi and English languages and place them on the reading room table for free reading of the public;
4. To circulate books and newspapers to the subscribers of the library;

5. To arrange for lectures which are instructive, educative, literary and patriotic and publish papers and pamphlets of like nature;
6. To make available all books and other reading material to all sections of the public freely in the library premises;
7. To open branch libraries in the town in conformity with the rules and regulations of the library; and
8. To create research facilities in Telugu literature and allied topics to scholars from various universities and colleges in Andhra Desa and elsewhere.

Library Collection

Being one of the oldest libraries in Andhra Pradesh, the collection that has gone into the library has great research value for present day researchers. In the first three decades of the 20th century, many stalwarts in such diverse fields as Literature, Fine Arts, Philosophy, Politics and Culture and also connected with the public life of the town were closely associated with this library and enriched its collection with personal gifts and donations. At the time of merger in 1920, Sarvajanika Pusthaka Bhandagaram possessed 5,322 Telugu and Sanskrit books, 2,246 English books and 153 manuscripts. The Vasuraya Pusthaka Bhandagaram possessed 2,800 Telugu and Sanskrit, 800 English books and 100 manuscripts. The Gowtami Library being the fusion of three libraries has the privilege of possessing very rich and valuable collection which can be found only in few libraries in Andhra Pradesh.[4]

Books and Periodical Collection

A majority of book stock consists of publications published before 1930s. Many of these books are first editions. At the time of government's take over on 19th February 1979, the library collection consisted of 31,004 printed books and the breakup is as follows: Telugu 15,242; English 14,362; Sanskrit 781; Hindi 719 and 719 bound volumes of periodicals in

Telugu, 520 in English and 702 volumes of miscellaneous nature.[5] The periodical collection mainly constitutes those published during the later part of the 19th century and the beginning of the 20th century. The old periodicals such as: *Sarada, Kavita, Vasavi, Manorama, AmudritaAndhra Grandha Chintamani, Sivadharma Prakashini, Hindu Sundari,* which reflect the culture of the Telugu people are among the very valuable collections of the library. These back volumes can rarely be found in other libraries in Andhra Pradesh and the research value of these back volumes can hardly be emphasized.

Manuscript and Inscription Collection

The successive managements of the library strove hard to acquire manuscripts and copper inscriptions which formed the basic sources of information on Telugu literature, culture and history. The manuscript collection constitutes paper and palmleaf manuscripts. A larger part of the manuscript collection was donated by Raja Vatsavai Jagapati Varma, Zamindar of Peddapuram. *Rigveda Samhita*, translated into Telugu by Nemani Venkata Narasimha Sastri, is one of the pride possessions of the library. Another invaluable manuscript the library possesses is *Vamsa Vriksha Pradarshini* which depicts vividly the lineages of famous personalities of the Puranas. In addition to these Telugu manuscripts, the Sanskrit manuscript collection contains, among others, *Parishanusekharam Chitprabha Vyakhya* of Kalluri Venkata Subrahmanyam Dikshit and *Manorama Sabdaratnam* of Gangadhara Bhattu. The other valuable manuscripts include *Kabiru Abhanganuchu, Samavedam* of Sripada Krishna Murthy. These are not yet printed and need critical examination and research. *Srimad Andhrikrita Padya Rigveda Samhita* rendered in Telugu poetry for the first time is another valuable manuscript. The other manuscripts worth mentioning are: *Iravata Charitram, Vedanta Saram, Sabdha Lakshana Sangraham.* [6]

Col. Colin Mackenji (1754-1821), an Englishman employed as Engineer during East India Company rule toured the entire South India in search of historical monuments and findings and recorded his impressions in his own handwriting.[7] He also got them recorded in local languages. His successors had given away these volumes to this library for preservation. As stated already, the library possesses six copper plates belonging to 14th century. These inscriptions related to the charitable deeds of a ruler of this region by the name Sri Kumara Giri Reddy. These are in Telugu script.[8]

As per the information provided in the filled-in questionnaire, in June 2001, the library possessed 68,028 printed books in Telugu, English, Hindi and Sanskrit, 1,500 bound volumes of periodicals, 420 palmleaf manuscripts, 30 paper manuscripts, 6 copper plates and 83 microfilm rolls. The library currently subscribes to 54 journals and 16 newspapers.

Arrangement of Collection

The whole book collection of the library has been broadly grouped under the following subject headings and accession registers maintained accordingly [9]

1. Arshagrandhas, Smritis, Srutis, Dharma Sastras, Puranas, Itihasas, Mahatyams, Vratas, Stotras, Religion, Philosophy and Geneology.
2. Poetry (ancient and modern), Satakas, Moral Poetry, Dandakams, Avadhanas and Chatuvulu.
3. Dramas, Prahasanams.
4. Novels
5. Prose — Vachana Kavyas, Stories, Puranisc Stories.
6. History — Histories of Countries, Biographies.
7. Oration — Social and Philosophical.
8. Sciences — Economics, Industries, Agriculture, Bharata Sastras, Astrology, Law, Domestic Science, Natural History, Biology, Geography, Constitutions, Civics,

Architecture, Medicine, Health and Hygiene, etc.

9. Linguistics — Dictionaries, Grammar, Alankara Sastras, Prosody, Criticism, History of Poets.
10. Songs, Kirtanams, Harikathas, Yakshaganas.
11. Vachakams (Textbooks)
12. Annual Reports, Rules and Regulations and Lists.
13. Periodicals
14. Sanskrit Works — Poetry, Drama and Fiction.
15. Hindi Works
16. Kannada Works
17. Oriya Works
18. Back Volumes of Periodicals
19. Palm leaf Manuscripts, Manuscripts in Telugu and Sanskrit.

The English collection has been grouped under the following broad subject headings: 1. History. 2. Politics. 3. Language and Literature. 4. All Varieties of English Books. 5. Medicine. 6. Poetry. 7. Religion. 8. Encyclopedias and Dictionaries. 9. Commerce. 10. Census of India, 1961. 11. Sciences. 12. English Novels. 13. English Tales and Stories. 14. Miscellaneous Collections. 15. Reference Books. 16. Dramas and 17. Prose. Of late, the library has started to reclassify its entire collection by Dewey Decimal Classification and cataloguing by AACR.

Research Value of the Collection

Being one of the oldest and foremost libraries in Andha Pradesh, it is but natural that library possesses varied and rich collections of significant research value. It provides a veritable goldmine for any research scholar engaged in the history, culture, language, literature and social and economic aspects of Andhra Pradesh. The rich personal collections donated by eminent literateurs and public men add to the value and prestige of the collection of the library as they are not available elsewhere. Because of this rich, valuable and rare collection, the universities in the state and elsewhere have recognised the Gowtami Library as one of the research libraries where much needed sources of information are available. Therefore, it is but natural that research scholars from universities in the state and also from other parts of India and in few cases, scholars from foreign countries like USA, UK and Canada visited the library in the past for collecting information.[11]

Rare Book Collections

As the library is more than a century old it is but natural that the library possessed very rare and valuable printed books of immense importance. The library has around 1500 rare books published before 1900 and about 8115 books published before 1923 and around 5000 books published up to 1950. In all 15000 rare books find a place in the library. The later collections include books in Telugu, Sanskirit, Hindi, Kannada, Tamil, English and Urdu languages. A very important feature of the collection was the Preservation of the first edition of Encyclopedia Britanniaca published in the year 1771 in 3 volumes[12].

Library Building

The library is housed in its own building with the premises covering an area of 3100 sq.yds. In the main old building sections such as Social Education wing, Periodical section are housed. The ground a floor of the new building constructed with M.P. Lads houses Reference and Rare book Section, Binding Section and Computer Sections. The first floor of new building houses Issue Counter and Reading Hall and stack area.

Library Staff

The library is managed by eleven staff members. The following table provides the number of sanctioned posts and posts that were vacant as on 31.03.05.

Category of Posts.	*No. of Posts Sanctioned*	*No. of Posts Vacant*
Gazetted Librarian	1	–
Asst. Librarian Grade I	1	–
Asst. Librarian Grade II	1	–
Card writers	3	1
Typist	1	–
Record Asst.	2	–
Sweeper	1	–
Watchman	1	–
Total	11	1

Book Collections

The total book collection as on 31.03.05 stood at 77,267. The following table provides number of books purchased by the library's own budget and books received from DPL, RRRLF and from the Public as gratis.

Net Book Stock as on 31.03.04	*No. of books added*			*Books received as gratis*	*Total*
	Books supplied by DPL/ RRRLF	*Book supplied by RRRLF Kolkata*	*Books Purchased*		
73,147	1169	108	2239	604	77,267

The language wise break-up of the total collection is as follows : Telugu 60,497, English 13,718, Hindi 2039, Urdu 359 and other languages 654.

Periodical Subscription

A total of 119 periodicals are received in the library during the year 204-05 in the languages such as Telugu and English. The following table provides figures for the periodical subscribed and received as gratis.

	Telugu			English			
	D	W	M	D	W	M	Total
Purchased	8	5	28	5	7	22	75
Gratis	6	3	20	–	–	15	44
Total	14	8	48	5	7	37	119

Membership and Readership

The total membership and readership of the library for the 2004-05 stood at 3988 and 2,29,075 respectively. Of the 2,29,075 readership 1,02,039 visited periodical section and 1,27,036 visited book section of the library.

Book Consulted and Lent

During the year 2004-05, a total of 171,479 books were consulted with in the library and 13,015 books were lent for home reading.

Book Collections Added

During the year 2004-05 books were added to the existing collections by purchase from the funds of the library and book received from DPL/RRRLF Scheme, Director RRRLF and through gratis from the public. The following table provides figures for books received from these four sources.

Sources	No. of titles	No. of Books	Total
By Purchase		2239	2239
DPL/RRRLF	1162	1169	1169
Director, RRRLF	108	108	108
By gratis	–	604	604
Total			4120

A total of 4120 books were added to the existing collections during the year 2004-05.

Extension Activities

In addition to normal library services, the library has under taken a number of extension activities such National Library week celebrations during the month of November, birthday celebrations of national leaders, organising book exhabitions, literary and cultural activities and forming reading circles. During the year 2004-05, the library celebrated birthday of NalamKrishna Rao the founder of the library and of Dr. B.R. Ambedkar, Dr. S.R. Ranganathan, Mahatma Gandhi and Independence day and Republic day celebrations. In addition, the library has organised 10 book exhibitions, 3 filmshows, 32 literary activities 12 cultural programmes and formed 6 reading circles.

An Estimation of the library

The library had its genesis before the formation of Andhra Desa Library Association and contributed greatly for the genesis and spread of library movement in Andhra Desa. Chilakamarthi Lakshmi Narasimham who presided over the First Andhra Desa Library Representatives Conference held at Bezawada on April 10, 1914 stated in his presidential address that perhaps he was chosen to preside over the conference because he happened to be the Librarian of Veeresalingam Library, Rajahmundry, one of the libraries merged later to form the Gowtami Library.

This leading library which has rendered yeomen service for the spread of knowledge among the people in general and contributed substantially for the growth of scholarship in Andhra Pradesh in particular receded to the background in its activities after Independence. The successive managements could not do much to keep up activities of the library. For nearly two and half decades the library has been completely neglected and this resulted in the colossal loss and damage of its valuable collection. No proper attention was given for the care and preservation of library's rich collection.

This deteriorating situation was averted by the Government of Andrha Pradesh when it took over the management of the library on 9th February, 1979. This takeover by the Government put a halt to further deterioration and enabled it to consolidate itself and render normal services to the user community. The Government of Andhra Pradesh should pay special attention for the development of this library as a research center and it should not be treated on par with other regional libraries in the state.

References

1. Sri Gowtami Grandhalayam, Rajhmundry. *Annual Report*, 1919.
2. *Grandhala Pragati*, Part 1. (Vijayawada, A.P. Library Association, 1962), p.1.
3. Sri Gowtami Library, Rajahmundry. *Rules and Regulations*, p.1.
4. Sri Gautami Library, Rajahmundry. *Brochure*, p.2.
5. Sri Gowtami Library, Rajahmundry, *Annual Report, 1978-79*.
6. Brief note circulated by Sri Gowtami Library, Rajahmundry, n.d., p.1.
7. Ibid, p.1.
8. Ibid, p.2.
9. A.A.N. Raju, *History of Library Movement in Andhra Pradesh (1900-1956)*. (Delhi, Ajanta Publications, 1988), pp.46-47.
10. Ibid, p.47.
11. Ibid, p.49.
12. A.R. Chandrika. Sri Gowtami Regional Library, Rajahmundry. In National Confrerence on Reorientation of Library Services in India, 18-20, August 2007. *Sonvenir*, (Vijayawada, A.P. Library Association, 2007), p. 66.
13. Narasimham, Chilakamarthi: "Presidential address to the First Andhra Desa Library Representatives Conference", Bezawada, April 10, 1914, IN *Grandhalaya Pragati*, Part 1. (Vijayawada, A.P. Library Association, 1962), pp.1-7.

Source : *Annual Report of Sri Gowtami Govt. Regional Library, Rajahmundry, 2004–05.*

F

ZILLA GRANDHALAYA SAMSTHAS (ZGSS)

The Zilla Grandhalaya Samsthas were constituted under section 9(1) of the A.P. Public Libraries Act, 1960 one for each revenue districts and also one for the twincities of Hyderabad

ZILLA GRANDHALAYA SAMSTHAS (ZGSs)

and Secunderabad. These were reconstituted in 1988-89 under section 10 of the Act (as amended by Act. No. 13 of 1987) one for twincities of Hyderabad and Secunderabad and one each for other twenty two (22) revenue districts in the state.

The ZGSS of each district consists of members nominated by the government from among the residents of the district (three) who have rendered eminent.service in the field of education or public libraries; one member nominated by the government from among the presidents of the governing bodies of the aided libraries in the district; one member nominated by the government from among councillors of either Municipal Corporations or the Municipalities of the districts; Two members nominated by the government from among the presidents of Mandal Panchayats in the district ; the District Education officer (DEO) concerned Ex-officio; the Deputy Director of Adult Education of the district, Ex-officio, the librarian, District Central Library, Ex-officio, Who shall be the Member Secretary. The Government shall nominate one of the non-official members as the chairman of the Zilla Grandhalaya Samasthas. The same composition of ZGSS shall apply to Hyderabad City Grandhalaya Samstha also except that the presidents of the Mandal Panchayats and District Panchayat officers are not members of that Samastha.

Objectives of ZGSS

Most of the ZGSS in the state, with few exceptions, have listed the following as their objectives :

1. To establish, equip, maintain and develop an integrated, comprehensive and efficient library services in the district.
2. To develop infrastructure facilities viz; buildings, furniture and equipment to public libraries in the district.
3. To augument the supply of books and periodicals to all public libraries in the district.

4. To prepare and implement long term and short term plans for improving library services in the district; and
5. To raise finances and regulate their usage for the promotion of library services in the district.

The following sections of this chapter briefly deal with 23ZGSS alphabetically with respect to the establishment of the ZGS, total number of libraries, accommodation, staff position book stock, membership, readership, boooks consulted, books lent for home reading, purchase of books and books received from other agencies, librarycess collection, development indicators, extension activities and status of privately managerd public libraries.

The following abbreviations are used in the succeeding pages.

BDC	: Book Deposit Centre
BL	: Branch Library
DCL	: District Central Library
DPL	: Director of Public Libraries
LLA	: Local Library Authority
ML	: Mobile Library
RL	: Rural Library/Regional Library
SCL	: State Central Library
VL	: Village Library
ZGS	: Zilla Grandhalaya Samstha.

F.1. Zilla Grandhalaya Samstha (ZGS) : Adilabad

Adilabad district consists of 13 towns, 52 Mandals and 1559 villages. The Zilla Grandhalaya Samstha (ZGS) was formed in 1958 with three Branch Libraries (BLS) to startwith. The District Central Library was established in the 1959. The district is a border district to Maharashtra and therefore the influence of Marathi language is very much evident in the district. In almost six Mandals, Marathi is spoken by the people. The collection in the libraries is more on Marathi langauage. Gradually the situation changed and Telugu language gained importance after formation Andhra Pradesh in 1956. At present the library collection in the libraries consists of five languages such as Marathi, Urdu, Telugu, English and Hindi. The collection on literature is more in Marathi and Urdu.

Number of Libraries

The type and number libraries functioning in the year 2003 is shown in the following table

Type of library	*No.*
District Central Library (DCL)	1
Branch Libraries (BLs)	51
Rural Libraries (RLs)	3
Mobile Libraries (MLs)	2
Book Deposite Centres (BDCs)	25
Total	82

The DCL and 48 BLs were managed by professionally qualified people. Six BLs were manage by Record Assistants/ one BL by Attender and one BL by Parttime worker. As on 31st March 2002 there were 23,916 Male, 19,692 Female and 2,153 child totaling 45,761 registesed borrowers in the ZGS.

During the year 2006-07 the number of sanctioned libraries were 165 of which 87 were functioning and 78 were not functioning. The following table provides figures for various types of libraries sanctioned, functioning and not functioning by the end of 31.03.07.

Category of library	*No. of Libraries Sanctioned*	*No. of libraries functioning as on 31.03.07*	*No. of libraries not functioning as on 31.03.07*
DCL	1	1	–
Br. Lib Grade I	–	–	–
Br. Lib Grade II	5	5	–
Br. Lib Grade III	42	38	4
Br. Lib. R. Asst.	7	7	–
Village Libraries	3	3	–
Mobile Libraries	3	–	3
BDCS	61	32	29
Aided libraries	8	–	8
Panchayat Libraries	34	–	34
	165	87	78

Note : R. Asst. means Record Asst. P.T. Lib means Parttime Librarian. Some of the BLS were managed by Record Assts and Parttime Librarians. In the above table Aided libraries and Panchayat Libraries does not come under sanctioned libraries. Actually the libraries sanctioned during the year 2006-07 are DCLI does not come undersantioned libraries BLs 55, VLS3, MLS3 and BDCS 61.

Library Staff

The following table provides figures for various categories of library staff working in ZGS in the year 2003 and also number of sanctioned and vacant posts.

S.No.	*Category*	*Sanctioned Posts*	*Vacant Posts*
1.	District Central Librarian	1	–
2.	Senior Asst	–	1
3.	Junior Asst.	–	1
4.	Typist	–	1
5.	Dy. Librarian	–	1

6.	Grade II Librarian	6	2
7.	Grade III Librarian	42	1
8.	Record Asst.	10	3
9.	Attender	21	–
10.	Part time workers	33	23
11.	Daily wagers	4	1
	Total	108	33

From the above table it can be inferred that out of 108 sanctioned posts, 33 posts were lying vacant due to ban imposed by the government on new recruitment and filling up of existing vacancies. Almost one third of the posts of different categories were vacant. It is rather difficult to run the ZGS and its BLS effectively with the lack of sufficient staff.

During the year 2006-07 sanctioned posts of various categories rose to 129 of which 55 posts were vacant. The following table provides figures for sanctioned and vacant posts.

Category	*Sanctioned*	*Vacant*
DCL/Secretary	1	–
Dy-Librarian	1	1
Librarians, Grade II	6	3
Librarians, Grade III	43	6
Sr. Assistant	1	–
Jr. Assistant	1	1
Typist	1	1
Record Assistants	10	5
Attenders	21	7
Part time workers	33	24
Rickshaw pullers	3	2
Part time librarians	4	3
Part time Watchmen	4	2
Total	129	55

Library Buildings

The DCL and 9 BLS have their own buildings. Four BLS were functioning under rented buildings and rest of the BLS were functioning in rent free buildings such Gram Panchayat buildings.

During the year 2006-07, 11 libraries were housed in own buildings, 2 in rented and 42 in rent free buildings. The following table provides figures for type of libraries and nature of library buildings.

Type of library	*Own Bld.*	*Rented Bld*	*Rent free Bld.*
DCL	01	–	–
BLS	10	02	39
VLS	–	–	3
Total	11	02	42

Book Collections

As on 31st March 2002, total book collection at DCL was 33,805 and in all BLS 2,07,242. In RLS the total collection was 4260 totalling 2,34,821 books in the entire public library system. The languagewise break up was as follows :

Telugu	1,89,885
English	21,304
Hindi	14,206
Urdu	6,801
Other languages (including Marathi)	2,625
Total	2,34,821

During the year 2006-07 the total book collection stood at 302902. The following table provides figures for the book collections available in various types of libraries as on 31.03.07.

DCL	33805
BLS	264618
VLS	4303
MLS	176
Total	302902

Periodical Collection

During the year 2006-07 the ZGS has subscribed to 1033 periodicals. The following table provides figures for periodicals subscribed in Telugu, English, Hindi, Urdu and other languages.

The language wise break-up is that out of 61 periodicals subscribe to DCL : Telugu 31, English 17, Hindi 9, Urdu 3 and others 2. Out of 914 periodicals subscribed to BLS : Telugu 732, English 96, Hindi 38, Urdu 40 and others 83. Out of 26 periodicals subscribed to VLS : Telugu 21, English, Hindi 14. 32 Telugu titles are subscribed to BDCS.

Membership

The total membership of the ZGS as on 31.03.2007 stood at 29372. The break-up was DCL 5650, BLS 23722, VLS 210. There has been 5.93% increase in the membership during the year 2006-07.

Readership

The total readership of ZGS as on 31.03.07 stood at 1956473. The breaking was DCL 256942, BLS 1687003, VLS 12528. There has been 78.32% increase of readership during the 2006-07.

Book Consulted

A total of 245999 books were consulted during the year 2006-07. The break-up was DCL 55053 and BLs 190946. There has been an increase of 70.76% of book consultation during the year 2006-07.

Books Lent for Home Reading

A total of 1,88,871 books were lent for home reading during the year 2006-07. The break-up was DCL 28482 and BLs 160389. There has been 39.55% increase in book lending during the said period.

Category of Library	Telugu				English				Hindi				Urdu				Other languages				
	D	W	FN	M	D	W	FN	M	D	W	FN	M	D	W	FN	M	D	W	FN	M	Total
DCL	7	6	3	15	3	5	3	6	2	3	3	2	–	–	–	–	1	–	–	–	61
Gr II Libraries	28	19	10	42	8	10	2	8	5	2	–	–	5	1	1	5	2	–	–	–	148
Gr III Libraries	168	260	70	135	34	18	2	14	18	6	2	5	12	8	2	6	6	–	–	–	766
VLS...	5	6	2	8	1	1	1	1	–	–	–	–	–	–	–	–	–	–	–	–	26
BDCS	32	–	–	–	–	–	–	–	–	–	–	–	–	–	–	–	–	–	–	–	32
Total	240	291	85	200	46	34	8	29		10	5	7	20	9	3	11	9	–	–	–	1033

No. of books received from different sources

In addition to purchase of books from its own budget the ZGS has received books from DPL, RRLF, Kolkata and also form the public as gratis. The following table provides figures for the reciept of books from various sources during the year 2006-07.

Sources	*No. of books*	*Language wise break-up Telugu*	*English*	*Urdu*	*Hindi*	*Others*	*Total*
By Purchase	14401	10949	2996	130	326	–	14401
DPL/RRRLF	6957	6025	583	16	223	110	6957
DPL/RRRLF	3228	1105	2105	–	18	–	3228
Direct or, RRRLF	439	–	134	–	305	–	439
Gratis	112	90	16	–	5	–	112

Extension Activities

In addition to celebrating national holidays and birth and death anniversaries eminent Indians, the ZGS has been celebrating National Library week every year during November 14-20 by organising essay writing, debating, painting and sports competitions. During the year 2006-07, the ZGS at its DCL and BLS have organised and conducted 202 extension activities, cultural activities and inservice training programmes. The break up was : inservice training programmes 46, book exhibitions 52, literary activities 52 and cultural activities 52.

Development Activities

During the 1999-2000 with the financial support from RRRLF, Kolkata Rs 2,10,492 worth storage material was acquired and distributed to 51 BLS and RLS. Again in the year 2000-2001 Rs 17,9701 worth almirahs and book racks were purchased and distributed to BLS at Nirmal, Bhainsa and Laksetipeta. In the year 1999-2000 Rs. 11.95 lakhs worth books in different languages were purchased and distributed to BLS with the funds received under janmabhoomi programme. Library buildings were constructed for BLS at

Mudhol and Narsapur. For Bhainsa BL building, RRRLF, Kolkata released a grant of Rs 200,000 as first instalment and construction work would be commenced shortly. For nine BLS land was accquired. The Grampanchayat at Tansi gave building freely for establishing BL.

Future Plans

The ZGS wants to computerwise the DCL and provide Internet facility and filling the vacancies at the earliest. With the funds expected from RRRLF, MPLADS and donations from the public, the ZGS wish to construct library buildings, acquisition of storage materials for BLS and to open competitive examination resources centre at the DCL.

What Lies Ahead

During the year 2001-02 the ZGS realized a sum of Rs 16,80,815 as library cess from 866 Gram Panchayats and 7 Municipalities. The government has sanctioned a grant of Rs 79,43,000. But the cess collection was partial. Many Municipalities and Grampanchayats does not release library cess to the ZGS in time. Consequently the ZGS was not able to meet its commitments and facing several problems. The apathy of the government and imposition of ban or recruitment and opening up of new BLS stunted the growth and development of public library system in the district. Unless streamling of library cess collection and lifting of ban was not done the expansion of library services to all the village having population of 5000 and more was very difficult to achieve. The ZGS has shown some progress during the year 2006-07 in respect of book collections, members, readership, book consultation with in the premises of DCL and BLS and book lending for home reading. But still a long way to go to realise its cherished objectives.

Sources : 1. K. Ramadevi, 'Andhra Pradesh lo Zilla Grandhalaya Samsthalu: Adilabad Zilla' *Grandhalaya Sarvaswamu*. V64, N3, May 03, pp. 2-5.

2. *Annual Report of Zilla Grandhalaya Samstha, Adilabad, 2006–07* (Mimeographed).

F.2. Zilla Grandhalaya Samstha (ZGS): Anantapur

Anantapur district played a prominent role in the genesis and spread of library movement not only in Rayalaseema but also in Andhra pradesh. In the year 1952 Local library authority (LLA) was formed for Anantapur District as per provisions of Madras Public Libraries Act of 1948. Pappuru Ramacharyulu a prominent personality of Rayalaseema became the first chairman of LLA of Anantapur. The District Central Library came into being in 1952 and it was housed temporarily in Ramachary's house as suitable building was not available immediately. Ramacharyulu strove hard to have a building for the District Central Library in the year 1965 with an open auditorium called 'Bhuvana Vijaya Mandapam constructed in 1969. During the stellar leadership of Kaulluri Subha Rao another prominent public figure and politician of Rayalaseema who served as chairmen of LLA from 1954 to 1960, a large number of Branch librarians (BLS) were established in the semi urban and rural areas of Anantapur District, and took effective steps for the collection of library cess from the local bodies.

No. of Libraries

As on 31.03.2007 the ZGS has 140 libraries of various types. The following table provides figures for various types of libraries.

	Type of library	*No*
1.	District Central Library (DCL)	01
2.	Branch Libraries (BLS)	69
3.	Village Libraries (VLS)	09
4.	Book Deposite Centres (BDCS)	61
	Total	140

Library Staff

As on 31.03.2007 the ZGS has sanctioned strength of 124 staff members of various categories of which 46 posts were lying vacant. The following table provides figures for categories of sanctioned staff, presently working and vacant posts.

Category of Post	*Sanctioned*	*Now Working*	*Vacant*
1. DCL	01	01	–
2. Libr Grade I	04	02	02
3. Libr Grade II	08	–	08
4. Libr Grade III	50	38	12
5. Sr. Asst.	01	–	01
6. Jr Asst.	02	02	–
7. Record Asst.	18	14	04
8. Attender	40	21	19
Total	124	78	46

Library Buildings

It is one of the first local library authorities (Presently Zilla Grandhalaya Samastha) in the state to have own library building for the District Central Library at Anantapur in 1965. The following table gives us an idea of the library buildings in the district public library system as obtained by the end of 31.03.07.

Type of Library	*Own Bld*	*Rented Bld*	*Free Bld*	*Total*
District Central Library	01	–	–	01
Branch Libraries	20	10	39	69
Rural Libraries	9	–	–	9
Book Deposit Centres	06	55	–	61
Total	36	65	39	140

Book Stocks

The total book stock as on 31.03.07 stood at 5,91,092.

The language wise break-up of book stock in different libraries was as follows :

	DCL	BLS	VLS	MLS	Total
(a) Telugu	25334	433980	10557	–	469871
(b) English	13308	67539	1327	–	82174
(c) Hindi	1496	12026	48	–	13570
(d) Urdu	544	2035	–	–	5178
(e) other languages	1059	21829	10	–	22898
Total	41741	537409	11942	–	5,91,092

Category Wise Break-up

(a) Children books	7953	107259	1050	–	115212
(b) Reference books	1965	916444	545	–	94154
(c) Text books	1876	16016	501	–	18393
(d) Books for neoliterates	–	–	–	–	–
(e) Fiction books	18235	166208	7669	–	192112
(f) Non-fiction books	11712	156282	2177	–	170171
Total	41741	537409	11942	–	590042

Periodicals Subscribed

During the year 2006-07, the ZGS has subscribed to a total of 1491 Periodicals for the DCL, BLS and VLS. The language wise break-up is as follows :

(a) Telugu	1240
(b) Enlgish	219
(c) Hindi	–
(d) Urdu	16
(e) other languages	16
Total	1491

Registered Borrowers

The usage of the library collections is indicated by the enrollment of registered borrowers by the ZGS. During the year

2006-07, the ZGS has 40652 registered borrowers which consists 5728 at DCL, 34543 at all BLS and 381 at all VLS. The following table provides for category wise break-up of membership obtained at DCL, BLS and VLS.

Category	*DCL*	*BLS*	*VLS*	*Total*
(a) Professionals	1275	2950	75	4300
(b) Farmers/Agriculturists	704	5792	35	6531
(c) Businessmen	314	5117	34	5465
(d) Students	896	7386	127	8409
(e) Housewives	112	3196	25	3333
(f) Employees	1431	5181	32	6644
(g) Unemployed	996	4921	53	5970
Total	5728	34543	381	4065

Readership

The number of readers who visit the district public library system is indicative of usage of library collections. During the 2006-07 a total of 1,66,8,874 readers visited the DCL, BLS, VLS and BDCS. The following table provides break-up figures of readers who visited these libraries.

Names of sactions	*DCL*	*BLS*	*VLS*	*BDCS*	*Total*
(a) Periodicals section	187961	1035644	–	–	1223605
(b) Book section	67282	177987	–	–	1668874

Books Consulted

The number of books and other types of reading materials consulted by the user community is another indication of usage of library collections. The following table provides figures for the number of book consulted within the libraries and type of books consulted during the year 2006-07.

Type of book consulted	*DCL*	*BLS*	*Total*
(a) Text books	23746	15056	38802
(b) Ref. books	7149	21211	28360
(c) Non fiction	10813	36217	47030
(d) Fiction	20083	39562	59644
Total	61790	112046	173836

Books Lent

There is correlation between the number of regist borrowers and the number of books lent to them. A total of 71,433 books were lent for home reading during the year 2006-07. The following table provides the type of books lent for home reading by DCL and BLS.

Type of books	*DCL*	*BLS*	*Total*
(a) Fiction	4119	33610	37729
(b) Non-Fiction	1373	32331	33704
Total	5492	65941	71433

Extension Activities

Extension activities are another important mechanism through which the library services and its collections are publicised to attract more readers. During the year 2006-07 the ZGS through its DCL, BLS have organised a total of 208 programmes of various types. The following table provides figures for various types of activities carried out by the ZGS.

Type of Programmes	*DCL*	*BLS*	*Total*
(a) Book exhibitions	02	52	54
(b) Film shows	04	47	51
(c) Lectures	10	17	27
(d) Classes	–	–	–
(e) Discussions	02	13	15
(f) Seminars/Conferences	01	07	08
(g) Staff training classes	–	–	–
(h) Other programmes	01	52	53
Total	20	188	208

Aided Libraries

There are ten public libraries run by private managements in the districts which have recognised by the DPL for grant in aid. One of such library is Edward Cornation Reading Room established in 1926 at Dharmavaram. None of these libraries have received any aid either from the ZGS, Anantpur or from DPL, Govt of A.P.

Growth Indicators for Seven Year Period ie; 1995 to 2002

The Anantapur Grandhalaya Samstha (LLA) achieved marked progress in respect of acquisitions of books, enrollment of new members, visitors to libraries, lendings of books for home reading, library buildings and collection of librarycess. The following table provides, progress achieved in the mentioned indicators from 1995 to 2002.

Future Plans

The Grandhalaya Samastha committee intends to provide reading material useful for competitive examinations in all Branch Libraries. Computersation of District Central Library and Branch Libraries in a phased manner and provision of text book sections in all branch libraries is another important item in the agenda of future plans. With funds from Raja Rammohan Roy Library Foundation, Kolkata (RRRLF) MPLALDS, EAS, Janmabhumi, the committee intends to consturct library buildings for branch libraries. With a view to render better library services to user community, workshops and refreshers courses are conducted at regular intervals to the library staff. If the need arises library staff also serve as volunteers and supervisors in adult education centres. With the support and cooperation fromt the Gram Panchayats and Vidya Committees in the district, reading materials to be supplied for rendering libraray services where there are no branch libraries in the rural areas.

Indicators	*1995-96*	*1996-97*	*1997-98*	*19898-99*	*1999-2000*	*2000-01*	*2001-02*
Books	4,13,880	4,42,960	4,33,720	4,38,001	4,62,181	4,67,092	4,73,054
Membership	20,763	34,670	34,917	33,750	33,552	34,128	35,167
Visitors to libraries	12,04,534	6,99,125	7,29,123	9,21,452	10,55,751	1,18961	12,76,667
Book lending	2,00,149	2,59,816	2,20,001	1,28,206	1,12,831	1,13,113	89,509
Library Building	–	–	–	1	6	–	2
Librarycess collection	14,61,149	21,98,836	25,70,575	28,41,570	33,04,291	31,31,352	36,26,197

Present Position of Private Libraries in the District

During the thick of the library movement many libraries were established in the district by energetic youth for the cause of independence, spread of adult education, social reforms and eradication of untouchability. Due to the ravages of time many of these libraries have disappeared from the scene. But some of them have survived and rendering useful library services to the community even today. Mention may be made of : 1. Edward Cornation Reading Room and Saraswati Nilayam, Dharmavaram, 2. Sri Sarada Mitra Grandhalaya Mandali, Betapalli (Gutti Tq), 3. SriVijaya Vidyardhi Grandhalayam, Belaguppa (Kalyanadurgam Tq), 4. Gramaseva Mandira Grandhalayam, Nimmapuram, (Kalyanadurgam Tq), 5. Arya Vysya Grandhalayam and 6. Sanghamitra Reading Room, Anantapuram.

Stalwarts of Library Movement

Anantapur District was fortunate in having stalwarts of the library movement like Pappuru Ramacharyulu (1898-1972), Kalluru Subha Rao (1897-1972), Battula Venkata Rama Reddy and scores of others who devoted their lives for the spread of library movement in the district and helped to carve out niche in the history of library movement not only in Rayalaseema but also in the entire Andhra Pradesh.

Sources : 1. R.Sarada, "Andhra Pradesh lo Zilla Grandhalaya Samsthalu : Anantapuram Zilla". *Grandhalaya Sarvaswamu*, V63, N7, October 2002, pp. 2-5.

2. R. Sarada, 'Anantapuram Zilla lo Grandhalayodhayamam'. *Grandhalaya Sarvaswamu*, V63, N7, Octo. 2002, pp. 6-8.

3. Zilla Grandhalaya Samstha, Anantapur : *State Administration Report for the year 2006-07*. (Mimeographed).

F.3. Zilla Grandhalaya Samstha (ZGS):Chittoor

The Chittoor District Local Library Authority was formed in the year 1952 as a result of Madras Public Libraries Act, 1948. Eminent Personalities like Dr. Kattamanchi Ramalinga Reddy popularly known as C.R. Reddy and world renowed philosopher Jiddu Krishna Murthy and the first qualified director of Public Libraries, Govt. of A.P., K. Raghava Reddy hail from the district. During his stewardship as a director he worked ceaselessly for the growth and development of Zilla Grandhalaya Samasthas in the state.

No. of Libraries

In the year 2004-05 the Chittoor Grandhalaya Samastha in addition to District Central Library, has 69 Branch Libraries (BLS) 38 book Deposit Centres (BDCS) and 7 Village Libraries (VLS). In addition, the system has 1 women's library 2 childrens libraries. The following table shows the type of the library and their numbers.

Type of Library	*Nos.*
District Central Library	1
Branch Libraries	69
Women's Library	1
Childrens Libraries	2
Village Libraries	7
Book Deposite Centres	38
Total	118

Library Staff

The sanctioned posts of all categories for the Zilla Grandhalaya Samastha was 166 of which 60 posts were lying vacant in view of the ban on recruitment imposed by the state government.

The following table provides figures for various types sanctioned posts and the number of vacant positions.

S.No.	Type of Post	Sanctioned Posts	Vacant Posts.
1.	Secretary (Librarian)	1	–
2.	DyLibrarian	1	–
3.	Sr. Assistant	1	–
4.	Jr. Assistant	1	1
5.	Typist	1	1
6.	Grade I Librarians	3	2
7.	Grade II – do –	9	3
8.	Grade III – do –	59	13
9.	Record Assts	5	4
10.	Attenders	31	10
11.	Night Watchmen/Sweepers	4	–
12.	Village Library Assts	7	7
13.	Part time workers	39	19
	Total	166	60

Library Buildings

The Committee of ZGS was striving hard to provide own library buildings to all its branch libraries. The Districts Central Library and some of the Branch Libraries were housed in the own library buildings. Eleven branch libraries were housed in rented buildings. Rest of the BLS were housed in the free buildings. Village libraries and Book Deposit Centres were also housed in free buildings. The following table provides figures for library buildings such as own, rent free and rented for housing various types of libraries as on 31.03.2005.

Type of Library	Own	Rented	Rent free	Total
DCL	1	–	–	1
BLS	17	9	43	69

Development Activities

During the years 1991-96, with the financial support from RRRLF, Kolkata storage material such as almirahs, racks worth

Rs 2,32,080 was purchased for 603 branch libraries. In the 2002-03 RRRLF supplied 4006 books worth Rs. 2,98,998.

Book Collection

As on 31.03.2005 the total book of the ZGS at its all types of libraries stood at 468367. The following table provides figures for the total books available at different types of libraries.

Type of Library	*Total books*
DCL	45363
BLS	423025
Total	468388

The total book stock includes 8214 books received under DPL/RRRLF matching grant scheme and also 281 from RRRLF, Kolkata, 993 books purchased from ZGS own funds and 195 books as gratis during the year 2004-05. The language wise break-up is Telugu 402076, English 34978, Hindi 12887, Urdu 2977 and other languages 15154.

Periodicals subscribed

During the year 2004-05 the ZGS has subscribed to a total of 1402 periodicals to its libraries. The following table provided figures for the number of periodicals of various frequencies subscribed for the libraries.

Type of library	*No. of Periodicals Subscribed*
DCL	63
BL Grade I	116
BL Grade II	195
BL Grade III	1028
Total	1402

The total includes 231Dailies, 260 Weeklies, 64 Fort nightlies and 567 Mohntlies in Telugu and 73 Dailies, 72 Weeklies, 9 Fortnightlies and 88 Monthlies in English and only one monthly in Hindi.

Membership

During the year 2004-05 the total membership stood at 38674. The break-up is as follows :

Type of library	*Total membership*
DCL	5493
BLS	33181
Total	38674

Readership

During the year 2004-05 a total of 2561018 readers visited the district public library system to use its services. The following table provides figures for number of readers visited each type of public library.

Type of Library	*No. of readers visiting Periodical section*	*Book section*	*Total*
DCL	163488	48478	211966
BLS	1757814	5914238	2349052
Total	1921302	639716	2561018

Book consulted

A total of 397320 books were consulted during the year 2004-05. The following table provides figures for total books consulted at DCL and BLS.

Type of library	*Total books consulted*
DCL	36974
BLS	360346
Total	397320

Books lent for home reading

A total of 242396 books were lent for home reading by the ZGS libraries during the year 2004-05. The following table provides figures for books lent by DCL and BLS.

Type of library	*Total books lent*
DCL	11504
BLS	230892
Total	242396

Books Added by Purchase ; etc

During the year 2004-05 the ZGS has purchased 917 books worth Rs 133622 from its funds. It has received a total of 8195 books under DPL/RRRLF matching scheme and 281 books directly from RRRLF, Kolkata. It has also received a total of 53 books as gratis.

Library cess

Library cess is one of the most important sources of revenue to the ZGS in the state. During the year 2004-05, the ZGS has realised a sum of Rs 1,41,63,285 as librarycess from the muncipalities and local bodies in the district. The following table provides figures for the cess realised from these local bodies.

Name of the local body	*Cess Realised during 2004-05*
Municipal Corporation	–
Municipalities (5)	1,19,28219.00
Gram Panchayat's	2235066.00
1. Notified (63)	2176069.00
2. Non-notified (1093)	58997.00
Total	1,41,63,285.00

Extension Activities

During the year 2004-05, the ZGS has organised a number of extension activities and celebrated national events. The District Public Library System has organised 3 workshops, 70 book exhibitions, 25 filmshows, 85 literary activities and 440 cultural activities.

Future Plans

The library committee plans to computerise District Central Library and instal Internet facility. With the financial support from RRRLF, Kolkata, MP, LADS and funds from Zilla Grandhalaya Samastha, the ZGS committee intends to construct library buildings for Branch Libraries.

Stalwarts of the Library Movement

Mention may be made of some of the prominent persons who devoted their engieres for the spread of library movement in the district before independence. These persons include B. Narsimha Rao, Vatambati Venkatarayashresthi, T. Godvindaswamy Shreshti, C.V. Rangam Shresthi, B. Ramanujualu Reddy and Srinivasa charyulu.

Sources : 1. C. Udaya Kumari, Andhra Pradesh lo Zilla Grandhalaya Samsthalu : Chittoor Zilla. *Grandhalaya Sarvaswamu* V64, N5, August 2004. pp. 2-5.

2. *Annual Report of Zilla Grandhalaya Samstha : Chittoor District*. 2004-05.

F.4. Zilla Grandhalaya Samstha (ZGS) : East Godavari

East Godavari District is one of the developed districts of Andhra Pradesh. It consist of 57 revenue mandals and 1317 habitated villages. The district played a prominent role in genesis and development of library movement in Coastal Andhra region. Eminent telugu literaturer and social reformer Kandukuri Veeresalingam and the father of library movement in Andhra pradesha Padmasri Ayyanki Venkata Ramamiah hail from this district.

East Godavari Zilla Grandhalaya Samstha (ZGS) was established in 1950 with the head quarters at Kakinada as a result of Madras Public Libraries Act, 1948. The District Central Library (DCL) was also established in 1950 and initially located at Brahma Samajam building.

No. of Libraries

As on 2006-07 in the ZGS, there were 215 libraries of various types. The break up is as follows :

Type of library	Sanctioned strength	Non functional Number
District Central Library (DCL)	01	0
Branch Libraries (BLS)	97	–
Rural Libraries (RLS)	51	7
Book Deposit Centres (BDCS)	61	18
Mobile Libraries (MLS)	05	0
Total	215	25

In the light of the above table one can conclude that the DCL and all the 97 BLS are functioning. Out of 51 RLS only 44 and out of 61 BDCS only 43 are functioning. All the 05 MLS stopped functioning.

Library Buildings

The building for DCL was constructed in the year 1977 during the chairmanship of K.V.Kondala Rao who served as a chairman of ZGS for almost 15 years from 1971-1985. The first floor was constructed in the year 1985, which provides for a meeting hall and technical sections. In the ground floor Newspapers section, Reference section, Lending section. Office, of Secretary, ZGS and Chairman's office have been located.

The building for BL at Malikipuram was constructed in the year 1991on the free land given by the philanthropists of the village. The building for BL at Kothapeta was constructed in the year 1999. The following tables provides the position of library buildings.

Lib. Buildings	Own blds.	Rented blds.	Free accommodation	Total
1. DCL	1	–	–	1
2. BLS	50	14	33	97
3. RLS	2	–	42	44

Library Staff

The sanctioned posts for the ZGS was 204. But of out

of these, only 156 posts have been filled up. Forty six posts have been lying vacant and were not filled up due to governments ban on recruitment of staff in the ZGSS of the state. Sixty staff members posses CLSC certificate and seven staff members BLISc degrees.

Staff Position

The total sanctioned posts as on 01.04.07 was 273 of which 72 posts were vacant. The following table provides figures for various categories of sanctioned posts and the posts vacant under each category. Forty libraries were working with single persons.

Category of post	*Sanctioned*	*Vacant*
Dist. Central Librarian/Secretary, G.S.	1	–
Libn Grade I	6	3
Libn Grade II	11	2
Libn Grade III	47	12
Senior Asst	1	–
Junior Asst	2	–
Typist	2	–
Binder	2	–
Record Asst	1	–
Attender	51	9
Watchman	80	25
Village Libn (Rural)	51	8
Part time workers	18	12
Total	273	72

Library Collections

As on 31.03.07 the DCL posses 53,761 books. In all the BLS taken together the total books collection was 9.70 lakhs. A total of 1,99,032 readers visited the DCL during the year 2000-2001. In the same year a total of 20,49,420 readers visited all BLS in the ZGS library system and had 89,007 registered borrowers.

Progress Achieved During Five Year Period

The following table provides an idea as to the progress achieved by the ZGS during five year period ie; 1995-96 to 1999-2000.

Indicators	*1995-96*	*1996-97*	*1997-98*	*1998-99*	*1999-2000*
Books (in lakhs)	9.30	9.57	9.53	9.67	9.70
Membership (in lakhs)	0.68	0.71	0.76	0.75	0.77
Library visitors (in lakhs)	21.50	21.00	23.00	21.00	21.00
Books lent for home reading (in lakhs)	7.81	7.75	6.87	6.09	6.00
Buildings constructed	2	0	1	2	10
Librarycess collected (Rs in lakhs)	42,47,333	47,01,139	48,83,295	50,67,155	4,45,041

The govt has sanctioned 26 BDCS for the year 2001-02.

The total book collection in the ZGS Public library system during the year 2006-07 was as follows :

Net book collection as on 31.03.07 was 1116515. The break-up was as follows :

DCL	69,287
BLS	897,205
VLS	123,489
MLS	26,534

The language wise break-up was as follows :

Telugu	990189
English	100450
Hindi	21487
Urdu	1419
Other languages	2610

The total number of periodicals subscribed was as follows:

Telugu	2218
English	322

Membership

The total membership of the ZGS as on 31.03.2007 was 95,886 and the break-up was as follows :

DCL	10,554
BLS	76,440
VLS	6487
MLS	2385

An overall increase of 2.63% was witnessed during the year 2006-07.

Readership

The total readership during the 2006-07 was 343,6046. The break-up was as follows :

DCL	225797
BLS	2665548
VLS	510292
MLS	–
DBCS	–

There has been an increase of 7.88% of the readership in BLS and 1.01% increase of readership in VLS.

Books Consulted

A total of 5,45,830 books were consulted during the year 2006-07. The break-up was as follows :

DCL	28438
BLS	41,9827
VLS	97565
MLS	–
BDCS	–

There has been an increase of 2.60% in books consultation.

Books Lent for Home Reading

A total 4,52,118 books were lent for home reading during the year 2006-07. The break-up was as follows :

DCL	5971
BLS	376,475
VLS	69,772
MLS	–
BDCS	–

Books Purchased and Received from DPL/RRRLF

The following table provides figures for books purchased from ZGS funds and books received from DPL under matching grant from RRRLF and also directly from RRRLF, Kolkata.

	Titles	*Books*
By Purchase	–	39417
DPL/RRRLF	–	4846
Director, RRRLF	–	388
Gratis	3466	3466

The following table provides figures for distribution of books languagewise purchased from ZGS funds to BLS.

	BLS	*VLS*
Telugu	27383	3792
English	6629	263
Hindi	–	–
Total	34012	4055

Achievements

With the funds received from RRRLF, Kolkata storage material worth Rs5.80 lakhs was purchased and supplied to all BLS in the district. In the year 2000-01 funds received from ITDA, new buildings were constructed for BLS at Y.

Ramavaram and Gangavaram. The building for Sakhinetipalli BL was completed in 2001-02.During the 2001-02 sites were acquired for construction of buildings for BLS at Kajuluru, Kattamuru, Gollaprolu, Jaggampeta and Peddapuram. A total of 13 staff members had actively participated in 'akshara sankranti' programmes as volunteers and made 200 persons as literates. In the years 2000-01 and 2001-02 the ZGS has paid Rs 5 lakhs each as matching grant to RRRLF, Kolkata. As a result, construction of library buildings at Rajolu, Kirlampudi, Peddapuram for BLS has been started. The ZGS has spent Rs 12.86 lakhs during the year 2001-02 for acquisition of books for the library system.

Progress achieved

The ZGS has added 56,185 books to its existing collections during the year 2006-07. The book consultation was increased to 7,628 and books issued rose to 4,568 when compared with the year 2003-04. Nine new buildings were constructed to BLS at Places such as : 1. Kesanapalli, 2. Rajanagaram, 3. Korukonda, 4. Lingamparthi, 5. Jaggampeta, 6. Rojole, 7. Peddapuram, 8. Kirlampudi and 9. Thondangi. The ZGS has also acquired six new sites for construction of library buildings at : 1. V.L. Kattamuru, 2. Allavaram, 3. Uppalaguptham, 4. Makavaram, 5. Manapalli and 6. Maredupalli. The ZGS has received the following public donations from 2003-04 to 2006-07

It was a matching donations from the public and also MPLADS funds.

1. B.L. Velangi - ZGS + Public donations (Rs 1.55 + 1.5 lakhs)
2. B.L. Gollaprolu - ZGS + Public donations (Rs. 1.0 + 2.0 lakhs)
3. B.L. Atreyapuram ZGS +Public donations + M.P. Funds (Rs 1.50 + 1.50 + 2.0 lakhs).

The ZGS had set up Competitive Examination Reference unit at DCL, Kakinada during the year 2002-03. In the 2006-07 with the funds from M.P. LADS, computer room was renovrated for installing two servers. LAN points were fixed in all the important sections of DCL.

The ZGC has been actively celebrating National Library Week every year during the month of November 14-20 by arranging essay writing, debating, painting, quiz competitions and distributing prizes to the winners. During the year 2006-07, it has spent Rs 27,500 for conducting NLW at the DCL and BLS.

Future Plans

In the comming five years begining from the year 2002 ZGS wants to establish Reference Section concerning competitive examinations at the DCL and 5 Grade I Libraries. Computerisation of in house operations at the DCL and five Grade I Libraries. With the funds from RRRLF, Kolkata, 'Food for Work Programme', OPLAD and support from the public, the ZGS wants to take up construction of new library buildings. Again with the support from RRRLF it want to purchase of storage material and conducting workshops and refresher courses to the professionals working in the ZGS. With the close collaboration with open schools the ZGS wants spare its professional staff to spare their services to open school students and neoliterates and thereby contributed to growth of literacy in the district. To establish BDCS in hospitals and jails so as to meet the information needs of patients and prisoners. Lastly but not the least to accelerate the process of librarycess collection to the tuen of rupees one crore for the 2002-03 with the participation of the chairman, the secretary and other library staff in the cess collection drive.

Stalwarts of the Library Movement

The District has produced a number of stalwarts who have devoted their life for the cause of library move not only in East Godavari district but actively participated in state and national levels. Mention may be made of Kandukuri Veeresulingam (1848-1919), Chilakemarti Lakshmi Narashimam (1867-1946), Nalamkrishna Rao (1881-1961) and Chelikani Bhavan Rao. Kandkuri constructed a Town hall in Rajahmundary in the year 1891 and established free library in its premises. He was instrumental in the renaissance movement of telugu language, literature and culture and social movements in Andhradesa in the second half of the 19th century.

Chilakamarthi served as a first President of the library established by Nalam Krishna Rao in Rajahmundry. He presided over the first Andhra Desa Bhandagarula Mahasabha at Bezawada held on April 10,1914 and propounded what is known as 'Grandhalaya Vedam'. He also participated in the third Andhradesha Grandhalaya Mahasabha held at Nellore in 1916 and the fourth Andhra Desha Grandhalaya Mahasabha held at Barua in 1917.

Nalam Krishna Rao the poet, social reformer and a nationalist closely worked with Veressalingam and established Veerasalinga Grandhalayam in Nalam choultry and later the name changed as 'Sarvajana Pustaka Bhandagram' (Public library) in 1914, which in later years become nucleus for the genesis of the present Gautami Library. He served as first Secretary of Andhradesha Grandhalaya Sangham. He presided order the 11th Andhra Desha Grandhalaya Maha Sabha held at Eluru in 1926.

Chelikani Bhavana Rao was the spirit behind the survival and working even today, of Sri Suryaraya Vidyananda Grandhalayam established in 1915 at Pitikapuram. He served as Vice president, Jt.secretary and member of executive committee of Andhra Desha Grandhalaya Sangham (ADLA) for several years. For a number of years he served as Hon.Secretary of ADLA East Godavari District Branch. He was instrumental for the establishment and growth of several private libraries in the district with his advice and support.

Sources : 1. D. Ananda Mohan Bose, 'Andhra Pradesha lo Zilla Grandhalaya Samsthalu: Toorpu Godavri Zilla'. *Grandhalaya Sarvaswami*, V63, N5, August 02, pp.2-6.

2. P. Chiranjivinikumari and H. Subha Rao, 'Charitra putallo Toorpu Godavari'. *Grandhalaya Sarvaswarum*, V63, N5, August 02, pp. 7-9.

3. Zilla Grandhalaya Samstha Kakinada : *East Godavari District Annual Report for 2006-07*. (Mimeographed).

F.5. Zilla Grandhalaya Samstha (ZGS) : Guntur

Guntur district is one of the politically, culturally, socially, economically and educationally advanced districts of Andhra pradesh. The district consists of 15 towns, 57 Mandals and 692 villages. It played a prominant role in the spread of library movement during the begining of 20th century. It was estimated that by the year 1939 there were 207 libraries established in the district. The famous boat libraries organised by one of the tallest leaders of library movement, Paturi Nagabhusanam on behalf of Sevashram at Pedapalem (Tenali Tq) carved a niche in the history of library movement in the Andhradesa before independence.

The Guntur District ZGS came into being in April 1950 as a result of Madras Public Libraries Act, 1948. The District Central Library (DCL) was established in 1952 at Guntur. Later Branch Libraries (BLS) were established at different places in the district.

No. of libraries

As on 2003 the ZGS has 284 sanctioned libraries of various types under its jurisdiction. Of the total, 130 libraries were not functioning due to various reasons. In the year 1972 Prakasam District was formed by taking away certain areas from Guntur district. As a result of this development 12 BLS from Guntur district were transferred to newly formed Prakasham district. These are : Chirala, Santaravaru, Addanki, Maddipadu, Yedugulapadu, Parachuru, Karamchedu and Uppukonduru. The following table provides information about the type of libraries and the number.

Type of library	*No. of Libraries Sanctioned*	*No. of Libraries not working*
Dist. Central Library (DCL)	01	0
Branch Libraries (BLS)	97	0
Rural Libraries (RLS)	44	13

Book Deposite Centres (BDCS)	69	58
Mobile Libraries	01	01
Aided Libraries	72	58
Total	284	130

Strictly speaking Aided libraries does not come under the administrative control of the ZGS. They are libraries (Private) managed by voluntary organizations and some of them were very old and established during the thick of the library movement. The ZGS provides annual grant for their functioning and rendering library services to the public.

Mobile Libraries

As per the norms prepared by the Department of Public Libraries, Govt. of Andhra Pradesh, efforts have to be made by ZGS in the State to open a BL in a habitat for a population of 5000 and above. It the population of the habitat is above 1000 but less than 5000, mobile libraries services have to be provided to such habitats by the nearest DCL or BL as their auxiliary service. The ZGS Guntur has taken steps and introduced mobile library services in the following centres as shown in the table.

Libraries	*Attached Villages*
Guntur	1. Pedakakani, 2. Nallapadu, 3.Budampadu, 4. Gorantla, 5. Takkilapadu, 6. Lalpuram, 7. Etukuru, 8. Aukireddipalem.
Tenali	1. Angalakuduru, 2. Burripalem
Chirala	1. Jandrapeta (Shifted to Prakasham Dt)
Repalle	1.Sajjavaripalem, 2. Penumudi, 3. Karumuru, 4. Oleru.
Muppalla	1. Indumallu
Amritaluru	1. Pedapudi
Sattenapalli	1. Irukupalem
Gurazala	1. Charlagudi Palem

Library Staff

The total sanctioned staff working under the ZGS was 270 as on 2002 and the break-up is provided in the following table.

Type of Post	*Nos*
District Central Librarian (DCL)	01
Superintendent	01
Grade I Librarians	07
Grade II Librarians	12
Grade III Librarians	59
Senior Assistants	01
Junior Assistants	02
Typists	02
Record Assts	26
Binders	02
Driver	01
Attenders	59
Watchmen	33
Part time workers	20
Rural Librarians	44
Total	270

Of the total staff 01 Grade I Librarin,12 Grade II Librarins, 06 Grade III Librarins, 01 Junior Asst, 06 Record Assts, 09 Attenders, 05 Watchmen, 20 part time workers, 13 Rural librarians totaling 73 post were lying vacant due to governments ban or new recruitments and filling up vacancies. This policy of the government is hampering the effective functioning of libraries under the ZGS.

Library Buildings

Library building is an important item in infrastructure for a public library system. The ZGS has strived hard to have its own buildings for housing libraries both urban and rural areas.

The following table provides an idea as to the provision of buildings for various types of libraries established in various parts of the district.

Type of Library	Own Blds	Rented Blds	Free Blds	Total
1. District Central Library (DCL)	01	–	–	01
2. Branch Libraries (BLS)	57	15	24	96
3. Rural Libraries (RLS)	21	–	23	44
Total	79	15	47	141

The above table shows that 79 libraries were housed in own buildings, 15 in rented and 47 in rent free buildings.

Book Collections

As on April 2000 the ZGS under its library system posses a total of 9,38,300 books in Telugu, English and Hindi. The following table provides figures for book collections in various types of libraries.

Type of library	Total book collection
Dist. Central Library (DCL)	55,267
Grade I Libraries	1,11,147
Branch Libraries (BLS)	7,03,307
Rural Libraries (RLS)	65,751
Mobile Libraries (MLS)	2,282
Total	9,38,300

Achievements

The ZGS had several achievement to its credit for rendering quality library services to the reading public. Some of them are briefly presented. During the year 1999-2000 the ZGS had spent Rs 30 lakhs for acquistion of books in Telugu, English, Hindi and Sanskrit languages. During the year 1998-

99 with the financial assistance from RRRLF kolkata storage material worth Rs 4.67 lakhs was purchased and distributed to BLS. From the years 1996-97 to 1999-2000 with the financial support from RRRLF MPLADS, Janmabhumi Programme 12 library buildings were constructed. With the support, expertise and infrastructure from National Institute of Rural Development (NIRD), Hyderabad Public Information KIOSK was started in Grade I Library at Tenali. The following table provides growth indicators such as : books, membership, visitors, books lent for home reading, buildings constructed, library cess collected for a five year period ie., from 1995-96 to 1999-2000.

Indicators	*1995-96*	*1996-97*	*1997-98*	*1998-99*	*1999-2000*
Books (in lakhs)	9.34	9.39	9.40	9.31	9.37
Members (in lakhs)	0.49	0.49	0.50	0.50	0.50
Library visitors (in lakhs)	26.10	25.50	26.18	24.40	22.54
Books lent (in lakhs)	10.33	9.09	8.57	8.10	07.31
Buildings constructed	–	5	–	3	4
Librarycess received (Rs. in lakhs)	84.84	39.02	57.12	38.55	65.20

The total book collection at the end of 31.03.2007 stood at 1072675. The break up of the collection language wise was as follows :

1. Telugu	946233
2. English	97994
3. Hindi	23260
4. Urdu	3444
5. Other languages	1744
Total	1072675

The category wise breakup of the toal collection was as follows :

1. Children books	152784
2. Reference books	54768
3. Text books	39319
4. Books for Neoliterates	22804
5. Bounded periodical volumes	4084
6. Fiction books	464390
7. Non fiction books	334526
Total	1072675

Periodicals Subscribed

The total number of periodical titles subscribed during the year 2006-07 for the entire district public library system stood at 3746. The language wise breakup was as follows :

1. Telugu	3349
2. English	397

The periodicity wise breakup of the periodicals subscribed was as follows.

Dailies	822
Other than dailies	2924

Registered Borrowers

The total number of registered borrowers for the entire district public library system as on 31.03.07 was 69792. The breakup is as follows. Men 53,782, women 12,796 and children 3214. The category wise breaking is as follows.

1. Professionals (Doctors, Lawayers, Engineers etc)	1981
2. Farmers	17900
3. Businessmen	9837
4. Students	13151
5. House wives	9707
6. Employees	10338
7. Unemployeed	7378
Total	69792

Readership

The total readership as on 31.03.07 stood at	3591156
No. of readers who visited periodicals sections of DCL and BLS	2741670
No. of readers who visited book sections	849486

Books Consulted

The total number of books consulted during the year 2006-07 stood at 591831. The figures for the types of books consulted is as follows :

1. Text books	42801
2. Reference books	91200
3. Non-fiction books	167091
4. Fiction books	290739
Total	591831

Extension Activities

During the year 2006-07, the ZGS which includes DCL, BLS, VLS, BDCS has conducted 2668 programmes for which the break-up is given below :

1. Book exhibitions	242
2. Film shows	208
3. Reading circles	139
4. Lectures	251
5. Classes	96
6. Discussions	126
7. Seminars	2
8. Conferences	–
9. Staff Training Programmes	22
10. Other programmes	1582
Total	2668

Books Lent for Home Reading

During the year 2006-07 a total of 591831 books were

lent for home reading to registered borrowers. The books lent by DCL, BLS, VLS and BDCS was as follows :

DCL	52612
BLS	326352
VLS	106883
BDCS	105984

Aided Libraries

There are 13 private aided libraries and 08Grampanchayat Libraries and 01 Cooperative Society Library functioning in the district which are eligible for grant in aid. The DPL or the ZGS Guntur have not sanctioned any grant to these aided libraries during the year 2006-07. There are about 61 privately managed registered public libraries in the district which also do not get any financial support either from ZGS or form DPL, Govt. of Andhra pradesh.

Future Plans

In the comming five years (from 2003 onwards) at the DCL and 6 Grade I Branch Libraries it was planned opening of reference service concerning competitive examinations. Computerisation of library operations at DCL and six Grade I Branch Libraries and provision of separate textbook sections in these libraries. To repair the library buildings and provision of necessary infrastructure for computerisation and installation of Internet facility. With the funds from RRRLF, Kolkata and MPLADS, construction of buildings for Branch libraries and also supply of storage materials and reading equipment. To impart professional training through work shops and refreshers courses to staff working in the ZGS continuously so as to enable them to render quality library services to the reading public. To enable the staff to the extent possible to work as supervisers/volunteers in Adult Education Centres. To supply reading materials/ equipment useful to neoliterates at Adult and Continuing Education Centres. To establish cordial relations with primary and secondary schools nearby and supply the required reading materials to them and there by inculate reading habits among school going children. To strive for the provision of library services in hospitals and jails in the district.

Source : 1. R. Sarada, 'Andhra Pradesh lo Zilla Grandhalaya Samsthalu Guntur Zilla.' *Grandhalaya Sasvaswamu*. V62, N12, March 02. pp. 2-9.

2. Zilla Grandhalayasamstha, Guntur. *Administrative Report for the year 2006-07* (Mimeographed).

F.6. Hyderabad City Grandhalaya Samstha

After police action in 1948 the former Hyderabad state was integrated into Indian Union. In 1956 Andhra Pradesh was formed and Hyderabad city as its capital. Hyderabad is the fifth largest city and become a centre for higher educational, Management, R & D and of late for Information technology insituations. It is the smallest district in Andhra Pradesh. Hyderabad City Grandhalaya Samastha (HCGS) was formed in 1961 as per the provisions of AP Public Libraries Act, 1960. The Central Library Secundrabad and City Central Library at Hyderabad were established in 1960 and 1961 respectively. Later Branch Libraries were established in various parts of twin cities. It was established with an aim of providing free library service to the residents of twin cities by way of opening one branch library for every 25,000 population. The Hyderabad City Grandhalaya Samastha was catering to the information needs of the twincities reading public by establishing branch libraries (BLS) and exclusively libraries for children, women and to cover distant city areas with Mobile Libraries (MLS). The following table provides figures for different types of libraries functioning under HCGS as on 01.04.2005.

Type of library	*No.*
City Central Library (CCL)	1
BLS Grade I	3
BLS Grade II	6
BLS Grade III	76
Total	86
MLS	3
Aided libraries	40
Total	129

In addition to above libraries, there were 192 recognised aided libraries (private libraries) functioning in the twincities. Some of these were recognised by HCGS for grant in aid. In the year 2000-01, the HCGS sanctioned grant in aid from its funds a sum of Rs 2,52,000 to 42 recognised aided libraries.

Library Staff

To manage 89 libraries of various types and the mobile libraries, HCGS requires sufficient qualified staff. The following table provides figures for sanctioned and vacant posts.

Category	*Sanctioned Posts*	*Vacant posts*
Hyderabad City Grandhalaya	11	3
City Central Library (CCL)	59	8
Branch Libraries (BLS)	176	45
Mobile Libraries (MLS)	12	3
Total	258	59

For city Central library (CCL) at AshokNagar, Hyderabad 62 posts were sanctioned. These posts consists: 1 City Central Librarian, 3 Grade I Librarians, 13 Grade II Librarians, 9 Grade III Librarians, 13 Record Assistants, 8 Attenders, 8 Watchmen, 2 Gardners, 1 Sweeper, 1 Film operator and 1 Electrician. During the year 2004-05 the number of vacant posts rose to 93 due to retirement of library staff and non filling up of vacancies.

Library Buildings

As on the year 2000-01, the ZGS has its own library buildings for its City Central. Library (CCL) at Ashok Nagar, Nagarjuna colony, Sanatnagar LIC Colony. The Muncipal Corporation of Hyderabad ows to HCGS a sum of Rs 9,61,88,852 towards librarycess. In lieu of the cess amount, the Municipal Corporation handed over 56 of its buildings, mostly community halls, to HCGS for locating its BLS. Four BL are housed in rent free buildings and eighteen (18) BLS are functioning in rented buildings. The following table provides figures for accomodation as obtained on 31.303.2005.

Category of Library	*Own*	*Rented*	*Rent free*	*Total*
CCL	1	–	–	1
BLS	61	17	7	85

It appears that no new buildings were constructed during the year 2004-05. With the financial support from RRRLF, Kolkata, plans and financial estimates were submitted to concerned authority in the year 2002 for construction of library buildings to BLS at : 1. Mahmoodnagar, Golconda Mandal, 2. Bansilalpet, Secundrabad Mandal, 3. Agapura, Nampally Mandal and Taranaka, Maredpally Mandal with an estimated cost of Rs 200,000/ for each BL building. But the work was not yet started untill 31.03.05.

Silver Jubilee

The Grandhalaya Samstha celebrated Silver Jubliee (1961-1986) in November 1986. During the 25 years of its existence it has made significant progress in various facets of public library development. The following table provides figures for the number of books added to the City Central Library and Branch Libraries in the twincities of Hyderabad and Secandrabad.

Year	*No. of books added*	*Total at the end of the year*
1961-62	2276	2276
1970-71	1598	1,78047
1980-81	42133	5,86,197
1985-86	25,575	7,44,040

The number visitors to the City Central Library and forty branch libraries during the past 25 years had greatly increased. The following table provides figures for the number of persons enrolled as registered borrowers between the years 1964-65 and 1984-85.

Year	Enrolled during the year	Total at the year end
1964-65	338	338
1972-75	4816	15261
1980-81	3368	27252
1984-85	4458	38741

The other indicators of public library services such as number of visitors, books consulted and books lent had greatly increased. The following table provides figures for these three indicators between the year 1964-65 and 1985-86.

Year	Visitors	Books consulted	Books lent out
1964-65	489031	60801	9675
1974-75	2270586	580286	675280
1984-85	2343924	863174	1341351
1985-86	2608626	1158614	1306624

Source : Hyderabad city Grandhalaya Samastha : Silver Jubliee (1961-1986). *Souvenir*. (Hyderabad, Hyderabad city Grandhalaya Samastha, 1986). Annexures V, IX and X.

City Central Library (CCL)

As stated already it was established in 1961 at Himayat Nagar in a rented building. The foundation stone was laid on 9th October, 1969 by Sri V.V. Giri, President of India. In 1974 a spacious library building with modern facilities was constructed at Ashok Nagar and library was shifted to its new premises.

This library over the years has transformed as one of the presigeous public libraries in Andhra Pradesh. This was the first and fully computerised public library in the state. All the in house operations have been completely automated. Internet facility was provided with 16 computers and special cabinets were provided for the purpose. In addition to offering and organising literary, cultural and social services, the following services were offered to the public by the library.

1. Providing audio-visual materials to the clientele and offering information, education through three moblie library services.
2. Providing well stocked text book and reference sections and helping especially to the student community.
3. Meeting information and knowledge requirements of the user community with the help Internet and reference services.
4. With the spacious conference hall and open air theatre help organising cultural, social, educational activities and functions and colloborating with voluntary organisations for the said purpose.
5. Offering library services to all people in the society without bias to any caste, religion, language, gender and education, and
6. Extending library services to children and women by opening special sections in BLS.

As on 31st March 1985 the City Central Library (CCL) has fifty four staff members of various categories on its rolls. It has been offering services to the user community with the following sections: viz,

1. Main lending section, 2 Children's section, 3. Peroidical section for gents, 4. Periodical section for ladies, 5. News papers section 6.Technical section, 7. Text book section, 8. Reference section, 9. Periodicals Preservation Section and 10. Book-bin. The total book stock at CCL as on 31st March 1985 was 1,03,879 and membership stands at 9,551. During the year 1984-85 a total number of 2,87,47 vistited the library at an average of 1038 readers per day. During the same year a total number 2,94,596 books were consultled at an average of 1,063 books per day. A total number 2,48,888 books were lent for home reading at an average of 898 books per day. The following table provides figures for total book collection available in some of the import sections of CCL on 31.3.1985.

Sections	Total Books available
Lending Section	71,047
Childrens Section	13,233
Text book Section	11,037
Reference Section	8,562
Book bin Section	16,473

Source : Hyderabad City Grandhalaya Samstha's Report. 1984-85. (Hyderabad City Grandhalaya Samstha, 1985) 31p.

Book Collections

The City Central Library (CCL) as on the year 2000-01 consists books on the following languages.

Telugu	61,063
English	66,056
Urdu	15,687
Hindi	23,595
Marathi	3,229
Kannada	3,516
Tamil	2,915
Sanskrit	2,500
Total	1,78,561

The library subscribes in seven languages to 30 dailies, 261 monthlies and has 19,327 registered borrowers. Daily 1580 readers visit the library and on an average consult 1009 books and other materials and borrow 93 books. It also organises 257 educational, pultural literary and social programmes in a year. For the year 2001, the CCL got "Southern Zone Best Library Award" from RRRLF, Kolkata.

As on 31.03.2005 the total book collection at HCGS stood at 1361877. The following table provides figures for book collection available at CCL and BLS.

Category of Libraries	*Book as on 31.03.05*
CCL	1,71,128
BLS	1111743
MLS	79006
Total	13,61877

No. of Periodicals subscribed language wise

A total of 245 Periodical titles were subscribed by CGS during the 2004-05 except City Central Library (CCL), Hyderabad. The following table provides figures for periodical titles subscribed languagewise by the BLS.

No. of Books Available Languagewise

The total book collection 13, 61, 877 available at HCGS during the year 2004-05 is shown languagewise in the following table.

Category of Library	*Telugu*	*English*	*Hindi*	*Urdu*	*Others Langs.*	*Total*
CCL	57655	62931	24413	14287	11878	171164
BLS	819487	130745	59670	91066	10554	1111522
MLS	54317	5704	6541	7877	4819	79258
Total	931459	199380	90624	113230	27251	13,61944

Special facilities

In order to help the students in their educational endeavour text book sections were provided in the following BLS.

1. City Central Library, Ashok Nagar
2. Central Library, Secundrabad
3. Branch Library, Shah Alibanda
4. Branch Library, Nampally
5. Branch Library, Khairatabad

Category of Libraries	*Telugu*			*English*			*Hindi*			*Urdu*			*Others*			*Total*
	D	W&F	M	D	W&F	M	D	W&F	M	D	W&F	M	D	W&F	M	
Grade I BLS	5	5	15	9	18	19	3	4	3	3	2	6	1	4	–	92
Grade II BLS	5	8	11	5	16	17	1	2	3	2	2	2	1	5	1	82
Grade III BLS	5	9	12	4	12	13	2	1	1	2	2	2	1	3	2	71

6. Branch Library, Phoolbagh
7. Branch Library, Malakpeta.

The text books in the above libraries except BLS at Malakpeta and Phoolbagh open for 12 twelve hours i.e from 8 AM to 8 pm. New Text Books useful to Inter to PG students are added every year to these text book sections. Every day hundreds of students use these text book sections. For example at CCL. Ashok Nagar at least 500 student daily visit the text books section. Efforts are on to establish a Competitive Examinations Reference Unit at the CCL for the benefit of those appearing for national and international competitive examinations. Similarly efforts are on to supply books on competitive examinations for all the BLS.

Childrens Libraries

Specially there is a childrens library at chudibazar. In addition the following libraries have childrens sections.

1. City Central Library (CCL), Ashoknagar. In addition to children's section, there is a provision for kindergarten section with play articles, globes, maps etc.
2. Central Library, Secundrabad
3. Branch Library, Shah Ali Banda.

Women's Libraries

The HCGS has established three women's libraries at Vijayanagar colony, Malakpeta colony, Yerramanzil colony. These libraries work from 10.30 AM to 4.30 PM.

Progress Achieved During Four Years Period

The HCGS has achieved appreciable progress with respect to books, membership, readers, book lent, buildings constructed and library cess realised. The following table provides figures for four year period 1999-2000 to 2002-03.

Indicators	*1999-2000*	*2000-01*	*2001-02*	*2002-03 (Up to 31.08.02)*
Books (in lakhs)	11.992	12.37	12.48	12.89
Membership (in lakhs)	0.66	0.67	0.70	0.72
Readers (in lakhs)	29.08	31.54	32.46	15.32
Books Lent (in lakhs)	6.86	7.31	6.85	3.84
Buildings Constructed	1	0	0	0
Librarycess realised (Rs. in lakhs)	216.81	406.08	400.08	200.44

A.V. Services

For the benefit of youth and neolterates HCGS arranges Audio-visual programmes on every Sunday from 6.00 PM to 7.30 PM to screen 16 MM films. On every week from Tuesday to Saturday 16 MM film shows are also arranged in one BL for the benefit of user community. Everyday at 7 .00 PM DD News Cast is also shown on T.V in addition to all important telecasts. All the Grade I Libraries have colour T.V. sets.

Akshara Sanskranti (Literacy Compaign)

HCGS actively participating in aksharasankranti programmes which are meant to propagate literacy in the society and achieved designed results.

It has established 25 akshara sanskranti centres in 25 BLS under its juridication. With cooperation and support from voluntary organisations it has been organising a number of programmes for promotion of adult education programmes. For organizing these programmes each BL has been spending Rs 500/.

Mobile Library Services

Since 1973, HCGS has been organising mobile library services (MLS) for the benefit far flung localities where there were no BLS. It has 3 mobile vans through which library services are extended.

Mobile Library I

This was started in 1973. The van covers areas such as : Barkatpura, Vijayapuri, Indiranagar and extended to 36 points in these areas. There were 36,000 books in the mobile library and 5000 registered borrowers.

Mobile Library II

This was started in the year 1985. This mobile van covers areas such as : Old Bolakpur, Brindavan apartments, Arun apartments and covers 72 points. There were 25,000 books in the mobile library and 3000 registered borrowers.

Mobile Library III

This was introduced in the year 1989. This Van covers areas in the old city such as : Yakutpura, Bag-e-Jahanara, Kurmaguda and covers 70 points in the area. The library has 14,000 books and 1000 registered members.

Digitisation

With the technical and financial support and cooperation from Carneige Mellon University ; USA, digitisation of valuable and old books have been taken up at CCL, Hyderabad. Books in English, Telugu, Persian, Arabic, Urdu and Sanskrit were taken up for digitisation. The scanning work was started vigorously at specially designed air conditioned hall at CCL. The following table provides figures for book scanned at the City Central Library (CCL), Hyderabad from 01.12.02 to 30.03.07.

	Scanned		*Cropped*		*OCR*	
Language	*Books*	*Pages*	*Books*	*Pages*	*Books*	*Pages*
English	5645	2004733	5645	2004733	5645	2004733
Persian	–	–	–	–	–	–
Urdu	384	54507	384	54507	–	–
Arabic	2	974	2	974	–	–
Telugu	15369	3052778	15369	3052778	–	–

Hindi	62	1501762		15017	–	–
Sanskrit	1614	645869	1614	645869	–	–
Total	23076	5773878	23076	5773878	5645	2004733

Membership

As on 31.03.05 the total membership stood at 80651. The following was the break-up of the membership

CCL	22620
BLS	49074
MLS	8957
Total	80651

Readership

The total readership during the year 2004-05 stood at 3861837. The following was the breakup figures of readers at different types of libraries.

CCL	359119
BLS	3502718
Total	3861837

Books Consulted

Book consultation and lending for home reading are two important services offered by the public library system of HCGS. A total number of 1219882 books were consulted in the public library system of HCGS. The following figures show the number of books consulted at CCL and BLS.

CCL	419722
BLS	800160
Total	1219882

Books Lent for Home Reading

During the year 2004-05 a total of 816799 books were lent for home reading by HCGS. The following figures indicate the number of books lent for home reading by various types of libraries.

CCL	22753
BLS	760289
MLS	33757
Total	816799

Book Collections Added

Book collections are added to the existing collections by purchase, books recieved from other sources and also by gratis. During the year 2004-05, HCGS has not purchased any books from its funds. But it received books from the DPL, RRRLF, Kolkata and gratis from the public. The following table provides figures for books received languagewise from various sources.

Language	*DPL/RRRLF*	*RRRLF, Kolkata*	*Gratis*
Telugu	5995	–	–
English	837	216	11
Hindi	280	–	145
Urdu	78	333	–
Other Languages	155	–	–
Total	7345	549	156

Extension Services

In addition to traditional library services, the CCL has been rendering extensions services vigorously to reachout the community at large. The following services are being provided regularly.

Meeting Place

The CCL has specious meeting hall with a capacity for 200 guests in the first floor of its building. In this hall meetings, conferences, library weeks and showing films are held regularly. Cultural, educational, literary and social organisations in the twincities have been utilizing this conference hall for their activities by paying nominal rent. On first sunday of every month, the CCL with the cooperation of 'Yuvabharati', a literary organisation organises programmes on personality development. Various literary, cultural, social and educational organisations conduct their programmes within the premises of CCL.

City Central Library of HCGS is a hub of social, educational and cultural activities of the twin cities of Hyderabad and Secundrabad. The spacious conference hall and open air theatre provides a congenial atmosphere for holding various types of extension activities. During the year 2004-05, the HCGS conducted about 305 extension activities. The following figures indicate number of programmes carried out by various types of libraries.

Category of library	*Conferenc es/seminars*	*Training Programmes*	*Exhibitions*	*Literary activities*	*Cultural activities*
CCL	1	2	1	85	80
BLS	–	–	–	70	70
Total	1	2	1	155	150

Future Activities

HCGS wants to computerise 8 identified nondal BLS in the second phase. Later computerisation shall be extended to remaining BLS. It wish to have Hyderabad City Libraries Net works called HCGS LIBNET. To digitise the collections CCL, Ashok nagar, Hyderabad. To launch a website on City Central Library, Ashok Nagar. To open a separate section at CCL with books and other reading materials for the benefit of those appearing for competitive examinations, and later the same facility extended to all BLS. To carryout necessary repairs, extensions to library buildings of 56 BLS and if necessary construct new library buildings. To develop land scape gardens at all BLS.

What Lies ahead

The HCGS is the richest Grandhalaya Samstha in the entire state of Andhra Pradesha. On an average the Samstha gets Rs 5 crores as librarycess from the Municipal corporation of Hyderabad (now Greater Hyderabad Municipal Corporation).There was and is no financial problems faced by the HCGS unlike other Grandhalaya Samsthas in the state. With the formation of GHMC, the jurisliction of the Samstha has increased and has to cover a population of 70 lakhs. The present 89BLS were not able to cover the information requirements of growing population. Many out lying areas in the city were not covered BLS or MLS.

The ban is imposed by the government for opening new BLS, recruitment of new staff and filling up of existing vacancise has come in the way of expansion of litrary services in the twin cities. HCGS is a typical example of suffering from bureaucratic hinderance where by it was not able to utilise the available abundant financial resources for its expansion and was not able to do justice to those who pay librarycess and other reading public of the twincities. The sucessive managing committees HCGS have partly to be blammed for this sorry state of affairs.

Source : 1. R.Sarada : 'Hyderabad Nagara Grandhalaya Samstha.' *Grandhalaya Survaswamu*, V64, N1, April 03, pp.2-7.

2. *Annual Report of City Grandhalaya Samstha*, Hyderabad 2004-05 (Mimeographed).

F.7. Zilla Grandhalaya Samastha (ZGS) : Kadapa

The District Central Library (DCL) Kadapa was established in 1952 under Local Library Authority (LLA) of Kadapa district as per the provisions Madras Public Libraries Act. Andhra State was formed in 1953 and in 1956 enlarged state of Andhra Pradesh (Visalandhra) was formed by merging the Telangana area with Andhra State. The Andhra Pradesh Public Libraries Act, an integrated Act, came into being in 1960. All the twenty districts of the new state came under the provisions of the new act. As per the provisions of the new act branch libraries, rural librariess and book deposit centres were established inn Kadapa district.

No. of Libraries

As on March 31,2005 there was one District Central Library, 3 Grade I libraries, 6 Grade II libraries and 47 Grade III, one rural library and 37 book deposite centres were functioning in the district.

Total Book Collection

The total book collection in the entire district public library as on March 31, 2005 was 3,41,07. The break-up is : Telugu 2,94,000, English 35,863, Hindi 7,764, Urdu 2,755, others 654. There were 26,560 registered borrowers who have been borrowing books from the public library system.

No. of Readers

In the year 2005 a total of 15,58,263 readers visited the libraries. A total of 1,51,150 books have been lent for home reading and a total 4,26,139 books have been consulted within the libraries.

Library Buildings

Some of the Municipalities and Gram Panchayats and philanthrophists have come forward for construction of library buildings for housing libraries in the districts : For example in

Brahmamagarimatham building was constructed freely and handed over to Zilla Grandhalalya samstha for opening a branch library : The Grama Panchayats of D.Nandyala, Bojjavari Palley, Badwel donated land freely for the construction of library buildings. The collector of the District was trying to release funds from ZGS funds for the construction of library buildings at Badwel and Valluru. The Grama Panchyatas of Rlykoduru and Verraballi have started construction of library buildings. The following table provides an idea as to the present position of library buildings in district public library system.

Type of Library	*Own*	*Rented*	*Free*	*Total*
District Central Library (DCL)	1	–	–	1
Branch Library (BL)	7	4	44	55
Rural Library (RL)	–	–	1	1
Book Deposit Centres (BDC)	–	–	37	37
Total	8	4	82	94

Staff Position

Out of the 141 sanctioned posts, presently 73 persons of all categorised have been working leaving 68 posts including professional, administrative and class IV to be filled up. The Secretary Ms B.N. Jyoti opines that "inspite of staff shortage every effort is being made to utilize the available resources bothmen and material to the maximum benefit and thus endeavour to fulfill the objectives of Kadapa Zilla Grandhalaya Samstha and march ahead for offering better library services to reading public at large".

Future Plans

The Library Committee of Zilla Grandhalaya Samstha recognised the need for computerisation of library operations. To start with it intends to computerise first the District Central Library (DCL) followed by Grade I libraries in the district. To have own library buildings to all branch libraries (BLS) in a phased manner. To equip Branch Libraries with proper furniture and equipment. To air condition the District Central Library with an estimated cost of Rs 1.9 lakh of rupees to make reading within the library more confortable and enjoyable and also to enable those who appear for competitive examination to spend more time in the library. To strengthen book collections in the Branch Libraries by acquiring more useful reading material. Lastly but not the least to undertake binding of not only all newly acquired books but also damaged books so as to extend life of books.

Stalwarts of Library Movement

During the formative stages of library move many stalwarts devoted their life and strove hard for the spread of movement not only in the district but also in the entire Rayalaseema. Foremost among there were Vedam Venkata Krishna Sarma, Bhadri Sitaramayya, K. Gundu Rao, Viruru Pichaiah, Gullapalli Punnaiah Sastri and Polepalli Venganna Shresthi.

Source : B.N. Jyoti, 'Andhra Pradesh lo Grandhalaya Samsthalu : Kadapa Zilla. *Grandhalaya Sarvaswamu*, V66, N8, Nov. 2005, pp. 2-6.

F.8. Zilla Grandhalaya Samstha : Karim Nagar

The District was formed in the year 1897 and was called Sarkar Elgandala. In the year 1900 the Hyderabad State was reorganised and the name of the district was changed as Karimnagar. The district comprised of three revenue divisions and fourteen tulukas. In the year 1985, the revenue divisions were abolished and in their place 56 revenue mandals were created. There are 1098 Villages and 1009 Grampanchayats in the district.

Number of Libraries

As on 31.03.05, the Grandhalaya Samstha had 107 libraries of various types which is shown in the following table.

Type of Library	*No. of Libraries*
(a) District Central Library (DCL)	1
(b) Branch Libraries (BLS)	58
(c) Village Libraries (VLS)	4
(d) Book Deposit Centres (BDCS)	30
(e) Mobile Libraries	
1. Vans	–
2. Rickshaws	14
3. Cycles	–
Total	107

It appears that out of 30 BDCS sanctioned 29 were not yet opened.

Library Buildings

The various types of libraries run by the ZGS are housed in own/rented and rent free buildings. The following table provides figures for the library buildings.

Types of library	*No. of Libraries*	*Own Building*	*Rent free Building*	*Rented Building*	*Total*
DCL	1	1	0	0	1
BLS	58	11	22	25	58
VLS	4	0	4	0	4
BDCS	14	0	14	0	14
Total	77	12	40	25	77

Out of 77 libraries 12 libraries have own buildings, 40 are housed in rent free buildings and 25 are housed in rented buildings.

Staff Strength

As on 31.03.2005, the ZGS had a total strength of 93 staff of various categories of post such as : DCL (1), Librarian Grade I (1), Librarian Grade II (4), Librarian Grade III (48) Record Assistants (12), Attenders (12), Watchmen (12) and other posts such as : Senior Asst (1), Supernintendent (1) and Typist (1). In addition, the ZGS have 53 part time posts which include : village librarians, sweepers and part time workers.

Book Stocks

The total book stock of the DCL, BLS, VLS and BDCS as on 31.03.05 is shown in the following table

DCL	*BLS*	*VLS*	*BDCS*
29467	36725	2199	0

The language wise break-up is as follows :

(a) Telugu	17273	259442	1877	0
(b) English	6459	22715	223	0
(c) Hindi	3324	11319	48	0
(d) Urdu	2217	12539	51	0
(e) Other languages	143	141	0	0
Total	29476	36725	2199	0

The categorywise break-up is as follows :

(a) Children books	870	63427	650	0
(b) Reference books	2850	20240	50	0
(c) Text books	3270	11791	0	0
(d) Books for Neo literates	0	9107	250	0
(e) Fiction books	13136	104939	9550	
(f) Non-fiction books	9350	96302	4940	
Total	29476	367625	494	0

Periodicals Subscribed

During the year 2004-05 the ZGS had subscribed to periodicals of various frequencies in various languages to DCL, BLS and VLS. The following table provides the number of periodicals subscribed to these types of libraries.

	DCL (1)	*BLS (58)*	*VLS (4)*
By purchase	45	812	26
By gratis	5	92	2
Total	50	904	28

The languagewise break-up is as follows :

(a) Telugu	25	799	25
(b) English	18	92	2
(c) Hindi	0	0	0
(d) Urdu	7	13	0
(e) other languages	0	0	0
Total	50	904	27

The frequencywise break-up is as follows :

(a) Dailies	17	293	8
(b) Other than dailies	33	665	19
Total	50	904	27

Registered Borrowers

The following table provides figures for registered borrows at DCL, BLS and VLS as on 31.03.05.

DCL (1)	*BLS (58)*	*VLS (4)*
4973	21213	71

Genderwise break-up.	*DCL (1)*	*BLS (58)*	*VLS (4)*
(a) Men	4355	16810	66
(b) Women	423	1616	5
(c) Children	0	2097	0
Total	4973	20523	71

Categorywise break-up	*DCL*	*BLS*	*VLS*
(a) Professionals (Doctors, Lawyers, Engineers etc)	551	672	21
(b) Famers/Agriculturists	598	4065	21
(c) Businessmen	1067	5098	18
(d) House wives	345	1342	0
(e) Students	1176	5227	7
(f) Employed	695	2353	9
(g) Unemployed	631	3170	8
Total	4973	20523	66

Readership

The following table provides figures for number of readers visiting the DCL, BLS and VLS during the year 2004-05.

DCL (1)	*BLS (58)*	*VLS (4)*
149595	1181441	12154

Section wise usage of library resources

(a) Periodical Section	99742880	086	10229
(b) Book Section	49853297	407	1925
(c) Both the Sections	149595	1183632	12154

Books Consulted

The following figures give an idea as to the number of books consulted by the readers at the DCL and BLS during the year 2004-05 24335 190086

Type of Books Consulted

1.	Text books	10150	27519
2.	Reference books	5800	32413
3.	Non-fiction	6730	67518
4.	Fiction	1655	64589
	Total	24335	191839

Library cess

Librarycess is one of the most important sources of revenues of ZGSS in the state. During the year 2004-05, the ZGS had realised a total of Rs 89,05,61000 as library cess from the Municipalities and Grampanchayats.

Extension Activities

Extension activities are very important activites for public libraries to attract more readers into their fold and drive home the role played by these libraries for the development of society. During the year 2004-05, DCL (1) BLS (58) and VLS (4) have organised a total of 198 extension activities which include book exhibitions, filmshows, reading circles, lectures, training classes, discussions, seminars and conferences. Of the total of 198 programmes, the DCL had carried out 30 programmes, the BLS 163 and VLS 4 programmes.

Source : *Annual Report of Zilla Grandhalaya Samstha. Karimnagar for the year 2004-05.* (Mimeographed).

F.9. Zilla Grandhalaya Samstha (ZGS) : Khammam

Khamman district was formed in the year 1953. Before 1953, it was part of Warangal District. It has completed 50 years of formation in the year 2002 and celebrations were held on a grand scale. It consists of 4 Revenue Divisions, 46 Mandals, 4 Municipalities, 21 Notified Panchayats and 754 Gram panchayats. Khamman Zilla Grandhalaya Samastha (ZGS) was formed in 1958 with the District Central Library (DCL) along with two Branch Libraries (BLS), and the number rose to 19 BLS and 5 Rural Libraries (RLS) in 1981.

No. of Libraries

In the year 1986 during the tenure of N.T.Rama Rao as a Chief Minister, the Government of Andhra Pradesh took a momentus decision to establish a Branch Library (BL) in every Mandal in the state. As a result of this revenue policy a BL was established in every Mandal of the state.

Khamman district was no exception. As on the year 2003 the ZGS has 119 libraries of various types. The following table provides figures for various types of libraries functioning in the district as on 01.04.2002.

Type of Library	*Nos*
District Central Library (DCL)	01
Branch Library Grade II	01
Branch Libraries (BLS) Grade III	47
Rural Libraries (RL)	02
Book Deposit Centres (BDCS)	26
Panchayat Libraries (PLS)	11
Total	88

Library Staff

The following table provides figures for sanctioned posts and vacant in 2003.

S.No	Type of post	Sanctioned	Vacant
01.	District Central Librarian	01	–
02.	Grade I Librarian	01	–
03.	Grade II Librarian	01	–
04.	Grade III Librarians	44	11
05.	Sr. Assistant	01	–
06.	Jr. Assistant	01	–
07.	Typist	01	–
08.	Record Assistants	08	02
09.	Attenders	20	03
10.	Watchmen	03	03
11.	Village librarians	08	07
12.	Sweepers	01	–
13.	Part time workers	34	32
	Total	124	58

Out of 85 sanctioned posts, 17 post were lying vacant and not filledup due to ban imposed by the government on filling up vacancies and creation of new posts, by the ZGS as on 30.03.02.

Library Buildings

The following table provides figures for library buildings for housing various types of libraries in the ZGS.

Type of Library	Own bld	Rented bld	Free bld	Total
District Central Library (DCL)	01	–	–	01
Branch Libraries (BLS)	31	05	12	48
Rural Libraries	3	–	05	08
Total	35	05	17	57

Out of 57 libraries it is encouraging to see that only five libraries are housed in rented buildings, thereby saving meagre financial resources of the ZGS which can be used for other purposes.

Book Stocks

As on 31.03.02 the total book stock of the ZGS stood at 336506 books. The following table provides figures for the total book stock available in various types of libraries.

Types of Library	*Total book stocks*
DCL	30769
BLS	280482
VLS	21529
MLS	3726
Total	3,36,506

Out of the total collection DPL/RRRLF supplied 3825 books, RRRLF, Kolkata 460 books and book purchased from ZGSS funds 1439 and books received as gratis 2480 books.

Periodicals Subscribed

During the year 2001-02, the ZGS had subscribed to a total of 934 periodicals of various frequencies in Telugu, English and Hindi. The following table provides figures for the number of periodicals subscribed by various types of libraries.

Type of Library	*Telugu*				*English*				*Urdu*				*Total*
	D	*W*	*F*	*M*	*D*	*W*	*F*	*M*	*D*	*W*	*F*	*M*	
DCL	7	7	2	16	3	5	1	5	2	–	–	–	48
BLS Grade II	5	5	–	13	3	3	–	–	–	–	–	–	29
BLS Grade III	144	152	–	397	42	6	–	15	–	–	–	–	756
VLS	1			7	–	–	–	–	–	–	–	–	8
BDCS	26	22	–	45	–	–	–	–	–	–	–	–	93
Total	183	186	2	478	48	14	1	20	2	–	–	–	934

Language Wise Collection

The book collection of the ZGS consists of books in Telugu, English, Hindi and Urdu. The following table provides figures for languages wise collections available in various types of libraries.

Category of Library	*Telugu*	*English*	*Hindi*	*Urdu*	*Other Languages*	*Total*
DCL	19244	8439	1831	1221	34	30,769
BLS	237693	23412	13080	6220	77	280482
VLS	19781	1527	218	3	–	21529
MLS	3526	200	–	–	–	3726
Total	280244	35578	15129	7444	111	336506

Membership

As on 31.03.02 the total membership of the ZGS stood at 24251. The following table provides figures for total membership at different types of libraries of the ZGS.

Types of library	*Total membership*	*Percentage of increase*
DCL	3302	50%
BLS	19941	99%
VLS	666	16%
MLS	342	–
Total	24251	87%

An overall increase of 87% was achieved in the enrollment of new members than the previous year.

Readership

A total of 1078275 readers visited the district public library system during the year 2001-02. The following table provides figures for the total number of readers availed library services at different types of library functioning the under the ZGS.

Category of library	*No. of readers*	*Percentage of increase*
DCL	80394	
BLS	987012	11.39%
VLS	7606	37.30%
Total	107,8275	

There had been an increase of 11.39% and 37.30% in readership respectively at BLS and VLS.

Books Consulted

During the year 2001 - 02, a total of 219741 books were consulted at different types of libraries under the ZGS. The following table provides figures for the total books consulted at various types of libraries.

Type of library	*Total books consulted*	*Percentage of increase*
DCL	5262	
BLS	213367	7%
VLS	1112	–
Total	219741	6%

An overall 6% increase was achieved in book consultation than the previous year.

Books lent for home reading

During the year 2001-02, a total of 230186 books were lent for home reading. The following table provides figures for the books lent by different types of libraries.

Types of library	*Total books lent*	*Percentage of increase*
DCL	12968	–
BLS	215297	–
VLS	1921	62%
Total	230186	

VLS had achieved 62% increase in lending of books than the previous year.

Book Collections

The ZGSS had acquired books by purchased and books recieved from DPL/RRRLF, Director, RRRLF and by gratis and added to its existing collections. The following table provides figures for the books acquired and added to the collections during 2001-02.

Mode of acquisition	*No. of Titles*	*No. of books*
By Purchase	187	7950
DPL/RRRLF	686	3825
Director, RRRLF	460	460
By gratis	248	248

Library cess

Librarycess is one of the most important sources of revenue to the ZGSS in the state. During the year 2001-02. the ZGS had received a total sum of Rs 3228505.00 from the local bodies in the district. The following table provides figures for the cess amount realised from the local bodies.

Name of the local body	*Cess realised*
Municipalities (4)	2860993.00
Notified Gram Panchayats (21)	323497.00
Non notified Gram Panchayats	44015.00
Total	3228505.00

Extension Activities

During the year 2001-02, the libraries under the ZGS had celebrated National Library Week during 14-20. November. With the cooperation of local educational institutions book exhibitions, lectures by eminent personalities, competitions such as general knowledge quizz programmes had been organised by the DCL and BLS. A total of 74 programmes were conducted. In addition, the staff of the ZGSS had actively participated in Janambhoomi and Clean and Green programmes and 60 works were completed under these programmes.

Progress Achieved

During the year 2000-01 with the funds from RRRLF, Kolkata, the ZGS has purchased storage material worth Rs 17,250 and supplied to BLS. From the year 1994 to 2000-01, the ZGS has constructed 26 library buildings with funds from IJRY and buildings for 5 more libraries were under construction. The staff of ZGS have actively participated in 'akshara sanskranti', 'janambhoomi' and social service programmes and helped to change illiterates into literates. The Districts collector of Khammam has honoured M.V. Rajeshware Rao, Branch Librarian, Vaira Branch Library for his active participation in the literary and social service programmes on the republic day in the year 2002.

The following table provides figures for the progress achieved during five year period from 1995-96 to 1999-2000

Indicators	*1995-96*	*1996-97*	*1997-98*	*1998-99*	*1999-2000*
1. Books (in lakhs)	3.37	3.41	3.46	3.48	3.54
2. Members (in lakhs)	0.23	0.24	0.24	0.25	0.25
3. Readers (in lakhs)	9.20	8.61	10.31	8.94	9.50
4. Books lent (in lakhs)	3.20	3.00	3.14	2.98	3.25
5. Buildings constructed	3	5	3	3	3
6. Librarycess realised (in lakhs)	20.91	16.32	14.09	21.017	20.14

Future Plans

In the comming five years the ZGS was planning to open competitive exams reference section in some of the important BLS. To computerise and provide Internet facility in the DCL. Later by stages computerise all BLS and network with DCL. To construct library buildings for BLS and acquire storage materials with the funds from RRRLF, Kolkata and MP and MLA LADS. To extend library services by stages to all Gram Panchayats in the district. To impart professional training to the library staff by conducting work shops and refresher courses at regular intervals, so that they can offer better library services to the user community. To actively participate in 'akshara sankranti' programmes by the library staff as supervisions and volunteers and help to achieve complete literacy in the district. To raise funds from the donors for every library and put the donations with fixed deposit and use the interest accured there to for developmental activities and transform BLS in to self supporting institutions. Lastly but not the least to transform BLS and other libraries in the district to instill reading habits among the public.

Sources : 1. V. Sankara Reddy, 'Andhra Pradesh lo Zilla Grandhalaya Samsthalu : Khamman Zilla'. *Grandhalaya Sarvaswamu* V64, N4, July 03, pp. 2-6.

2. *Annual Report of Zilla Grandhalaya Samstha : Khammam District, 2002-03*. (Mimeographed).

F.10. Zilla Grandhalaya Samstha (ZGS) : Krishna

Before independence Krishna district was one of the largest districts of the country extending its boundaries from Rajahmundry to Macherla and Machilipatnam to Munagala Paragana. In the year 1904 Guntur district was carved out from Krishna district and again in the year 1925 West Godavari district was also carved out from Krishna. In the year 1959 certain areas were transferred to neighbouring Nalgonda district effecting changes in the boundaries. Over the years the district achieved phenomenal growth and development in agriculture, industry and politically more concious and produced a number of stalwarts in the fields of education, social reforms, library movement and politics. The district consists of 19 towns, 48 mandals and 942 panchayats.

Local Library Authority (LLA) for Krishna district was formed in the year 1950 at Machilipatnam (Bandar) as a result of Madrass Public Libraries Act, 1948. The District Central Library was established in 1952 at Machilipatnam, the district headquarters.

No. of Libraries

As stated already District Central Library (DCL) was established in the year 1952 at Machilipatnam, the district headquarters. As on 31.03.04, the total numbers of libraries functioning under the ZGS was 243. The following table provides the break-up of these libraries.

Type of Library	*Nos*
District Central Library (DCL)	1
Grade I Libraries	7
Grade II Libraries	18
Grade III Libraries	83
Branch Libraries (BLs) Managed by	30
Record Assts	30
Rural Libraries (RLs)	16
Mobile Libraries	47
Book Deposite Centres (BDCS)	41
Total	243

Out of 243 libraries 1 childrens library was functioning at Machilipatnam established in 1960 and women's libraries were functioning at Gudivada established in 1961 and Patamatalanka (Vijayawadwa) established in 1968. To meet the reading requirements of educated prisoners two libraries were opened in the year 2000 at Machilipatnam and Vijayawada jails. The Grade I Library-Tagore Memorial Library named after Rabindranath Tagore at Vijayawada on Bandar road was fully developed with modern facilities to meet the information needs of urban educated population. It consist of five divisions viz : General, Reference, Textbooks, Newspapers and Magazines and Mobile.

Library Staff

Krishna district ZGS has earned name and fame as one of the best ZGSS in the state. The credit of bringing to the top position goes to its former secretary V.Chandrasekhar Rao who served the ZGS for almost 20 years the longest period in the history of Krishna ZGS. As on 31.03.04 the total staff structure of all categories of posts was 299.

The break-up is as follows :

Typs of post	*Sanctioned posts*	*Vacant posts*
Dist Central Librarian (DCL) and Secretary	1	
Grade I Librarians	8	4
Grade II Librarians	20	10
Grade III Librarians	57	22
Record Assistants	43	15
Attenders	67	30
Part time posts	11	10
Watchmen	51	34
Village Librarians	34	22
Administrative Staff Working in ZGS Office		
Senior Assistant	1	
Junior Assistants	2	
Typist	1	
Binder	1	
Driver	1	
Cleaner	1	
Total	299	147

Out of the 299 sanctioned posts, 147 posts of various categories are lying vacant.

Library Buildings

The following table provides an idea as to the number of libraries housed in own/rented/free library buildings.

Type of Library	*Own Blds*	*Rented Blds*	*Free Blds*	*Total*
1. Dist. Central Library	1	–	–	1
2. Branch Libraries	53	15	40	108
3. Rural Libraries	3	–	31	34
Total	57	15	71	143

The above table shows that the ZGS own only 57 buildings and most of the BLS and RLS were housed either in rented or rent free buildings. The scenario is not encouraging. Efforts have to be made to tap the financial support from RRRLF, MP and MLA LADS and other governmental programmes for construction of more library buildings.

The acquisition of sites for construction of buildings at Vatsavai, Nandigama, Nagayalanka, Guduru, Vanukuru, Reddygudem and Mudinepalli are under process. The construction of library buildings at Kornkollu, Ibrahimpatnam, Tiruvuru, Pedaparupudi and Chanubanda having sites were not taken up yet.

Growth Indicators

The ZGS has made significant progress with respect to acquisition of books, registered borrowers, visitors to libraries, books lent for home reading, books consulted within the library premises, buildings constructed and library cess collected. The following table gives an idea as to the progress achieved during five year period from 1995-96 to 1999-2000.

Indicators	*1995-96*	*1996-97*	*1997-98*	*1998-99*	*1999-2000*
1. Books (in lakhs)	12.19	12.34	12.19	3.48	12.04
2. Members (in lakhs)	00.68	00.66	00.68	00.68	00.68
3. Visitors (in lakhs)	21.28	19.88	18.09	17.49	16.81
4. Books Lent (in lakhs)	04.70	03.90	02.25	02.63	02.17
5. Books consulted (in lakhs)	03.61	03.49	03.54	03.51	03.21
6. Buildings constructed	4	3	2	5	1
7. Lib cess collected (Rs. in lakhs)	56.94	74.66	69.59	79.32	66.47

Book Stock

As on 31.03.04 the total book stock stood at 12,72,332 which includes books purchased by ZGS from its own funds and books received from DPL under RRRLF matching grant, directly from RRRLF and as gratis from the public. The following table provides figures for book stocks available at DCL, BLS, VLS and MLS and also books weeded out during the year 2003-04.

Category of Libraries	*Book stocks 31.03.03*	*DPL/ RRLF*	*RRRLF*	*ZGS*	*gratis funds*	*Total*	*Books weded out 31.03.04*	*Net book stocks on*
DCL	54575	374	320	–	69	55338	501	54837
BLS	11,59,051	3838	1594	1471	1143	1167100	3496	1163604
VLS	42704	–	–	–	46	42750	–	42750
MLS	11141	–	–	–	–	11141	–	11141
Total	12,67474	4212	1914	1471	1258	12,76,329	3997	12,72,332

Of the total book stock of 12,72,332 available in the district public library system by the end of 31.03.04, the break-up of the total book stock language wise is shown in the following table.

Category of Library	*Telugu*	*English*	*Hindi*	*Urdu*	*Other Languages*	*Total*
DCL	38,350	12,011	3610	248	438	54,837
BLS	1,082,414	62,371	17,231	495	1,093	11,63,604
VLS	42,357	228	3	162	–	42,750
MLS	11,106	35	–	–	–	11,141
Total	11,74,407	74,645	20,844	905	1531	12,72,332

Periodical Subscription

During the year 2003-04, the ZGS has subscribed to a total of 3220 periodical titles of various frequencies of which Telugu periodicals constituted 2857, followed by English 363. Of the total 2857, Telugu periodicals dailies constitute 486, weeklies 455, fort nighlies 167 and monthlies 1749. Likewise of the total 363 English periodicals dailies constitute 114, weeklies 112, fort nightlies 20 and monthlies 115.

Memberships

The total memberships by the end of 31.03.04 stood at 83935. The following table provides the break-up of membership as per the category of library.

Category of Libraries	*Membership as on 31.03.03*	*New members added*	*Members withdrawn*	*Not membership as on 31.03.04*
DCL	3.973	180	26	4127
BLS	63,191	4217	195	67,213
VLS	2627	21	–	2648
MLS	9947	–	–	9947
Total	79,738	4,418	221	83,935

Readership

The total readerships by the end of 31.03.04 stood at 20,20,910 and break-up of membership as per the type of library shown in the following table.

Type of library	*2003-04*
DCL	130408
BLS	1859929
VLS	30573
MLS	–
BDCS	–
Total	20,20,910

If appears that there was an increase of 6.96% in the total membership than the year 2002-03.

Books Consulted

The total books consulted during the year 2003-04 in the entire public library system stood at 3,94,318. The following table provides figures for the total books consulted at different categories of libraries.

Category of Libraries	2003-04
DCL	28277
BLS	358153
VLS	7888
MLS	–
BDCS	–
Total	3,94,318

It appears that there has been an increase of just 1.27% readership in the year 2003-04.

Books Lent for Home Reading

During the year 2003-04, a total of 263522 books were lent for home reading by district public library system. The following table provides figures for library wise lending of books.

Category of library	2003-04
DCL	18803
BLS	240927
VLS	3792
MLS	–
BDCS	–
Total	263522

It appears that there has been an increase of just 0.18% in book lending.

Librarycess

Library cess is one of main sources of revenue for the ZGSS in the state. During the year 2003-04, the ZGS has realised as sum of Rs 84,65,929 as library cess from the following local bodies in the district :

1.	Municipal corporation	21,00,000
2.	Municipalities	27,83,690
3.	Panchayats	33,36,221
4.	Industrial area, Kondapalli	2,46,018
	Total	84,65,929

Extension Activities

During the year 2003-04, the ZGS has a total of 61 activities which include book exhibitions, film shows, literary and cultural activities. It has been actively celebrating National Library Week during November 14-20 every year. For the 36th National Library Week (14-20-11-03) celebrations the ZGS has spent a sum of Rs 50,000.

Achievements

In the year 1999-2000 books worth Rs 16,44,992 in Telugu, English and Hindi were acquired. An amount of Rs 2,31,102 was spent for acquiring storage material for BLS. In the years 1997-98 and 2000-01, with the funds form MPLADS and ZGS funds 10 library buildings were constructed spending an amount of Rs 13,19,000. In the year 1999-2000 an amount of Rs 8,80,740 was spent towards acquisition of periodicals and magazines. Library cess to the tune of Rs 66,47,700 was collected from local bodies as per the provisions of A.P. Public Libraries Act, 1960.

Future Plans

The ZGS wish to strengthen the Reference Division of Tagore Memorial library at Vijayawada. To start with, strengthening of Competitive Exams Reference Divisions at Grade I Libraries and later extending the same to all BLS. Computerisation of DCL and provision of Internet facility was high on the agenda of the ZGS. To strive for own library building to all BLS in the system and impart training to the working professional on the development and trends in the field of LIS so as to offer quality services to reading public. To organisej and conduct adult literacy centres. To supply reading materials to neo-literates. To extend library services from BLS through RLS to village people where the are no libraries with the support and cooperation from village education Committees of Grampanchayats.

Sources : 1. Andhra Pradesh lo Zilla Grandhalaya Samsthalu Krishana Zilla, *Grandhalya Sarvasmamu*, V62, N11 Feb 02. pp. 2-8.

2. *Annual Report of Zilla Grandhalaya Samstha, Krishna District 2003-04.*

F.11. Zilla Grandhalaya Samstha (ZGS) : Kurnool

Local Library Authority, Kurnool District came into being in 1950 as a result of Madras Public Libraries Act, 1948. In the year 1953 the District Central Library (DCL) was established in 'Musanmazil' building near Clock Hospital (Gadiyaram Ashpatri). In October 1953 Andhra State was formed and Adoni Branch Library from Bellary District was transformed to Kurnool district. From 1954 to 1963 seventeen Branch Libraries were .established. Untill the year 1966-67 only eleven Branch Librarians (BLS) were additionalty established. As a result of formation of Prakasam district in 1967 the BLSS at Markapuram, Giddaluru and Kambam were transferred to the new district. In the year 2002 there were 59 BLS functioning in the district public library system. Due to the efforts of former Chairmen of ZGS B. SubbaReddy and K. Kesava Reddy and also with the support of K. Vijaya Bhaskar Reddy the then Finance Minister (later Chief Minister) of Andhra Pradesh a newly constructed District Central Library (DCL) was inaugurated in August 1977.

No. of Libraries

The following table presents position of libraries as in the year 2002.

Type of library	*Nos*
District Central Library (DCL)	1
Branch Libraries (BLS)	58
Village Libraries (VLS)	5
Book Deposit Centres (BDCS)	29
Total	90

Library Staff

Almost all Zilla Grandhalaya Samathas (LLAS) in the state, with no exception to Rayalaseema were suffering from shortcage of man power to render effective library services to reading public. The sanctioned staff of all categories was 132 of which 63 posts lie vacant. Almost 50% of the posts were not filled up due to governments ban on recruitment. In the year 2002 the staff position was as follows : District Central Librarian (1), Grade II Librarians (12), Grade III Librarians (42), Senior Asst (1), Junior Assts (2), Record Assts (9), Attenders (35), Village librarians (5), Part time workers (22).

Library Buildings

The ZGSS in the state were not able to have own library buildings especially for the Branch Libraries (BLS) due to non availability of suitable land in semi urban and rural areas. Majority of ZGSS have only few own library buildings. Mostly the libraries are housed in rented or freely given buildings. The following table provides the position of library buildings in the district in the year 2002.

Type of Library	*Own Blds*	*Rented Blds*	*Free Blds*	*Total*
Dist. Central Library (DCL)	1	–	–	1
Branch Lib Bld	9	22	27	58
Village Lib Bld	–	–	5	5
Book Deposit Centre Bld	–	–	26	26
Total	10	22	58	90

Growth Indications

The Kurnool ZGS has achieved notable progress during the past five decades in respective of : acquisition of books, enrollement of members, visitors to the libraries, lending of books for home reading, collection of librarycess and construction of new library buildings. The following table gives us an idea as to progress achieved from 1996-97 to 2001-02.

Indicators	*1996-97*	*1997-98*	*1998-99*	*1999-00*	*2000-01*	*2001-2002*
Books	3.10	3.10	3.10	3.24	3.24	3.46
Members	0.20	0.20	0.20	0.21	0.22	0.25

No. of readers visited	10.42	11.03	10.57	11.56	11.44	13.33
Books Lent for home reading	2.58	1.94	1.24	1.43	0.96	0.86
Libcess collection (Rs. in lakhs)	9.01	23.46	31.44	25.49	32.59	39.48
New Lib Bld	–	–	–	2	–	–

In respect of construction of new library buildings the progress was dismal. During the six year period only two new library buildings were constructed.

Future Plans

The Kurnool Zilla Grandhalaya Samstha intends to computerise the library operations in phased manner to begin with DCL followed by Grade I libraries. To utilise the funds received from RRRLF, MP. LADS, EAS and Janmabhoomi programme for the construction buildings for Branch Libraries (BLS). With the permission of Director of Public Libraries, Govt of A.P. to open 25 BDCS in rural areas. To open ready reference section and special section for women readers at the DCL.

Stalwarts of Library Movement

Kurnool district has the distinction of producing one of the top most leaders of Andhra Pradesh in Gadicharla Hari Sarvottam Rao who dedicated his entire life for the cause of freedom movement, library movement and adult education movement not only in Andhradesa but also the entire country. Mention may be made of other prominent leaders who strove hard for the spread of the movement in the district include K. Narasing Rao, Desapandya Subha Rao, Kaipa Subhabmanya Sarma and Vavilala Parambramha Sastri.

Source : A Lalita, 'Andhra Pradesh lo Zilla Grandhalaya Samsthalu : Kurnool Zilla'. *Grandhalaya Sarvaswamu*. V63, N8, Nov. 2002, pp. 2-5.

F.12. Zilla Grandhalaya Samstha (ZGS) : Mahboobnagar

The District was named after Mir Mahboob Alikhan (1869-1911) the sixth Nizam of former Hyderabad State. This is the second biggest district in the state. The District was formed in 1870 in the name of Nagar Kurnool. In the year 1883 the district headquarters were shifted from Nagarkurnool to Mahboobnagar. Before 1985, the district consisted of four revenue divisions and thirteen talukas. In the year 1985 the revenue divisions were reorganised into 64 revenue Mandals. Presently the district consists of 16 Panchayat Samithis, 1553 villages and 1104 Grampanchayats.

No. of Libraries

The following table provides figures for types of libraries functioning under ZGS in the district during the year 2006-07.

S.No	Type of Library	Number
1.	District Central Library (DCL)	1
2.	Branch Libraries (BLS)	66
3.	Village Libraries	15
4.	Book Deposit Centres	46
	Total	128

Book Collection

The total book collection in the district public library system including the DCL as on 31.03.2007 stood at 3,39062. The collection at DCL stood at 3,05,6192 and at Village libraries stood at 4026 and at Book Deposit Centres was 1830. The language wise break-up of collections at DCL and BLS is shown in the following table.

Languages	DCL	BLS
Telugu	14,472	2,55,716
English	6777	26,919

Hindi	2,262	13,588
Urdu	1,937	9,312
Other languages	139	84
Total	25,587	3,05,619

Category wise Collection

The following table provides category wise book collection available at the DCL and BLs.

Category	*DCL*	*BLS*
Children books	2,287	75,292
Reference books	5,878	23,547
Text books	560	10,258
Books for neoliterates	2,229	29,909
Fiction books	6075	1,03,717
Non-fiction books	8,558	62,896
Total	25,587	3,05,619

Periodicals Subscribed

The ZGS has subscribed to 1,368 periodicals during the year 2006-07 to DCL, BLS, VLS, Mobile library and BDCS. The following table provides figures for periodicals subscribed and received by gratis.

	DCL (1)	*BLS (16)*	*VLS (15)*	*ML (1)*	*BDCS (50)*
By subscription	40	1,051	30	2	100
Gratis	20	123	–	–	–
Total	**60**	**1,176**	**30**	**2**	**100**
Frequency wise break-up					
Dailies	17	495	30	2	100
Other than dailies	43	681	–	–	–
Total	60	1,176	30	2	100

Language wise break-up					
Telugu	38	1,088	30	2	100
English	17	59	–	–	–
Hindi	1	10	–	–	–
Urdu	4	19	–	–	–
Total	60	1,176	30	2	100

Registered Borrowers

The number of registered borrowers by the end of 31.03.07 stood at 36,852. The break-up is as follows :

DCL	*BLS*	*VLS*	*BDCS*	*MLS*	*Total*
3957	32,303	592	–	–	36,852

Categories of Borrowers

The registered borrowers consists of cross section of public who use collections of DCL, BLS and VLS. The following table provides figures for various categories of borrowers.

S.No Category of Borrowers	*DCL (1)*	*BLS (66)*	*VLS (15)*	*BDCS (50)*	*MLS (1)*
1. Professionals (Doctors, Lawyers, Engineers etc)	239	1,715	592	–	–
2. Farmers/Agricultu-ralists	394	5,172	–	–	–
3. Businessmen	1,310	5,334	–	–	–
4. Students	196	6,724	–	–	–
5. Housewives	663	3,459	–	–	–
6. Employees	415	3,518			
7. Others	740	6,381			
Total	3,957	32,303	592	–	–

Books Consulted

Consultation of library collections within the library is one of the common services offered by public library. Duirng the year 2006-07 a total of 1,12,215 books were consulted at the DCL and BLS. The following is break-up of types of books consulted by the readers.

Type of book consulted	*DCL (1)*	*BLS (66)*	*Total*
(a) Text books	2,532	1,05,683	1,12,215
(b) Ref. books	2,300	23,301	
(c) Fiction	868	33,889	
(d) Non-fiction	832	28,355	

An average of 22 books were consulted in the DCL and 368 books in the BLS per day.

Books Lent

Lending of books for home reading is another important service rendered by the DCL and its Branch Libraries. During the year 2006-07 at total of 7,436 books were lent by DCL and 1,38,239 books were lent by 66 BLS, totaling 1,45,675 books. The following figures deal with the type of books lent by DCL and BLS.

	DCL (1)	*BLS (66)*	*Total*
(a) Fiction books	5,400	72,010	77,410
(b) Non-fiction	2,036	66,229	78,265
Total	7,436	1,38,239	1,45,675

The total percentage of population covered of the District is 30,77,051 of which urban area population is 3,42,192 and rural area population is 27,34,859. The total literates in the urban areas is, 1,09,994 and in the rural areas it is 76,148. The population covered by library services in the urban areas was 32% and in rural areas it was just 2% a total 34% of the population covered by library services in the district.

Library Buildings

The Districts Central Library (DCL) is housed in its own

building. Of the 66 BLS and 15 VLS, 37 have their own buildings and the rest ie 45 BLS and VLS are housed in rent free buildings. Under food for work programme, the Govt. of A.P. has sanctioned funds for the construction of library buildings for BLS at Dameragidda, Lingala, Dharur and Gopalupeta. The ZGS has acquired 400 sq yds of land under the instructions of District collector at Diet College at Mahaboob nagar. The local MP A.P. Jitender Reddy, sanctioned Rs. 10 lakhs from MP LADS funds.

From the funds of Chairman, Zilla Parishat, Rs 10 lakhs were sanctioned. D.Vitta Rao, M.P., sanctioned Rs 3.70 lakhs from his MPLADS fund. With these funds compound wall and the first floor of the library building was constructed.

The RRRLF, Kolkata has sanctioned 4 lakhs each for construction library building for BLS at Danwada and Koyilukonda. The building for Kesavapeta BL was constructed with the financial assistance of Rs 4 lakhs from RRRLF, Kolkata. The following table provides figures for library buildings.

Type of Library	*Own Blds*	*Rented Blds*	*Free Blds*	*Total*
1. Dist. Central Library	1	–	–	1
2. Branch Libraries	45	21	–	66
3. Village Libraries	2	13	–	15
4. Book Deposite Centres	–	46	–	46
Total	48	80		128

Library Staff

The sanctioned staff strength of various categories of posts in the year 2006-07 was 161. The following table provides figures for various categories of sanctioned posts.

Name of the post	*Nos*
District Central Librarian	1
Junior Asst	1
Typist	1

Librarians Gr I	2
Librarian Gr II	1
Librarians Gr III	53
Record Assts	15
Attenders	14
Watchmen	1
Sweepers	72
Total	161

To manage village Libraries (VLS) and Book Deposit Centres (BDCS) 15 partime village librarians and 46 part time BDC librarians have been working.

Extension Activities

The extension activities include book exhibitions, filmshows, forming reading circles, arranging leactures, organising seminars and conferences and conducting orientation programmes for the staff members. During the year 2006-07, the ZGS has organised 48 activities at the DCL level and 1586 at the BLS level. The following table provides figures for the various types activities conducted by the ZGS.

Type of activity	*DCL*	*BLS*
Book exhibitions	5	246
Film shows	4	19
Reading Circles	1	175
Lectures	3	194
Classes	5	189
Discussions	5	188
Training Programmes	2	2
Other Programmes	23	573
Total	48	1586

Private Libraries in the District

Not much is known about the state of private libraries in the district. The Director of Public Libraries (DPL) has recognised six libraries in the district for grant in aid. These are :

1. Madina Public Library (1963), Mahaboobnagar,
2. Yuvajana Seva Sangam Library (1975), MNagar
3. Sri Andhra Yuvajana Library (1960) Chennipad,
4. Hindi Prachara Samithi (1964), Narayana Peta,
5. Sri Netaji Yuvajana Sangham (1976), Peddamaroor, and
6. Sri Sitaramanjaneya Library (1963), M Nagar. These libraries are not receiving any grant either from the ZGS, Mahaboobnagar or from DPL, Govt. of Andhra Pradesh.

Source : *Zilla Grandhalaya Samstha, Mahaboob Nagar. State Administrative Report, 2006-07.*

F.13. Zilla Grandhalaya Samstha (ZGS) : Medak

Medaks district consist of 3 revenue divisions, 45 Mandals, 44 major gram panchayats and 5 municipalities. The Districts Central Library (DCL) was establised in 1958 at Sangareddy, the district headquarters. Later in 1959 three Branch Libraries (BLS) were established at Jogipeta, Medak and Siddipeta. In the year 1960 Local Library Authority (LLA) was formed as per the provisions of A.P. Public Libraries Act, 1960. In addition to Telugu, Hindi, Urdu, Marathi and Kannada languages are spoken by the people of Medak district.

No. of Libraries

The following table provides figures for the types of public libraries functioning in the district under Medak Zilla Grandhalaya Samastha (ZGS) in the year 2004-05.

	Type of Library	*Nos*
1.	District Central Library (DCL)	01
2.	Branch Libraries (BLS)	46
3.	Rural Libraries (RLS)	06
4.	Book Deposit Centres (BDCS)	61
	Total	114

The DCL and 27 BLS were managed by qualified library staff. The rest of 19 BLS were managed by Record Assistant/ Attenders.

Book Collection

As on 31st March 2005 the book collection stood at 2,58,6,30.

The break-up of book collecltion language wise was as follows.

	Language	*No. of books*
1.	Telugu	2,05,802
2.	English	23,913

3.	Hindi	14,711
4.	Urdu	14,195
5.	Sanskrit	09
	Total	2,58,630

Periodicals Subscribed

During the year 2004-05, the ZGS has subscribed to 121 periodicals for its libraries. The following table provides figures for the periodicals subscribed languagewise.

Language	*DCL*	*BLS/VLS*	*Total*
Telugu	58	19	77
English	22	05	27
Hindi	02	02	04
Urdu	08	05	13
Total	90	31	121

Membership

As on 31st March 2005 there were 27717 registered borrowers in the ZGS. The break-up was as follows :

DCL 2753, BLS 19316, RLS 242 and BDCS 1853.

Readership

During the year 2004-05, a total 19,56,209 readers visited the libraries of the ZGS. The following table provides figures for the total readership visited various types of libraries.

Type of Library	*Total readership*
DCL	63510
BLS	15,66,717
VLS	78,352
BDCS	2,47,630
Total	19,56,209

Books Consulted

During the year 2004-05 a total 2,76,917 books were consulted by the readers in all the libraries. The books consulted include text books, reference books, competitive examinations books and books on fiction.

Books Lent for Home Reading

During the year 2004-05 a total of 2,09,607 books were lent for home reading by all the libraries of the ZGS. Out of 27,717 registered members 13,234 members borrowed 2,09,607 books which include reference and text books and also books on competitive examinations and books on fiction.

Books Added During the Year

The ZGS has purchased 26,937 books from its funds. In addition, it has also received 146 books from RRRLF Kolkata and 671 books from DPL/RRRLF Kolkata and 397 books from the public as gratis.

Library cess

During the year 2004-05 an amount of Rs 48,99,094 was realised towards library cess from the following local bodies :

1.	APIIC, Patancheru	Rs 4,62,769
2.	Municipalities	Rs 25,63,438
3.	Notified Panchayats	Rs 16,72,004
4.	Non Notified Panchayats	Rs 2,00,883
	Total	Rs 48,99,094

Library staff

The following table provides figures for sanctioned posts and existing vacancies of various categories of posts in ZGS as on 31.03.2005.

S.No	Type of Post	No. of Sanctioned Posts	No. of Vacant Posts
1.	Secretary/District Centre Librarian (DCL)	01	–
2.	Dy. Lilbrarian (Grade I)	01	01
3.	Jr. Assistant	01	–
4.	Typist	01	–
5.	Grade II Librarians	04	03
6.	Grade III Librarians	34	08
7.	Record Assts	12	02
8.	Attenders	17	–
9.	Watchmen	06	02
10.	Gardner	01	–
11.	Sweeper	01	–
	Total	79	16
12.	Part time Village Librarians	06	06
13.	Part time Workers	24	24
	Total	30	30

Almost one fourth of the posts were vacant due to ban imposed by the government on new recuritments and filling up of existing vacancies.

This policy of the state government was effecting proper functioning of libraries in the district and rendering quality library services to the reading public.

Library Buildings

Having own library buildings for all the BLS in the district is a major problem faced by all the ZGSS in the state. Medak district is no exception in this regard. In 2004-05, DCL and 21 BLS and 1 RL having their own library buildings.

Twenty nine BLS/RLS are housed in rent free buildings and 2 BLS are housed in rented buildings. For BLS at Kodbaram, Jinnaram, Kaudipalli, Hatnurla, Papannapeta, library buildings were under construction with the funds worth Rs 400,000/- for each library received under 'food for work programma'. With the funds received from RRRLF, Kolkata construction of library buildings were undertaken for BLS at Patancheru and Sivampeta. In the 2003, the RRRLF again sanctioned Rs 4.00 lakhs each for construction of buildings for BLS at Mulugu and Miraoddi.

RRRLF's Support

During the year 2001-02, the RRRLF, Kolkata granted Rs 1,50,000 for construction of building for BL, Rs 10,000 for childrens library, Rs 47,344 for purchase of books and storage materials for 11 BLS, and Rs 10,000 for conducting refresher courses to staff member, and Rs 20,000 for purchase of a cycle and books for Book Deposit Centres. Again for the year 2002-03 the RRRLF sanctioned Rs 600,000 in the installments for construction of library buildings for two BLS, Rs.100,000 for purchase of racks and almirahs for five BLS; Rs 20,000 for purchase of books to childrens library ; Rs 80,000 for purchase of cycles and books for four BDCS; Rs 25,000 for conducting refresher courses to library staff.

The RRRLF, Kolkata again in the year 2001-02 supplied 3939 books worth Rs 3,00,869 to the ZGS, Medak. The Director of Public Libraries, Govt. of AP with the matching grant from RRRLF, supplied 453 titles worth Rs 55,644. In the year 2002-03, the RRRLF Kolkata supplied 606 titles worth Rs 75,888. In the same year the Director of Public Libraries, Govt of AP with the matching grant from RRRLF supplied 4564 titles worth Rs 3,74,760. This shows that RRRLF has been supporting the public library system in AP in a big way by releasing funds for construction of library buildings, acquisition of reading materials and storage materials and enhancing professional competence of the staff by releasing considerable funds for conducting refresher courses/workshops/orientation programmes and seminars at regular intervals.

Grants Received from RRRLF, Kolkata

During the year 2004-05 the following grants were received from RRRLF, Kolkata by the ZGS.

1. Construction of buildings for Branch Library at Nangnoor Rs 4,00,000.
2. Purchase of children books Rs 100,000.
3. Purchase of storage material Rs 50,000.
4. Development of Rural BDCS. Rs 40,000.

A proposal for computerisation of DCL was sent to RRRLF, Kolkata.

Future Plans

The ZGS, Medak wants at the first instance to fill up the existing vacancies and carryout necessary repairs to DCL for its modernisation and computerisation and provision of Internet facility. To computerise the BLS in a phased manner and provision of Internet facility. To tap the required financial reasources from RRRLF, Food for work programmes, Janambhoomi programme, MP, MLA LADS, JRY. funds to have own library buildings and supply required reading and storage materials to all BLS. To open competitive exams materials sections in some of the BLS located in Assembly constituency headquarters and stock degree level text books within five years. Extend library services in a phased manner to all gram panchayats. To upgrade the existing Grade III BLS in the Municipalities and Assembly constituency headquarters to Grade II Libraries. To conduct at regular intervals refresher courses and orientation programmes to staff members so as to render better library services to the reading public. To elicit donations from the philnthrophists and put that money along with part of library deposit money in a bank under fixed deposit and utilise the interest accrued for developmental activities of DCL and BLS. To conduct cultural programmes and celebrate rational and international events regularly including national library week and to convey the importance of libraries and their services to readers and strive to achieve total literarcy in the district.

Sources : 1. T. Pulliah. Andhra Pradesh lo Grandhalaya. Samsthalu, Medak Zilla. *Grandhalaya Sarvashwamu* V65, N3, June 04, pp. 1-4, 10.

2. *Zilla Grandhalaya Samstha, Medak District Annual Report*, 2004-05. (Mimeographed).

F.14. Zilla Grandhalaya Samstha (ZGS) : Nalgonda

Nalgonda district is politically very concious among the districts of Telangana. The district has played a significant role in the spread of library movement in Telangana and establishment close relationship between the leaders of Telangana and Andhra regions before independence. The district consists of 59 Mandals, 48 Major Pancyatas and 1,127 Minor Panchayats. The Nalgonda District Grandhalaya Samastha was formed in 1955 as per the provisions of Hyderabad Public Libraries Act, 1955. The District Central Library was established in 1958 at Nalgonda the district headquarters.

No. of Libraries

The following table provides figures for types of libraries functioning under ZGS in the district during the year 2006-07.

S.No	Type of library	Number
1.	District Central Library (DCL)	01
2.	Branch Libraries (BLS)	60
3.	Rural Libraries (RLS)	04
4.	Book Deposit Centres (BDCS)	58
	Total	123

Book Collection

The total collection of books in the district as on 31.03.07 was 2,86,903 of which the collection in DCL was 31,852, in BLS 2,09,785 and in RLS 4,182. A collection of 3,860 books were added to total collection received from RRRLF, Kolkata on matching grant scheme, received through Director of Public Libraries, Govt. of Andhra Pradesh. In addition, 613 books were gifted by RRRLF directly to the ZGS. A total of 8,733 titles were added with the funds of ZGS. Donors gifted 170 very useful titles. The break-up of the collection languagewise was as follows :

Telugu	2,41,091
English	29,669
Hindi	9747
Urdu	6359
Other languages	37
Total	2,86,903

No. of Periodicals

The total number of periodicals in the DCL and BLS in the District as on 31.03.07 was 1760. The break-up is as follows :

Telugu 1590, English 154, Hindi 6 and Urdu 10.

Library Buildings

The ZGS had strived hard to have own library buildings for majority of BLS. This was a notable and remarkable achievement when compared with other ZGSS in the state. This shows the result of streneous efforts made by members of sucessive library committees and secretaries of the ZGS. The following table provides figures for library buildings.

Type of Library	*Own bld*	*Free bld*	*Rented bld*	*Total*
District Central Lib (DCL)	01	–	–	01
Branch Libraries (BLS)	48	10	02	60
Rural Libraries (RLS)	02	03	–	05
Total	51	13	02	66

It is very significant to not that only two BLS are housed in rented buildings, which is remarkable achievement on the part of Nalgonda ZGS, which the other ZGSS in the state should emulate. The Nalgonda ZGS could save its meagre financial resources and utilise the money and thus saved rental expenditure for strengthening infrastructure facilities in BLS. In addition, the ZGS could acquire land for three library buildings of which two sites were registered in favour of ZGS. In the year

2003 an auditorium was constructed on the first floor of DCL building. In the 2003, the ZGS received Rs 2 lakhs grant from RRRLF and with that amount a building was constructed for BL at Kolanupaka and womens and childerens library was started at Nalgonda.

Library Staff

The sanctioned staff strength of various categories posts in the year 2002 was 93 of which 26 post were lying vacant due to governments ban on recruitment and filling up of existing vacancies. The ban has come in the way effective functioning of libraries in the district. The following table provides figures for various types of sanctioned posts and vacancies against team.

S.No	*Type of Post*	*Sanctioned posts*	*Vacancies*
1.	District Central Library (DCL)	01	–
2.	Grade I Librarians	03	03
3.	Grade II Librarians	03	02
4.	Grade III Librarians	56	10
5.	Sr. Assistant	01	–
6.	Junior Assistant	01	–
7.	Record Assistants	02	–
8.	Attenders	18	05
9.	Watchmen	08	06
	Total	93	26

Due to non filling up vacancies there are instances where one person has been made incharge of two or three BLS. Fifteen BLS were managed by part time workers. The library services are being effected by this type of arrangement. The ZGS yearly spends Rs 70 lakhs on salaries and a pensions.

Language Wise Availablility of Books

During the year 2004-05 a total of 291,664 books in

different languages were available in various types of libraries. The following table provides figures for the books in different languages.

Category of Library	Telugu	English	Hindi	Urdu	Total
DCL	1389	567	31	27	2014
BLS	243051	31212	6633	5918	286814
VLS	2740	63	33	–	2,836
Total	247180	31842	6697	5945	291664

Membership

During the year 2004-05, the total membership of the ZGS stood at 10625. The break-up of membership according to type of library is given in the following table.

Types of library	Total membership
DCL	4136
BLS	6085
VLS	404
Total	10625

There has been 14% increase in the membership than the previous year.

Readership

During the year 2004-05 the total readership stood at 6520104 in the entire district public library system. The break-up as per type of library is given in the following table.

Type of library	Total readership
DCL	403126
BLS	6079166
VLS	37812
Total	6520104

There has been an increasing of 103.42% readership during the year than previous year.

Books Consulted

A total of 482282 books were consulted during the year 2004-05 in the district public library system. The following table provides figures for total book consulted at different types of libraries.

Type of Library	*Total books consulted*
DCL	43213
BLS	439069
Total	482282

There has been an increase of 15.40% in readership during the year than last year.

Books Lent for Home Reading

During the year 2004-05 a total of 449707 books were lent for home reading by the libraries under ZGS. The following table provides figures for total books lent for home reading by various type of libraries.

Type of Library	*Total books Rent*
DCL	18456
BLS	428832
VLS	2419
Total	449707

There has been an increase of 8.46% in books lending during the year 2004-05 than last year.

No. of Books Received from Other Sources

During the year 2004-05 a total of 4555 books were recieved from DPL/RRRLF matching scheme. The ZGS has also received 310 books from RRRLF Kolkata and 170 books as graitis form the public.

Library Cess

Library cess is one of the important source of revenue

for the ZGS in the state. During the year 2004-05, the ZGS has realised a sum of rupees 3347418 and Rs 4031622 as librarycess. The following table provides figures for the library cess received from local bodies such as Municipalities and Grampanchayats.

	Name of the local body	*Cess realised during 2004-05*
	Municipalities (4)	Rs 40,316,22
	Grampanchayats	
1.	Notified (48)	Rs 394,507
2.	Non-notified (1127)	Rs 40765
	Total	3347418.00

	Name of the local body	*Cess realised during 2004-05*
	Municipalities (4)	Rs 3386359
	Grampanchayats	
1.	Notified (48)	Rs 394507
2.	Non-notified (1127)	Rs 78605
	Total	4031622

Extension Activities

During the year 2004-05, the ZGS has organised few confrences, book exhibitions, literary and cultural activities. The DCL has organised 4 conferences, arranged 1 book exhibition, 6 literary activities and 10 cultural activities. The DCL and BLS have actively celebrated National Library weeks during November 14-20, 2004 and organise election, essay writing and painting competitions for children and students.

Progress Achieved

The ZGS achieved a remarkable progress in having own library buildings of BLS and this is a record in Telangana area. During the past 4 to 5 years the ZGS constructed buildings for BLS at Nakerkal, Gauraram, Ketapalli, Vemulapalli, Nampally, Gurrampodu, Chunduru and Rajampeta with the funds flowing from MPLADS, EAS and Jannambhoomi schemes and programmes. Land was acquired at Yadagigutta, a pilgrim centre and the temple authorities of SriLakshmi Narasimha Swamy Devasthanam got constructed a beautiful library building and handed over to the ZGS authorities. To strive hard to get funds from RRRLF every year and acquire storage materials such as furniture, book racks and almirahs, cycles, trunk boxes and provide them for BLS. To keep the library premises neat and clean and colouring and white washing all BLS in the district to attract more readers.

Future Plans

To increase the library cess collection to 20 to 25% more than the previous year and iniate necessary measures in this regard and also to ensure financial stability to ZGS. To get funds from RRRLF for construction of buildings to BLS at Arvapalli and Mathampalli. To arrange two programmes every month in all BLS for the benefit of children and senior citizens. To conduct continuous and adult educations programmes in all the BLS and establish community learning centres. To open 'competition book cell' in all BLS and help unemployed youth in their career endeavours and conduct free classes in career guidence and counselling with the support of well qualified experts. To enhance part time workers salary from Rs 750-Rs 1250 and entrust the job of cess collection to these workers. Lastly but not the least to endeavour to have own buildings to all the BLs in the district.

State of Private Libraries

Nalgonda district has played a very significant role in the spread of library movement in Telagana. One of stalwarts of the library movement Kodati Narayana Rao hailed from this district and learnt first lessons of popular public library movement. The other stawarts of movement Madapati Hunumanah Rao and Survaram Pratapa Reddy learnt their first steps of the movement in the district. During the thick of the movement it was estimated that there were nearly 120 libraries functioning in the district. Most of these libraries have disappeared from the scene and presently 3 to 4 libraries have survived. The ZGS has to come forward to revive these 'private' libraries and support them both financially and otherwise.

Source : 1. R.V.S. Siva Ramakrishna 'Andhra Pradesh lo Zilla Grandhalaya Samsthalu : Nalgonda Zilla. *Grandhalaya Sarvashumamu*, V64, N4, July 04, pp. 2-6.

2. *Annual Report of Zilla Grandhalaya Samstha, Nalgonda, 2004-05*

F.15. Zilla Grandhalaya Samstha (ZGS) : Nellore

Nellore district carved out a prominent place in the history of Andhra Pradesh. Two of the Kavitrayas Tikkana and Yerrana who wrote Mahabharata in Telugu hail from this district. Potti SriRamulu freedom fighter and nationalist who sacrified his life for achievement of Andhra state also hailed from this district. The district consists 7 towns, 46 Mandals and 1105 villages. The ZGS of Nellore district was formed in 1952 at Nellore town the district head quarters. The District Central Library (DCL) was also established in 1952.

No. of Libraries

The following table provides figures of number of various types of libraries functioning under the ZGS in the year 2004.

Type of library	*Nos*
District Central Library (DCL)	1
Branch Libraries (BLS)	58
Grade I	2
Grade II	5
Grade III	48
Managed by Record Assts	4
Rural Libraries (RLS)	11
Mobile Libraries (MLS)	2
Book Deposit Centres (BDCS)	26
Total	98

Book Collections

The total book collection under the ZGS library system in the year 2004 was as follows :

Types of Libray	*No. of Books*
Dist Central Library	37,938
Branch Libraries	3,50,189
Rural Libraries	17,514
Mobile Libraries	9,443
Total	4,15,084

Library Buildings

To have own library building for the DCL, the late A.C. Subba Reddy, when he was Municipal chairmen gave land freely in the heart of town for the construction of the buildings and foundation stone was laid in 1967. Due to technical and financial problems construction of the building was put on back burner. The present building from where the DCL was functioning was acquired from 'Rebala' family with the condition that the building should named after the late Rebala Pattabhirami Reddy in whose name the building was named. The following table provides figures for library buildings under the ZGS in the year 2004.

Type of Library	*Own bld*	*Rented bld*	*Free bld*	*Total*
Dist Central Library (DCL)	1	–	–	1
Grade I Library	–	2	–	2
Grade II Library	1	1	3	5
Grade III Library	15	1	32	48
Libraries Manage by Record Assts	2	1	1	4
Rural Libraries	8	–	7	15
Total	26	5	43	74

Book Collections

The total book collection in the district public library system in the 2004 was 4,15,084 books. The break up is given in the following table.

Type of Library	*No. of Books*
Dist Central Library (DCL)	37,938
Branch Libraries (BLS)	3,50,189
Rural Libraries (RLS)	17,154
Mobile Libraries (MLS)	9,443
Total	4,15,084

Membership

The number of registered borrowers and readers who visited the libraries in 2004 is given in the following table.

Type of library	*Members*	*Readers*
Dist. Central Library (DCL)	5,240	65,903
Branch Libraries (BLS)	26,432	15,63,537
Total	35,672	16,29,440

Periodical Collections

The following table provides figures for periodicals subscribed by the ZGS in Telugu and English during the 2001-02.

Type of Library	*Telugu*			*English*			*Total*
	D	*F*	*M*	*D*	*F*	*M*	
DCL	06	10	20	03	05	10	54
Grade I Libraries	04	10	20	02	09	08	53
Grade II Libraries	03	04	16	04	02	10	39
Grade III Libraries	04	02	19	02	04	13	44
Village Libraries	02	–	19	–	–	–	21

Books Consulted

During the 2001-02, a total of 1,54,523 books were consulted by the readers in the district public library system. The following table provides figures for total books consulted in various types of libraries.

Type of library	*Total books consulted*
DCL	6101
BLS	1,34,848
VLS	13,304
Total	1,54,253

Books Lent for Home Reading

During the year 2001-02, a total of 1,63,262 books were lent for home reading by various types of libraries managed by the ZGS. The following table provides figures for the books lent by the libraries.

Type of library	*Total Books Lent*
DCL	7,707
BLS	1,46,593
VLS	8,962
Total	1,63,262

Books Received from Other Agencies

During the year 2001-02, the ZGS had received books from the following agencies.

	No. of books	*No. of titles*
1. DPL/RRRLF Scheme	685	3,814
2. Director, RRRLF	4378	933
3. By Gratis	280	29

Librarycess

Librarycess is one of the most important sources of revenue for ZGSS in the State. The following table provides figures for the cess realised during 2001-02 from the local bodies.

Name of the local body	*Amount realised*
1. Municipalities (3)	2,72,402
2. Notified Gram Panchayats	3970000
3. Non-notified Gram Panchayats (951)	

Extension Activities

The libraries functioning under the ZGS had been organising National Library Week every year during November

14-20. During the year 2001-02 fifty five BLS had celebrated NLW. In addition the DCL and 4 BLS have arranged five book exhibitions. The extension activities were far from satisfactory.

Achievement

During the year 2004 storage material worth Rs 2,72,860 was acquired and distributed to BLS. Construction of library buildings with the funds received from 'Janambhoomi', MP and MLA LADS, EAS Scheme, and voluntary contributions. The ZGS collected library cess vigorously from the local bodies. Acquisition of vacant land costing Rs 2 lakhs for the construction of Branch Library building.

Future Plans

To start with in the first phase establishment of competitive exams Reference sections in DCL and two Grade I Libraries and slowly extending the said facility to all BLS in a phased manner. To undertake necessary repairs for computerisation and provision of Internet facility at the DCL. To tap funds from different sources for the construction of library buildings and purchase of books to BLS. To establish liason with Adult Education Centres by the staff and extend library services to such centres. To establish close relations with Primary and Middle schools in the vicinity and inculcate reading habits among school children.

Sources : 1. R. Sarada, Andhra Pradesh lo Zilla Grandhalaya Samsthalu : Nellone Zilla, *Grandhalaya Sarvaswamu* V64, N11, Feb 04, pp. 1-5.

2. *Annual Report of Zilla Grandhalaya Samastha, Nallore District.* 2002-2003. (Mimeographed).

F.16. Zilla Grandhalaya Samstha (ZGS) : Nizamabad

Nizamabad district was formed in the year 1876 during the region of Asafzahis. Presently the district consists of 3 Municipalities, 36 Mandals, and 719 Gram panchayats. The District Central Library (DCL) was established in 1959 at Nizamabad town, the district headquarters along with 2 Branch Libraries (BLS) at Kamareddy and Armoor. Local library Authority (LLA) was formed in 1960 as per the provisons of A.P. Public Libraries Act, 1960. The people of the district speak Telugu, Hindi, Urdu, Marathi and Kannada languages.

No. of Libraries

The following table provides figures for various types libraries functioning under Zilla Grandhalaya Samastha as on 31st March 2003.

Type of Library	*No*
District Central Library (DCL)	1
Branch Libraries (BLS)	43
Rural Libraries (RLS)	30
Book Deposit Centres (BDCS)	26
Total	100

జిల్లా గ్రంథాలయ సంస్థ, నిజామాబాద్

The District Central Library and 29 BLS were managed by qualified staff and 15 BLS were managed by Record Assts/ Attenders.

Book Collections

The total collection at the DCL as on 31st March, 2003 was 34,432 at all the BLS 3,83,200, at all the RLS 64,782 totaling 4,82,414 books in the district public library system. The language wise break-up was as follows :

1.	Telugu	3,95,815
2.	English	41,692
3.	Hindi	22,186
4.	Urdu	20,047
5.	Other languages	2,675
	Total	4,82,414

Library Staff

The sanctioned posts for ZGS as on 31st March 2003 was 135 of which 34 posts were vacant. The following table provides figures for different types of posts and vacancies against each post.

S.No	*Type of Post*	*Sanctioned Post*	*Vacancy*
1.	Secretary/District Central Libraian (DCL)	01	–
2.	Dr. Librarian (DL)	01	–
3.	Sr. Assistant	01	01
4.	Jr. Assistant	01	–
5.	Typist	01	01
6.	Grade II Librarians	02	–
7.	Grade III Librarians	32	06
8.	Record Assistants	13	03
9.	Attenders	24	05
10.	Watchmen	08	01
11.	Rural Libray Organisers	30	11
12.	Part time workers	20	06
	Total	135	34

More than one fourth of the posts of various categories were vacant in the ZGS due to governments ban on new recruitment and filling up existing vacancies. Lack of required staff had hampered the library services.

Libray Buildings

The ZGS has own library buildings for the DCL, 16 BLS and 01 Rural library. Twelve BLS were housed in rented buildings and 15 in rent free buildings.

Development Activities

With funds received from RRRLF, Kolkata storage materials ie, almirahs and racks worth Rs. 2,92,350 were purchased in the year 1998-99 and distributed to 43 BLS and twenty two RLS. In the year 2000-01 RRRLF sanctioned Rs 4.00 lakhs for construction of buildings for BLS at Bhiknoor and Rs 18,000 for purchase of furniture to BLS at Varni, Bhiknoor and Bodhan. Again in the year 2000-01 RRRLF has sanctioned Rs 6 lakhs for construction of library buildings for BLS at Armoor and Sadasivanagar, and Rs 48,000 for purchase of racks for 8 BLS, Rs 40,000 for the purchase bicycles and books for BDCS at Neela and Arsapalli, Rs 10,000 for conducting refresher courses and orientation programmes for library staff. Again in the year 2002-03 RRRLF has sanctioned Rs 1 lakh for purchase of storage material for 10 BLS, Rs 20,000 for children's library, Rs 40,000 for the purchase of bicycle and books for BDCS and Rs 3,60,000 for the construction of library buildings for BL at Velpur.

For the year 2001-02 the Director of public libraries, Govt. of A.P. with the matching grant from RRRLF supplied 4,437 titles. Again for the year 2002-03, the ZGS received 3908 titles worth Rs 2,33,289. Again for the year 2003-04 the ZGS received 3,569 titles worth Rs 3,50,000. The above actions show that RRRLF has been supporting the ZGSS in the state in a big way for construction of library buildings, acquisition of books, providing storage materials and helping to conduct training programmes for the library staff.

Future Plans

The ZGS would like to strive in every possible way to fill up the existing vacancies and computerise DCL and Provision of Internet facility for the benefit of library users.

With the funds from RRRLF, MPLADS and supplementing with ZGS funds construction of library buildings to the BLS. To under take necessary repairs and modifications for moderisation and computerisation of DCL. In future the ZGS strives to have own library buildings to all BLS RLS in the district by tapping financial resources from various schemes of the government. In the year 2003 it wants to purchase computer system and computerise official records.

Source : A. V. N Raju, 'Andhra Pradesh lo Grandhalaya-Samsthalu Nizamabad', *Grandhalaya Sarvaswamu*, V64, N7, Oct 03. pp. 5-8.

F.17. Zilla Grandhalaya Samstha (ZGS) : Prakasam

Ongole district was formed in the year 1972 by merging certain areas from the neighbouring districts, Nellore, Kurnool and Guntur. The district was renamed after Sri Tangturi Prakasham Pantulu on 12.5.1972 the great freedom fighter and first Chief Minister of Andhra which was formed in 1953 and to prepetuate his memory in recognition of his sacrifies and contributors, for the cause of telugu people. To concide with the birthday of Prakasam Pantulu Prakasam district Grandhalaya samastha was formed on August 23, 1973 as a consequence of A.P. Public Libraries Act of 1960. Initially the ZGS consisted 20 BLS transferred from Guntur 12, Nellore 5 and Kurnool 3.

No. of Libraries

Comparatively Prakasam district ZGS was younger than most of the ZGSS in the state. But it strove hard to establish BLS in various parts of the district to provide library services to the reading public. The famous 'Saraswata Niketanam' library is in the district at Vetapalem. The following table provides figures for the libraries functioning in the district as on 31.03.05.

Type of Library	*Nos*
District Central Library (DCL)	1
Branch Libraries (BLS)	65
Rural Libraries (RLS)	27
Book Deposit Centres	40
Total	133

Library Staff

The sanctioned posts of all categories for the ZGS as on 2003 was 164 of which 45 posts were lying vacant for years due to ban imposed by the government on filling up vacancies and creation of new posts. The following table provides figures for various types of sanctioned posts and existing vacancies.

Category	*Sanctioned posts*	*Vacancies*
District Central Librarian	1	–
Grade I Librarians	2	–
Grade II Librarians	4	–
Grade III Librarians	47	2
Junior Assistants	2	–
Typist	1	1
Record Assistants	26	4
Attenders	14	4
Watchmen	8	5
Part time workers	59	29
Total	164	45

Library Buildings

The District Central Library was established in 1974 in a rented building. Later on 'Saraswati Grandhalayam' functioning in the heart of the town was taken over and the DCL was relocated in the building of Saraswati Grandhalayam in April 1974. The vast vacant place around Saraswati Grandhalayam was acquired in February 1975 and the foundation stone for new building was laid in December 1975 and the new building was inaugurated 1978. The following table provides information about library buildings as on 31.03.05.

Type of Library	*Own Blds*	*Rented Blds*	*Free Blds*	*Total*
1. Dist. Central Library	1	–	–	1
2. Branch Libraries	15	15	35	65
3. Village Libraries	1	–	25	26
Total	17	15	60	92

Book Collection

The total books collection of the ZGS as on 31.03.05 stood at 4,43,658. The break-up of language wise and category wise was as follows :

	DCL	*BLS*	*VLS*	*Total*
Languagewise Break-up	35157	379903	28598	4,43,658
Telugu	24375	347682	27962	400019
English	9522	24969	579	35070
Hindi	1107	6415	42	7564
Urdu	60	470	8	538
Other languages	93	367	28598	4,43,658
Total	35157	379903	28598	4,43,658
Categorywsie Break-up				
Children's books	1437	80853	15206	97,406
Ref. books	6350	20442	1276	28068
Text books	2909	9832	1064	13805
Books for neo literates	260	7978	413	8651
Bound periodical volumes	658	9796	37	10491
Fiction books	9149	133708	6425	149282
Non fiction books	14394	117294	4177	135865
Total	35157	379903	28598	443658

Periodical Collections

A total of 1437 periodicals were subscribed by the ZGS during the year 2004-05. The break-up by purchase, gratis, language and frequency is as follows :

(a)	By purchase	58	1117	105	1280
(b)	By gratis	–	146	11	157
	Total	58	1263	116	1437

By language

Telugu	34	1173	113	1320
English	24	87	3	114
Hindi	–	3	–	3
Urdu	–	–	–	–
Total	58	1263	116	1437

By frequency

Dailies	12	282	25	319
Other than dailies	46	981	91	1118
Total	58	1263	116	1437

Registered Borrowers

The ZGS had a total of 35411 registered borrowers as on 31.03.05. The breakup was follows :

	DCL	*BLS*	*VLS*	*Total*
Genderwise break-up				
(a) Men	3574	23774	1337	28685
(b) Women	298	4166	173	4637
(c) Children	121	1894	74	2089
Total	3993	29834	1584	35411
Category wise break-up				
(a) Professionals	401	948	59	1408
(b) Farmers/Agriculturists	330	4618	539	5487
(c) Businessman	860	5078	161	6099
(d) Students	800	5863	266	6929
(e) House wives	231	3130	104	3465
(f) Employees	725	5571	249	6545
(g) Unemployed	646	4626	206	5478
Total	3993	29834	1584	35411

Readership

A total of 1648980 readers used the ZGS public library system during the year 2004-05. The break-up was as follows:

189107 134850 95023 1648980

The following figures show the number of readers used periodical and book sections of the district public library system.

Public Library system	*DCL*	*BLS*	*VLS*	*Total*
(a) Periodical section	142434	983834	64120	1190398
(b) Book Section	46673	381016	30893	458582
Total	189107	1364850	95013	1648980

Books Consulted

A total of 320623 books were consulted by the readers during the year 2004-05. The break-up was as follows :

51595 249283 19745 320623

The following figures indicate the type of books consulted.

(a) Text books	9723	29233	1872	40828
(b) Ref books	27700	50078	2526	80304
(c) Nonfiction	3452	78285	6740	88477
(d) Fiction	10720	107814	8607	127141

Books Lent for Home Reading

During the year 2004-05 a total of 201798 books were lent for home reading. The books lent by various types of libraries is provided in the following table.

	DCL (1)	*BLS (65)*	*VLS (27)*	*Total*
Types of book lent	7709	178089	16000	201798
1. Fiction	5945	103886	10608	120439
2. Non-fiction	1746	74203	5392	81359
Total	7709	178089	16000	201798

Progress Indicators

During the five year period ie., 1997-98 to 2001-02 the progress achieved in respect of acquisition of books, membership, readers, books lent, buildings constructed and cess realised is shown in the following table.

Indicators	*1997-98*	*1998-99*	*1999-2000*	*2000-01*	*2002-02*
Books (in lakhs)	4.41	4.41	4.38	4.57	4.62
Membership (in lakhs)	0.29	0.30	0.30	0.30	0.33
Readers (in lakhs)	10.52	9.90	10.66	12.26	13.64
Books lent (in lakhs)	1.65	1.87	1.82	1.49	1.23
Buildings constructed	1	–	–	–	–
Librarycess realised (Rs. in lakhs)	26.75	25.62	31.81	28.42	30.31

The progress achieved in construction of library buildings was negligible.

Future Activities

With the funds form RRRLF and with an expenditure of Rs 10 lakhs work has been started to computerise District Central Library and install Internet facility. To have an auditorium on the first floor of DCL. To construct library buildings for BLS with the financial support from RRRLF, Kolkata funds from MP LADS and other developmental projects of the state government. In addition to the present 26 BDCS functioning in the district, and opening up more BDCS to cover many villages to provide library services to more readers. Provisions of Competitive Examinations Reference Units not only in the District Central Library but also in BLS, opening up of text books sections in BLS. To organise 'akshara sankranti' programmes for the propogation of literacy in the district. To increase library readers and enhance library memberships to an appreciable figures.

Source : 1. K. Sri Krishna 'Andhra Pradesh lo Zilla Grandhalaya Samsthalu : Prakasam Zilla'. *Grandhalaya Sarvaswamu*. V63, N12, March 03, pp. 1-6.

2. *Zilla Grandhalaya Samstha Prakasam District Administrative report for the year 2004-2005*. (Mimeographed).

F.18. Zilla Grandhalaya Samstha (ZGS) : Ranga Reddy

RangaReddy district came into being on 15 August 1978 and named after K.V. RangaReddy, a very prominent political leader of Telangana region. The district was formed by bifurcating Hyderabad district and adding few areas from Nalgonda and Mahaboobnagar. The district consists of 12 Municipalities 37 Mandals and 1055 villages. As per the provisions A.P. Public Libraries Act 1960, RangaReddy Zilla Grandhalaya Samastha (ZGS) was formed in 1979 and District Central Library (DCL) was also locat at Vikarabad. This library was established in the year 1959 as a district library of the then Hyderabad district. After the formation of RangaReddy district ZGS, the library was transformed as DCL.

No. of Libraries

The RangaReddy district is surrounds Hyderabad district and most of Branch Libraries were established in the rural areas surrounding Hyderabad urban areas. The following table provides figures for types of libraries functioning under the ZGS as obtained during the year, 2004-05.

	Type of Library	*Nos*
1.	District Central Library (DCL)	01
2.	Branch Libraries (BLS)	51
3.	Rural Libraries (RLS)	17
4.	Book Deposit Centres	116
5.	Aided Libraries	2
6.	Mobile Libraries	3
	Total	190

Book Collections

The total book collection in the DCL as on 2006 was 56,094. The break-up was as follows : English 10,028, Hindi 6,900, Urdu 3,743, other languages 110. The library subscribes to 7 dialies, 5 weeklies, 2 fortnightlies, 23 Montilies in Telugu, 3 Dailies, 4 Weeklies, 1 Fortmightly and 2 Monitlies in English and one daily newspaper in urdu and Hindi.

The ZGS has 51 Branch libraries. The total collection in all the BLS is as follows : Telugu 3,98,504, English 34,124, Hindi 20,869, Urdu 17,025 other languages 12 totaling 4,71,824 books. All the BLS taken together subscribe to 270 dailies, 300 weeklies, 104 fortnightlies, 866 montilies in Telugu. In English thes BLS subscribed to 93 dailies, 115 weeklies, 39 fortnightlies and 100 monthlies in English. These libraries also get 13 dailies in Hindi and 1 weekly and 23 dailies in Urdu totaling 1929 periodicals in all languages.

There were 17 Rural libraries (RLS) under ZGS as on March 2005. In these libraries a total collection of 43,521 was available and the breakup is Telugu 42,410, English 640, Hindi 335 and Urdu 136. These libraries subscribe to 37 Dailies, 55 Weeklies, 26 Fortnightlies, 83 Monthlies in Telugu and in English 19 Dailies, 7 Weeklies, 8 Monthlies and in Hindi 1, Urdu 1 daily papers.

Book Deposit Centres

There were 64 BDCS. The ZGS was thinking to increase

the number of BDCS and to have one BDC in each village. These centres works 3 hours a day. The centres subscribe to 120 dailies, 116 weeklies, 58 fortnightlies and 138 monthlies in Telugu and 13 dailies, in English totaling 445 periodicals.

Library Staff

The sanctioned posts and vacancies in the DCL was given in the following table as on 31.03.05.

Category	*Sanctioned posts*	*Vacant posts*
Dy Librarian (Grade I)	1	1
Grade II Librarian	1	1
Grade III Librarian	1	0
Attender	1	1
Watchmen	3	1
Total	7	4

Out of seven sanctioned posts four post were vacant and not filledup due ban on recruitment and filling up of existing vacancies imposed by the government. With just 3 staff members it was rather difficult to manage DCL. The following table provides figures for staff position as obtained in 2004-05.

Category	*Sanctioned posts*	*Vacant posts*
Grade II Librarians	3	2
Grade III Librarians	29	8
Record Assts	15	5
Attenders	11	1
Watchmen	17	6
Total	75	22

With just 53 staff members of various categories it was rather difficult to manage 51 BLS in the district and offer better library services to user community. There are instances where BLS were run by Watchmen/Attenders in the state public library system. The following table provides for staff position in the Rural Libraries (RLs).

Category	*Sanctioned posts*	*Vacant posts*
Rural Librarians	17	4

Library Buildings

Out of 52 libraries in the district only 26 libraries have own library buildings. Twenty four libraries were housed in rent free buildings and two were housed in rented buildings. With the funds form RRRLF Kolkata 2 buildings were under construction. For BL at Vennachedu Rs 4 lakhs in two instalments, BL Shemirpata Rs 2 lakhs in one instalment, BL Kotupalli Rs 2 lakhs, BL Yalal Rs 2 lakhs, BL Bantaram Rs 2 lakhs were recieved. The library building for Pudur BL was yet to be started. Thirteen village libraries are housed in rent free buildings.

Membership

As on 31.03.05 the total membership stood at 34364. The following table provides figures for total membership at different types of libraries under ZGS.

Type of Library	*Total Membership*
DCL	2814
BLS	30444
VLS	1106
Total	34364

Readership

As on 31.03.05 the total readership stood at 21,98,282. The following table provides figures for total readership at different types of libraries under the ZGS.

Type of Library	Total Readership
DCL	1,09,174
BLS	17,21,479
VLS	1,30,803
BDCS	2,36,826
Total	21,98,282

Books Consulted

During the year 2004-05 a total of 392607 books were consulted in different types of libraries under the ZGS. The following table provides figures for book consulted.

Type of Library	Total Book Consulted
DCL	13477
BLS	304504
VLS	26418
BDCS	48208
Total	392607

Books Lent for Home Reading

During the year 2004-05 a total of 188602 books were lent for home reading. The following table provides figures for book lent by various types of libraries under the ZGS.

Type of Library	Total Books lent
DCL	7003
BLS	164092
VLS	17507
Total	188602

Books Added During the Year

During the year 2004-05, the ZGS has added 63 books by purchase from the ZGS funds.It has received a total of 5812 books from DPL/RRRLF matching grant scheme. It has also received a total of 381 books directly from RRRLF, Kolkata and 1801 books as gratis from the public.

Extension Activities

The ZGS has been celebrating national events such as Independence and Republic days and also National Library Week every year during 14-20 November. During the year 2004-05 it organised 1 inservice training programme, 65 book exhibitions, 219 literary activities and 69 cultural activities. These were organised by DCL and BLS.

What Lies a Head

The ZGS, Ranga Reddy District is financially very sound and in a better position than majority of ZGSS in the state except Hyderbad City Grandhalaya Samastha (HCGS). The total library cess collected during the year 2005-06 was Rs 5,22,35,167 which was fairly good amount. But unfortunately due to various reasons especially lethargy on the part of sucessive managing committees, the services of ZGS could not be expanded to cover villages having 5000 population and above with BLS. The district has 12 municipalities in addition to village punchayats and these were not fully covered by sufficient number of BLs. To certain extent government's policies such as ban on recruitment, opening of new BLS, filling up of existing vacancies are some of the stumbling blocks which have come in the way of exampansion of library services in the district. Let us hope that the government will lift the ban and allow the ZGS to open more. BLS with its own funds and meet the information requirements of highly concentrated educated and unemployed youth and other sections of society in the district.

Sources : 1. R. Sarada, 'Andhra Pradesh lo Zilla Grandhalaya Samsthalu : Ranga Reddy Zilla. *Grandhalaya Sarvashwamu* V67, N5 August 2006. pp, 1-4.

2. *Zilla Grandhalaya Samstha. Ranga Reddy District. Annual Report 2004-05* (Mimeographed).

F.19. Zilla Grandhalaya Samstha (ZGS) : Srikakulam

The District was formed in 1930 by merging certain areas from Ganjam and Visakhapatnam districts. It consists of 3 Revenue Divisions, 38 Mandals, 1 Municipality 3 Nagar Panchayats, 1106 non notified panchayats and 16 notified Panchayats. The Srikakulam Zilla Grandhalaya Samastha (ZGS) was formed in 1952 as a result of Madras Public Libraries Act, 1948. The progress was not satisfactory. It was only in 1956 after the formation of Andhra Pradesh three branch libraries were established. Gradually by the end of 1981 the ZGS consisted 19 BLS and 5 rural libraries. In the year 1986 the ZGS opened a branch library for each Mandal.

No. of Libraries

As on 31.03.03 ZGS consists of 1 Districts Central Library (DCL), 42 Branch Libraries (BLS) 5 Rural Libraries (RLS) 1 Mobile Library (ML) and 5 Aided Libraries (ALS) and 26 Book Deposit Centres (BDCS).

Library Staff

As on 31.03.03 the sanctioned staff of the ZGS was 103 consisting Professional, Semi Professional, Administrative and class IV employees. Of the sanctioned posts 1 Grade I Librarian, 8 Grade III Librarians, 2 Record Assts, 11 Attenders, 5 Rural Librarians, 20 part time workers post were lying vacant for several years due to government's ban on recruitment. The break up of the 103 sanctioned posts are : 1 District Central Librarian, 1 Grade I Libn, 1 Grade II Libn, 33 Grade III Libns, 2 Junior Assts, 1 Typist, 11 Record Assts, 22 Attenders, 1 Watchman, 24 part time workers and 5 part time librarians.

Library Buildings

The District Central Library (DCL) is housed in its own building. In addition, 7 Branch Libraries were housed in own buildings and 22 Branch Libraries and five village libraries were housed in rent free buildings and 11 BLS were housed in rented buildings. The Buildings for BLS at Naupada, Meliyaputtu and Garo were constructed with MPLADS funds released by K. Yerram Naidu, M.P. Srikakulam, and the buildings for BLS at Lolugu and Yecherrla were constructed with MPLADS funds released by P. Anandagajpati Raju, Bobbili MP and buildings for BLS at Regidi and Amadalavalsa were constructed with the funds released by K. Kalavenkata Rao, Member, Rajya Subha. Eight sites are under process of acquisition for BLS at Vanagram, Sompeta, Sarubujjili, Laveru, Barua, Pathapatnam, Nandigam and Bhamini. The building for BL at Seethampeta is under construction.

Book Stocks

The total book stock as 31.03.03 of the ZGS stood at 165469. The following table provides figures for the total book stock available at DCL and BLS and also books added by purchase, books supplied by DPL/RRRLF scheme, books directly recieved from Director, RRRLF and books received under gratis.

Type of Library	*Stocks on 31.03.02*	*Books Supplied by DPL*	*Books Supplied by RRRLF*	*Books Received under gratis*	*Books weeked*	*Total*
DCL	21065	549	366	313	1501	20792
BLS	128612	3158	219	359	240	132108
VLS	6957	236	–	–	–	7193
MLS	5376	–	–	–	–	5376
Total	162010	3943	585	672	1741	165469

It appears that no books were purchased during the year 2002-03 from ZGS funds.

Periodical Subscription

During the year 2002-03, the ZGS has subscribed to 931

periodicals of various frequencies of which Telugu 798, English 131 and other languages 2. Out of 242 periodicals 29 magazines were newly subscribed during the year 2002-03. The following table provides for language and library wise break-up of figures.

Type of Library	*Telugu*				*English*				*Hindi*				*Total*
	D	*W*	*F*	*M*	*D*	*W*	*F*	*M*	*D*	*W*	*F*	*M*	
DCL	7	5	4	28	3	7	3	19	–	–	–	–	76
BLS	161	137	63	318	37	26	8	24	–	–	–	2	776
VLS	6	4	3	10	1	–	1	2	–	–	–	–	27
BDCS	26	26	–	–	–	–	–	–	–	–	–	–	52
Total	200	172	70	356	41	33	12	45	–	–	–	–	931

Language Wise Break-up of Book Stocks

The following table provides figures for availability of books language wise in various types of libraries functioning under the ZGs as on 31.03.03.

Category of Library	*Telugu*	*English*	*Hindi*	*Urdu*	*Other Languages*	*Total*
DCL	12702	6384	1617	83	6	20792
BLS	12201	7616	2119	38	234	132108
VLS	6727	289	175	–	2	7193
MLS	5123	238	15	–	–	5376
Total	146653	14527	3926	121	242	165469

Membership

As on 31.03.3 the total membership of the ZGS stood at 11,936. The following table provides library wise break up figures of membership.

Type of Library	Total membership as on 31.03.03	Percentage of increase
DCL	2528	108%
BLS	8551	115%
VLS	264	106%
MLS	593	–
Total	11936	

There had been an increase of 108% in the membership at DCL, 115% at BLS and 106% at VLS, when compared with previous years figures.

Readership

During the year 2002-03 a total of 798912 visited all the types of libraries functioning under the ZGS. The following table provides figures for the number of readers visited the libraries.

Types of Library	No of readers	Increase
DCL	85363	179%
BLS	688430	121%
VLS	21119	–
BDCS	4680	–
Total	798912	122%

On the whole there had been 122% increased in the readers when compared with previous years figures.

Books Consulted

During the year 2002-03, a total of 101558 books were consulted by the readers in various types of libraries under the ZGS. The following table provides figures for total number of books consulted in various types of libraries.

Type of Library	Total books consulted	Percentage of Increase
DCL	6200	145%
BLS	92788	117%
VLS	1070	–
BDCS	1500	–
Total	101558	101%

It appears that there had been 101% increase in book consultation than the previous year. The readers had consulted books on life histories, software, science and technology, general knowledge and books on competitive examinations.

Books Lent for Home Reading

During the year 2002-03, a total 46,827 books were lent by the libraries for home reading. The following table provides figures for books lent by various types of libraries.

Type of Library	Total books Lent	Percentage of Increase
DCL	3264	134%
BLS	40001	117%
VLS	362	–
MLS	80	114%
Total	46827	128%

It appears there had been an increase of 128% in book lending than the previous year.

Librarycess

Library cess is one of the most important sources of revenue for the ZGS in the state. During the year 2002-03 a sum of Rs 1,55,107.00 was received from the local bodies. The following table provides figures for the amount of recieved from the local bodies.

Name of the local body	*Amount recieved*
Municipalities (4)	113958.00
Notified Grampanchayats (16)	249036.00
Non notified Grampanchayats (1090)	174113.00
Total (1110)	1557107.00

Grants Received from RRRLF, Kolkata

Rajah Rammohan Roy Library Foundation, Kolkata is a funding agency for the development of public libraries in the country, which was established by government of India in the year 1972. During the year 2002-03, the ZGS has received an amount of 2,25,000.00 for the projects submitted by the ZGS. The following table provides information about the name of the scheme, the number of proposals submitted under the scheme and the amount received as a grant from RRRLF.

Name of the scheme	*No of proposals submitted*	*Total amount received*
1. Storage and Display	10	100,000
2. Childrens libraries	2	20,000
3. In service trainig	1	25,000
4. BDCS	4	80,000
Total		2,25,000

Developmental Activities

With the financial support from RRRLF, Kolkata during the year 2000-01, book storage material worth Rs 1.28 lakhs was purchased and equipped 40 Branch libraries (BLS). From the year 1996-97 to 2000-01, with the funds from MPLADS own library buildings were constructed for six branch libraries. The ZGS staff fully participated in the governments akshara sanckranti programme and contributed for the eradication of illiteracy in the district.

Future Plans

In the comming five years the ZGS plans to introduce in the DCL and other BLS reference service which will be useful to those readers who appear for competitive examinations. Opening up of text book section at the DCL. To computerise DCL and provide Internet facility. Computerise BLS in the phased manner and network with DCL. To equip the DCL and BLS with reading and storage materials, and to construct new library buildings with the support from RRRLF, Kolkata and also funds from MP and MLA LADS. Conducting workshops and refreshers courses to professional staff at regular intervals to enhance their professional skills for rendering better service to the reading public. To establish a branch library at the newly created Lakshminarasmpeta Mandal in the district. To participate vigorously in 'akshrasankranti' programme by the ZGS staff as volunteers and supervisors and help in enhancing the percentage of literacy in the district.

Sources : 1. R.S Venkatpati Raju, 'Andhra pradesh lo Zilla Grandhalaya Samsthalu : Srikakulam Zilla.' *Grandhalaya Sarvasamu*, V63, N6, Sept 02. pp 2-4.

2. *Annual Report of Zilla Grandhalaya Samstha, Srikakulam District,* 2002-03 (Mimeographed).

F.20. Zilla Grandhalaya Samstha (ZGS) : Visakhapatnam

Visakhapatnam district falls part of North coastal region of Andhra Pradesh. Before independence it was the largest district in the country. After independence the district was bifurcated twice transfering certain areas to Srikakulam and Vizianagarm districts. In addition to Visakkapatnam city the district head quarters, the district consists 14 towns, 42 mandals and 3695 villages.

No. of Libraries

The ZGS of Visakkapatnam district was formed in 1954 along with the District Central library (DCL) and seven branch libraries (BLS). Gradually the strength of BLS increased by the year 1981 and consisted 61 Branch Libraries (BLS), 5 Rural Libraries (RLS) and 61 Books Deposit Centres (BDS). After the formation of Vizianagaram district in 1981, 19 BLS were transferred to Vizianagaram District ZGS. Consequently the number of libraries in Visakkapatnam ZGS came down to 1 DCL, 42 BLS, 7 RLS. In 1986 Govt of Andhra Pradesh taken a policy decision to establish a BL in every mandal of the state. As a result of this policy, in 21 mandals of the district new BLS were established. The position of libraries by the end of 31.03.05 in the district is shown in the following table.

Type of Library	*Nos*
District Central Library (DCL)	1
BLS	59
VLS	7
BDCS	50
MLS	4
Total	121

Library Staff

Out of 132 full time posts sanctioned for the ZGS, 38

posts were lying vacant and there by hampering effective library services to the reading public. The government policy of ban on recruitment came in the way of public library development in the State and Visakkapatnam district was no exception in the regard.

Library Buildings

Of the 12 libraries functioning in the district, 36 BLS have own library buildings, 28 BLS were housed in rent free buildings and 8 BLS were housed in rented buildings. In the year 1995 with an estimated cost of Rs 3,75,000 a building was constructed by the ZGS to house Grade I Library at Yelamanchili. The building was named as "Arudra Vignana Mandiram" after the famous telugu litterateur 'Arudra'. In the year 1999 under Employees Assurance Scheme (EAS) first floor was constrructed costing rupees five lakhs and named as Sri" Samavesa Mandiram" after the revoluntionary telugu poet Sri" Srirangam Srinivasa Rao. Various literary and cultural progammes were being organised in the confrence hall.

With the funds released by G.Srinivasa Rao, Member of Parliament, Anakapalli, building was constructed costing 2 lakh rupees for housing a rural library at Upamaka Agraharam. In addition, library buildings were constructed at Yetikoppaka, S.Rayavaram, Chidikada for housing BLS with the funds sanctioned by G. Srinivasa Rao MP under MP LADS scheme. Under "Telugu Grameena Kranti Padhakam" 'a State Government's scheme' library buildings were constructed at Vaddadi, Sabbavaram, and Makavaripalem to house BLS. For Rolugunta BL, Konathala Ramakrishna, Member of Parliament, Anakapalli sanctioned funds under MPLADS for the construction of library buildings.

Book Stock

By the end of 31.03.05 the total book stocks in the ZGS stood at 550741. The following table provides figures for book stocks available in various categories of libraries.

Category of Library	*Total book stocks*
DCL	51,397
BLS	4,77,401
VLS	21943
Total	5,50,741

The language wise break up of the above collection is as follows :

Language	*DCL*	*BLS*	*VLS*	*Total*
Telugu	310	425915	21574	478507
English	16925	39181	348	56,454
Hindi	3203	10891	17	14111
Urdu	96	238	1	335
Other languages	155	1176	3	1334
Total	51397	477401	21943	550741

The category wise break up of the total collection is as follows :

1. Children's books	4400	105541	6935	116876
2. Ref books	5989	14709	1373	22071
3. Text books	992	4656	219	5867
4. Books for neo literates	–	2054	120	2174
5. Bound periodicals	404	770	0	1174
6. Fiction books	9000	438746	5335	190081
7. Non fiction books	30612173	925	7961	212498
Total	51397477	401	21943	550741

Periodicals Subscribed

During the year 2004-05 the ZGS has subscribed to 2287 periodicals of different frequencies and received 150 as gratis totaling 2437 periodicals. The following table provides figures fro periodicals subscribed to various libraries and language wise beak up also.

	DCL	BLS	VLS	BDCS	Total
Subscribed	69	2018	92	108	2287
Gratis	38	112	–	–	150
Total	107	2130	92	108	2437
Language wise break up					
Telugu	70	1835	89	108	2102
English	37	294	3	–	334
Total	107	2130	92	108	2437

Registered Borrowers

During the year 2004-05 the ZGS has 40121 registered borrowers and the breakup is as follows :

34425	4301	–	1395	40121

The breakup of the total figure 40121 genderwise is as follows :

	DCL	BLS	BDCS	Total
Men	3480	25992	1088	30560
Women	683	5530	167	6380
Children	138	2903	140	3181
Total	4301	34425	1395	40121

Readership

During the year 2004-05 a total of 1816506 readers visited the district public library system. The breakup is follows.

DCL	BLS	VLS	Total
128691	1602298	85517	1816506

The various sections of the libraries used by the readers is as follows :

Periodical section	107963	1158813	49259	1316035
Book section	10250	312476	28468	351464
Other sections	10478	130739	7790	149007

Books Consulted

During the year 2004-05 a total of 229002 books were consulted within the libraries of various types of ZGS. The following figures indicate the number of books consulted.

DCL	BLS	VLS	Total
5218	205679	18105	229002

The type and number of books consulted is provided in the following table.

Type of books	*DCL*	*BLS*	*VLS*	*Total*
1. Text books	800	13733	2567	17100
2. Ref books	1518	32982	2610	37110
3. Nonfiction	1700	87557	9319	98576
4. Fiction	1200	71407	3609	76216
Total	5218	205679	18105	229002

Books Lent

During the year 2004-05, a total of 185542 booking were lent for home reading by different libraries of the ZGS. The following figures indicate the number books lent by the libraries.

1. Fiction	5592	95386	4923	79641
2. Non fiction	2000	72486	5155	97641
Total	7592	167872	10078	185542

Extension Activities

During the year 2004-05, the ZGS has organised 236 programmes. The break up is follows. Book exhibitions 36, Film shows 10, Reading circles 56, Lectures 16, Training classes 2, Discussions 29 and National Library Week celebrations 87.

Private Libraries

The ZGS has recognised 12 privately managed public libraries for grant in aid. The Hindu Reading Room,

Visakhapatnam was established in 1917 and supposed to be one of the oldest libraries. But none of these libraries received grant in aid either from the ZGS or from the DPL, Govt of Andhra Pradesha during the year 2004-05.

Acheivements

During the year 1999-2000 with the financial support from RRRLF, Kolkata, storage material worth Rs 2,64,156.00 was acquired and distributed to 69 BLS and RLS. Between the years 1997-98 to 2000-01, two library buildings were constructed with the funds from MPLADS. The ZGS acquired three building sites for construction of library buildings.

Future Plans

The first priority of the ZGS was to fill up vacant posts. During the first phase, provision of reference service and material for competitive examinations in the DCL and five grade I Libraries. Later the said facility is to be extended to all BLS. Computerisation of library operations and provision of Internet facility in a phased manner begining with DCL and later extending to all BLs. Establishment of text books sections in BLS. With the financial support from RRRLF and funds from MPLADS and donations from the public taking up of building construction and supply of storage materials for BLS. To participate vigorously in 'akshara sankranti' programmes for the propagation of literacy in the district and also conduct various types competitions for neo literates and supply relevant reading materials. To extend library services to those villages where there are no BLS and BDCs. Efforts are being made to construct 10 library buildings with a total amount of Rs 20 lakhs and securing Rs 14 lakhs as matching grant under "food for works programme". The RRRLF, Kolkata has also sanctioned Rs 3.75 lakhs for the construction of library building at Kothakota village.

Conclusion

The Visakkapatnam ZGS has made rapid strides in having own library buildings for almost all BLS except 10 which were housed in rented buildings. Efforts are being make to have own library buildings for these 10 BLS also. The collection of library cess was also encouraging. If the vacant post are filled up at the earliest the ZGS will be in a position to offer quality library services to its reading public.

Source : 1. R. Sarada 'Andhra Pradesh lo Zilla Grandhalaya Samsthalu : Visakkapatnam Zilla'. *Grandhalaya Sarvashwamu* V63, N2, May 02, pp. 2-5.

F.21. Zilla Grandhalaya Samstha (ZGS) : Vizianagaram

Vizianagaram district is a part of Northcoastal Andhra Pradesh and came into being on June 1,1979 talking away certain areas from SriKakulam and Visakkapatnam districts. The district consists of 2 Revenue Divisions, 38 Mandals 4 Municipalities, 17 Major Panchayats and 931 Panchayats.

The Vizianagram district Zilla Grandhalaya Samastha (ZGS) came into being in 1981 by transfering 19 branch libraries from Visakkapatnam and SriKakulam districts.

No. of Libraries

The number of libraries during the year 2004-05 consists of 1 District Central Library, 4 Grade II Libraries and 33 Grade III Libraries (Branch libraries) and 4 Rural Libraries 41 Book Deposit Centres, 4 Aided libraries totaling 87 libraries.

Library Staff

The sanctioned staff of ZGS during the year 2004-05 was 90 consisting professional, semiprofessional and non professional categories. Of the sanctioned staff 23 posts were vacant due to governments ban on recruitment and non professional categories were working in the district public library system. The breakup is 1 District Central Librarian, 1 Grade I Librarian, 21 Grade III Librarians, 1 Senior Asst, 2 Junior Assts, 1 Typist, 6 Record Assts, 10 Attenders, 6 Watchmen, 15 part

time workers, 1 Rural librarian. In the District Central Library 10 staff members belonging to various categories are working.

Library Buildings

The construction of own building for the District Central Library (DCL) was taken up in 1986. The Branch Libraries at Kumili, Devupalli, Pusapatirega, Moida, Denkada, Gumma lakshmipuram, Terlam and S.Kota were constructed with funds from MP LADS. Free sites were given by the panchayats for construction of buildings for Branch Libraries at Badangi; Gajularega, Bondapalli and Garividi.

The following table provides status of library buildings housing various types of library in the ZGS, Vizianagaram during the year 2004-05.

Type of Library	*Own Blds*	*Rented Blds*	*Free Blds*	*Total*
1. Dist. Central Library	1	–	–	1
2. Branch Libraries (BLS)	6	16	15	37
3. Village Libraries (VLS)	–	–	2	2
Total	7	16	17	40

The ZGS has to go a long way in constructing library building of its own to house BLs.

Book Collections and Visitors

The total books stock in the district library system during year 2001-02 was 36,001 and had 4,243 registered borrowers. During the same period a total of 1,03,650 readers visited the library system and a total of 8,299 book were lent for home reading, and also a total of 18,039 books were consulted within the premises of libraries.

Developmental Activities

During the year 2000-01 with the support of RRRLF, Kolkata book storage material worth Rs 1.28 lakhs was purchased and supplied to branch libraries. During the year 2000-01 and 2001-02, with the funds released by Members of Parliament under MPLADS new buildings were constructed for branch libraries.

Stalwarts of the Library Movement

The District has produced many stalwarts of the library novement. Mention may be made of Jayanti Rama Lakshmana Murthy, Jayanti Kameshwara Rao and Bangari Naidu, who devoted their energies for the spread of library movement in the district. Ramalakshaman Murthy established 'Sri Rama Jayanti Library' at Jaggapuram, Gantyada Mandalam in 1945 and for the last six decades the library has been rendering yeomen service to the rural people of the region. This library inspired other library workers in the region to establish rural libraries at places such as : Budatanapalli, Vasanta, Pedamajjipalem, Tandrangi, Murapaka and Chipurupalli. Ramalakshaman Murthy has been serving as a member of ZGS since its establishment in 1981.

Future Programmes

The ZGS wish to establish Competitive Examination Reference unit at DCL and computerise inhouse operations with Internet facility. It also wants to strengthen text book sections in all BLS. With the financial support from RRRLF, Kolkata and MPLADS funds the ZGS wants to augument book collections at the DCL and BLS, and construction of own buildings for BLS. To improve efficiency of the staff members for renderings effective library services to the user community, the ZGS is planning to conduct training classes and deploy library staff in literacy programmes of the state government as volunteers/supervisors. It also wants to lend reading materials to continuing education centres of Education Department from the nearest BL. Establishing linkages with nearby Primary and Upper primary schools to cultivate reading habits and inculcate moral values among school going children is another import future programme. Lastly but not the least providing library services in the village habitations where BLS are not opened, through panchayat/village educational committees by lending reading materials from the nearest Branch/Village Libraries.

Sources : 1. M.V.S. Krishnaveni. 'Andhra Pradesh lo Zilla Grandhalaya Samsthalu : Vizianagaramu Zilla.' *Grandhalaya Sarvaswamu*, V64, N5, August 2003. pp. 2-4.

2. *Zilla Grandhalaya Samstha, Vizianagaram Action Plan for the year 2004-05*. (Mimeographed).

F.22. Zilla Grandhalaya Samstha (ZGS) : Warangal

Warangal was the seat of Kakatiya rulers and mirrors Kakatiya valour, culture and arts and carved a niche in the history of Andhradesa. Warangal is second biggest city in Telagana region after Hyderabad. Presently it is a centre for higher educational institutions in Engineering, Medicine, Pharmacy and General Education. Higher Educational institutions like Kakatiya University, National Institute of Technology (former Regional Engineering College) and number of degree colleges were located in warangal city. The famous Raja Raja Narendra Andhra Nilayam established in 1904 was also located in Hanamkonda, twin city of Warangal. The district was established in 1905 during the region of Asaf Zahis. It consists 981 minor and 46 major panchayats. Warangal ZGS came into being in 1961 as per the provisions of AP Public Libraries Act, 1960.

No of Libraries

The ZGS could establish only 17 Branch Libraries (BLS) untill 1981 and later the number increased to 54 BLS. The following table provides figures for different types of libraries functioning under ZGS in the year 2004-05.

Type of Library	*Nos*
District Central Library (DCL)	01
Grade I Libraries (BL)	01
Grade II Libraries (BLS)	03
Grade III Libraries (BLS)	49
Rural Libraries (RLS)	19
Book Deposit Centres (BDCS)	58
Total	131

In the year 2004 Internet Centre was established at DCL.

Book Collections

As on March 31,2005 the total book collection at the DCL and all the BLS was 335969 of which the collections at DCL stands 33245, the BLS 285607 and RLS 17117. As against last year, this year (2003) an additional collection of 35967 books were added to the total collection out of which 5,972 books were received from RRRLF, Kolkata. The break-up of the total collection language wise was as follows :

Language	*Total collection*
Telugu	2,65,425
English	38,134
Hindi	15,961
Urdu	15,225
Other languages	1224
Total	335969

No. of Visitors

The number of visitors in 2002-03 to all the BLS was 12,92,517 to Rural libraries 1,37,026, to Book Deposit Centres 56,326 a totaling 16,95,293. The figure increased to 18,78,722 in the year 2003-04, thus achieving an increase of 11% in number of visitors to public libraries in the district. A survey was conducted by the authorities of the ZGS which revealed that 74% of readers consulted news papers and periodical section and only 24% of readers consulted general, reference and text book sections of libraries. The survey also reavealed that everyday 700 to 800 readers visit DCL, and 80 to 90 visit each BL and 25 to 30 visit each RL.

Library Buildings

In the ZGS only one third of BLS have their own library buildings. Five BLS were house in rented buildings and the rest in rent free buildings. For eight (8) BLS land was acquired and registered for construction of buildings. The following figures provide the status of library buildings in the ZGS as on 31.03.04.

1.	Own library buildings	19 BLs
2.	Free library buildings	53 BLs
3.	Rented library buildings	04
	Total	76

In the past RRRLF, Kolkata sanctioned a sum of Rs 48,000 for purchase of storage materials for 8 BLS. It has also sanctioned Rs 10,000 for conducting orientation programmes to staff members and Rs 50,000 for the development of BDCS. RRRLF also sanctioned Rs 2 lakhs each for construction of buildings for BLS at Dornakal, Narmatta and Nallachelli. The construction work was completed and ready for inauguration.

Library Staff

The ZGS was facing acute shortage of staff and 30% of

the sanctioned posts were vacant. The following table provides staff position as obtained in the year 2004-05.

S.No	Type of Post	Sanctioned Post	Vacant post
1.	District Central Libraian (DCL)	01	–
2.	Grade I Libns	02	–
3.	Grade II Libns	05	03
4.	Sr Assistant	01	–
5.	Junior Asst	01	–
6.	Typist	01	01
7.	Grade III Libns	47	18
8.	Binder	01	01
9.	Record Assts	06	02
10.	Attenders	13	04
11.	Watchmen	13	01
12.	Gardener	01	–
13.	Part time Sweepers and Workers	64	48
	Total	156	78

From the above table it was evident that out of 156 sanctioned posts, 78 posts of various categories were lying vacant due to ban imposed by the government on recruitment and filling up of vacancies. This policy of the government is hindering the growth, development and expansion of public library services not only in warangal district but also entire Andhra Pradesh.

Membership

The total membership as on 31.03.05 stood at 38440. The membership at various categories of libraries is shown in the following table.

Type of Library	Total membership
DCL	9205
BLS	28087
VLS	1148
Total	38440

There has been 133% increased in library membership than the previous year.

Readership

The total readership at the DCL and BLS as on 31.03.05 stood at 1973389. The following table provides figures for total readership at all types of libraries under the ZGS in the district.

Type of Library	*Total readership*
DCL	302621
BLS	1430928
VLS	101352
BDCS	137488
Total	1973389

There has been 121% increase in the readership than the previous year.

Books Consulted

During the year 2004-05 a total of 219886 books were consulted in different types of libraries of the ZGS. The following table provides figures for total number of books consulted.

Type of Library	*Total no of book consulted*
DCL	53894
BLS	152370
VLS	12550
BDCS	1072
Total	219886

Books Lent for Home Reading

A total of 166571 books were lent for home reading during the year 2004-05. The following table provides figures for total books lent by various types of libraries functioning under the ZGS.

Type of Library	*Total books lent for home reading*
DCL	28726
BLS	128400
VLS	6747
BDCS	2698
Total	166571

Librarycess

Library cess is one of the most important sources of revenue for the ZGS in the State. During the year 2004-05, the ZGS has realised a total sum of Rs 1,23,29,254.00 as library cess from municipalities and gram panchayats in the district. The following table provides figures for the cess contributed by the local bodies to the ZGS.

	Name of the local body	*Cess remitted to ZGS*
	Municipal Corporation (1)	Rs. 1,08,29,434
	Municipality (1)	Rs. 6,95,529
	Grampanchayats	
1.	Notified (46)	Rs. 5,86,397
2.	Non-notified (9810	2,17,894
	Total	1,23,29,254

Future Plans

The ZGS was planning to computerise DCL at Hanamkonda with an estimated cost of Rs 4 lakhs in the year 2004-05. In the years to come with an estimated cost of Rs 15 lakhs, acquisition of latest books and books on competitive exams and equip all BLS. Purchase of furniture and other storage materials with a cost of Rs 5 lakhs and supply to these BLS which were facing shortage of furniture. To establish a separate text book section at DCL with a cost of Rs 3 lakhs. To arrange for Competitive Exams Reference Unit (CERU) at the DCL with an expenditure of Rs 2 lakhs. To establish community learning centres as an auxiliaries to all BLs in the district.

In addition to the above future plans the young and dynamic chairman of ZGS, Dr. Pola Natraj identified four strategic actions to improve the image of the ZGS among public. These are : 1. In the official programmes in addition to organising festivals, training programmes to staff members, visits and inspections, organising cultural programmes to attract more readers, 2. To provide conducive atmosphere in all BLS, to provide computerised library services and to construct more library buildings for BLS and at the DCL premises construction of mini auditorium to be named after late 'Kaloji' the great peoples poet who hailed from the district and also to collect rare and valuable documents, 3. to arrange for library stalls at the district level 'Science fairs' so as to create awareness among the students about libraries and in the premises of libraries, organising book exhibitions frequently and arrange for lectures by experts for the benefit those appearing for competitive examinations and, 4. To strive relentlessly for strengthening financial resources of the ZGS by collecting library cess arrears from Panchayats and Municipalities in the district and make efforts to get salary and pension grants from the government in time by bringing pressure on the administration.

Above all under the dynamic leadership of the chairman of the ZGS, Dr. Pola Natraj, 'book collection week' festivals were arranged at all the BLS in the district and collected 9500 books from the donors. Under the chairmenship of the District Collector, with prominent citizens as members 'Library development action committee' was constituted.

Sources : 1. R.V.S. SivaramaKrishana 'Andhra Pradesha lo Zilla Grandhalaya Samsthalu : Warangal Zilla'. *Granadhalaya Sarvaswamu*, V65, N6, Sept 04, pp. 2-69.

2. *Annual Report of Zilla Grandhalaya Samstha, Warangal District, 2004-05. (Mimeographed)*.

F.23. Zilla Grandhalaya Samstha (ZGS) : West Godavari

The West Godavari district was formed in the year 1925 and its headquarters are at Eluru. The district achieved all round development especially in agriculture and regarded as rice bowl of Andhra Pradesh. The district consists of 14 towns, 46 mandals and 839 villages. The Local Library Authority (LLA) of the district was formed in 1950 as a consequence to Madras Public Libraries Act, 1948.

No. of Libraries

The Zilla Grandhalaya Samastha (ZGS) of the West Godavari district consists of : 1 Districts Central Library (DCL), 71 Branch Libraries (BLS), 37 Rural Libraries (RLS) and 86 Book Deposit Centres (BDCS), totaling 195 libraries of all types. Besides, 156 aided libraries (private libraries) were also functioning in the district. The present strength of BLS is not satisfactory taking into account the population of district. If we set aside 86 BDCS, there were only 109 BLs working inthe district. Among 109 libraries, 36 are Rural libraries of which 16 RLS were not functioning.

Library Buildings

The following table provides an idea as to the position of library buildings in the district as on 31.03.05.

Type of Library	*Own Blds*	*Rented Blds*	*Free Blds*	*Total*
1. DCL	1	–	–	1
2. BLS	41	11	19	71
3. RLS	–	–	18	18
Total	42	11	37	90

Library Staff

The sanctioned posts for the ZGS as on 2002 was 278 of all categories of which 129 posts were lying vacant due to governments ban on recruitment in ZGSS. The non filling up of vacant posts was affecting the management of BLS and offering better library services to the reading public. The following table provides information about various categories sanctioned posts and vacant posts as on 31.03.05.

S.No	*Category*	*Sanctioned Posts*	*Vacant posts*
1.	District Central Libraian (DCL)	1	–
2.	Grade I Libns	6	3
3.	Grade II Libns	3	2
4.	Grade III Libns	53	7
5.	Sr Assistant	1	–
6.	Junior Asst	1	–
7.	Typists	2	2
8.	Record Assts	21	48
9.	Attenders	39	10
10.	Watchmen	5	1
11.	Part time Village librarians	36	18
12.	Part time Worker	36	30
	Total	204	51

Development Indicators

The following table provides for the development indicators for a six year period from 1995-96 to 2000-01 with respect to books, membership, visitors, books lent, new buildings and library cess collected.

Indicators	*1995-96*	*1996-97*	*1997-98*	*1998-99*	*1999-2000*	*2000-01*
Books (in lakhs)	8.83	8.92	8.94	9.06	8.88	7.23
Visitors (in lakhs)	60.63	63.43	63.02	63.74	63.70	67.74
Membership (in lakhs)	17.92	16.94	17.01	16.12	15.87	14.88
Books lent for home reading (in lakhs)	05.17	04.12	03.95	03.97	03.98	01.69
New Buildings	–	–	–	2	3	2
Library cess collected (Rs in lakhs)	96.03	27.87	23.29	41.45	48.49	93.49

During the year 1999-2000, the ZGS had spent Rs 6.19 lakhs for acquisition of books in Telugu, English and Hindi. Between the years 1997-98 and 2000-01, with the funds received from 'Janambhoomi', M.P. and MLA LADS and contributions received from voluntary organisation, the ZGS had constructed five new buildings for BLS. It has also acquired site worth rupees five lakhs for Bhimavaram branch library. With an estimated cost fo Rs 14.50 lakhs and matching grant form RRRLF, Kolkata two library buildings were constructed. The Library staff have actively participated in 'aksharasankranti' programme for the cause of adult literacy programmes in the district.

Library Facilities

In Eluru, the district headquarters the ZGS opened childrens library the only one in the district. Two womens Branch Libraries were opened at Eluru and Tanuku. In these two BLS the facility of home delivery of books was introduced. In the DCL at Eluru a text book section was opened in the year 1970 for the benefit of student community.

Book Collection

As on 31.03.05, the total book collection of the ZGS stood at 827784. The ZGS has received a total of 6388 books under DPL/RRRLF matching grant, 245 books from RRRLF, Kolkata, added 787 books from ZGS funds and received 17527 books as donations. The following table provide figures for book collections available at DCL, BLS and VLS.

Category of Libraries	*DCL*	*BLS*	*VLS*	*MLS*	*Total*
	83169	681687	62928	–	827784

Periodicals Subscribed

During the year 2004-05 the ZGS has subscribed to 2653 Telugu and 515 English Periodicals and 1801 Telugu and 431

English news magzines. The following table provides figures for subscription of periodicals to various types of libraries.

Category of Libraries	*DCL*	*Grade I BLS*	*Grade II BLS*	*Grade III BLS*	*VLS*	*Total*
	171	391	129	2335	275	3301

Book Collections

The total collections of the ZGS as on 31.03.05 stood at 803390. The following table provides break-up figures of book stock available in various types of libraries.

Category of Library	*Telugu*	*English*	*Hindi*	*Urdu*	*Other Languages*	*Total*
DCL	58098	20532	4075	214	263	83182
BLS	594413	44432	13234	851	609	653539
VLS	66155	426	74	13	01	66669
Total	718666	65390	17383	1078	873	803390

Membership

The total registered membership of the ZGS library system by the end of 31.03.05 stood at 70851. The following table provides figures for total readership at various types of libraries.

Type of library	*Total readership*
DCL	5270
BLS	62323
VLS	3258
Total	7085

There has been increase of 2.23%, 2.73% and 5.64% of membership at DCL, BLS and VLS respectively when compared with the year 2003-04.

Readership

By the end of 31.03.05 the total readership of the District Public Library System stood at 19796981. The following table provides figures for total readership at various types of libraries.

Type of library	*Total readership*
DCL	164532
BLS	1646844
VLS	165605
Total	1976981

There has been an increase of 2.55%, 4.48% of readership at DCL, VLS when compared with the year 2003-04.

Books Consutled

A total of 389257 books were consulted during the year 2004-05 at all categories of libraries under the ZGS. The following table provides figures for total books consulted at DCL, BLS and VLS.

Type of library	*Total number of books*
DCL	10740
BLS	163901
VLS	26519
Total	201160

There has been a decrease of 18292 books for home reading during the year 2004-05 when compared with the year 2003-04 a total 27.01% decrease in books lent for home reading.

Librarycess

Library cess is one of the main sources of revenue for the ZGS in the state. During the year 2004-05 the ZGS has realised a sum of Rs 10860136, and a sum of Rs 27364284 was due from the local bodies in the district. The following table provides figures for the total amount realised from the Municipalities and Grampanchayats and total cess amount due as on 31.03.05.

Name of local body		*Cess realised during 2004-05*	*Total cess due as on 31.03.05*
Municipal Corporation		–	–
Municipalities (8)		Rs 7297917	Rs 266884503
Gram panchayats	201		
Notified	687	Rs 3562219	Rs 480281
Total	888		
Total	896	Rs 10860136	Rs 27364284

Extension Activities

During the year 2004-05 the ZGS has organised a total of 469 activities consisting : conferences and seminars (7), book exhibitions (71), film shows (11) literary activities (131), cultural activities (212) and reading circles (37). These programmes were carried out at DCL, BLS and VLS. During the National Library Week (14-11-2004 to 20-11-2004) 72 libraries have organised various types of programmes by spending an amount Rs 18,055.00.

Future Plans

In the comming years at the DCL and Grade I Libraries, the ZGS was planning to open special reference section useful to those appearing for competitive examinations. Later the said facility shall be extended to other BLS in the district. To introduce in a phased manner computerisation at DCL and other BLS. To digitise the collections at DCL. To establish text book sections in all BLS. In addition to construct to new library buildings with the support from RRRLF, MP and MLA LADS, improving the physical facilities at the DCL and BLS. To train the library staff by conducting refresher courses and work shops and improve their professional skills and capacities to render better services to the user community. To extend cooperation and support to adult education centres. To establish cordial relations with local school authorities and inculcate and promote reading habits among school going children.

Sources : 1. R.Sarada, 'Andhra Pradesh lo Zilla Grandhalaya Samsthalu', Pachima Godavari Zilla.' *Grandhalaya, Sarvashuamu* V63, N3, June 02, pp. 2-5.

2. *Annual Report of Zilla Grandhalaya Samstha, West Godavari District*, 2004-05. (Mimeographed).

G

Library Committees

Committee means "a body of persons delegated to consider, investigate, take action on, or report on some matter." Committees or commissions are constituted at different levels ranging from international to local to get feed back on the working of various branches of the government or institutions or on social, economic or educational development of societies or the state of affairs of particular social phenomena. In the field of public library development many committees/ commissions were appointed by the governments of the countries of the world to find out the state of affairs of public libraries and suggest suitable recommendations for their improvement and development.

In the year 1924 the Board of Education, Government of UK appointed a committee under the chairmanship of Sir F. Kenyon to explore the adequacy of public library acts which were in operation in country. In 1957, the Ministry of Education, Government UK appointed another committee under the chairmanship of Sir Sydney Roberts to examine the structure of public libraries in England and Wales. Like the two committees in the UK, committees were appointed by many countries of the world to look into the state of affairs of public libraries and recommend suitable measures for their development. India is no exception in this regard.

The Government of Bombay, during the British rule, appointed a committee in 1939 under the chairmenship of

A.A.A. Fyzee to report on the development of libraries in the Bombay presidency. This committee mostly dealt on the establishment of Regional Libraries (RLS) in the then multi lingual Bombay Presidency. After independence, Government of India appointed a committee in 1958 under the chairmanship of K.P. Sinha, the former Director of Public Instruction, Bihar. The report submitted by this committed titled Report of Advisory committee for libraries and is popularly known as Sinha Committed Report. The Government of Tamil Naidu also appointed a committee in 1974 under the chairmanship of V.N Subbarayan to look into the working public libraries in the state.

As for Andhra Pradesh is concerned two committees were appointed by the Government of Andhra Pradesh to look into the working of A.P. Public Libraries Act, 1960 and working of private libraries in the state. The first committee was appointed in 1976 under the chairmanship of Justice Gopal Rao Ekbota and the second committee was appointed in 1978 under the chairmanship of Vavilala Gopala Krishnayya. The information about these two committees is presented in the following sections.

G.1. Andhra Pradesh Public Libraries Act, 1960 Review Committee, 1976 (Ekbote Committee)

Introduction

The Andhra Pradesh Public Libraries Act, 1960 came into force on Ist April 1960. During the course of its implementation, certain amendments were brought to the Act to meet the changing needs of public library development in the state. The Act was in operation for nearly three decades. The administrators, professionals who manage the public library system in the state at different levels and also the library workers and persons who devoted their lives for the cause of library movement in the state and also professional intellectuals felt the need for go into thoroughly the working of A.P. Public Libraries Act, 1960 and suggest necessary amendements to the Act for its proper functioning. Several conferences, Seminars were also held by the professionals in this regard and requested the government to appoint an expert committee to have a second look on the working the Act. The result of this professional representation and pressure was the appoint of a Review Committee (Ekbote Committee) appointed in 1976 by the Government of Andhra Pradesha.

Appointment the Review Committee

The Government of Andhra Pradesh through its G.O. Ms No. 198 dated February 25,1976 appointed A.P. Public Libraries Act Review committee to go into the working of the A.P. Public Libraries Act, 1960 and the administration of public library system in Andhra Pradesh and suggest amendments to the existing provisions in the Act under the chairmenship of Justice Gopal Rao Ekbote, retired Chief Justice of Andhra Pradesh with 13 members drawn from public library movement, academic libraries, legistative assembly and legistlative council and officials from the government. Among others the committee consisted of eminent personalities such as Vavilaka Gopala Krishnayya, KodatiNarayana Rao, M. Bhojo

Reddy, and K. Raghava Reddy, Retired Director of Public Libraries and Professor R. Sripati Naidu, Librarian, SriVenkateshwara university, Tirupati.

The terms of reference were :

1. To examine the provisions of A.P. Public Libraries Act, 1960, the Rules issued there under vis-a-vis the Maha rashtra Act, 1967 and the Mysore (Karnataka) Public Libraries Act, 1965 and suggest suitable amendments whenever necessary.
2. To suggest suitable new provisions for incorporation in the Act to carryout the purposes of the Act.
3. To go into the administration of the Act and Rules issued there under and point out bottlenecks in implementing them and suggest remedial measures for the smooth working of the Act and Rules.
4. To suggest amendements and new provisions, the committee may interview the persons interested and working in the field of libraries both at headquarters and in the districts.

Before submitting the report, the committee visited states of Maharashtra, Madras and Karnataka where library legistlation was in operation and how it was working in these states. It has also circulated a detailed questionaire to elict opinion from the public library personal, library workers, library oragnizers, educationists and administrators and those involved in public library development. It has also received memoranda from library bodies and individuals and heard views of individuals who appeared before the committee.

The committee submitted its report in the year 1978. It is a voluminous report consisting 14 chapters with 13 appendices. These chapters deal with : History of library movement in A.P., the Public administration, Finance, School and Children's libraries, Selection of books and other library materials, Institutional and Private libraries, Planning of library services, Library building programmes, Library cooperation and Interlibrary loan, Library education and Conclusions. At the end, the review committee appended a list of 134 recommendations chapter wise, covering different aspects of public library development such as : 1. State Library Authority, 2. Directorate, 3. State Library Council, 4. The State Central Library, 5. Regional Libraries, 6. Zilla Grandhalaya Samsthas (ZGSS), 7. Finance, 8. School and Children's Libraries, 9. Selection of books and other library materials, 10. Institutional and Private Libraries, 11. Planning of Library Services, 12. Library Building Programme, 13. Library Cooperation and Inter library loan and 14. Librarians and training, The list of recommendations were given in the annexure.

Fate of the Review Committee Report

Like any other committee appointed by the governments at the Central and States level, the Report of the Review Committee was put in cold storage. The major recommendations with financial implications were not implemented so far. Especially the recommendations pertaining to : State Library Council, State Central Library, Regional Libraries, Finance, Institutional and Private Libraries, Planning of Library Services, Library Building Programme, Library Cooperation and Inter Library Loan were not fully implemented and incertain cases recommentations were partially implemented where there was no financial implications. Certain amendments suggested for in the Act were not carried out.

It is almost three decades since the submission of the Report to the government for its implementation. The need for implementation of major recommendations of the Ekbote Committed Report was brought to the notice of the government from time to time by Professional associations, Staff Associations, Library Administrators and also by organising seminars and conferences. But till today the major recommendations which have far reaching implications and effects on public library developmented. It appears that the authorities at the helm of affairs have completely forgotten the Ekbote Committee Report.

In the office of the Department of Public Libraries the Ekbote Committee Report is gathering dust. It has now only academic value and interest and being told to the sucessive batches of students of Library and Information Science about the recommendations of the Review Committee on various facets of public library development in the state.

Annexure : Ekbote Committee

List of Recommendations

For convenience we give below a list of our recommendations.

Chapter III (c)—Minister to be the State Library Authority:

(1) The Minister in charge of Libraries should be the State Library Authority, charged with the duty of implementing the Act. It will be his duty to superintend and promote the improvement of the Library service, provided by library authorities and to secure the proper discharge, by them of their functions. It shall be his statutory duty to establish, equip and administer a State library system providing comprehensive and efficient library services, free of charge, to all the citizens in the Stale.

(2) He shall have the necessary powers of overviewing the functioning of the libraries under the Act, and to act in default, on failure, to perform any duty by any library authority.

(3) He shall also be authorised to make rules under the Act, on the advice of the State Library Council, including the power to make rules governing standards of library service.

(4) The Minister must have power to act in default of any library authority.

(5) He shall also specify, lay down. and publish the standards of library service, and see that those standards are strictly observed and that he shall keep the standards under continuous review.

(6) Provisions to these effects may be incorporated in the Act.

Chapter III(d)-Diectorate :

(7) The Director should ordinarily be a person who possesses academic and professional qualification and has adequate administrative experience.

(8) The Director should be relieved of the technical work assigned to him in the present Act. Instead those duties as referred to above be assigned to the State Central Library.

(9) The Director in addition to the present duties should be empowered to exercise powers as mentioned above.

(10) (a) The Director's post should be ultimately a co-ordinate post to that of any Director in the Department of Education. His pay and status should be co-ordinate with such office.

(b) The post of Director should be a selection post to be filled only on merit.

(11) The Director should have three cells in the Directorate:

(a) Administration.

(b) Inspection.

(c) Audit.

(A) A deputy Director's post on the administrative side should be created for the above said purposes.

(B) A Deputy Director's post may be created and a senior experienced professional man be appointed to carry on the work of inspection. He would be assisted by Junior professionals.

(C) The auditors must also be qualified and experienced persons. The Audit unit should be headed by an officer of the rank of at least an Assistant Director.

(12) The Director should prepare report annually and submit the same to the State Library Council before it is presented to the legislature. Such a report would include the findings of the inspection and audit parties. The report should be critical and analytical with a view to throw light upon the working of the library system in the State.

(13) The Department of the Public Libraries under the Director be expanded, improved and strengthened. Financial provision of lae Directorate has to be increased.

Chapter III (e)— State Library Council:

(14) The State Library Committee should here after be called State Library Council.

(15) The State Library Council should have 17 members as detailed above.

(16) Instead of Minister of Public Libraries as at present to head the body, the body should have a Chairman elected by the State Library Council at its first meeting from amongst its non-official members.

(17) The term of office and other procedure for holding meetings of the Council shall be the same as at present.

(18) The Council will perform two functions :

(a) On their own initative tender advice on all matters under the Act or otherwise and as they think fit.

(b) They also will advise on all matters specially and specifically referred to them by the Minister or Director of Public Libraries. Its main work would be to watch and guide the acheivement of standards and the general working of the Act including the development and coordination of library services.

(19) The Slate Library Council shall also be library Authority for the Stale Central Library and all Regional Libraries. The body when it sits as the Library Authority for the State Central Library shall have the powers and functions as are conferred on it under the rules made bv the Government. When the State Library Council sits as a Library Authority for the State Central Library, the Librarian of the State Central Library shall be its Member-Secretary

(20) The Council will report every 6 months or a year its findings, regarding the working of the Public Libraries Act.

Chapter III (f)—The State Central Library :

(21) The State Central Library should be developed only as a reference and research library

(22) It should stock books, periodicals and other non-book materials meant for referance and research.

(23) It should develop reprographic section, by acquiring the most modern equipment.

(24) It should discharge, all the functions enunciated by us above and provide leadership in all activities in the field of libraries.

(25) It should arrange exhibitions and other extension activities on a more meaningful and larger, scale.

(26) The bibliographical work, the union catalogue work and the bibliography of children's literature and for the blind should be carried by the State Central Library in co-ordination with Regional Libraries. The Government should give special grants for this important and urgent work.

(27) The Classification and card cataloguing should be

centrally organised by the State Central Library in co-ordination with the Regional Libraries and the District Central Libraries

(28) The book selection work, the selection of periodicals and newspapers should be entrusted to the Stale Central Library which would constitute a Book Selection Committee and do the work in consultation with the District Central Libraries and the Regional Libraries

(29) It should organise a survey and research unit and continuously carry on survey and research on different aspects of the library work.

(30) The Inter Regional Library loan and loan of books and Periodicals to and from outside the State should be organised by the State Central Library.

(31) The State Central Library ought to provide documentation and information services to all and in particular to the Legislative Houses and other departments of the State Govern ment.

(32) The State Central Library should plan short and long term library services throughout the State.

(33) It should supervise and aid library education in the State.

(34) The State Central Library should be responsible for production of literature for neo-literates and of children of different age groups and blind people and supervise the work of book production council.

(35) It should prepare annual report on the functioning of the libraries in the State.

(36) It should perform such other functions as are entrusted to it by the State Library Council or the Government.

(37) There should be a Slate Central Library Authority for the State Central Library and the Regional Libraries. Its composition should be on the lines suggested by us. Its powers and functions should be such as are conferred

on it by Rules made under the Act by the Government keeping in view the character of the State Central and Regional Libraries.

(38) The definition "State Regional Library" in Section 2 (12) be changed as "Regional Library".

(39) The State Central Librarian's status should be that of a Deputy Director.

Chapter III (g)—Regional Libraries :

(40) There should be only three Regional Libraries : One at Guntur, the other at Tirupathi and the third at Warangal. They shall as at present be wholly financed by the State Government.

(41) Reference books and other library material of that nature existing in the Vishahapatnam and Nizamabad Regional Libraries be transferred to Regional Libraries of Guntur and Warangal respectively.

(42) The status of the Regional Librarians should be that of Assistant Director.

(43) The Regional Libraries at Vishkhapatnam and Nizamabad be developed as Branch Libraries of the concerned District Central Library

(44) The Regional Libraries shall by reference Libraries and shall not be lending libraries except to the extent permitted for the reference section and that too to an institution recognised for that purpose.

(45) The functions of the Regional Libraries will be as mentioned above. Their powers and duties will be as stated earlier.

(46) The growth of all the three Regional Libraries suggested by us should be ensured on equal basis and discrimination of every kind should be avoided, so that the people of the three regions will have equal access to reference and research material.

Chapter III (h)-Zilla Grandhalaya Samsthas :

(47) Revenue District as at present should continue to be the unit of the library service. It will serve the entire district consisting of both urban as well as rural areas.

(48) The composition of the Zilla Grandhalaya Samstha should be as above.

(49) There should be a District Central Library in each district. The Zilla Grandhalaya Samsthas should be empowered to open Branch Libraries, Deposit Stations and Mobile Librarie etc., in accordance with the Rules prescribed, so that the entire district will have the library service on the basis of equality.

(50) Amendments to the provisions of the Act and the rules made thereunder should be effected as suggested by us.

(51) The rule requiring administrative sanction of the Director of Public Libraries for every expenditure even when provided in the approved budget should be deleted.

Chapter III (h) (B)-Zilla Graudhalaya Samstha for the Twin Cities of Hyderabad and Secunderabad:

(52) The composition of the Zilla. Grandhalaya Samstha for the City of Hyderabad and Secunder abad should be on the lines suggested above.

(53) The relevant provisions of the Act should be amended on the above lines.

(54) Except twin cities of Hyderabad and Secunderabad, in no other city a separate Zilla Grandhalaya Samstha need be constituted.

Chapter III (i)—Employees of the Department of the Libraries :

(54-A.) Section 19-A be replealed and instead, provisions on the lines of Section 15 of the Mysore Public Libraries Act be introduced.

Chapter IV. Finance :

(55) The Government should maintain a separate fund called the State Library Fund.to meet expenses for development of library services in the State.

(56) A cess at the rate of six paise per rupee on the following taxes be levied and collectted by the agencies which collect the tax and be remitted to the State Library Fund apart from the cess collected on property tax which is being remitted to the respective Zilla Grandhalaya Samatha Library Fund.

(a) Sales Tax.

(b) Vehicles Tax.

(c) Land Revenue.

(57) In addition to the matching grant provided in Section 21 (3) of the Act, the Government should contribute an amount not less than the total amount of cess collected on the above said three taxes or 10% of the education budget whichever is higher.The Government congribution on the cess collected on sales tax, vehicles tax and land revenue should be credited to the state Library Fund. The grant should be increased as and when new areas are covered by the library service.

(58) The Central Government should contribute a certain percentage of their education budget for the development of libraries in the country and distribute the same equitably amongst all the States. Contingent grants and grants based on relative population should be avoided.

(58-A) The Local bodies, that is to say, the Municipal Corporation, the Municipalities, Zilla Parishads, Panchayat Samithis and Village Panchayats should contribute an amount not less than $1\frac{1}{2}$% of their total budget to the Zilla Grandhayala Samsthas library fund in whose district these local bodies function.

(59) The Government should help the backward districts by evolving suitable criteria in order to ensure equal library service to the people of the State.

(60) The cess collected on the property tax as well as the land revenue, sales tax and vehicles tax should be deducted by the Government at source and remitted to the library funds of each district or the State Library Fund as the case may be. A provision on the lines of Kerala Bill be enacted to that effect in our Act.

(61) The ban or the restriction put by the Government on the expansion of the library service and employment of library staff should immediately be lifted.

(62) The budget demand relating to public libraries should be separated from the education budget and such a demand should be moved in the Legislature by the Minister for Public Libraries.

Chapter-V. Libraries Role in Eradicating Illiteracy :

(63) The Government should constitute an ag;ncy on a permanent basis or entrust this to public libraries after strengthening the department, to fight against Illiteracy on a war footing so that the agency could carry on the work mostly in the rural areas.

(64) The library service should participate and co-opearate in the campaign of removing lliteracy by organising library service stocked with books and other non-book material such as audio-visual materials for that purpose.

(65) The Government should have its own publications for neo-literates, particularly in Telugu language as well as should encourage private publishers, authors and illustrators suitable for writing, illustrating and producing literature of the type mentioned above for neoy-literates.

(66) A book develops-at council should be appointed by the

Government as stated above.

(67) From the assitance which the State gets from Raja Ram Mohan Roy Library Foundation, highest priority should be given for the purchase of audio-visual materials with a view to organise the campaign for the removal of illiteracy in the rural areas.'

(68) The Central Institue of Indian Languages should be requested to prepare a film on how to learn Telugu script, if they have not already made.

(69) Each library,particularly in the rural area, should stock books and other reading materials helpful to the neo-literates.

Chapter -VI.—School and Children's Libraries:

(70) The comprehensive Education Bill, at present pending before the Legislative Assembly, should contain a provision for the establishment, equipment, and administration of school libraries in every pre-primary, primary and secondary school. In any event, the library law should contain provisions for making it compulsory to have a children's section in each Public Library.

(71) Every Primary and Secondary School should have a well-equipped library. It should have enough stock of books and other reading material. Wherever it exists, it should be improved according to definite plans, so that it would be made available to all children at school, as well as teachers teaching in such schools.

(72) (a) One teacher from each school should be given training in library services with education in the child psychology so as to be helpful to the children in their library work.

(b) Courses in children's library services should be made a part of training of teachers in all teacher-educational institutions.

(73) The school libraries should have co-operative arrangements with Public Libraries of sections so as to have a smooth change over from child-hood to adolescence developing libraryhabits. There should be continuous joint planning on a local and area-wide basis by those who are responsible for school and college libraries, so that complete and co-ordinated library services may be provided to the children.

(74) Selection of the books for schools must be made by the school committee and the librarians of the Public Libraries, to avoid duplication and to enrich the collection.

(75) The school libraries should provide books and reading material not only to help the education process, but 'o develop an attitude and habit of self and independent reading in the children,

(76) Every Public Library should have a Children's Section housed in attractive place. The Public Libraries must organise various programmes such as exhibition of children's books and reading material, filmshows, story-telling programmes, dramas and other cultural activities for the children.

(77) Every children's library and children's section in a Public Library, as far as possible, should be placed under the charge of a trained librarian with knowledge of child psychology.

(78) Books for children written in Telugu and other languages spoken in the State should be got written from competent persons and illustrators. Writers and publishers in this field should be appropriately encouraged by offering awards, prizes or royalties or by guaranteeing minimum sale of their books. The books and their content and designs in such cases should be approved by the department. Such a production should include books designed to keep the neo-literate reading, whether child or adult.

(79) That special consideration should be given to the library services for mentally and physically handicapped children, in particular, the blind and the orphans and delinquents housed in institutions.

(80) The Public Library planning and their activities should be designed to encourage the growth of school and academic libraries, the development of centralised school library programmes and the attainment of school library standards.

(81) Public Libraries with the co-operation of school, college and university libraries should be able to meet the growing needs of part-time, private and other students who appear for examinations through correspondence courses.

(82) The school libraries should be made to work all the year round and should be utilised for at least eight hours a day, if not longer.

(83) Nothing would be more dangerous to a growing school than to neglect its library or to give it a low priority. On the contrary, the school library should become an important centre of attraction on school campus. The Government should, therefore, provide sufficient funds for establishing school libraries.

Chapter VII (a) —Implementation of the Press and Registration of Books Act, 1867 and the Books Delivery Act, of 1954

(84) The penalty clauses of both the said Acts should be made, by amendment, more stringent so as to act as deterrent for those who violate the provisions of the said Acts.

(85) The machinery for the implementation of these two Acts must be strengthened and every possible effort should be made to effectively implement the Acts.

(86) The Book Slection Committee of the State should select books for the public libraries only from the list of the books delivered under the two Acts, and refuse to select any book not so delivered. If necessary, a provision may be made in this behalf in the library Act, or rules made thereunder.

Chapter - VII (b) — Selection of books and other library material :

(87) The selection of books and periodicals should be made by a Selection Committee or Committees constituted by the State Library Council.

(88) Such Selection Committee should consist of various interests represented by experts and librarians. It should meet as often as should be required.

(89) The Zilla Grandhalaya Samsthas should have their own selection committees both for suggesting material to be selected by Selection Committee, as well as, for the purchase of materials out of the list prepared by the Committee.

(90) Once the Selection Committee selects materials, then it should not require anybodys approval, it should be treated as final selection. The two provisos to Section 13 (1) (b) of the Act should be substituted by the following provisos "Provided that the books that may be stocked in the libraries shall be selected from the list of books approved from time to time by the Book Selection Committee constituted by the State Library Council the aggregate value whereof shall be not less than 75% of the provision made in the budget of the Samstha for the purpose of this clause."

"Provided further that a Zilla Grandhalaya Samstha is at liberty to purchase books upto the value of 25 % of the budget provision for the year." Every delay in selection and remitting the list of books so selected, to the Zilla Grandhalaya Samsthas be scrupulously avoided.

(91) Selection of books should be made keeping *in* view the purposes mentioned above.

(92) The number of books should be increased in the manner suggested above.

Chapter - VII (c.) — Removal of Unwanted Material :

(93) Material no longer useful, obviously pernicious material, material damaged beyond repairs be systematically removed in order to enliven the library system.

(94) Weeding out of the material should be done periodically but with great care and caution. A Committee consisting of experts should be appointed and it is only on their advice and in any case under the supervision of a high library authority the process of weeding out should be completed.

(95) The same or separate committee may be constituted for the purpose of separating the pernicious stock of books from the general stock of books and reading material.

Chapter - VIII — Institutional and Private Libraries :

(96) The Zilla Grandhalaya Samsthas should immediately carry on a survey regarding the existing association owned public libraries. This survey should cover not only the number of such libraries but the area which they serve, the book-stocks they have, the periodicals and newspapers they make available to the readers, their financial and administrative position and whether their bookstock has been classified and catalogued properly etc.

(97) Grant in aid rules be prepared by the Government *in* consultation with the State Library Council classifying the association-owned public libraries for the purposes of

grant. Such grants should be made with a view to upgrade their standard with a view to bring them on par with the State Library Service.

(98) There should be an attempt to get absorbed in the State Library system small association owned libraries so that larger units of libraries can serve the people comprehensively and efficiently.

(99) The departmental libraries should offer technical advice and assistance to the institutution libraries and bring them within the system for the purpose of inter-library co-operation including inter-library loan.

(100) The-Act should have a provision for amalgamation of institutionally owned Pubic Libraries.

Chapter - IX—The Planning of Library Services :

(101) The State Library Council should be constituted as a State Planning Authority to prepare State Library Service Plan which would be approved by the Government.

(102) Before finalising the plan at State level, a survey of each District as suggested above shall be carried on and the findings noted.

(103) The Zilla Grandhalaya Samsthas in the light of these surveys should prepare District Plans keeping in view the existing library service provided by all kinds of libraries and then make plan for covering the remaining area by providing different kinds of library service. Such plans then will be submitted to the State Planning Authority for their integration into a State Plan.

(104) The plan so finally approved by the Government will be implemented in a phased manner.

(105) Section 14 of the Act and Rules 15 and 16 of the Rules be substituted by provisions in the Act on the lines of the Comprehensive Education Bill now pending before the State Legislature.

(106) As a measure to take library service to the door steps of the people there can be no better method than providing services of Mobile Library in each revenue division of a district, apart from other methods adopted such as opening of Branch Libraries, Village Libraries, Book Deposit Centres, Mobile rickshaws' etc.

Chapter - X—Library Building Programme :

(107) To meet the existing as well as future needs for considerably improving the public library premises and for many new buildings, a higher priority should be given as soon as possible by the State and Central Governments to provide in a phased manner capital expenditure for sites, premises for public libraries so that the whole building programme could be completed in 10 to 15 years.

(103) The Government should constitute a study group of experts consisting of architect, engineer, librarian and Chairman of the Zilla Grandhalaya Samstha to investigate the economic planning of library premises and buildings.

(109) The Urban Land Ceiling Authority should be requested to set apart suitable sites in the towns and cities to which the relevant Act is made applicable for public libraries. The librarians of the concerned Ziila Grandhalaya Samasthas should be asked immediately to indicate their needs to the said authorities.

(110) The Urban Development Authorities should be requested to set apart suitable sites or buildings for libraries while planning.

(111) The study group suggested should not only inquire into the existing needs but also into future needs and estimate costs so that in a phased manner the building programme may be taken up. The Committee also should prepare

alternative building plans which be adopted to varying situations.

Chapter - XI—Library Co-operation and Inter-Library Loan :

(112) The State Central and Regional Libraries should be statutorily authorised to organise inter-library loan in the State and the Regions respectively along with the scheme of inter availability of tickets.

(113) Section 8 has to be accordingly amended. Rules regarding the inter-library loan and the inter availability of tickets should be framed by the Government after consulting the State Library Council.

(114) The Librarians should be trained for these purposes.

(115) Adequate bibliographies and union catalogues should be kept in the State Central Library and the Regional Libraries.

Chapter - XII—Librarians and their training :

(116) There should be a library training course for training library assistants or library technicians in the course now known as certificate course. There should be arrangement for irservice training for librarians.

(117) The basic general qualification for admission to this course should not be lower than a first or second class pass in Intermediate or Junior College.

(118) Before the students are admitted to the school, written and oral aptitude tests should be rigorously taken so that only persons suitable for the profession will be admitted.

(119) Pre and Post apprenticeship of not less than three months in a recognised library should be insisted on for the purpose of admission for training in the school.

(120) The duration of the course should not be less than 150 working days of five hours a day, each hour being of 60 minutes.

(121) The course can be run either by the Department of Public Libraries or by a recognised Library School. But the Governmnent in either case shall extend all possible help.

(122) The syllabus and curriculum should contain the aspects mentioned above. The present syllabus is required to be revised in the light of the above discussion.

(123) The Government should constitute a small but effective committee of experts to draft syllabus for (a) Library Course ; (b) Teachers training for teachers who teach in the schools or for their re-training ; (c) inservice training of the librarians as well as the teachers. This ought to be done without any more delay as it is affecting the library service

(124) There should be uniform syllabus, duration of period and examination etc., for the course run by the Association and/or Department.

(125) The library law should provide a central authority preferably the State Central Library to organise and/or supervise work of library education which includes library course for inservice training as well as training of teachers.

(126) Inservice training should be organised by the State Central Library periodically in cooperation with the library association. Such training could be organised either at the State Capital or at the district level.

(127) The Library Schools should gradually build up their own laboratories and for doing so, the Government should extend to them financial help. Till such laboratories are developed, the schools should make arrangements with different kinds of good libraries situa-led near about the place where the school is located.

(128) In the training of librarians for public libraries, a course in adult education administration and techniques should be added. Similarly, library administration and library

extension methods should form part of training of adult edudcation workers.

(129) In order to attract talented men and women for the development of library service, the librarians should be offered appropriate status and pay.

(130) More text books and other books on library science should be written in Telugu or translated from, foreign languages ; glossaries of technical terms in library science should be compiled with a view to assisting the early publication of library science books in Telugu, and for such publications adequate direct or indirect Government subsidies should be given. These books should also be written or translated for the purpose of training of teachers and inservice training of librarians.

(131) Professional associations of librarians should be recognised and financial help should be given to them by the Government.

(132) The teachers in library school should take tutorials, adopt, seminar and discussion method of teaching rather than relying only on lectures. Case study method should also be followed.

(133) Teachers should know new methodology of teaching and if necessary undergo training for that purpose.

(134) At least part of the teaching staff in a library science school should be- full-time.

Note : For recommendations made with regard to additions to or deletions from the Act, please see Chapter XI11.

(Sd.)

Chairman and Members.

Source : *Report of the committee appointed by the Government of Andhra Pradesh in February, 1976 to review the working of the Andhra Pradesh Public Libraries Act, 1960 and suggest amendments to the Act.* (Hyderabad, Dept. of Public Libraries, Govt. of A.P. 1978), pp. 99-108.

G.2. Committee on Private Libraries, 1978 (Vavilala Committee)

Introduction

Libraries have been established in Andhra Desa including Rayalaseema and Telanagana region as part of peoples movement. These were established owing to the initation, enthusiasm and drive of selfless individuals and groups of dedicated workers willing to work at the grass root level for the spread of library movement in every nook and corner of Andhra Desa and Telangana regions. The urge to educate themseleves and spread knowledge among the people through library service appeared during the nineteenth century and steadily rose like a groundswell. In the year 1800, a private library belonging to Paravasthu family was declared open for public. In 1872 H.H. Sri Sankararadhya established a library at Secundrabad in 1872. Manthena Adinarayamurthy established Saraswati Nilayam at Visakkapatnam in 1866 supposed to be the first public library on modernlines. In 1898 Sri Gawtami Grandhalayam was established in Rajahmundry. In Telangana Region, Srikrishna Dearaya Andhra Bhasha Nilayam was established in 1901 at Hyderabad followed by Sri RajaRaja Narendra Andhra Bhasha Nilayam in 1904 at Hanamkonda. Likewise many libraries were established in Andhra and Telangana regions for the spread of library movement.

It was estimated that by the end of 1913 there were nearly 163 libraries functioning in different parts of Andhra Desa. By the end of 1920 there were about 720 public libraries in Andhra and Telangana regions which were established and managed by the associations and voluntary organisations with the support of public donations and membership of subscriptions. After independence, their survival and existence become a big question mark. The public support had slowly come down and many libraries have disappeared were from the scene. Some of them struggling hard to survive and render service to the public. The Ekbote committee aptly summarized the state of affairs of these libraries by stating that "there were libraries which are more than 75 years old in state. Some of the libraries have very ancient and rich collections of books and manuscripts. Some of them, however, are languishing because of lack funds and proper administration while some others are torn with bends and dissensions."[2]

Ekbote Committee Recommendations

For the rejunavation of these libraries. Which were dubbed erroneously as private libraries the Ekbote committe recommended the following :

"1. The Zilla Grandhalaya Samasthas should immediately carryon a survey regarding the existing association owned public libraries. This survey should cover not only the number of such libraries but the area which they serve, the book stocks they have, the periodicals and news papers they make available to the readers, their finanicial and administrative position and whether their book stock has been classified and categoriesed property etc.,

2. Grant in aid rules should be prepared by the government in consultation with the state Library council classifying rhe association, owned Public libraries for the purpose of grant. Such grants should be made with a view to upgrade their standard with a view to bring them on par with the state Library service.

3. There should be an attempt to get absorbed in the state library system small association owned libraries so that larger units of libraries can serve the people comprehensively and efficiently.

4. The departmental libraries should offer technical advice and assistance to the institutional libraries and bring them within the system for the purpose of inter library

cooperation including inter library loan.

5. The Act should have provision for amalagation of institutionally owned libraries."[3]

As stated else where the report of the Ekbote committee was put in cold storage. After two years the government of Andhra Pradesh appointed another committee to look into the state of affairs of 'Private Libraries' which Ekbote committee termed as" Institutional and Private Libraries."

Appointment of the Committee on Private Libraries

The Government of Andhra Pradesh through its Go. MS. No 766 Education (E) Department dated 19.07.1978 costituted a committee on private libraries with Vavilala Gopala Krishnayya as chairmen and Kodati Narayana Rao and M.Bhoj Reddy as members and the Director of Public Libraries as Convenor:

Terms and Conditions of the Committee

The terms and conditions of the committee were as follows :

"1. To review the role played by private libraries to render library service."

2. To suggest measures as to how best private libraries can help in the cause of library movement.

3. To identify good private libraries in the state.

4. To evolve a system of grant in aid to private libraries for their promotion, and

5. To submit its report to the Government within a month from the date of its cocnsitution."[4]

Committee Report

The committee submitted its report in November 1978. It is breif report consisting just three chapters and supported by three tables. Chapter 1: deals with Early efforts and History of Library movement, Chapter 2: Role of Private Libraries and Chapter 3: Norms to identification and Grant-in-Aid.

To get first hand information on the state of affairs of private libraries in the state, the committeed visited important places in Andhra Pradesh and had discussions with the workers in the fields of library movement, received representations from individuals, organisations and associations and also visited important privately managed libraries. The committeed also attended two seminars organised by Guntur Zilla Grandhalaya Samastha (ZGS) at Narasaraopeta on 06.10.1978 and another one at Hyderabad on 22.10.1978 jointly organised by Srikrishna Devaraya Andhra Bhasha Nilayam, Institute of Library Science and Academy of Library Science and documentation.[5]

Recommendations

Chapter 3 of the Report deals with "Norms for identification and Grant-in-Aid". The norms for identification and grant in aid is provided in the annexure. The committee estimated the existence of 2,155 private libraries functioning in the state. Out of which only 969 libraries were in receipt of grant-in-aid. In addition to recommendation made in chapter 3, the committee further made certain general recommendations which were shown in the annexure.

Fate of the committee report

Like Ekbote committee report, the Vavilala committee met the same fate of non-implementation of major recommendation. Hitter to Zilla Grandhalaya Samasthas (ZGSS) were giving grant in aid to recognised and select Aided Libraries (Private Libraries) for the purchase of books, periodicals and furniture to the extent of 85% of the total expenditure incurred and the Director of Public Libraries sanctioned to the extent of 50% subject to a maximum of Rs

800.00. These grants to the Private Libraries have been, of late, stopped by Zilla Grandhalaya Samasthas as well by the Department of Public Libraries, with few exceptions. The reason for the stoppage of grant-in-aid to private libraries was the accute financial problems faced by the ZGSS due to governments policies and programmes. Many Private libraries have disappeared from the scene and few are struggling to survive.

Many representations were made from time to time to the concerned authority for full and and immediate implementation of Vavilala committee report. But these representations had no impact on the Government. The situation obtaining in private libraries had turned from bad to worse as the financial support from the ZGSS and Department of Public Libraries has completely dried up. It is three decades since the submission of the Report. There is no hope of its implementation. Like Ekbote Committee Report, the Vavilala committee Report also gathering dust on the shelves in the office of the Department of Public Libraries. The consquences of non-implementation of the recommendations of the Vavilala committee is the deterioration in the functioning of private libraries, which some of them, have played glorious part in the genesis, growth and spread of library movement in Andhra Pradesh.

References

1. C. Gopinatha Rao. *Library Movement in Andhra Pradesh*. (Hyderabad, Dept. of Public Libraries, govt. of A.P., 1981), p.1.
2. *Report of the committee appointed by the Government of Andhra Pradesh in Felraversy 1976 to the review the working of A.P. Public Libraries Act, 1960* and to suggest ammendents to the Act (Hyderabad, The Director of Printing, Govt of AP, 1978), p.72.
3. Ibid, pp. 74-75.
4. *Report of the committee on private libraries*, November, 1978. (Hyderabad, Dept of Public Libraries, effort of A.P., 1978), p. V.
5. Ibid., pp. VI to VII.

Annexure
Report of the Committee on Private Libraries

Recommendations

Keeping in view the several activities that are expected of these libraries and to ascertain views of library workers and managements of such libraries in the state, the Committee toured extensively in the districts and obtained suggestions from several quarters. After considering these suggestions the Committee makes the following recommendations :

Identification

1. (a) A Library established and run by any non-official organisation and registered under the Public Libraries Act is a Public Library.

A Library run by a village Panchayat, Municipality or any other local body and registered under the Public Libnaries Act is a Public Library,

A Library established and run by an organisation and registered under the Trust Act or Societies Act and registered under the Public Libraries Act is a Public Library,

Every Library other than those managed by the government, Zilla Grandhalaya Samstha, local body, or. public and open to the public must be registered with the Director of Public Libraries afresh though they were registered under the different Acts and recognised by the Director of Public Libraries.

(b) The term 'Private Libraries', has been used by government in the Order appointing this Committee to identify libraries run the by agencies other than government and quasi-government ones. However, the attention of the Committee was drawn to the fact that in the economic and industrial sectors the term 'private' is used in connection with individual or group profit as opposed to'public benefit'. These libraries, on the other hand organised by voluntary groups of enthusiasts, are run entirely for Public benefit and the larger good of the people with their active participation. In this sense they are 'Peoples' libraries. The Committee therefore decided to call them 'peoples' libraries (Poura Grandhalayam),

2. (a) A Library/reading-room/club should be registered with the Director of Public Libraries without charging any fees and a register showing these should be maintained by the Directorate. The application for registration should be processed by the librarians of the concerned district central library. Presently such registration is done under the Registration of Societies Act, 1867 or 1350 F. as the case may be. A provision for registration with the Director of Public Libraries and other items mentioned above should be made in the Andhra Pradesh Libraries Act, by amending it suitably. Pending such amendment, the concession of reduction in the registration fee under the Societies Registration Act, 1860 and Public Societies Registration Act, 1350 F. in Andhra & Telangana from Rs. 50 to Rs. 5 given to Rural Youth Clubs and Manila Mandals in G.O. Ms. No. 949, PR (T & III) Dept., dated 8-11-66 may be extended to these libraries,

(b) A Library/reading- room should have been organising service at least for a minimum period of 2 years immediately preceding the date of registration to enable it to gain eligibility for grant and/ or franchise in the elections for membership of Zilla Grandhalaya Samstha,

(c) The Library/reading-room/club should be open for all members of society for consultation within the premises without restriction on the basis of caste, creed, religion or sex and free of charge,

(d) A Library/reading-room/club should be working for at least 3 hours in a day,

(e) (i) A Library should have a minimum of 500 books and be subscribing to at least 2 dailies and 5 other periodicals,

(f) A reading-room/club should be subscribing to at least 2 dailies and 8 other periodicals. Such reading-room/club should within a period of 2 years from the date of registration acquire or strengthen heir existing book-stock to the minimum of 500 books, A Library/reading-room/club should provide space for at least 10 readers to sit and study,

(g) A Library/club should provide facilities for homelending of books, and

(h) The application for registration/grant of every library should be supported by a statement of accounts duly audited by a registered auditor. But libraries with a book-stock of 500 and below and reading rooms and clubs should be exempted from this condition.

Grants-in-aid

In the matter of fixing up quantum of grant for these libraries/ reading-rooms/clubs some weightage will have to be given to units belonging to backward and tribal regions. For this purpose, Andhra Pradesh State may be recognised as falling into three distinct regions viz., (a) Ordinary/normal region, (b) Backward and drought affected regions and slums sector in urban areas and (c) tribal ageencies.

The committee is of the view that there should be a minimum grant for every library/reading-room/club. Such a grant should not be less than Rs. 200 so as to enable it to run its day-to-day services. It should however be eligible to special/ additional grants for books, furniture, equipment etc.

A. Normal Grants

1. Normal area libraries for purchase of books and periodicals:

Management Share	Government Share
1/3	2/3

The entire expenditure on books and periodicals is admissible for assessment of the grant and grant would be worked out on the basis of 1 : 2.

The grant towards staff salary shall be equivalent to 50% of the grant on books and periodicals or actual expenditure whichever is less.The grant towards other expenditure i.e. Rents, Rates, Taxes, Book Binding and other contingencies shall be equivalent to 50 % of grant on books and periodicals or actual expenditure which ever Is less.

B. Special Grants :

	Library share	*Government grant*
1. (i) Building Construction	40%	60%
(ii) Library equipment like typewriter, catalogue cards, duplicator, Rubber stamps, Trays Dater, Book-Racks/ Shelves,Lighting equipment,book ends, Film slides, Records, Maps, Microfilm recorders and all allied materials	40%	60%
(iii) Library furniture—Tables, Chairs, Issue counter, Trays, Book trolleys, Display racks, book exhibition stands and all allied materials	40%	60%

Every care should be taken to provide for a book-rack or shelf per 1,000 books added to the collection.

2. Backward, Drought affected, Slum and Tribal Areas :

In respect of items under this head i.e., recurring and non-recurring, libraries in these regions should get grant at a higher rate viz. library's share 25% and Government Grants 75%.

C. Additional Grants

In addition to these, libraries should be given special grants for taking up work in the following areas also.

1. Adult Education Programme: For stocking reading material useful for neoliterates and extending assistance in this programme, an amount of Rs. 1,000 per annum may be provided (remuneration for teacher as already provided in the National Adult Education Programme of the Government of India)

2. Text Books : In the villages and other Non-urban areas a quiet place for young students to sit and study is hardly available because of large size of anaverage family and the little space and lighting facility available at home. It is therefore necessary that libraries should take the responsibility for providing such special accommodation. The centre should be open for at least 4 hours in a day and should provide accommodation for at least 6 students. A special grant of Rs. 1,000 per annum for first 3 years and Rs. 500 per annum thereafter may be provided for this activity after due inspection and verification.

3. Children's Section : These libraries should be given special grants for organising special cells for children. The grant may be Rs. 1,000 per annum for the first 2 years and Rs. 500 per annum thereafter.

Every one of these libraries should be required to provide special accommodation and facilities for women, farm and factory workers and attend to their conveniences.

D. Release of Grants :

Libraries shall furnish all required documents including audited accounts together with the application for grant not later than the end of July every year. Grant for the year shall be released before the end of December of the year to enable libraries to maintain an even flow of service.

Libraries having a book stock of 500 copies need not submit audit report.

Inspection

Next, for purpose of inspection and supervision of the working of these libraries they may be categorised as indicated below :-

(a) Libraries having Book stock of 15,000 and above shall be inspected by the Director of Public Libraries or an Officer authorised by him,

(b) Libraries having Book stock of above 5,000 and below 15,000 shall be inspected by the Librarian, District Central Library or a grade I Lbrarian authorised by him, and

(c) Libraries having Book stock of below 5,000 shall be inspected by any Branch Librarian.

Other Issues

The Committee further makes the following general recommendations :

(1) Generally no branch Library should be opend by a Zilla Gran-dhalaya Samstha at a place where a public library is already functioning;

(2) Organisers/Librarians of these libraries should be exposed to an intensive course of training in basic skills of librarianship for a period of a week or 10 days;

(3) The Endowment Department may be requested to exempt the amounts contributed to these libraries from the payment of their "Contribution";

(4) Since the state receives financial help to the extent of 2 lakhs per annum from Raja Rammohan Roy Library Foundation scheme as its share the Committee feels that Government, may provide books to private libraries to the extent of 50% of the total books purchased instead of giving the entire benefit to the Zilla Grandhalaya Samstha libraries and Government libraries;

(5) All government and quasi-government publications tracts on special subjects intended for distribution may be supplied to all private libraries also keeping these libraries on mailing lists;

(6) As part of the library system these libraries should be

allowed to participate in the inter library loan scheme and other schemes of library co-operation;

(7) In a federal country like ours the Central Government also has to shoulder responsibility towards maintenance and improving the tone and content of library service through grants from out of its funds. The Advisory Committee on Libraries of theGovt. of India headed by Sri K.P. Sinha in its report 1959 (Page 112) advocated a matching grant from the centre to the State Library Fund. The fact that 'Education' is now a subject on the 'concurrent list' also lends additional weight to this plea. We therefore reiterate the recommendation of the Ekbote Committee (Page 54) that the Central Government should also earmarks some percentage of its Education budget for the purpose. In the circumstances we recommend that the State Government take steps to prevail on the Central Government to allocate funds and make a beginning in this behalf.

The Committee is convinced that once a beginning is made by providing for liberal grants as recommended above the entire library net work in the state will begin to hum with life and pave the way for improved service for after all the character and personality of a people will depend on what they are given to read and think about. We look forward to saying with Andre Maurios—

"*Tell me what you give your people to read
and I will tell you what you are*",

	(Sd.) Vavilala Gopalakrishnayya	Chairman
Hyderabad,	(Sd.) Kodati Narayana Rao	Member
Dt. 10-11-78.	(Sd.) Bhoj Reddy	Member
	(Sd.) M. V. Venkata Reddy	Convenor

Source : *Report of the committee on Private Libraries, November, 1978* (Hyderabad, Dept of Public Libraries, Govt. of Andhra Pradesh, 1978), pp. 20-24, 27-28.

H

PROFESSIONAL ASSOCIATIONS AND ORGANISATIONS

The Oxford English Dictionary (OED) defined the term 'Profession' as "a vocation in which a professed knowledge of some department of learning or science is used in its application to the affairs of others, in the practice of an art bounded upon it". A professional means a person who practices a profession for the purpose livelihood and serves the society for its progress. The term 'association' means an organization of persons having a common interest. The persons who practice librarianship as a profession can come together to form an organisation to safe guard the interest and strive hard for the development of the profession. Through a professional body/ bodies the members strive hard to serve the society with dedication and sense of purpose. A profession has certain attributes and library profession is no exception in this regard. The attributes of any profession in general indicates that it :

1. involves knowledge based and promoted intellectual activity.
2. has basic philosophy on which the activities are formulated and implemented.
3. has distnict and special techniques, methods, practices and skills with which it grows and helps the society at large.
4. requires extensive and intensive education and training.

5. has set of principles, ethics and social work of conduct and behaviour.
6. has a social recognition and status to its members in the society.
7. has an organization/association to work together for the cause of the profession.
8. sets of specific norms and standards for entry in training.
9. has some guide lines and norms for the conduct if its members in relation to society.
10. imposes responsibilities and duties along with rights.
11. sets aside personal profit or gain against service to society.

These professional associations and organization serve the cause of professional development by actions and activities such as : 1. providing a meeting place for the professionals to come together at regular intervals for exchange of views on professional matters, 2. acting as a representative organisation of the profession to inter act with the government and other agencies and to bring to their notice the problems faced by the professionals, 3. safe guarding the interests of the members, 4. bringing out professional literature such as news letters, journals, state of the art reports, to disseminate results of research and developments, 5. conducting continuing education programmes such as : short and long term refresher courses, workshops, seminars and symposia, 6. strive to enhance professionals image and status by enforcing code of ethics, work standards and 7. improving the image of the profession and professionals in the eyes society and thereby earn respect to the profession.[2]

Like other professional organisations, we have several library associations and organisations at various levels - national state, regional, district and local. These associations/ organisations are meant for different target groups such as : Public, Academic School, College and University, Special,

Technical, Agricultural, Government librarians, information scientists document lists and LIS teachers. In Andhra Pradesh there is no dearth for such as associations. Infact Andhra Pradesh has distinction of having founded the first library association for the whole country namely Andhradesa Grandhalaya Sangham (Andhradesa Library Association) founded in the year 1914 at Vijayawada. The following sections briefly deal with some of the prominent library associations/ organisations which have been functioning and rendering significant services for the cause of library profession and professionals in Andhra Pradesh. Some Associations rendered yeomen service and disappeared from the scene due to passage of time and political and administrative changes. Some are just on paper and dormant for several years. Presently Andhra Pradesh Library Association (APLA), Vijayawala and Academy of Library Science and Documentation (ALSD), Hyderabad are the only two professionals organisation which are active and contributing to the growth of the profession through their activities.

Reference

1. L.S. Ramaiah Library Profession. In *Library and Society* (Course material BLISC) (Hyderabad, Dr B.R. Ambedkar Open university, 2003) p. 29.
2. S. Sunderashan Rao and T.V. Profullachandra. Library Associations in India with special Reference to Andhra Pradesh. In 53 All India Library Conference of ILA, Dec 13-16, 2007. *Souvenir* (Hyderabad, Dept of Lib & Inf. Sc., OU., 2007) p. 55.

H.1. Andhra Pradesh Library Association (APLA), Vijayawada

Introduction

Libraries have been established in Andhra Desa as a part of the peoples movement. The movement spread owing to the initiation, enthusiasm and drive of selfless workers, willing to work at the grass root level. The democratic character of the movement was proclaimed by Ch. Lakshminarasimham, in his presidential address to the First Andhra Desa Library Workers Conference held on 10th April, 1914, under the auspices of Ram Mohan Library at Bezawada. He stated that "Knowledge should be available to all as universally as the air we breathe, the water that quenches thirst and the sun's energy that sustains the life.*[1] The driving force behind this great movement is Andhra Desa Library Association (ADLA).

Genesis

The First Andhra Desa Library Workers Conference held on 10th April 1914 at Bezawada passed several resolutions concerning the spread of the library movement. As a result of the fourth resolution, Andhra Desa Granthalaya Sangham (ADLA) was founded on 10 April 1914 and it was the first library association of its kind for the entire country. The conference elected Mocherla Ramachandra Rao as its first President, Ch. Lakshminarasimham and S.V. Narasimha Sastri as Vice-Presidents and Nalam Krishna Rao and Ayyanki Venkata Ramanayya as General Secretaries of Andhra Desa Library Association.

The State of Andhra Pradesh was formed on 1st November 1956 with the merger of Telugu speaking districts of former Hyderbad State. As a consequence to this change the name of the association was changed in 1957 as the Andhra Pradesh Library Association (APLA) to extend its jurisdiction and activities over the entire State. The

Headquarters of the association is housed in Sarvothama Bhavanam at Vijayawada constructed by the Library Trust which was established in 1946.

Objectives

The Association was established with the following objectives for the spread of librarymovement not only in Andhra but also in other regions of the country and abroad where Telugu people live:

1. Establishing, maintaining and promoting libraries, reading rooms, social education, language institutions and cultural organizations.
2. Propagation of knowledge and education among the general public through all possible means and activities.
3. Spread of library movement through conferences, pilgrimages, symposia, exhibitions and spring festivals.
4. Promotion of Andhra culture, literature and language through the publication of books, pamphlets and journals.
5. Training of librarians and social education workers and preparation of roster of such workers for the spread of the movement
6. Conducting, debating and competitions for the spread of Telugu language and library science and awarding prizes for the winners in the competitions.
7. Preparing and publishing classified lists of books in Telugu for the benefit of scholars.
8. Establishing branch offices of the association at regional, district and taluka levels for the spread of the movement
9. Cooperating with individuals and institutions whose objectives are similar to the objectives of the association.
10. Making efforts for effective implementation of A.P. Public Libraries Act, promoting reading habits among the

people, and helping them to lead peaceful and orderly civic life.

Constitution

The Andhra Pradesh Public Library Association (APLA) is a registered body as per the provisions of the Act No. 21 of 1860. The constitution of the Association passed through in three stages in its chequered history. The first constitution was framed in 1918 and the new constitution was adopted in 1938 and amended in 1957 after enlarging its jurisdiction to the entire state of Andhra Pradesh. According to the 1957 constitution there are nine categories of individual and institutional membership, which constitute the General Body of the Association. It meets once in two years to elect the Managing Committee and has authority over the affairs of the Association. The Managing Committee has one President, five Vice-Presidents, one Secretary, one Treasurer, five Assistant Secretaries and one hundred members or one fifth of the total membership whichever less. In order to carry out day to day activities of the Association, the constitution provides for an Executive Committee which consists of President, Secretary, Treasurer, Vice-Presidents, Joint Secretaries and eight members. This is a three-tier constitutional structure providing representation to all regions, institutions and individual members.

Membership

The constitution of the Association provides for three types of membership, viz: (1) Honorary membership, (2) Life membership and (3) Ordinary membership.Honorary members both individual and institutional are proposed and approved by the Executive Committee. The life membership consists of three sub-categories. Those who contribute Rs. 1,000 are enrolled as Chief Patrons, those who contribute Rs. 250 are enrolled as Patrons, those who conlribute Rs. 150 are enrolled as Life members and those who contribute Rs. 10 are enrolled as ordinary members.[5]

Activities

The Association through its multifarious activities such as meetings, conferences, library pilgrimages, spring festivals propogated the significance of the role of libraries in social and economic development. It cultivated and spread the notion that library is a centre of knowledge and information, and therefore, of great public concern and interest. It emphasised the democratic and public character of libraries so that they shall be accessible to all. The Association encouraged the establishment of special sections for children and women in libraries. Ayyanki Venkata Ramanayya who studied the Baroda library movement of 1917 introduced special divisions for women and children in libraries and devised a special scheme for classifying the Telugu books on the basis of Baroda Scheme."[6]

Organisation of Village Libraries

The association as one of its prime activities strove hard for the organisation and development of village libraries. The village library was considered to be the prime centre for rural development. It helped the establishment of several hundreds of rural libraries not only to serve the literate people but also to educate illiterate masses. The association worked hard to bring home to people that the village library is an information centre and pivot of social and cultural life of the village. In the words of Ayyanki "To us the library is a social service centre for the whole village for human activity with life and animation for the uplift of the country."[7]

No activity which contributed to the reconstruction of the society was beyond the scope of the village library's work. Newton Mohan Dutt stated that "Andhra Desa has developed quite a new type of library incorporating in its organisation among others, the hoary indigenous institution of Hindu temple and the ancient village community and the modern public library."[8] The rural libraries, to mention a few, Sri Veeresalinga Kavi Samajam at Kumudavalli, Sri Balasaraswati Library at Angaluru, the Krishna Devaraya Library at Baruva and Saraswata Niketanam at Vetapalem entered into very heart of the life of the village community and took special interest in adult educaton and literacy including education of women and even prepared them for competitive examinations.[9]

The association for the first time drew attention of all to the immense potentiality of rural library service. In the words of G.Hari Sarvottama Rao "It has kept the torch of service for the culture of our rural population burning. In fact it is the first association in India to draw attention to rural library and its organisation."[10]

Library Conferences

Holding of annual conferences at different places in Andhra Desa for the popularisation of library movement became a regular feature for ADLA. From 1914, the Association conducted these conferences which were well attended by the members of the association and delegates from libraries. The Association also encouraged and supported District and Taluk Library associations to hold conferences for the spread of library movement. Since 1916 district conferences were held at Tenali, Repall, Ongole, Palnadu, Vijayawada, Gudivada, Tanuku and Bhimavaram.[11]

The association strove hard to maintain its links with library movement in Telangana region. To foster cultural and emotional integration of the Telugu people of the two regions, it organised five Annual Conferences at Singaeni Colleries (1944), Kyaturu (1946), Suryapeta (1950), Janagama (1953) and Khammam (1957). The first four conferences helped greatly in achieving emotional integration and immensely contributed for the realisation of Visalandhra in 1956.

Commenting on the Singareni Conference, Vavilala Gopalakrishnayya states that "It was at Singareni that the two streams, one from British India and the other from Hyderabad State merged to become a bigger stream".[12]

During the first twenty five years of its existence, i.e. from 1914 to 1939, the Association through its annual conferences and resolutions adopted therein on various aspects greatly succeeded in bringing to the notice of the government and to the public, the problems faced by the libraries. These resolutions dealt with: (a) support of the government and local bodies to libraries, (b) management of libraries, (c) adult education, (d) ADLA, (e) establishment of Central Library for Andhra Desa, (e) encouragement to authors, (g) collection and preservation of manuscripts and other documents of historical importance, and (h) uplift of depressed classes.[13]

It is interesting to note that these conferences attracted not only library workers but also political leaders and social workers. In these conferences, papers and reports on various aspects of library movement and profession were presented and discussed. These conferences had a great publicity value and stimulated interest in the people towards library movement. The impact of these conferences were very great on the spread of library movement. The list of annual conferences held from 1914 to 2009 is provided in the annexure.

Library Pilgrimages

This was another indigenous method developed by the Association to popularise library movement. Ayyanki Venkta Ramanayya who conceived the idea of library pilgrimage states the purpose as "to inculcate among the youth the value of library services and examine the state of affairs of the libraries and suggest ways and means for their improvement"[14] A pilgrimage batch consisting of about 12 library workers, who in turn, divide themselves into six sections, viz. (1) Advance Information Section, (2) Bhajan Section, (3) Exhibition Section,

(4) Gramphone Section, (5) Lectures Section and (6) Magic Lantern Section.

The pilgrimage is executed in the following manner: First, the Advanced Information Section reaches the target village and sticks the posters on the walls and contacts elders and others associated with libraries. The Exhibition Section organises exhibition of books, magazines and other reading materials near the venue of the public meeting. The Gramophone Section plays records. The Bhajan Section goes round the village singing songs and announcements of the public meetings. The Lecturing Section delivers lectures on several aspects of library movement. At the end of the meeting the Magic Lantern Section shows instructive and informative pictures on health, cooperation and library services. Later, the party of library workers hold discussions with the villagers, establish a library if there is no library and offer suggestions for the improvement of services of existing libraries. After the conclusion of the programme, the party leaves for another vilage.[15]

The library pilgrimages were conducted from 1937 to 1951 for the spread of the movement. These pilgrimages inspired the villagers and created an awareness of library movement among them. These also encouraged the use of libraries by the public and promoted adult education. These pilgrimages were conducted on a sound footing in coastal districts of Andhra Desa and also helped the growth and rehabilitation of rural libraries and the recruitment of full time and part time voluntary library workers to manage the rural libraries. West Godavari District had a greater impact of these library pilgrimages on the growth of rural public libraries.[16]

Mobile Library Services

Another significant method invented by ADLA to stimulate interest of the common man in library service was to introduce mobile library service. A special cart fixed with four bicycle wheels was used to circulate books in the neighbouring villages by the Kuppam village Library in Chittoor District. A bullock cart was used for the same purpose in Pedasangallu village in Krishna District. In Machilipatnam, the Friends Union Library used bicycles to lend books to its clientele in the town. The Saraswata Niketanam, Vetapalem employed men to circulate books in nearby villages. Ayyanki devised convenient book boxes to send books for circulation to villages and he exhibited the boxes at Fifth Andhra Desa Library Conference held at Visakhapatnam in 1918.[17]

Another unique and novel method adopted for the spread of library services was the introduction of 'Boat Library Publicity; and Boat Library Service', the 'Boat Library Publicity' was undertaken as far back as in 1,918 by A. Kaleswara Rao, S.V. Narasimha Sastri, D.Subbavadhani, Ayyanki Venkta Ramanayya and B. Suryanaryana. According to the plan drawn by Ayyanki, library publicity was carried out on the boats touching the villages of Palakoderu, Yandagandi, Gagaraparu, Cherukuganama, Kesavaram, and Pippara in West Godavari District.

Paturi Nagabhusanam was a pioneer in conducting 'Boat Library Service'. He conducted this service for seven years from 1935 to 1942 on behalf of Pedapalem's Sevasram Mandiram on the Buckingham Canal from Tenali to Nizampatnam. Likewise Sarvajana Vidya Pradayini Library at Sangam Jagarlaumudi in Tenali (Tq) also introduced boat library service for the commuters on boat[18]. This unique experiment helped to create reading habits among the travellers and contributed for the spread of library movement.

Spring Festivals

The Association strove hard to utilize all the possible avenues for the spread of the library movement. It conducted spring festivals to enlist popular support in spreading the message. During the spring season, most of the villagers have free time and students had their vacation. To utilize the services of the students, the association devised and executed Spring Festival Programmes to educate the public and to spread the library movement.[19] The important activities undertaken during these festivals were book exhibitions, public meetings, sports and cultural activities, establishing libraries and reading rooms, collection of books and donations of furniture and money for the libraries and the association and enlistment of new members. The utilisation of youth force for constructive activities added a new dimension for the spread of the movement. The Eighth Andhra Desa Library Conference held at Pamidipadu in 1923 through resolution No.8 lent support to conduct such spring festivals and honour eminent scholars and sculptors in the villages.[20]

Adult Education

Promotion of adult education had been one of the important activities of the Association since its inception. It wanted to make the library movement truly a people's movement. The Association to sustain the adult education programmes launched by the village libraries, arranged lectures, got prepared and supplied teaching and reading materials. G. Harisarvothama Rao, who was President of the Association for several decades did yeomen service for the cause of adult education. As honorary director of several training centres for adult literacy, he organised workshops of training for a large number of elementary teachers in the methods of teaching adult literacy classes.

When the Government of Madras prohibited Adult Education Programmes in 1941, the ADLA convened special Conference on Adult Education at Tenali. This conference protested against the decision of the Government to ban adult education classes and demanded its early repeal. Since 1942, the Association had also organised Adult Education Conferences as part of its Annual Conferences as sectional meetings. These sectional meetings provided an opportunity for the workers of adult literacy programmes to exchange ideas and experiences and promoted a feeling of fellowship. Books and materials of adult literacy programmes were exhibited at these meetings. In collaboration with sister organisations, ADLA conducted adult education classes at several places during the years 1940-1955. The duration of these courses varied from one week to three months.[21]

Library Legislation

The Association felt the need for the establishment of more libraries and their efficient management. It believed that library legislation was essential to ensure proper flow of funds and orderly development of libraries. Right from the first library conference, it has urged the government to allow the local bodies like Municipalities, Zilla and Taluka Boards to give financial assistance for the sustenance of libraries.[22] As a result of representations and resoulutions, the government permitted local bodies to support the libraries. At several of its annual conferences, the association urged the Government of Madras to bring the library act on the statute books. In the early part of 1947, through a petition to the government, the Association reiterated the need for library legislation.

The Government of Madras published a draft bill in the Gazette on 9th December 1947 prepared by S.R. Ranganathan, with certain modifications for public opinion."[23] The Association held a special conference at Patamata on 16th January 1948 to discuss the draft bill. The draft bill was discussed and comments and suggestions were offered for the improvement of the bill."[24] The Association appointed a sub-committee to suggest amendments to the draft bill in consonance with the resolutions passed at the special conference. The Madras Public Libraries Act came into force from 1st April 1950. The Association convened another special meeting of secretaries of District Library Associations at Bezawada on 30th August 1952 to consider and suggest measures for proper implementation of the Act.

After the formation of Andhra Pradesh in 1956, a Sub-Committee of the State Library Committee consisting of five members including P. Nagabhusanam, Secretary of APLA was appointed by the Government of A.P. to consider the two Acts, i.e. Madras and Hyderabad. In 1960 when the A.P. Public Libraries bill was refereed to the select committee, the Association played a significant role in shaping the bill. The Act came into force from April, 1960."[25]

Library Science Education

TheAssociation recognised the need for trained personnel for managing the libraries. To train librarians, the Association conducted two courses before 1966 namely (1) 'Grandhalaya Pravesika' and (2) 'Grandhalaya Visarada'. Two hundred sixty four persons were trained in 'Grandhalaya Pravesika' in ten batches and sixteen persons were trained in 'Grandhalaya Visaradha' in two batches.[26] It established a School of Library Science in 1966 which was recognised by the Government of A.P. Since then it is conducting a Certificate Course in Library Science regularly in Telugu. It is now named as Sri P.Naga Bhusanam School of Library Science.

Publications

The Association has been active right from its inception in the publication of professional and other useful literature in library science and adult education for the benefit of professionals. The publications deal with various aspects of librarianship. These can be categorised as: (1) bibliographies, (2) books and monographs, (3) annual reports, (4) conference proceedings and souvenirs and (5) miscellaneous publications. It also published authoritative works in agriculture.[27]

Grandhalaya Sarvasvamu

In 1915 the Association started a periodical entitled *Grandhalaya Sarvasvamu* in Telugu. At the beginning it was started as a quarterly and continued for two years. From volume 3 (1918) it was published as a bimonthly. It ceased publication in 1922 and reappeared in 1928. However from Volume 6 (1938), it was published as monthly. Again it ceased publication in 1938, after completing 11 volumes. After independence, ADLA revived its publication with Volume 12,1948.This periodical has passed through several vissicitudes during its long and arduous career."[28]

This periodical did yeomen service for the spread of library movement in Andhra Desa. It helped create proper atmosphere for the establishment of libraries and through them, to spread knowledge among the people. During the early period, prominence was given in its columns to literary, historical and cultural fields with special reference to the activities of the Association. During 1930s and 1940s it assumed nationalistic character and strove to propogate adult education and constructive programmes of Gandhiji.[29] Beside publishing learned articles on libraries, library movement, adult education and literature, it also covered all important news items relating to the library. It is the oldest of all vernacular library periodicals published in the country.

Conclusion

Andhra Pradesh Library Association, formerly ADLA, the first professional association for the whole country did yeomen service for the spread of library movement and growth and development of public libraries, especially rural public libraries in Andhra Pradesh. It produced stalwarts of the library movement like S.V. Narasimha Sastri, Ayyanki Venkata Ramanayya, G.HariSarvothamaRao, Vavilala Gopalakrishnayya, Paturi Nagabhushanam, and Kodati Narayana Rao. It ceaselessly endeavoured for the spread of knowledge and education among the people. It played a very significant role in the enactment of A.P. Public Libraries Act of 1960. Through its numerous publications it enriched library science literature in Telugu. Its journal *Grandhalaya*

Sarvasvamu provided an opportunity to young and budding professionals to express their views on various aspects of library movement and adult education. It is rather sad to note that this premier professional organisation slowly slackened its activities after the formation of Andhra Pradesh.

After passing away of Sri Paturi Nagabhushanam, his daughter and very able sucessor, Dr. (Mrs) R.Sarada took over the reigns of the Association and accelerated its activities by organising seminars, conferences and bringing out *Grandhalaya Sarvaswamu* very regularly and in a new format with several innovations. The Association is marching ahead with confidence to celebrate centenary year in 2014.

References

1. *Grandhalaya Pragati*. Part-I. (Vijayawada; A.P. Library Association. 1962). p. 83.
2. *Andhra Desa Grandhalaya Charitra* 1914 Vrittantamu. (Bezawada; ADGS. 1915.)
3. A.P. library Association. Objectives, Rules and Regulations. Vijayawada; APLA. 1968. p. 1-2
4. Ibid. p. 4-5.
5. Ibid. p. 3-4.
6. A. VenkataRamanayya. *Grandhalaya Jyoti* (Vijayawada; Saraswati Samrajyamu. 1973.) p. 215-23, 332-34.
7. A. Venkta Ramnayya. *Light of the Library*. (Vijayawada; Saraswati Samrajyamu. 1973.) p. 4.
8. N.M. Dutt. *Baroda and its Libraries*. (Baroda; Central Library. 1928). p. 54.
9. A. Venkata Ramanayya. *Light of the Library*, p. 42.
10. G.Hari Sarvottama Rao. Address to Tenth All India Library Conference, 1953. In. M.V. Rao, ed. *Sarvottaama Jivitam*. (Vijayawada; APLA. 1965). p. 216.
11. *Grandhalaya Pragati*. 3 Parts. (Vijayawada; APLA. 1962.1964. 1969).
12. V. Gopala Krishnayya. *Library Movement in Andhra Pradesh*. (Hyderabad; Department of Information & Public Relations, Govt. of A.P. 1977). p. 4.
13. *Grandhalaya Pragati*. Part 1, p. 141-164. Part 2. p. 190-214.

14. A. Venkata Ramanayya *Grandhalaya Jyoti.* p. 274.
15. H. Adiseshuvu. *Grandhalaya Tapasvi B. Tirupati Raju.* (Kumudavali, Sri Veeresalinga Kavi Samaja Grandhalayam, 1971). p. 110-103.
16. *Grandhalaya Sarvaswamu.* 1936,10, p. 113.
17. A. Venkata Ramanayya. Grandhalaya Jyoti. p. 298.
18. V. Venkatappayya. *Mana Grandhalayaodhyamamu* 9200-1950 AD).Manuscript, p. 73.
19. Ibid. p. 75.20. *Grandhalaya Pragati.*Part-1, p. 156.
21. C.A.Bose. *A study ofA.P. Library Association.* (Jaipur; DepL of Adult Education, Univ.ofRajasthan, 1973).
22. *Granthalaya Pragati*, part 1, p. 145.
23. V. Venkatapayya, *Andhra-Telegana Grandhalaya Pragati.* (Eluru; Sanchalana Sahit, 1973). pp.30-31.
24. *Grandhalaya Pragati*, part 2, pp. 198-200.
25. V. Vcnkatappayya, *Andhra Pradesh Grandhalaya Chattam.* (Vijayawada; Navaratna Book Centre, 1985). p.19.
26. K. Sarada. *A.P. Library Association* (Waltair; Andhra Unviersity Press. 1978). pp. 83-84.
27. A.A.N. Raju, 'Library Literature in Telugu', In Agrawal, S.N. et al, eds. *Perspective in Library & Information Science.* (Lucknow; Print House (India): 1982). p. 168.
28. Ibid. p. 178.
29. A.A.N. Raju, *History of Library Movement in Andhra Pradesh, 1901-1956.* (Delhi; Ajanta Publications. 1988). p. 253.

Annexure

The following table lists the annual conferences held from 1914 to 2009.

S.No.	Year	Place	President of the Conference
1.	1914	Bezawada	Chilakamarti Lakshmi Narasimham
2.	1915	Rajahmundry	P. Ramarayanim
3.	1916	Nellore	K. Nageswara Rao
4.	1917	Baruva	B. Venkatapati Raju
5.	1918	Visakhapatnam	K. Venkata Krishna Rao
6.	1919	Madras	S. Venkata Narasimha Sastri
7.	1920	Mahanandi	Ch. Virabhadra Rao
8.	1923	Pamidipadu	D. Gopala Krishnayya
9.	1925	Machilipatnam	G. Rangayya Naidu
10.	1926	Pedacherukuru	V. Ramadas
11.	1926	Eluru	N. Krishna Rao
12.	1927	Anantapuram	R. Anantha Krishna Sarma
13.	1928	Guntur	Ch. Bhanumurti
14.	1931	Guntur	B. Seshagiri Rao
15.	1933	Bezawada	B. Sitarama Raju
16.	1933	Bezawada	Ch. Narasimha Rao
17.	1934	Kakinada	V. Ramadas
18.	1934	Kakinada	B. Sitaramayya
19.	1934	Madras	D. Trivikrama Rao
20.	1935	Visakhapatnam	S. Ramaswami
21.	1937	Bezawada	V. Venkateswara Sastri
22.	1941	Rajahmundry	M. Ramachandra Sastri
23.	1942	Pedapalem	S. Pratapa Reddy
24.	1942-3	Hindupur	M. Lakshminarayana Rao
25.	1944	Singareni	B. Ramakrishna Rao
26.	1946	Kyaturu	P. Venkata Rama Reddi
27.	1950	Suryapeta	P. Rama Murthi
28.	1951	Chagalamarri	M. Rangayyapappa Rao
29.	1953	Jangoan	S. Bhagavatham

S.No.	Year	Place	President of the Conference
30.	1957	Khammam	M.V. Krishna Rao
31.	1966	Vijayawada	Kalluri Subba Rao
32.	1967	Nellore	Durgabai Deshmukh
33.	1969	Tirupati	M.Anantasayanam Iyyenagar
34.	1981	Warangal	T. Hayagrivachari
35.	1986	Kovvuru (W.G.)	Kodati Narayana Rao
36.	1992	Vijayawada	V.GopalaKrishnayya
37.	1995	Anantapur	Dr. P.S.G. Kumar
38.	2009	Guntur	Prof. V.VishwaMohan

H.2. Academy of Library Science and Documentation (ALSD), Hyderabad.

Genesis

The formation of Andhra Pradesh on linguistic basis in 1956 with Hyderabad as its capital was a land mark in the history of modern India. Hyderabad city since 1956 witnessed remarkable growth and development of educational institutions, R & D Institutions, Industries, Scientific laboratories management training institutions and defence laboratories. As consequence to this growth and development a number of academic and special libraries, documentations centres and information centres have come into being. These libraries, documentation and information centres have been managed by a number of specialists librarians and documentalists. Their number has been increased gradually and some of the senior professionals felt the need for a professional association so as to come together and exchange professional ideas and contribute to the development of the profession and professionalism. In the words of K.H. Bandegeri one of the founder members of ALSD "urged by adesire to grow and develop and to turn out more productive work, a few enthusiestic and devoted librarians got together, deeply deliberated and established a new organisation in Hyderabad last year [1965] for the advancement of library science and documentation technique"[1].Thus ALSD came into being on the auspicious day of ugadi, the Telugu new years day on April 2, 1965 and was inaugurated by M.R. Appa Rao, Minister for Cultural Affairs, Government of Andhra Pradesh at the State Central Library (SCL), Hyderabad. The Academy had the fortune of receving blessings from the father of library science in India Dr. S.R. Ranganathan and eminent librarian B.S. Kesavan.

Aims and Objectives

Promotions of research and advanced studies in library science and documentation was one of the prime objectives as enshrined in the constitution of the Academy. S. Pandurangam[2] and L.S. Ramiah[3] have listed the following objectives of the Academy.

1. "to promote research and advanced studies in library science and documentation.,
2. to provide a common forum for the intellectuals in the field to meet and exchange ideas.,
3. to improve professional standards ;
4. to strive to improve service conditions of persons in the profession.
5. to promote publication and distribution of professional literaure.
6. to promote and organise further education and training of persons engaged in or intending to engage in the profession.,
7. to make available specialist services as consultants or otherwise to organisations and individuals;
8. to cooperate with other organisations having similar aims and objectives;
9. to establish a library for the Academy; and
10. to perform such other functions as are incidental or conducive to the attainment of the objectives of the Academy."

The above objectives were really high sounding and elaborate indeed and to achieve the above objectives the Academy understook activities like seminars, symposia, extension lectures, reporting on national and international conferences, review of current topics contained in professional journals, books and reports. The Academy also arranged workships and visits to prominent libraries, conducting short term training courses, advisory services and undertake special projects on behalf of other institutions and organisations.[4]

Membership

Membership constitutes the back bone for any association especially for a professional body like ALSD. It draws its strength and vigour from the members and thier active cooperation and participation in its activities. The membership of ALSD consists of six categories viz; 1. Patrons, 2. Life members, 3. Ordinary members, 4. Associate members, 5. Student members and 6. Institutional members. Any person professionally qualified with a minimum of two years service in the field can become a member. Associate members are those who are in the profession but not fulfilling the requirements prescribed for a member. Students pursuing professional courses CLIS, BLIS, MLISC can also become members of the Academy with certain restrictions.

During the last four and half decades of its existence the membership of the Academy has grown impressively consisting of persons working in various types of libraries including LIS teachers hailing mostly from Andhra Pradesh and few members from other states of India. As on 2007 ALSD has about 550 members most of them being life members.

The General body elects the managing committee and a president for a two year term. The president elect in turn nominates other office beares and constitutes various sub committees to carryout various activities of ALSD.

The managing committee consists of a president, 2. Vice presidents, General Secretary, Joint Secreatry, Treaurer and 11 members. The list of presidents and secretaries who served the association since 1965 to the present is provided in annexure.

Activities

During the four and half decades of its existence the Academy has carried out its activities to the satisfaction of professionals at the local, regional and national levels by organising National Conferences/Seminars, lecture programmes, education and training programmes, study circle meetings, compilation of union catalogues, institution of gold medal, and visit to libraries, advisory and consultancy service and bringing out a news letter. These activities are briefly presented in the following paras.

National Conferences

ALSD has so far organised four national conferences and a seminar by inviting national professionals associations such as Indian Library Association (ILA) and Indian Association of Special Libraries and Information Centres (IASLIC). In the very second year of its genesis it has invited IASLIC to hold its fourteenth All India Seminar at Hyderabad from 17-20, December, 1966. The two themes of the seminar were 1: Procurement of government publications and technical reports and 2. Devaluation and its impact on development. In the year 1973 it has invited Indian Library Association to hold its 20th All India Library Conference from 9-12 july, 1973 at Hyderabad on the theme "How to achieve optimum utilisation of Existing National Library Resources." Again in the year 1981 the Academy invited ILA to hold it, 27 the All India Library conference from 9-12 January 1981 at Hyderabad on the theme" stock verification." After a gap of nearly two decades the Academy again invited ILA to hold its 44 All India Library Conference from 25-28 February, 1999 at Hyderabad on the theme "Libraries and Information Services in the Electronic Era". These national conferences and seminars have brightened the image of Academy among the professionals in India and abroad and transformed it as one of the dynamic professionals associations in India.

Seminars

In addition to organising library conferences at the national level the Academy organised seminars workshops, symposia on current topics of professionals interest for the benefit local professionals. The following is some of the themes of the seminars and workshops.

1. Society and Libraries, 2. Problems of acquisition, 3. Public library system, 4. Libraries in the 1970's, 5. College libraries, 6. Stock Verification and losses, 7. International book year-Books for all, 8. Child in the developing world, 9. Ekbote committee report, 10. Adult education : Programmes, problems and prospects, 11. Document collections in libraries, 12. Resource sharing among special libraries in Hyderabad, 13. Rural libraries in AP, 14. Role of Associations in the development of library profession, 15. AP Library legistation : Problems and Prospects. The seminars organised between the years 1995 and 2005 are shown annexure-2.

Education and Training Programmes

For the benefit young and budding professionals the Academy has conducted a number education and training programmes with the active support and cooperation of seniors in the profession by using the infrastructure facilities available in some of the prominent academic and special libraries in the twincites of Hyderabad and Secunderabad. These programmes were well received by the professionals working in public, academic and special libraries. Through these programmes, the Academy was able to generate some funds for carrying out its activities. The following is the list of some of the prominent courses organised by the Academy.

Year	*Name of the course*
1971	Management of Information storage and retrieval
1978	Special library and information work
1979	Library and Information work
1980	Special libraries
1983	Indexing
1987	Cateloguing (AACR-II) Classification (DDC-19the Ed)

Special Lecture Programmes

Since Hyderabad is one of the important metropolitan cities of India, prominent libraries and information specialists and LIS professors from othe parts of India and abroad have been visiting the city from time to time. For the benefit the youngsters in the profession working at grass root level, the Academy has been inviting those specialists from India and abroad to deliver lectures on burning topics in LIS. A number prominent senior Indian librarians such as BS Kesvan, A. Neelamaghan, T.S. Rajagopalan, V.A. Kamath, Girija Kumar, S.Parathasarathy, D.R. Kalia, N.M. Ketkar, D.B.Krishana Rao, D.M. Chakravarthy, Jagadish Sharma, B.H. Krishana Murthy, N.P.Rao and foreign experts such as : Paul Kruse, John Russell, S.C. Sutton, Lester Asheim, George S.Bonn, Peter Lazar, Dennis Grogan, Abdul Nur, N.V. Turtanov, M.A. Fomichov and M.A. Shermakov have delivered special literatures on the topics of their speciality and professional interest. The following is the list of names of some speakers and topics of their lectures.

S.No	*Name of Speaker*	*Topic*
1.	S.C. Biswas	Acquisition policy and Indian book trade
2.	Collin Harris	User studies
3.	Girija Kumar	User education
4.	V.A. Kamat	International Information Systems
5.	T.A.V. Murty	Design and development of an Information system for small idustry
6.	T.S. Rajagopalan	ILA and Professional activities in India
7.	Kalpana Dasgupta	National Library of India : Retrospective and prospective.
8.	J.C. Binwal	Universe of Knowledge
9.	G.Bhattacharya	Professionalism and Librarianship
10.	Jane Beaumont	CD-ROM
11.	N. Robertson	Some approaches to the study of users in Information Retrieval.

The lecture programmes arranged by the Academy

between the year 1996 and 2007 are presented in annexure - 3.

Reporting Conferences and Seminars

Members of the Academy attending national and international conferences were requested to present a brief report on the proceedings of these conferences and seminars for the benefit of members who do not have the opportunity to attend them. Members of the Academy who have attended annual seminars/conferences of ILA, IASLIC, DRTC, USIS, ASRC and other international conferences presented reports in the past for the benefit of members. Of late this programme receded to the background due to unknown reasons.

Presentation of Papers

To encourage young professionals to participate in the seminars and conference conducted by the Academy and to share their professional experiences with the seniors, members were persuaded and prompted to present papers on topical interest. Mostly these are practice oriented and intended to project specific problems and experiences that the practicing librarians come across during their day to day work. A few of the topics on which papers were presented by the professionals were : Information retrieved in small industrial research library; Classified concept coordination; Human relations in libraries - case studies, Design of inhouse abstracting and indexing service in special libraries, Organisation of reprint literature and organisation of data banks in an industrial library.

Know Your Library

The twincities are dotted with very old, young and famous Public, Academic and Special libraries and Information Centres. The Academy arranged from time to time visist to such libraries to familiarise with the book collections, infrastructure and services offered by them. Problems preculiar to these libraries are also discussed during the visits. Twenty four such visits were arranged under the programmes and some of the libraries covered under such visits were Osmania university library, ASRC Library, ASCI Library, NIN Library, RRL Library, Bharat Guna Vardhak Samastha Library, City Central Library, Sir Nijamat Jung Memorial Library, District Central Libraries (DCLS) of RangaReddy and Medak districts.

Advisory and Consultancy Services

The Academ got recognition through its various professional activities as a professionals body which can offer its expertise for the benefit those which were not properly organised and managed their collections. Many libraries in the twincities invited the Academy to advise and reorganise their collections and services. The Academy was fortunate to have young, energetic and well qualified professional members to offer their services freely to accomplish advisory and consultancy services. Eight libraries have been benefited by such services and some of them were as follow : 1. Institute of Asia Studies, 2. A.P. Secretariat library, 3. Indian Institute of Economics, 4. Sir Nizamat Jung Library, 5. Directorate of Industries, 6. Y.M.I.S Library.

Special Projects

The Academy sucessfully completed compilation of two union catalogue projects offered by ICSSR and INSDOC, New Delhi. The ICSSR Project of the Union Catalogue of Social Sciences Periodicals in A.P. was completed in 1973. This union catalogue has recorded 1700 Social Science Periodical holdings available in 36 select libraries in Andhra Pradesh. The INSDOC project was for scientific periodicals and covers 3840 titles available in 51 important libraries in the twincities of Hyderabad and Secunderabad. The union catalogue was published in 1975.

Publications

The Academy broughtout its first publication containing

the papers and proceedings of the Seminar on 'Problems of acquisition of library material' held in 1970. It has also started publication of *ALSD New letter* in 1971 as a bimonthly and now *ALSD communication* (Q) for the benefit of its members. So far 125 issues were brought out untill september 2007.

Gold Medal

To mark a decade of its fruitful professional existence Academy instituted a gold medal with the Osmania University in the subject Library and Information Science from the Academic year 1975-76. The Gold medal is awarded annually to the student who stands first class first in BLIS examination.

ALSD, IASLIC Study Circle

In association with IASLIC, Kolkata, the Academy has been conducting ALSD, IASLIC Study circle meetings from 1980. Under this programme eight study circle meetings were held and some of the topics were discussed as follows.

S.No	*Name of the Person*	*Topic*
1.	G.Vijaya Kumar	Development of Scientific Periodicals
2.	M.V. Venugopal	Library Statistics
3.	P.Vyasamurthy	Reprographic methods
4.	R.P. Kumar	Origin and development of periodical literature in English.
5.	S.Hari Krishna Reddy	User Survey techniques.
6.	D.S.R. Murthy	Use of Computers at PID: A Retrospect and Prospect.

Conclusion

Urge to have professional association to promote the interests of LIS Professionals in Andhra Pradesh especially in the twincities of Hyderabad and Secundrabad resulted in the establishment of ALSD in 1965 by a group of committeed, enthusiastic and service minded senior professionals. During the first two and half decades of its existence the Academy through its mutlifarious activities established itself as one of the most dynamic library associations in the country. The founding fathers of this professional association led by K.H. Bendegeri, B.P.Shenoy, Abdul Mahmood, T.V. Ramanayya, N.B. Inmadar, R.S. Sastri and M.V Rao and scores of others with their professional commitment and contacts strived hard to see that Academy attains new heights in professional activities and programmes for the benefit its members. The various activities and programmes carried out by the Academy right from its inception was testimony of its dynamism and professional committment of its office bearers during the first twenty five years of its existence.

During the four and half decades of its existence the Academy could not find a roof over its head. The sucessive managing committees especially from 1980's strived hard to have building/flat for the Academy in the twincities. But this wish was not fulfilled so far. It remained as a distant dream.

Of late the Academy, it appears, lost its dynamism and professional committment and receded to the background. There was a marked decline in its professional activities and programmes.The successive managing committees inspite of their best efforts were not able to take it forward with more programmes and activities as was expected by its members. The reason for this declining trend may be attributed the lack of interest among the professionals to come forward and extend full support and cooperation to sucessive managing committees. What ever may be reasons for this downward trend let us hope that better days will soon come to the Academy to regain its past glory and move forward with dynamism and accelerated activities for the cause library profession.

Annexure - I

Table showing the past presidents and secretaries of the Academy from 1965 to 2009.

Period	*President*	*Secretary*
1965	?	?
1966-68	K.H Bendigeri	T.V. Ramanayya
1968-70	K.H. Bendigeri	T.V. Ramanayya
1970-72	Abdul Mahmood	N.B. Inamdar
1972-74	Abdul Mahmood	N.B. Inamdar
1974-76	A.K. Dasgupta	R.S. Sastry
1976-78	A.K. Dasgupta	M.R. Rishwadkar
1978-80	B.P. Shenoy	S.Pandurangam
1980-82	B.P. Shenoy	S.Pandurangam
1982-84	N.B. Inamdar	L.S. Ramaiah
1984-86	N.B. Inamdar	E. Rama Reddy
1986-88	S. Panduranga Reddy	N.Laxman Rao
1988-90	A.A.N. Raju	M.Sankara Reddy
1990-92	D.B. Eshwar Reddy	S.Harikrishna Reddy
1992-94	L.S. Ramaiah	S. Sundarshan Rao
1995-97	Dorothy Issac	J.Yadagiri Reddy
1997-99	M.V Venugopal	S.Harikrishna Reddy
1999-2001	E.Rama Reddy	M.Ramchander
2001-03	N.Laxman Rao	M.Ramchander
2003-05	J.Yadagiri Reddy	G. Narasimha Murthy
2005-07	V.Chandra Sekhar Rao	P.Venkata Ramana
2007-09	S.Sudarshan Rao	K.H. Sunitha
2009-11	M.Ramchander	C. Vidyadhar Bhatt

Source : *ALSD News letter/Communications*

Annexure - 2

Seminars Organised by the Academy between the years 1995 and 2008 is shown in the following table.

Date	*Collaborating body*	*Seminar theme*
9.12.95	ALSD and Hyderabad Book Fair Society	Book trade and libraries
13-19.08.99	ALSD	Internet Training Programme
05.12.99	ALSD and Hyderabad Book Fair Society	Status of LICS and Book trade in the new millenium.
04.06.2000	ALSD	LIS for distance leaners.
19.11.2000	ALSD	Electronic Information Resources sharing.
03.12.2000	ALSD and Hyderabad Book Fair Society	Electronic Book Publishing: Role of trade and libraries.
18.11.01	ALSD and SCL	Automation of Public libraries : Problems and perspectives.
9-11.05.08	ALSD	Workshop on D-Space
08.02.03	ALSD and Hyderabad Book Fair Society	Curbing book piracy
09.08.03	ALSD and Dept of Lib & Info Sc, osmania university	Modern trends in LICS
25-26.06.05	ALSD	Preservation and conservation of library material in public libraries in the digital environment.

Source : *ALSD News Letter/Communications* Nos. 78-79 to 126-127.

Annexure - 3

List of lecture programmes arranged by the Academy between the years 1996 and 2007.

Date	*Name of the Speaker*	*Topic*
30.02.1996	Faye Powell (USA)	Library services in the Electronic environment
09.11.1996	L.J. Haravu	Emerging opportunities in I.T. for librarians
01.10.1999	I. Phichev and Zelanor (Russia)	The INION and its activities
20.11.1999	Richard J.Cohen	Modern library services in IT environment : Expectation of users.
21.01.2001.	INR. Goudar.	Web as an effective media for LIS services.
28.01.2001	V. RaghavaSwamy	Geographical Information System
04.07.2001	D.B.Eshwar Reddy	Trends in Academic Librarianship in USA over the next five years.
06.08.2001	Rama Raju Urs	Digital libraries and health information
28.01.2002	Alan Hopknison	Joined up Library and Information services.
18.03.2002	E.RamaReddy	Library and Information services in Taiwan.
16.04.2002	Abhimanyu Acharya	Managing knowledge
08.08.2002	A Lahiri	Electronic Publishing and Future of libraries
12.08.2002	Lalji Singh	The Information overload
10.02.2003	Roshan Raina	Total Quality Management (TQM) in LICS.
29.02.2003	Isabella Nyffengger	Library services and trends in France
03.03.2003	Francis Tait	Latest developments of I.T. in libraries
05.01.2004	A.R.D Prasad	Librarians and digital library.
05.01.2004	R.S.R. Varalakshmi	Detamining and its application
09.01.2004	R.K. Chadha	Modern library and information services in I.T. environment

29.04.2004	T.Ramadevi	E-Learning Technology
19.11.2006	L.J. Haravu	Standards in library automation and networking
13.04.2007	C.K. Ramaiah	An overviews of electronic books and their use in libraries.
20.06.2007	Peter Jacso	Citation based and citation enhanced databases.
12.10.2007	M.Sridhar	Library - IPR with reference to the copyright law.
07.04.2008	E.RamaReddy	LIS Education in Thailand : A comparative Account.

Source : *ALSD News Letter/Communications*. Nos 78-79 to 127.

Reference

1. K.H. Bendegari, 'Academy of Library Science & Documentation, Hyderabad ; An account of its Activities'. In Fourth All India Seminar, Hyderabad Dec. 17-20, 1960. *Souvenir* (Hyderabad, Academy of Library Science and Documentation, 1966), p.14.
2. S Pandurangam, 'Academy of Library Science and Documentation'. In 27 All India Library Conference, 9-12 Jan. 1981, Hyderabad. *Sourvenir* (Hyderabad, Academy of Library Science and Documentation, 1981), p.1.
3. L.S. Ramaiah, 'Academy of Library Science and Documentation'. In *Hand Book of Libraries, Archives and Information Centres in India. Vol. 10. Professional Organisations & Associations,* ed by B.M. Gupta et al. (Delhi, Aditya Prakashan, 1990), pp.148-149.
4. N.B. Inamdar, 'Academy of Library Science & Documentation : What it is and what it does'. In 20th All India Library Conference, 9-12 July 1973. *Souvenir*. (Hyderabad, Academy of Library Science and Documentation, 1973), p.11.

Additional Source: ALSD Constitution 12 p (Mimeographed).

H.3. Hyderabad Library Association (HLA), Hyderabad

Genesis

The Hyderabad Library Association was established on January 26, 1951 in the former Hyderabad state by the stalwarts of the movement such as : Gopal Rao Ekbote, Sridhar Varman Naik, Krishna Mukund Ujlambkar, popularly known as K.M. Ujlambkar and scores of others.

Activities

For five years it worked ceaselessly for the spread of library movement and enactment of Hyderabad Public Libraries Act, 1955. It also started a Certificate and Diploma courses in library science in 1953 and 1954 respectively. It has also started a mobile library service to children in 1954 and started library study circle in 1953 which was inaugurated by Dr. S.R. Ranganathan.

Conferences

The Association organised the first All Hyderabad Library Conference in 1954 and the Second All Hyderabad Library Conference at the Boys Scouts Head Quarters, Secunderabad on December 17-19, 1955. The first day conference was devoted to opening of library exhibition. It was inaugurated by Dr. D.D. Shandarkar, Director of Public Instruction and Director of Public libraries, Government of Hyderabad. Inauguruting the conference, Gopal Rao Ekbote, Education Minister surveyed various steps that are being taken by the Hyderabad Government for the development of library movement. The three day conference was presided over by K.G. Saidain, Additional Secretary, Ministry of Education,Government of India. In its concluding session on the third day the conference adopted a number of resoulutions. The conference requested Osmania University to institute training courses in LIS. It has also requested the Government to accord recognition to the

Certificate and Diploma courses conducted by the Association. In another resolution it advocated open access system to be introduced in the State Central Library (SCL), Osmania University Library (OUL) and other college libraries in the state.

The Hyderabad Library Association organised the Tenth All India Library conference at Hyderabad from June 1-4, 1953. The conference was inaugauted by Devsingh Chauvan, Education Minister, Government of Hyderabad and Prof S. Dasgupta, Librarian, University of Delhi acted as president of the four day conference. The main function of the conference was arranged in Salar JungHall, Nizam college. The three day symposia were held in Arts college, Osmania University. The subjects discussed were Depth classification, Reference Service and Library Service in Five year plan.

Publications

During the short span of its existence the Association brought out four publications, three in Hindi and one in English The three Hindi publications were : 1. *Grandhalaya Varghikaran* (Library classification), 2. *Grandhalaya Suchi karan* (Library cataloguing), 3. *Grandhalaya Sastraka Panch Sutr* (Five Laws of Library Science), The English Publication was **The Hyderabad Public Libraries Act, 1955 and its Salient features.**

All the four books were authored by K.M. Ujlambkhar and priced at Re 1- each. The Association also broughtout a journal titled *Grandhalaya* (1955-1956) (Hindi and English) ; monthly journal of Hyderabad Library Association and edited by KM Ujlambkar, the main spirit behind HLA.

Merger with ADLA

After the formation of Andhra Pradesh in 1956 the HLA was merged with Andhra Desa Library Association (ADLA) paving the way for the formation of Andhra Pradesh Library Association (APLA).

Conclusion

In the short span of six years (1951-56) the HLA strived hard to spread library movement, public library development in the former Hyderabad state. It had the credit of moblising professional of opinion for having public library act in the state and got the Hyderabad Public Libraries Act, 1955 enacted by the then government of Hyderabad state. Through *Granthalaya*, the activities of HLA were communicated to the professionals at large and become medium for the young professionals to contribute articles in English and Hindi on Various facets of public library and professional development. Though its life span was very short it spread professional knowledge brilliantly to the nook and corner of Hyderabad state.

Source : *Granthalaya* V1-1955 to V2 - 1955.

H.4. Andhra Pradesh Public Libraries Association (APPLA), Hyderabad

Establishment

The Andhra Pradesh Public Libraries Association was established in 1963 as a successor to Hyderabad Library Association to safeguard the interests of public libraries established under the provisions Hyderabad Public Libraries Act (1955) and by voluntary organisations in Telangana region of Andhra Pradesh. The Association as claimed by its founder members to be the 'mouth piece' of the library minded population especially in Telangana region.

Objectives

The main objectives of APPLA are as follows :

"1. To unify all the public and aided libraries, reading rooms in Andhra Pradesh on a common forum and to expouse their cause in the library service,

2. To obtain adequate financial and technical aid available under the A.P. Public Libraries Act and rules framed there under and from other sources,

3. To promote efficient library service and form a trained class of library workers.

4. To cooperate with other organisations with similar objectives."

Activities

In order to achieve the above objectives, the Association has started 'School of Library Science' to provide LIS education for lay man and workers of small libraries. Untill 1973 the Association turned out 13 batches of students and trained about 325 students. The organisers of the course claimed that "it is an uniqu type of library education system with more lessons on practice than theory."

Another important activity of the Association was to participate in Local Library Authority (LLA) of Hyderabad and Secunderabad election held in 1965 by capturing all the six seats available for 'Aided Libraries' under section 10(1) (b) of AP Public Libraries Act, 1960. This provision has been deleted from the Act in the subsequent amendements to the Act. This was perhaps one of the important reasons for establishing APPLA to safe guard the interest of aided libraries by capturing the seats available for aided libraries on the managing committee of the LLA.

The Association had offered technical advice to the needy aided libraries to organise their collections on sound lines and offer better library services to the use community. As its activities were mostly confined to aided libraries, it wanted to expand and serve the interests of other libraries such as : departmental, special and technical. The Association thought of federation of libraries and launched "Andhra Pradesh Library Federation (APLF) and Sri Ramdev as its first president and A.W. Shakira as the General Secretary.

Both APPLA and APLF Associations in the twincities jointly sponsored the works for International book year 1972 and advised and guided the following libraries in organising book weeks.

1. Khavateen-i- Deccan Library
2. Rajasthani Hindi Pustakalaya
3. Hyderi Circulating Library
4. Sadar Anjuman Islam
5. Shoeb Memorial Library
6. Radiant Reading Room
7. Bharat Marathi Patasala
8. Bharat Abyhudaya Patasala Library
9. Youngmens Improvement Society Library.

These aided libraries are eligible for grant-in-aid from Hyderabad city Grandhalaya Samastha.

The APPLA in colloboration with APLF organised Greater Hyderabad Libraries Conference on 30th December 1973 at Hyderabad. Justice Gopal Rao Ekbote, the then chief justice of Andhra Pradesh in a message to the library conference opined that "Private efforts in establishing and running the libraries will continue to play a leading role in the spread of this movement. If this is realised then the private libraries so established and run will have to be supported by the State Library Authority and the Government, apart from public. It is natural that the public aided libraries should be persuaded to play a prominent role in the spread of the library movement."

Present Position

The Association slowly disappeared from the scene as most of its founder members become old and some of them passed away. The amendments brought to AP Public Libraries Act 1960 in 1987 (Act No. 13 fo 1987) replacing elected bodies to Zilla Grandhalaya samasthas by nominated bodies may be another reason for slowing down the activities of the Association and gradually receded to the back ground. Since 1973 its existence was not felt by the professionals of Hyderabad as few more rival organisations came into being for the cause of public aided libraries specially in the twincities of Hyderabad and Secundrabad.

Source : Greater Hyderabad Libraries conference. 30th December, 1973 *Souvenir*. (Hyderabad, AP Public Libraries Associations, 1973).

H.5. Andhra Pradesh Public Library Association (APPLA) Hyderabad

Genesis

There are two association with same name, the only difference being 'libraries association' the first one was established in 1963 and second one 'library association' which was established on 1st November 1966 by Dr. M.A.Mazeed Khan. The first one was established by M.V. Bharati, an advocate by profession and some of his library professional colleagues. It is not known whether the association established by Dr. M.A.Mazeed Khan, a pseudo professional, was successor or rival to the association established by M.V. Bharti and his collegues. The following paras briefly deal with the AP Public Library Association established by Dr. Mazeed khan.

Aims and Objectives

The aims and objectives of the association are to :

1. Promote library movement and improvement in library services in all its aspects,
2. Promote LIS education and training of lilbrarians.
3. Promote bibliographical study and research in LIS.
4. Provide assistance for the establishment and managing libraries, documentation and information centres.
5. Establish and maintain Central Reference Library and acquire books and other reading materials pertaing to library movement.
6. Publish bulletins, books and periodicals which will help realisation of the objectives of the association.
7. Organise library talks, lectures, filmshows and radio and T.V. programmes for the promotion of library movement and adult education.
8. Promote enactment of library legislation in the country.

9. Conduct general knowledge (GK) tests, essay writing competitions and award certificates to the successful candiates.
10. Convening meetings, seminars and conferences.
11. Felicitate eminent library workers who have rendered yeomen service in the field of libraries and award them certificates.
12. Obtain adequate financial support from the government for public aided libraries functioning in the state.

Activities

The activities of the Association in a nut shell include conducting seminars, conferences, workshops and organising education and training programmes for professional and semi professionals, bringing out publications and celebrating of National Library Week every year and conducting essay competitions, general knowledge tests to school students and bringing to the notice of the government the professional problems.

Education and Training Activities

To meet the trained manpower at the semi-professional level to manage branch libraries established by Zilla Grandhalaya Samasthas (ZGSS) in the state, the Association established "Central Insstitute of Library Science" in the year 1970 to conduct Certificate Course in Library Science (CLSC) of 5 months direction from 1971 to 1981 and said course was discontinued in 1982. The Association also conducted a short term of one month duration in Library Science for the benefit of youth and students. Punjabi University, Patiala has established its study centre at APPLA premises for its Diploma in Library Science Course on distance mode. The Central Institute of Library Science, conducted practical classes for students admitted to the said course. It has also got affiliation from Osmania University for conducting BLISC course in the year 1996 After running few batches, the course was discontinued.

Conferences and Seminars

During the course of its existence, the Association organised at regular intervals library conferences and seminars. It has organised three state level conferences. The first Andhra Pradesh Libraries Conference was held at State Central Library, Hyderabad from March 9-11, 1979. The conference discussed in separate sessions the problems faced by Public, Academic and Special libraries and LIS education. The Second Andhra Pradesh Libraries conference was held at Narsaraopeta, Guntur District on February 21,1980. A Seminar on "Standards for College Libraries" was also organised on the occassion. The conference had also organised three conventions devoted to public and academic libraries and LIS education. The third AP Public Libraries conference was held at Tirupati from December 10-12, 1982. Dr (Mrs) Suseela Kumar delivered keynot address on "Professional Image of Librarians". Special conventions were organised on public, academic and special libraries and on LIS Education. The fourth of AP Public library conference was held at State Central library, Hyderabad from October 5-7, 1986 Dr. B.P Barua of RRRLF, Kolkata delilvered the presidential address.

Publications

The Association has brought out an eight page monthly publication tittled *Library Today* (1979) and now ceased publication. The annual reports of the Association were also published in the news letter along with the results of All India General Knowledge tests conducted by the Association for some time. Besides the publication of '*Library Today*' the Associat has brought out the following publications mostly text books for the benefit of (CLIS/BLIS) students.

1. P.V.A Narasimham and M.A. Majeed khan. *Andhra Pradesh Public Libraries Act, 1960*. 1981.

2. A.K.Chakraborti, *An Introduction to Documentation Service*. 1981.
3. T.V. Ramanayya, *Elements of Library Organisation and Management*, 1981.
4. E.D. Livingston, *Rudiments of Library Cataloguing. Theory and Practice*, 1982.
5. M.A. Majeed Khan, *Handbook of Library Science Education in India*, 1982.
6. A. K. Chakraborti, *Reference Service*, 1983.
7. S.S. Sahi, *Rudments in library classification : Theory and Practice*.
8. M.A Majeed Khan, *Practical Guide to School Librarianship*.

Other Activities

The Association has rendered professional assistance to privately managed libraries for their effective functioning. It was also celebrating National Library Week during 14-20 November every year by organising lectures and essay competitions for children. Senior library workers were honoured for their meritorious services to the cause of library movement and public library development in the state.

Post Script

After passing away of MA Majeed Khan, the founder General Secretary, the activities of the Association have come to stand still. There was no body to come forward and take forward the Association and its activities. It is another public library association which had receded to the back ground after few decades of active work and service to the profession and professionals.

H.6. Organisation for the Protection of Libraries (OP Lib), Hyderabad

Genesis

The Organisation for the Protection of Libraries (OPLib) "a non profit library advocacy group consisting of LIS Teachers, Professionals, Students, Research Scholars, Authors and Library lovers all working together with a mission to bring about Library Rennaissance in Andhra Pradesh" came into being on Sunday the 4th December, 2005 at Hyderabad. The inaugural function of this body was held the City Central Library (CCL), Hyderabad. Kuchipudi Sambasiva Rao , Chairman, A.P. Grandhalaya Parishad, as chief guest and M/S Ch. Venkata Reddy (CPI Floor Leader), N. Narasimhaiah (CPM Floor Leader) G. Krishan Reddy (BJP Floor Leader) and T.Devender Goud (TDP Floor Leader) in AP Legislative Assembly as Guests of Honour.

The new organisation was launched "to bring change in the library services at the grass root level" by young, dynamic and enthusiastic professionals and some of them were unemployed. It is registered body under the AP Societies Registration Act no 2001 vide registration no 1502/october 2005.

Objectives

This young and fledgling professional organisation has set before itself ten objectives or commandments which are as follows:

"1. To contribute to the regeneration of libraries in Andhra Pradesh focussing on staffing, collection development and resource mobilization,

2. To build up reading habits among the general public, with special focus on children and disadvantaged groups in the society,

3. To serve as a facilitator for establishment of user managed libraries in schools, Orphanages, social welfare hostels, grampanchayats, etc,
4. To bridge gap between the information rich information poor sections of society.
5. To build up professional image of LIS profession by offering better library and information services,
6. To improve the career opportunities and promotional avenues that are available for Library and Information Science Professionals.
7. To introduce Internet & Community information services in all public libraries for people's empowerment.
8. To mobilize public support for libraries for collection development, construction of library buildings, purchase of equipments & furniture, provision of community information services, preservation of books etc.,
9. To raise the awareness of general public on the importance of libraries.
10. To organise continuing library education programmes for LIS professionals and library volunteers."

Office Bearers

The office bearers to carry out its objectives include : Honorany advisors, Honorary President, Working President, President, Vice Presidents, General Secretary, Joint Secretaries, Coordinator, Treasurer, Public Relation Officer, Liaison Officer and Executive Members. It appears there are too many office bearers to shoulder the responsibility and carryout stated objectives.

Membership

There are five categories of membership which the organisation wants to enroll and seek their support and cooperation to carryout its activities. The five categories are :

Honorary Advisor, which is free/by invitation, Distinguished Life Member which is also free/by invitation, Library and Information Science Professional (by subscription), Library Friend (Writers, Astistes, Media Persons, Readers etc) (by subscription) and Student/Research scholar (by subscription).

Stated Activities

The 'OPLib" has listed the following seven activities which it wants carryout for the protection, rejuvenation and revitalization of libraries in Andhra Pradesh : These are :

"1. Starting student managed school libraries in backward areas of Andhra Pradesh by enlisting support from corporate houses and philanthropists,

2. Starting of people managed public library community inforamtion resource centres in the backward areas of Andhra Pradesh by enlisting support from corporate houses and philanthropists,

3. Establishment of Friends of the Public Library Groups in all public libraries to mobilize public support for collection development, construction of library buildings, purchase of furniture and equipment etc.,

4. Representing to the Government on the urgent and imperative need for strengthening of manpower in libraries through filling up of all vacant posts of librarians existing at present and regular recruitment for future vacancies,

5. Launching of a state wide campaign involving eminent artistes, writers and media persons to publicise libraries among masses,

6. Organising training programmes for student volunteers on how to run a Small Public Library/School Library.

7. Publishing a website and a quarterly news letter to keep all the stake holders informed of developments."

H.7. Andhra Pradesh Zilla Grandhalaya Samsthas (ZGSS) Employees Association Vijaywada

Genesis

The Andhra Pradesha Zilla Grandhalaya Samsthas Employees Association was formed in the year 1964 at Kadapa to safeguard the interests of ZGSS employees of different cadres and promote the spread of library services in the state through dedicaded work. Initally the starting of the association was mooted by the Secretaries of Zilla Grandhalaya Samasthas. After the formation, for the first four years, the association worked vigorously and ceaselessly for enhancement of salaries of ZGS employees. Later it went into hibernation for some time. Presently it is functioning from Vijayawada.

The bye-laws of the Association were revised upto 11.01.03 and modifications came into force with effect from 15.03.03. Again the bye laws of the Association were modified, to meet the changing needs in the year 2005 and published in Telugu.

Objectives

1. To foster a spirit of unity and fraternity among employees in library services.
2. To provide efficient service to the people by improved methods of work, specialization of vocational and professionals techniques.
3. To secure all category of Zilla Grandhalaya Samstha employees improved wages and working conditions.
4. To secure full recognition and enjoyment of rights liberties to which Zilla Grandhalaya Samasthas are justly entitled.
5. To promote conciousness of rights and duties among Zilla Grandhalaya Samstha employees.
6. To advance the economic, social and cultural well being of members.

7. To under take educational, cultural activities such as seminars, study tours, conferences and other cultural functions.
8. To stand and working out such schemes as may be beneficial to members such as cooperative housing, consumer movement, mutual benefit fund etc.,
9. To federate with any association or union having similar aims and objectives.
10. To do all such other things as are incidental and conducive to the attainment of above objectives.

Of the above ten objectives, the first two are concerned with providing better library services to the people and the rest are centred around employees welfare and progress.

Activities

In order to revive the Association representatives from the districts met at Warangal in the year 1970 and resolved to revive the activities of the Association and formation of district units. The new body directed its energies to solve many pressing problems faced by the employees and represent to the concerned authority for redressal. K.Koteshawa Rao the then MLC representing teachers contituency extended full support and cooperation in solving the problems faced by the ZGSS employees. The following are some of the achievements of the Association.

1. Organised two state level conferences to discuss the problems of employees.
2. Taking to the notice of MLA'S the problems faced by ZGSS employees and their redressal by the government at the earliest.
3. Representing to the Chief Minister and the Minister for libraries to provincialise the services of ZGSS Employees. It achieved sucess in this regard.
4. Creating welfare fund for the employees, and
5. Establishing Association branches in the districts.

As recently as June 9,2008, the incumbent president and secretary of the Association submitted a memorandum to the Chief Minister for favourable consideration of following problems : 1. Opening of new branch library (BL) in every Mandal in the state, 2. Payment of salaries to the staff regularly by the first of every month, 3. Supply of government publications freely to the ZGSS. 4. Membership to the librarians in the Book Selection Committees constituted by the government at different levels, 5. Provision of minimum infrastructure facilities especially in branch libraries (BLS), 6. Payment of salaries to the staff through government treasuries, 7. Application of medical reimbursement scheme to ZGSS employees and 8. Filling up of the posts of librarians and Record Assistants on permanent basis without resorting to out sourcing methods.

Conclusions

During the first one and half decades of its existence this professional staff association had the fortune of having the services and guidence of senior librarians with the rank of secretary to ZGS. Later on, the Association slowly slipped into the hands of 'Juniors' who are current by running the affairs of the Association. Except submitting memorandums to the government at times no other activity such as professional development, seems to have taken place during the last one decade.

Sources : 1. V.Venkatappaiah, Ed. *Grandhalaya Darshini*, 1973. (Eluru, Grandhalaya Dharmanidhi, 1973). pp. 71-72.

2. *Grandhalaya Sarvaswamu*, V69, N4, July 2008. p. 32.

3. The Bye-Laws of AP ZGSS Employees Association. Revised upto 11.01.03. In *Hand book of ZGS Employees*.Comp.by Y.Narasimha Rao, (Vijayawada, AP ZGSS Employees Association, 2003).

I

Library and Information Science Education in Andhra Pradesh

Introduction

Andhara Pradesh, which consists of twenty-three districts, is the fourth largest among the states of Indian union in respect of population and fifth largest in respect of area. The enlarged state of Andhara Pradesh came into being by merging the nine-Telangana districts of former Hyderabad state with the then Andhara State in 1956. Hyderabad, of late become as "Cyberabad" has rightly been chosen as a capital for the enlarged state of Andhara Pradesh. During the past four decades the state has made rapid strides in all spheres. Especially in the field of Information Technology, Hyderabad has become a nerve center for the entire country. In the fields of higher education, scientific research and management the progress has been phenomenal. In the state, presently there are fifteen universities namely Osmania, Andhara, Sri Venkateshwara, Kakatiya, Nargajuna, Sri Krishanadevaraya, Acharaya N.G.Ranga Agricultural university, N.T.R.University of Health sciences, Potti Sri Ramulu Telugu university, J.N.Tecnological university, Sri Padmavathi women's university, Dr. B. R. Ambedkar open university, Dr. Ramanand Tirth Rural university, Dravidan university and University of Hyderabad, a central university. Besides these fifteen old universities there are three deemed to be universities namely Central Institute of English and Foreign Languages, Sanskrit vidya peet and Srri Satya Sai Institute of higher learning.

During the last five years ie since 2004 State government has established the following new general universities : 1. Telangana university; Nizamabad, 2. Yogivemana university, Kadapa, 3. Adikavi Nannaya university, Rajahmundry, 4. Satavahana university, Karimnagar, 5. Dr. B.R. Ambedkar university, Srikakulam, and 6. Palamuru university, Mahboob nagar.

The establishment of Hitech City, Indian Institute of Information Technology and Indian Business School of International repute brought Hyderabad on the world map of I.T. and management. Besides these universities a number of national laboratories research institutions and management institutes have been established in around Hyderabad City and also at places like Vishakapatnam, Tirupati and Vijayawada in the state. Hyderabad has now become a center for management and training institutions for the entire nation.

L.I.S. Education

After the formation of Andhara Pradesh an integrated public libraries act, 1960 came into force. This act ushered in a new era for the systematic and orderly development of public libraries in the state. The fast growth witnessed in higher educational institutions, the establishment of a number of R&D Institutions, national laboratories, management and training institutions, I.T.institutions both in public and private sectors especially in the vicinity of Hyderabad, Visakhapatnam, Vijayawada and Tirupati had greatly contributed for the growth and development of Academic, Special, Technical and Research Libraries and Information Centers throughout the state. This development has resulted the need for trained manpower in the field of library and information science for managing these L.I.C.s. During the course of the past four decades university departments and few institutions started offering L.I.S. courses at professional and semi professional levels. The demand for the required-trained manpower was by and large met by the existing institutions and university departments in the state. The existing L.I.S education facilities is briefly presented in the following paras.

Semi Professional Level

The courses offered at this level for the award of Certificate in Library Science (C.L.S.c) is primarily meant to train semi professionals to manage branch libraries (B.Ls) under Zilla Grandhalaya Samasthas (Z.G.S.s) and to work in a junior capacity in Academic and Special libraries and Information centers. The duration of the course is five months. The minimum qualification required for admission to this course is Intermediate. Fore most among the institutes, which offer C.L.S.c both in English and Telugu, is the Institute of Library science Hyderabad. The Government of Andhra Pradesh accorded recognition to this course. So far this institute has produced more than three thousand semi professionals since its inception in 1953. Another institute, which conducts C.L.S.c, is the Central Institute of Library Science managed by A.P.Public Libraries Association since 1970.The State Institute of Library Education, Research and Training (S.I.L.E.R.T) also conducts C.L.Sc course in English since November 1987. S.I.L.E.R.T. has been created by the Department of Public Libraries Govt. A.P. The other institutes which conduct C.L.Sc courses are: Vavilla School of Library Science (1994), Guntur, Ponugoti Educational Society (1996) Hyderabad and Paturi Nagabushanam School of Library science (1966) of A.P.Library Association, Vijayawada and Rayalaseerna Institute of Library Science (1989) Cudapah. These courses were recognized by the Govt. of A.P. The Commissioner of Examinations Govt. of A.P. conducts examination and awards the certificates. Sri Krishna Devaraya University, Anantpur and SriVenkateshwar

University, Tirupati were also conducting CLSC course through conventional and distance education mode. Presently the following: Institutions are offering CLSC Course in Library Science.

1. Institute of Library Science Kachiguda, Hyderabad.
2. Paturi Nagabhushanam School of Library Science, A.P. Library Association, Vijayawada - 520010
3. Central Institute of Library Science, Chaderghat, Abids, Hyderabad (since discontinued)
4. Vavila School of Library Science, Arundelpet Guntur
5. Rayalaseema Institute of Library Science, 1-1720, Gandhinagar, Kadapa.
6. Gnana Sai Library Science Institute, Jedcherla, Mahboob nagar (Dt).
7. Naveen Vivekananda College of Library Science, H.No 16-11-477/2/1/1/A, Dilsukhnagar, SBI colony, Hyderabad.
8. State Institute of Library Education, Research and Training (SILERT), SCL Buildings, Afzulganj, Hyderabad.

University Level Courses

To meet the required-trained manpower at the professional level five universities in the state namely viz.: Osmania, Andhra, Sri Venkatswera, Sri Krishnadevaraya, and Dr.B.R. Ambedkar Open University and Kakatiya offer courses leading to the award of B.L.I.Sc., M.L.I.Sc. (one year), M.L.I.Sc. (two year), M.Phil and Ph.D. degrees.

Bachelors Degree Programme

Osmania University Hyderabad established the Department of Library Science in 1959 and initially instituted a P.G.Diploma course in Library Science in the same year. For three years it has also conducted C.L.S.c course and it was discontinued in 1962. In keeping with the trends and developments in L.I.S education and as per the recommendations of the U.G.C Review Committee, the P.G Diploma course was converted in to a degree course (B.L.S.c) from the academic year 1965-66. The duration of the course is of one academic year. Admission to the course is through an entrance test. Any graduate or post graduate of Osmania University or any other university recognized there to as equivalent with a minimum of 40% of marks in the aggregate in optional subjects is eligible to appear for entrance test. So far D.L.I.S, O.U has produced three thousand graduates and they are serving in various capacities in different types of libraries in the country and abroad. Few years' back Osmania University has given affiliation to five-degree collages to offer B.L.I.Sc. course. The syllabus is revised at regular intervals to meet ever changing needs of L.I.C.s

Andhra University, Visakhapatnam is one of the oldest institutions of higher learning in the country, which started courses in library science in 1930's. The university started a summer school of librarianship in 1934. It was switched over to one-year diploma course in the year 1937. The university also conducted a certificate course of three months duration during 1954-55 to 1961-62. This course was given up in 1962. A full-fledged Department of Library Science was established in 1967 for imparting training programmers in Library Science. This Department introduced Bachelors degree programme in 1968.

Sri Venkateswara University, Tirupati initially started with a certificate course of three months duration in 1971. After seven batches, the course was elevated to degree level leading to B.L.S.c of one-year duration in 1975. Sri Krishnadevaraya University, Anantapur also introduced bachelor's degree programme in Library Science to cater to the needs of professionals working in that area. The admission to these programmes is through an entrance test.

Masters Degree Programme

It was long felt need of library professionals in Andhara Pradesh to have masters degree programme in the state to meet ever increasing demand for library training at advanced level. The Department of Library and Information Science, Osmania University has taken lead in this direction and introduced for the first time in the state, M.L.I.S.c programme during the academic year 1978-79. Andhara University followed suit and introduced M.L.I.S.c programme from the academic year 1979-80. The other universities in the state namely: Sri Venkateswara, (1986-87) Sri Krishnadevaraya (1993-94) and Nargajuna have also introduced master's degree programmes in library and information science. Some of the universities in the state viz; Andhra, Srivenkateshwara, Nagarjuna and Srikrishna Devaraya have switched over to two year integrated MLIS Programme. But Osmania still continue with its BLISC/MLISC programmes each of one year duration. ICFAI university Hyderabad, a private university is also offering programmes in LIS. Kakatiya university, Warangal also started MLISC programme during the year 2004-05.

To provide an opportunity to working professionals, who could not obtain M.L.I.S.c degree, summer courses were introduced by Sri Krishnadevaraya and Osmania University. Osmania University started this programme in 1993. The duration of the course is for two summers of fourteen weeks for each summer. The admission to this programme is through an entrance test. This summer programmes have benefited a number of senior professionals working in Public, Academic, Special and Technical Libraries and Information Centers. Some of the universities in the state namely: Sri Venketswera, Nagurjana and Sri Krishnadevaraya have switched over to two year integrated M.L.I.S.c programme. Dr. B.R.Ambedkar P.G.Center of Andhara University at Etcherla, Srikakulam also offers two-year M.L.I.S.c programme.

Now this P.G. Centre has become Part of newly established Dr. B.R. Amedkar University, Srikakulam.

Distance Education Programmes

Dr.B.R.Ambedkar Open University (formerly A.P.Open University) taken lead for the entire country and introduced bachelors degree programme in library science from the academic year 1984-85. Kakatiya University, Warangal established School of Distance Learning and Continuing Education (S.D.L.C.E) in the year 1988. This school introduced B.L.I.S.c course during the academic year 1989-90, to provide L.I.S education to those who wish to pursue in that area. The Directorate of Distance Education (D.D.E) of Sri Venkateshwara University, Triupati also introduced C.L.S.c course of six months duration and B.L.I.S.c course of one year duration. Dr. B.R.Ambedkar Open University also started master's degree programme in 1999. In addition to these programmes through distance mode, Indira Gandhi National Open University (IGNOU) also offers B.L.I.S.c / M.L.I.S.c programmes and its study centers are located at Hyderabad, Vijayawada, Visakapatnam and Tirupati to provide counselling and contact programmes to its distance learners. University of Hyderabad started a P.G.Diploma programme on computer applications in Libraries in 1998. The School of correspondence courses Andhra university has also started BLISC programme through distance mode.

Research Degrees

Besides B.L.I.S.c, M.L.I.S.C and two year M.L.I.S.C programmes almost all the universities in the state offer research courses leading to the award of M.Phil/ Ph.D. degrees in library and information science.The D.L.I.S.c, Osmania University introduced M.Phil programme in 1994 and Ph.D. programme in 1989. Like wise facilities are available for pursuing these programmes at Andhara, Sri Venketswara and Sri Krishnadevaraya Universities in the state.M.Phil is a full time programme and Ph.D. is mostly part time programme in all the universities.

Dr. B.R. Ambedkar open university also introduced Mphil and Ph D programmes in LIS for the benefit of professionals.

Special Training Programmes

National Institute of Small Industry Extension and Training (NISIET) Hyderabad offers special training programmes in Information Storage and Retrieval Systems (ISRS), Management, Abstracting and Indexing both at national and international levels to train personnel working in Industrial Development Organizations, Corporate bodies and Documentation / Information centers. These intensive training programmes are of four weeks duration at the national level and ten weeks at the international level. The national programme is conducted twice a year and the International programme once a year.

Continuing Education Programmes

In addition to formal and regular programmes offered by the university departments and institutes several continuing educational programmes have also been conducted by these organizations and professional associations for the benefit of semi professionals and professionals in the state. Academy of Library Science and Documentation (ALSD) conducted an intensive short-term course on Management of Information Storage and Retrieval during summer 1971. Sri Venketswara University organized a summer institute for college librarians in 1971, which was sponsored by the U.G.C. The D.L.I.S.c, Osmania University organized a summer institute for college librarians in Telengana region for a period of four weeks in Nov-Dec 1977 and was sponsored by the U.G.C. Andhra University also conducted a summer institute for college librarians of Coastal Andhra in 1979 and was sponsored by the U.G.C. At the professional level the Department of Public Libraries, Govt.

of A.P conducted for the first time a five-day refresher course for B.L.I.S.c degree holders working in Zilla Grandhlaya Samsthas in the state. The said course was conducted at City Central Library Hyderabad in January 1980 for the benefit of the professionals working in Telengana region of Andhra Pradesh. The said programme was repeated by Andhra University and Sri Venkatswera University for the benefit of the professionals working in Coastal and Rayalaseema regions of the state. Again for the first time the Department of Public Libraries Govt. of A.P conducted a five day refresher course in December 1980 at three places in the state namely Hyderabad, Visakhapatnam and Triupati for the benefit of the professionals holding B.L.I.S.c degree.

The Department of Library and Information science, Osmania University has organized for the first time a six-day course on " Management of Public Library Services" from December 13-18, 1982. It was sponsored by the Department of Public Libraries Govt. of A.P. The said course was exclusively meant for the Librarians of District Central Libraries and Regional Libraries in the state. Osmania Library Science Alumni (OLSA) has organized the following refresher courses: 1. U.D.C (I.M.E), 1985,2.Computer Applications in Library Operations, 3.DDC-20th Edn and AACR-2.

Academic Staff College Osmania University has conducted seventeer refresher courses untill 2008, of four weeks duration sponsored by the U.G.C. The participants to this course are Lecturers in Library and information science, College Librarians and Assistant Librarians from the universities of southern and northeastern parts of India. These courses were designed to provide knowledge and exposure to Information Technology, Computer Applications in Libraries and Information Management. Academic Staff College of Andhra University has so far organized two refresher courses for the benefit of professionals. National Academy of Agriculture Research Management (NAARM),Rajendranagar Hyderabad has been offering training programs on CDS/ISIS.

These continuing education programs provided not only an opportunity to the professionals to meet fellow professionals and other seniors in the profession but also enabled them to gain new knowledge and understand new developments in the field of Library and Information Science.

Conclusion

It is hoped that the existing facilities for education for Librainship in the state would be able to meet the future demands for trained manpower for managing different types of Library Systems in the state and elsewhere in the country and abroad. It is the endeavor of the University Departments and other institutions in the state to offer quality LIS education and training keeping in view the needs and requirements of emerging Information society. Andhra Pradesh has carved out a special and enviable position on the LIS Education map of the country.

Sources

A.A.N. Raju, Library and Information Science Education in Andhra Pradesh.XXVII All India Library Conference, 9-12 Jan. 1981. *Souvenir*.(Hyderabad, Academy of Library Science and Documentation,!981). Pp.14-17

A.A.N. Raju, Facilities for Professional Education and Training in Hyderabad. XI IASLIC National Seminar, 26-29 Nov. 1984. *Souvenir*. (Hyderabad, Dept of Lib and Infsc, Osmania University,!984). Pp 6-8.

A.A.N. Raju, et al, eds. *Fifty Years of Library and Information Science Education in India. Seminar papers*. XV IATLIS National Seminar, 1997.(Hyderabad, Suchitritha Graphics, 1997).

J

Raja Rammohun Roy Library Foundation (RRRLF), Kolkata

Genesis

Raja Rammohun Roy Library Foundation (RRRLF) was established in May 1972 coinciding with bicentennial anniversary of Raja Rammohun Roy, the great social reformer, thinker and educationist of the 19th century India. The Foundation is an autoanomous organisation established by Government of India, presently under Department of Culture, Ministry of Tourism and Culture. It is registered under the West Bengal Societies Registration Act, 1961 and its head quarters is located at DD-34, Sector 1, Salt lake city, Kolkata 700064.

Objectives

The prime objective of the foundation is to promote and support public library movement and development in the country by extending necessary financial support to concerned agencies and with the support and cooperation from the state governments and voluntary organisations and societies who have been establishing and managing public libraries. The Foundations 'Memorandum of Association and Rules' has listed 29 objectives which it intends to achieve. These objectives may be summarised as :

"1. enunciation of national library policy and working towards its adaption by the Central and State Governments and perusading them to enact library legislation where such legislation does not exist;
2. helping build up national library system by integrating services of National Library, State Central Libraries, District Libraries and other types of libraries, for instance, through an inter library lending system;
3. providing financial assistance to libraries, to regional and national library associations and to other organisations engaged or intrested in the promotion of library development;
4. acting as aclearning house for ideas and information on library development;
5. promoting research in problems of library development; and
6. taking all such measures as may be found necessary to promote library development and its utilisation in the country."

Members of the Foundation

The foundation consists of the following members :

1. Minister, Department of Culture, Government of India or his nominee shall be the chairman,
2. Secretary, Department of Culture, Government of India, or his nominee
3. Thirteen persons to be nominated by the Government of India, four of whom are eminent librarians and nine educationists.
4. One representative each of the following organisations :
   (a) Indian Library Association (ILA)
   (b) Central Sahitya Akademi
   (c) National Book Trust India

5. Three persons nominated by the Government of India to represent respectively the Department of Education, the Ministry of Social Welfare and Ministry of Finance; and
6. Director, RRRLF is the Member Secretary.

Committees

To carryout its various activities concerning public library development a number of committees and sub committees are appointed from time to time viz; Book Selection Committee, Grants Committee, Research committee, Journal Committee etc.

Zonal Offices

In view of the vastness of the country and to carry out expanding activities, the Foundation has set up a Zonal Office cum Guest House in New Delhi, and three more Zonal offices at Mumbai (Western India), Chennai (Southern India), Kolkata (Eastern India). These Zonal offices are under the charge of Assistant field officers who are supposed to monitor the impact of and implementation of the assistance rendered by the Foundation to recipient Public Libraries, Institutions and Societies promoting public library development.

Schemes and Programmes

In order to augument the book collections in public libraries, the foundation has launched 'Assistance towards building up of adequate stock of books and other reading and visual materials.' The assistance under the scheme is rendered from four sources viz : matching source and non-matching source. Matching Schemes are operated from the matching contribution by the State Governments and equal share from the Foundation. Non-matching schemes are fully operated from the Foundation funds. In the matching scheme the responsibility of quality book selection, purchase and distribution of books is vested with the state authority. For example in Andhra Pradesh, the Director of Public Libraries, Government of A.P. is the State Authority. In the non-matching scheme, the Foundation is responsible for selection, purchase and distribution of books.

Matching Schemes

In addition to assist development of book collections in libraries the scheme also includes : 1. development of rural book deposit centres (BDCS) and mobile library services, 2. organisation of seminars, work shops and training courses, 3. to acquire storage and display of books equipments, 4. to acquire T.V. cum- UCP sets for educational purposes and 5. assistance for increasing accomodation in the existing library buildings and/or construction of new library buildings.

Non-matching Schemes

In addition to build adequate book collection in public libraries, the scheme includes to assist : 1. centrally sponsorred libraries such as Nehru Yuvak Kendras, 2. Organising seminars and conferences by National level organisations, 3. Voluntary organisations providing library services, 4 Children's libraries or children's section in existing public libraries, 5. Public libraries for celebrating centenary year/125th year/150th year/175year.

Promotional activities

Library legislation

Library legislation enables orderly development of public libraries at different levels and ensures governments support. There are many States in Indian which have not enancted library legislation. Besides being an aid giving body, the Foundation has been impressing those State governments which have not yet enacted library legislation, the need for the same.

Seminars

The Foundation on its own or in collaboration with other agencise such as National/State level Library Associations, University Departments, has been organising national seminars concerning public library development. For example during the year 2005-06, the Foundation in collaboration with Dept. Library and Information Science, Mizoram university organised a three day Seminar on "Bridging The Digital Divide - Public Library Services in the North East: Oportunities and Challenges" at Aizwal during May 19-21, 2005. Another National Seminar on the theme "Preservation and Conservation of Library Material in Public Libraries in Digital Environment" was organised by the Academy of Library Science and Documentation (ALSD) during 25-26 June 2005 at City Central Library, Hyderabad.

Another national seminar on the theme "Towards Excellance in Higher Education in Kerala Through IT Enabled Library Information System" was organised by Kerala Library Association during 5-7 May 2005 at Thiruvanthapuram.

Research Projects

The Foundation constituted a Research Committee in 1980 to advise it on the matters pertaining to research activities, its library and publications. The said committee formulated Guidelines for Public Library System & Services, which was published in *Grandhana* (V2, 1991) its official organ. It has also prepared a report on Missing Books and Remedial Measures in Libraries for submission to parliament.

Evaluation of Books

Publishers from time to time send their publication for selection by RRRLF under 'non-matching scheme'. These books are placed before the Book Selection Committee for evaluation and selection.

Library Statistics

A statical unit has been established in the Research wing to collect statistics on public libraries from different states and union territories through specialised institutions and organisations including library associations. The Foundation has also installed a computer for building up data bank of public libraries in India.

Publications

In order to publish original articles, survey reports, book reviews, short communications on public library development, the foundation started its academic journal titled *Granthana : Indian Journal of Library Studies* from January, 1990. but regularity of its publication was not ensured. The Foundation also published *Directory of Indian Public Libraries* edited by Dr BP Barua. It contains a select list of libraries assisted by the Foundation. Another publication of the Foundation is *Indian Libraries : Trends and Perspectives* edited by Dr. K.M George. It has also broughtout another publication tittled "*Raja Rammohan Roy and the New Learning*", a compilation of lectures on Raja Rammohan Roy. The books received for consideration under non matching scheme was brought out under the title "*List of Books Selected for Distribution among the Public Libraries in India*, 1993-94."

A quartarly News letter is brought out by the Foundation to communicates activities, programmes an schemes.

RRRLF Annual Memorial Lectures

To propogate the activities of the Foundation, RRRLF instituted Annual Memorial Lectures,

RRRLF Awards

To motivate the public libraries in the country for rendering better services to the user community, the Foundation has instituted national level RRRLF Awards for the best State

Central Library (SCL) in the Country and the best District Library (DL) in each of the six zones few year backs. The cash award for the best SCL is Rs 100,000/- and for each best DL in each zone is Rs 50,000/-. It has also instituted another award for contributing best professional article on development of public library services and systems/library information science. The contributors age should not exceed 40 years on 21st May in the year he/she contributes the articles. There are three awards with the cash component of Rs 5000/- as first prize, Rs 3000/ for second prize and Rs 2000/ for third prize.

National Level Fellowship

RRRLF has also institututed national level 'RRRLF Fellowship' few years back for those personalities who have contributed immensely to the library movement in the country through their active participation, organisational drive and/or intellectual contribution and leadership. The persons may be social activists, librarians, library and information scientists or heads of organisations involved in the propagation of reading habits among the communities for the spread of library movement. Initially the fellowship carried a cash of award of Rs 25,000 and has been enhancement to Rs 50,000 along with plaque and citation narrating the services redered by the Fellow in his field of work.

Foundations Library

The Foundations has established a library during 1981-82 at its headquarters specialising in the field of Library and Information Science (LIS). The library has a collection of 3828 books (as on 2005-06) in addition 9 video cassettes on LIS and also some CDs. It subscribed to 39 journals (which include both Indian and Foreign) and receives 3 journals as gratis.

Conclusion

It is more thean three and half decades since the establishment of RRRLF for the cause of public library development in the country. It is a centrally sponsored organisation and carrying out its activities with the financial support from Government of India. Undoubtly the foundation has achieved significant progress in promoting public library development and library services in the country. The states which have enacted public library legislation and as a result with a networks of public libraries at different levels in their respective jurisdictions have been benefitted by the 'Matching and Non-Matching' schemes introduce by the Foundation. In addition, its promotional activities such as : supporting seminars and conferences, operation of research projects, preparation of library statistics, publication of *Granthana*, the LIS Journal, and a News letter, institution of awards and fellowships have contributed in no small measure, for the rejuvenation of public library services in the country.

The thirty fourth annual report of the Foundation for the year 2005-06 states that over the last thirty four year the Foundation has covered about a little over thirty one thousand libraries at different levels.

State Central Libraries	28
Divisional and District Libraries	451
Subdivisional/Taluka/Tehsil libraries	501
Town and Rural libraries	30634
NYK [Nehru Yuvak Kendras]	272
Jawahar Bal Bhavans	49
Other	28
Total	32063

The coverage may be noteworthy. But still a lot of ground needs to be covered by the Foundation in the years to come.

The Foundation has to do much more in the realm of 'Privately managed public libraries' some of them have been established during the 19th and the begining the 20th centuries. These libraries are struggling hard to survive for want of finances, staff, books collections and infrastructure. There is greater need and responsibility on the party of the Foundation to carry out a survey on state of affairs of 'Privately managed and heritage' public libraries nation wide, and a 'Directory' has to be brought out on these libraries. The Foundation has to support the individual iniatives and the projects submitted by them on various facets of public library development for consideration and financial support. The projects under taken by the Foundation and financial assistance rendered to the public libraries in the country and the quality of book supplied to the public libraries needs to be properly evaluated and the impact of RRRLF on the 'Public Library Development' in the country has to be studied and assessed by a committee of experts. It is high time that the Department of Culture, Government of India takes iniative in this regard.

References

1. Raja Ram mohan Roy Library Foundation; *Memorandum of Association and Rules*. (Kolkata, RRRLF, 2004). 37p.
2. *Books for the millions at their Door steps : Information Manual.* (Kolkata, RRRLF, 1997). 109-p.
3. Raja Rammohan Roy Library Foundation. *Thirty Four Annual Report* 2005-06. (Mimeographed).

Index